PRINT CULTURE

PRINT CULTURES

A Reader in Theory and Practice

Edited by Caroline Davis

 macmillan
international
HIGHER EDUCATION

 RED GLOBE
PRESS

First published 2019 by
RED GLOBE PRESS

Red Globe Press in the UK is an imprint of Springer Nature Limited,
registered in England, company number 785998, of 4 Crinan Street,
London N1 9XW.

Red Globe Press® is a registered trademark in the United States,
the United Kingdom, Europe and other countries.

ISBN 978–0–230–28090–8 hardback
ISBN 978–0–230–28091–5 paperback

This book is printed on paper suitable for recycling and made from fully
managed and sustained forest sources. Logging, pulping and manufacturing
processes are expected to conform to the environmental regulations of the
country of origin.

A catalogue record for this book is available from the British Library.

A catalog record for this book is available from the Library of Congress.

Contents

List of Figures and Tables

Figures

Tables

Acknowledgements

The editor and publisher would like to acknowledge permission to reproduce the following extracts of copyright material:

PART ONE: PUBLISHING: THEORY AND PRACTICE

Stanley Unwin. 1960. *The Truth about a Publisher: An Autobiographic Record.* London: George Allen and Unwin, pp. 323–330. Reproduced with permission of HarperCollins Publishers.

Pierre Bourdieu. 1985. 'The market of symbolic goods'. *Poetics*, 14: 17–22 and 33–43. Reproduced with permission of Elsevier Science Publishers B.V.

Gérard Genette. 1997. *Paratexts.* Cambridge: Cambridge University Press, 1997, pp. 1–8. First published as *Seuils* (Éditions du Seuil, 1987). Used with permission of Cambridge University Press. © Cambridge University Press, 1997.

Lynne Spender. 1983. *Intruders on the Rights of Men: Women's Unpublished Heritage.* London: Pandora Press, pp. 1–14. Reproduced with kind permission of the author.

John B. Thompson. 2010. *Merchants of Culture: The Publishing Business in the Twenty-First Century.* Cambridge: Polity Press. Reproduced with permission of Polity Press.

Michael Bhaskar. 2013. *The Content Machine: Towards a Theory of Publishing from the Printing Press to the Digital Network.* London: Anthem Press, pp. 41–61. Reproduced with permission of Anthem Press.

PART TWO: AUTHORSHIP

Mary Ann Gillies. 2007. *The Professional Literary Agent in Britain, 1880–1920.* Toronto: University of Toronto Press, pp. 34–39. Reprinted with permission of the publisher, Toronto University Press.

Joe Moran. 2000. *Star Authors: Literary Celebrity in America.* London: Pluto Press, pp. 58–62. Reproduced with permission of Pluto Press.

Juliet Gardiner. 2000. '"What is an author?' Contemporary publishing and discourse and the author figure'. *Publishing Research Quarterly*, 16.1: 63–70. Reproduced with permission of Springer CCC.

Laura Dietz. 2015. 'Who are you calling an author? Changing definitions of career legitimacy for novelists in the digital era', in *Literary Careers in the Modern Era*, edited by G. Davidson and N. Evans. London: Palgrave Macmillan, pp. 196–201. Reproduced and revised with kind permission of the author.

George Landow. 2006. *Hypertext 3.0: Critical Theory and New Media in an Era of Globalization*, 2nd Edition. Baltimore: Johns Hopkins University Press, pp. 125–131. Reprinted with permission of Johns Hopkins University Press.

PART THREE: READERSHIP AND THE LITERARY MARKETPLACE

Q.D. Leavis. 1979. *Fiction and the Reading Public*. London: Penguin Books, pp. 19–30. With kind permission of Dr L.R. Leavis, Literary Executor Leavis Estate. Copyright © Q.D. Leavis.
Geoffrey Faber. 1934. *A Publisher Speaking*. London: Faber & Faber, pp. 19–24 and 28–29. Reproduced with permission of Faber & Faber Ltd.
Janice Radway. 1997. *A Feeling for Books: The Book-of-the-Month Club, Literary Taste, and Middle-Class Desire*. Chapel Hill, NC: The University of North Carolina Press, pp. 221–223 and 253–260. Copyright © 1997 by the University of North Carolina Press. Used by permission of the publisher.
Clive Bloom. 2002. *Bestsellers: Popular Fiction Since 1900*, Basingstoke: Palgrave Macmillan, pp. 82–92. Reproduced with the kind permission of the publisher and author.

PART FOUR: CENSORSHIP AND PRINT CULTURE

Sue Curry Jansen. 1991. *Censorship: The Knot that Binds Power and Knowledge*. New York: Oxford University Press, pp. 14–25. Reproduced with permission of Oxford University Press.
Lewis A. Coser. 1975. 'Publishers as gatekeepers of ideas'. *Annals of the American Academy of Political and Social Science*, 421: 14–22. Reproduced with permission of Sage Publications.
Alistair McCleery. 2013. 'The travels and trials of *Lady Chatterley's Lover*', in *Reading Penguin: A Critical Anthology*, edited by Donaldson, G. & Wootten, W. Cambridge: Cambridge Scholars, pp. 27–48. Published with the kind permission of Cambridge Scholars Publishing and the author. This chapter has been specially abbreviated and amended by the author for re-publication in this volume.
Archie L. Dick. 2012. *The Hidden History of South Africa's Book and Reading Cultures*. Toronto: University of Toronto Press, pp. 124–135. © University of Toronto Press 2012. Reprinted with permission of the publisher and the author.

PART FIVE: BOOKS, PROPAGANDA AND WAR

Peter Buitenhuis. 1987. *The Great War of Words: Literature as Propaganda, 1914–18 and After*. London: Batsford, pp. 12–20. Reproduced with kind permission of B. T. Batsford, part of Pavilion Books Company Limited.
Jane Potter. 2007. 'For country, conscience and commerce: Publishers and publishing, 1914–18', in *Publishing in the First World War: Essays in Book History*, edited by Mary Hammond and Shafquat Towheed. Basingstoke: Palgrave Macmillan, pp. 11–26. Reproduced with the kind permission of the author.

Valerie Holman. 2008. *Print for Victory: Book Publishing in Britain 1939–1945*. London: British Library, pp. 105–111. Reproduced with kind permission of the author.

Joe Pearson. 1996. *Penguins March On: Books for the Forces during World War II*. Penguin Collectors' Society, pp. 9–14. Reproduced with the kind permission of the author and the Penguin Collectors' Society.

John Hench. 2011. 'The American Publisher's Series goes to war, 1942–1946', in *The Culture of the Publisher's Series*, edited by John Spiers. Vol 1, Basingstoke: Palgrave Macmillan, pp. 198–206. Reproduced with the kind permission of the author.

PART SIX: COLONIAL AND POSTCOLONIAL PRINT CULTURE

Pascale Casanova, 2004. *The World Republic of Letters*. Cambridge, MA: Harvard University Press, pp. 115–119. Reproduced with permission of Harvard University Press. Copyright © 2004 by the President and Fellows of Harvard College.

Robert Fraser. 2008. 'School readers in the empire and the creation of postcolonial taste', in *Books without Borders Volume 1*, edited by Robert Fraser and Mary Hammond. Basingstoke: Palgrave Macmillan, pp. 89–93 and 99–104. Reproduced with the kind permission of the author.

Henry Chakava. 1992. 'Kenyan publishing: Independence and dependence', in *Publishing and Development in the Third World*, edited by Philip Altbach. London: Hans Zell, pp. 119–21. Reproduced with kind permission by Philip Altbach.

Graham Huggan. 2001. *The Postcolonial Exotic: Marketing the Margins*. London: Routledge, pp. 35 and 50–57, © 2001 Taylor & Francis Books, reproduced by permission of Taylor & Francis Books UK.

James Currey. 2008. 'Africa Writes Back: Heinemann African Writers Series—A publisher's memoir' in *Books without Borders Volume 1: The Cross-National Dimension in Print Culture*, edited by Robert Fraser and Mary Hammond. Basingstoke: Palgrave Macmillan, pp. 159–169 and p. 172. Reproduced with the kind permission of the author.

PART SEVEN: WOMEN AND PRINT CULTURE

Virginia Woolf. 1967. [1929] *A Room of One's Own*. London: The Hogarth Press, pp. 62–76. Copyright 1929 by Houghton Mifflin Harcourt Publishing Company and renewed 1957 by Leonard Woolf. Reprinted with permission of Houghton Mifflin Publishing Company. All rights reserved.

Urvashi Butalia and Ritu Menon. 1995. *Making a Difference: Feminist Publishing in the South*. Chestnut Hill, MA: Bellagio Publishing, pp. 15–22, 28–31 and 49. Reproduced with kind permission of the publisher, Philip Altbach.

Simone Murray. 2004. *Mixed Media: Feminist Presses and Publishing Politics*, London: Pluto Press, pp. 28–38. Reproduced with kind permission of the author and Pluto Press.

Mohanalakshmi Rajakumar and Rumsha Shahzad. 2015. 'She needs a website of her own: The 'Indie' woman writer and contemporary publishing', in *Literary Careers in the Modern Era*, edited by G. Davidson G. and N. Evans. London: Palgrave Macmillan, pp. 184–187. Reproduced with kind permission of the authors.

PART EIGHT: LITERARY PRIZE CULTURE

Richard Todd. 1996. 'Literary prizes and the media', in *Consuming Fictions: The Booker Prize and Fiction in Britain Today*. London: Bloomsbury, pp. 55–60. © Richard Todd, 1996, *Consuming Fictions,* Bloomsbury Publishing PLC.

Tom Maschler. 2003. 'How it all began', in *The Man Booker Prize: 35 Years of the Best in Contemporary Fiction, 1969–2003*. The Booker Prize Foundation, pp. 20–21. © Tom Maschler. Reproduced with the kind permission of the author and the Booker Prize Foundation.

Claire Squires. 2007. *Marketing Literature: The Making of Contemporary Writing in Britain*. Basingstoke: Palgrave Macmillan, pp. 97–101. Reproduced with the kind permission of the author and publisher.

Reprinted with permission of the publisher from THE ECONOMY OF PRESTIGE: PRIZES, AWARDS AND THE CIRCULATION OF CULTURAL VALUE by James F. English, pp. 187–192, Cambridge, MA: Harvard University Press, Copyright © 2005 by the President and Fellows of Harvard College.

PART NINE: CONGLOMERATION AND GLOBALISATION IN PUBLISHING

André Schiffrin. 2010. 'The future of publishing', in *Words and Money*. London: Verso, pp. 1–9. Reproduced with permission of Verso.

Walter Bgoya. 2001. 'The effect of globalisation in Africa and the choice of language in publication'. *International Review of Education*, 47. 3–4: 284–292. Reproduced with permission of Springer.

Angus Phillips. 2014. 'The global book', in *Turning the Page*. London: Routledge, pp. 99–116. Reproduced with kind permission of the author and Routledge.

Suman Gupta. 2009. *Globalisation and Literature*. Cambridge: Polity, pp. 159–170. Reproduced with permission of Polity.

Sarah Brouillette. 2007. *Postcolonial Writers in the Global Literary Marketplace*. Basingstoke: Palgrave Macmillan, pp. 49–61. Reproduced with kind permission of the author.

Every effort has been made to trace and contact copyright holders. The publishers would be pleased to hear from any copyright holder not acknowledged here so that this acknowledgement page may be amended at the earliest opportunity.

EDITOR'S ACKNOWLEDGEMENT

I would like to thank Jenna Steventon and Emily Lovelock at Red Globe Press for their excellent editing of this volume. I am also very grateful to Jane Potter and Claire Squires for their help in shaping the structure and contents of this book. My additional thanks go to Laura Schröder for her valuable research assistance, to my colleagues in the Oxford International Centre for Publishing for their help-ful advice, and to the School of Arts research fund at Oxford Brookes University for financial support. Most of all, I would like to thank the many students on the undergraduate and master's publishing programmes at Oxford Brookes, who have over the years contributed fascinating insights relating to print culture and the cul-ture of publishing.

1 Introduction

Print Cultures: A Reader in Theory and Practice is the first anthology of critical writings to concentrate on book, publishing and digital cultures in the twentieth and twenty-first centuries. These selected texts provide a comprehensive introduction to this rapidly developing and dynamic subject, and represent the main theoretical approaches and models as well as key historical and thematic analyses. This is a collection of essential reading for students and researchers wanting to know how the subject has developed, where it is now and its future directions.

Print culture studies can be defined as the study of the production, circulation and consumption of books and other communications media, in both printed and digital form. The focus of this field of study is three-fold. Firstly, it concerns print as an agent in cultural, social and political life; how the circulation of printed and digital texts affects society. Secondly, it involves the analysis of the material form of a publication, or in other words the significance of the physical form of the text. And thirdly, it uncovers the stories behind books and other publications, which lead to their creation, recognition and longevity. This field of study draws attention to people involved in the process of literary and cultural creation who are frequently assigned to the footnotes of history; not only the author, but also the publisher, literary agent, typographic designer, marketer and publicist, bookseller, and reader.

The terms 'print culture studies' and 'book history' have tended to be used interchangeably to describe this new and fast-developing academic field of study, but the term 'print culture', particularly in its plural form 'print cultures', encapsulates more accurately the multiple and competing cultures of contemporary and historical print and publishing discussed in this volume: the assortment of geographical and social contexts in which texts have been produced and circulated and the variety of different cultural institutions behind their production. These range from established publishing industries that are closely affiliated to, or controlled by, the state, to the alternative, often dissenting or subversive work of authors and publishers operating outside the mainstream. The studies in this anthology demonstrate the range of countries from which the study and theorisation of Anglophone print culture has emerged: the United Kingdom, the United States, the Caribbean, Kenya, South Africa, Nigeria, Tanzania and India. These studies also locate connections and mutually influential exchanges in international print culture, while acknowledging that these exchanges are frequently asymmetrical and uneven.

The study of print and publishing has conventionally taken place within the discipline of analytical bibliography, and has involved the technical analysis and historical investigations of individual books and editions. In the 1950s, however, new methods and approaches were introduced by historians Lucien Febvre and

1

Henri-Jean Martin in *L'Apparition de Livre* (1958), published in English as *The Coming of the Book* (1976), and later by Elizabeth Eisenstein (1979), to investigate the socio-materiality of texts: how literature and society have been influenced by the processes of textual production, distribution and consumption. These areas of scholarship have variously been termed the 'sociology of texts', 'book history', 'publishing studies' and 'print culture studies' (see Robert Darnton (1982), John Sutherland (1998), Finkelstein and McCleery (2006b) and Simone Murray (2007)). From the 1970s onwards, attention turned to contemporary institutions of literary and cultural production and has resulted in a number of sociological studies of late twentieth-century print culture (Coser et al. 1982; Lane and Booth 1980). The most influential of these is Pierre Bourdieu's sociology of culture (1971, 1993, 1996; see also Chapter 3 in this volume) which provides a framework for disclosing the systems of power and privilege in literary relations and for giving prominence to the role of the different agents, including authors, literary agents, editors and publishers, in the process of literary creation.

Scholarship in print culture has subsequently developed within a number of academic disciplines, including publishing studies, literature, social history, politics, law, sociology, library studies, information studies, geography, anthropology and art history, and this volume incorporates a number of methodological and theoretical approaches. The risk of such complexity is, as Robert Darnton famously stated, 'interdisciplinarity run riot' (1982, p. 67). In order to navigate a path through this potentially unwieldy subject, this volume maps out the main directions in which this field of research has developed and is continuing to develop, and identifies the main shifts in print and publishing history during the twentieth and twenty-first centuries.

One of the most significant shifts in print culture relates to changing patterns of ownership in the publishing industry, as it developed from family-owned and independent 'gentlemanly' firms in the early twentieth century to predominantly large multinational media conglomerates, with business interests spanning the globe, and with new players currently entering from the wings in the form of digital publishing start-ups. These changes precipitated debates and discussions that date back to the 1930s, when anxieties were expressed within the book trade and in the academy about the commercialisation of book publishing and reading, the rise of an undiscerning mass reading public, the tendency of the book trade to produce corrupting books for herd-like readers and the need for publishers to act as guardians of literature (see the extracts in this volume by Q. D. Leavis, Chapter 13 [1932]; Geoffrey Faber, Chapter 14 [1934]; and Mary Ann Gillies, Chapter 8 [2007]). As the publishing industry responded to new media and the developing marketplace for books in the mid-twentieth century, debates continued to centre on the publisher's role and responsibilities in negotiating the balance between culture and commerce (see extracts by Stanley Unwin, Chapter 2 [1960]; Janice Radway, Chapter 15 [1997]; and Clive Bloom, Chapter 16 [2002]). From the 1980s onwards, in the wake of the deregulation of markets in the United Kingdom and the United States, the publishing industry underwent fundamental changes in its patterns of ownership, when long-established family-owned imprints were taken over and absorbed within major multinational and multimedia corporations with headquarters in Europe and America (see extracts by Lewis A. Coser, Chapter 18 [1975]; Sue Curry Jansen, Chapter 17 [1991]; and André Schiffrin, Chapter 39 [2010]). Several scholars have examined how authorship and reading have been affected by structural changes in the publishing industry, in particular by the rise of literary celebrity culture, the ways in which authors have to promote themselves and the implications of literary prizes (see extracts by Richard Todd, Chapter 35 [1996]; Juliet Gardiner, Chapter 10 [2000]; Joe Moran, Chapter 9 [2000]; Tom Maschler, Chapter 36 [2003]; and James English, Chapter 38 [2010]).

The changing power structures in print culture have also come under scrutiny throughout the twentieth and twenty-first centuries, specifically the frameworks operating for the privileging and excluding of specific texts, authors, publishers and readers, and how these controls have been opposed or subverted. During wartime, the strong links between the political establishment and the publishing industry were particularly pronounced, and several of the chapters in this volume assess the ways in which British and American authors and publishers were co-opted by the state in the production of both censorship and propaganda during the first and second world wars, and the extent to which they and their readers were complicit in these arrangements (see extracts by Peter Buitenhuis, Chapter 21 [1987]; Joe Pearson, Chapter 24 [1996]; Jane Potter, Chapter 22 [2007]; Valerie Holman, Chapter 23 [2008]; and John B. Hench, Chapter 25 [2011]). Sue Curry Jansen argues that market censorship is more significant than state censorship in contemporary American publishing (Chapter 17). Other scholarship has drawn attention to the multiple ways in which writers, publishers and readers have contested and subverted state censorship, for example in Alistair McCleery's discussion of the ways in which *Lady Chatterley's Lover* avoided and circumnavigated obscenity scholarship in the early twentieth century (Chapter 19 [2013] in this volume) and Archie L. Dick's discussion of the means by which censorship in the apartheid period was resisted by black readers in South Africa (Chapter 20 [2012] in this volume).

Feminist publishers and scholars have sought, as Claire Squires notes, 'to remove the gendered construction of the "gentleman publisher"' (2007: 46), in exposés of systems of patriarchy in authorship, print culture and publishing, for example in the chapters in this book by Virginia Woolf (Chapter 31 [1929]) and Lynne Spender (Chapter 5 [1983]). The work of feminist publishers in establishing their own publishing firms, publishing feminist texts and recovering forgotten women's literature is reviewed in the extracts in this volume by Simone Murray (Chapter 33 [2004]) and by Mohanalakshmi Rajakumar and Rumsha Shahzad (Chapter 34 [2015]) while Urvashi Butalia and Ritu Menon (Chapter 32 [1995]) examine the particular challenges facing feminist publishers in the global south.

Postcolonial scholars have turned their attention to the implications of inequalities in knowledge production on a global scale, analysing the cultural, political and economic impact of the transnational and local book trade, and the emergence and constitution of reading publics in colonial and postcolonial contexts. The publisher's role, not just as an intermediary, but as an agent and gatekeeper in the production of print culture, is explored in this research, and there is particular attention to how such control over the production and circulation of printed books has adversely shaped literary and cultural development in these countries. One line of scholarship is concerned with the historical legacies of imperialism on the book trade, and the European publishing industry's involvement in the exercise of colonial and neo-colonial expansion (see extracts by Henry Chakava, Chapter 28 [1992]; Graham Huggan, Chapter 29 [2001]; and Robert Fraser, Chapter 27 [2008]), while other scholars have examined how print culture and publishing have been employed as a tool of independence, resistance and subversion in colonial and postcolonial contexts (see extracts by James Currey, Chapter 30 [2008]; and Archie L. Dick, Chapter 20 [2012]). Further recent scholarship has focused on the implications of a globalised, conglomerated publishing industry for authors, literature and publishers in the global south (see extracts by Walter Bgoya, Chapter 40 [2001]; Pascale Casanova, Chapter 26 [2004]; Sarah Brouillette, Chapter 43 [2007]; and Suman Gupta, Chapter 42 [2009]).

The most significant transformation in book and print culture during the last century has resulted from the digital revolution. A number of scholars embrace what Jay David Bolter (2001) termed 'the late age of print', arguing that the internet and digital publishing tools have liberated mass communication from control by a small elite: George Landow (Chapter 12 [2006]) celebrates the transformative potential of digital text, while Mohanalakshmi Rajakumar and Rumsha Shahzad (Chapter 34 [2015]) maintain that digital text offers new possibilities for women writers to tackle gender inequalities in the publishing industry. Other critics draw attention to the threats of digital disruption: for example, Laura Dietz (Chapter 11 [2015]) draws attention to the risk that new digital publishing poses to authors' careers, and John B. Thompson (Chapter 6 [2010]) points to the dangers associated with the possible disintermediation of the publisher from the publishing value chain. Michael Bhaskar (Chapter 7 [2013]) argues that digital technology is ambivalent, simultaneously offering the potential for individualism as well as centralisation, for freedom and for surveillance. Furthermore, several chapters grapple with the way that geographical boundaries are challenged by digital communications technology and publishing, and the extent to which new networks, connections and exchanges are being established that either challenge or reinforce traditional binaries between West and East, North and South (Walter Bgoya, Chapter 40 [2001]; Sarah Brouillette, Chapter 43 [2007]; Pascale Casanova, Chapter 26 [2004]; Angus Phillips, Chapter 41 [2014]; and Suman Gupta, Chapter 42 [2009]). These texts explore the dichotomy in twenty-first-century print and publishing culture, which on the one hand offers unique opportunities for individual expression and control, and for dissent and political opposition, as a result of digital technology and the internet, but on the other hand has become more centralised than ever before.

The book is organised into nine parts, each dealing with a specific concept or theme, and each consisting of an introduction and a selection of texts from leading theorists, historians and critics. The volume begins with an examination of publishing, authorship and readers in the literary marketplace, and then turns to censorship, propaganda and war, colonial and postcolonial print cultures, women and print culture, literary prize culture and globalisation and the book.

These readings in print culture shed light on the circuits of power operating in twentieth- and twenty-first-century print culture; they examine how the role of the author, the publisher and the reader have changed in response to socio-economic, political and ideological challenges, and explore the networks of textual exchanges underlying the publications of books and other texts. They offer important interventions in central, often paradoxical, issues in print culture studies: the ways in which the publishing industry, while corporate owned, also provides opportunities for individual and collective creativity; how print is employed as a means of enforcement of dominant ideologies, but conversely as a means of resistance; and how print and digital text has been used as a vehicle both for societal and political control and for radical social change.

SUGGESTED FURTHER READING

Darnton, R., 1982. 'What is the history of books?'. *Daedalus,* 111 (3), 65–83.

Finkelstein, D. and A. McCleery (eds), 2006b. 'Introduction', in *The Book History Reader.* London: Routledge, 1–4.

Howsam, L., 2014. 'The practice of book and print culture: Sources, methods, readings', in E. Patten and J. McElligott (eds). *The Perils of Print Culture: Book, Print and Publishing History in Theory and Practice.* Basingstoke: Palgrave Macmillan, 17–34.

McKenzie, D.F., 1999. *Bibliography and the Sociology of Texts.* Cambridge: Cambridge University Press.

Part One
Publishing: Theory and Practice

The publisher tends to be a hidden, somewhat overlooked figure in the process of literary and cultural production: while the author is more prominent and acclaimed, the publisher is often invisible. The key functions of the book publisher – acquisition and commissioning, editing, design and production, marketing and sales – are carried out behind the scenes and little attention is paid to the publisher's work in the shaping of the author's identity and public profile. This neglect is surprising, considering the historical and contemporary significance of publishing as a major culture-producing agency, and the fact that it is now a vast, global business.

As a subject of scholarship, the publishing industry has likewise failed to receive the same sustained research and theoretical attention of other creative cultural industries, for example journalism, television, film or museums. Several critics have commented on this academic lacuna: John Sutherland (1988: 576) pronounced that 'publishing history, though it flourishes with extraordinary juvenile vigour, lacks binding theoretical coherence' and Philip Altbach (1995: xxiii) described publishers as 'uninterested ... in systematically understanding the nature of their industry'. More recently, Simone Murray (2007: 3) has written of the 'inherited lack of theoretical and methodological rigour amongst the vocational wing of publishing studies' while Michael Bhaskar's (2013: 4) verdict is that 'Publishing has been thoroughly explored, both historically and in the present, but not adequately theorised'. Yet, although publishing as an academic subject has been widely overlooked, there have been some exciting new interventions in this field of study. This section highlights some of the ground-breaking texts in the theory and practice of publishing, while many other influential works theorising publishing and the role of the publisher are reprinted elsewhere in this volume (see extracts by Lewis A. Coser, Chapter 18 [1975]; Graham Huggan, Chapter 29 [2001]; Pascale Casanova, Chapter 26 [2004]; Sarah Brouillette, Chapter 43 [2007]; and Claire Squires, Chapter 37 [2007]). Collectively, these studies demonstrate a new concern with drawing the publisher out from the shadows and into the forefront of our understanding about the institutions that shape textual and literary culture.

Studies of publishing have traditionally been carried out within the industry itself, and take the form of official publishers' house histories, memoirs and biographies of prominent publishers. These texts, both corporate and personal, are employed as branding and publicity devices for the companies, a means of imparting prestige to the publisher's imprint. A famous example of the publishing memoir is reproduced in extract in Chapter 2: Stanley Unwin's *The Truth about a*

Publisher (1960). Unwin had an illustrious career as a publisher, initially working for his uncle T. Fisher Unwin, and then founding the British publishing house George Allen and Unwin in 1914. As President of the Publisher's Association from 1933, he championed British publishing interests abroad during and after the Second World War. But he is remembered most as the first publisher of J. R. R. Tolkien, having published *The Hobbit* in 1937 and *The Lord of the Rings* in 1954–5. Describing the world of the 'gentleman' publisher, who works in small independent firms and deals personally with authors, literary agents, printers and booksellers, his memoir provides a behind-the-scenes view of author–publisher relations and is full of anecdotes about the tribulations of publishers in the book trade. Unwin presents a vision of the ideal publisher, who pursues literary and cultural value, in contrast to 'dull' profit-seeking publishers.

The second extract (Chapter 3) in this section is Pierre Bourdieu's article 'The Market for Symbolic Goods' (1985), originally published as 'Le Marché des Biens Symboliques' (1971), which was his first full exposition of the field of cultural production and the role of the publisher in the process of 'symbolic production' (p. 19), or the creation of literary prestige and cultural value. Bourdieu, like Unwin, positions the publisher at the interchange of culture and commerce, but his analysis is significantly more complex. He dissects the systems of value operating within cultural institutions and identifies 'the social conditions underlying the production of the work and those determining its functioning' (1985: 142). The article begins with an assessment of the historical development of the two complementary cultural markets: the 'field of large-scale cultural production' (p. 17), which is defined as mass or popular culture, based on financial profits, dependent on the broadest possible audience and less susceptible to formal experimentation, and the 'field of restricted production' (p. 17), the art and literature that is conducive to innovation and marked by autonomy from the market and disavowal of economic capital. He describes the various authorities and institutions which compete for legitimacy to 'consecrate' literature and culture, including publishers, critics and academic institutions (p. 20). Focusing in particular on the way in which cultural value is conferred in the field of restricted production, the extract concludes with an illustration of the role of the publisher in making a literary judgement about whether or not to publish a work. For Bourdieu the publisher is thus not so much a literary 'discoverer', confident in his or her 'flair' to make judgements about an author's work (p. 24), but is instead a 'trader' in symbolic capital and economic capital, who operates alongside critics and educational institutions to assign recognition to certain authors (p. 25). Bourdieu developed these ideas further in *The Field of Cultural Production* (1993) and *The Rules of Art* (1996). His theoretical formulations have underpinned many subsequent studies of publishing and literary institutions, for examples see Peter McDonald (2002) and chapters in this volume by Casanova (Chapter 26 [2004]), James English (Chapter 38 [2005]) and John B. Thompson (Chapter 6 [2010]).

A further influential model for theorising the cultural interventions of the publisher is set out by Gérard Genette in *Paratexts: Thresholds of Interpretation* (Chapter 4 in this volume [1997: 1–8]), which stresses the importance of the material book as a site of communication. Genette suggests here that a book's paratexts constitute important interventions that intrinsically affect the meaning of the text to the reader, as 'liminal devices and conventions' that operate between author and reader, mediating between private and public spheres. 'Peritext' (p. 33) he defines as the authorial and publisher's interventions within the book, while 'Epitext' (p. 32) is the accompanying textual and non-textual material that surrounds a text. Genette hereby challenges the conventional approach in literary studies, in which the text is often studied in disembodied form, and urges attention instead to the physical form of the book.

A feminist theory of publishing and gatekeeping is proposed by Lynne Spender in *Intruders on the Rights of Men: Women's Unpublished Heritage* (Chapter 5 in this volume [1983]). She maintains that print and power are closely interrelated and that women have been 'excluded from or edited out of the printed words that make up our cultural heritage. They have been relegated to what constitutes an *unpublished heritage* of women's words and truths' (1983: xi). Spender argues that the male-dominated publishing industry has functioned as a gatekeeper, ensuring that male print culture is preserved: 'our patriarchal society is purposefully arranged so that men fill the decision-making positions and become the keepers of the gates ... Gatekeeping thus provides men with a mechanism to promote their own needs and interests at the expense of all others' (p. 39). Her main assertion is that 'Print, the conveyor of truth and creator of knowledge, does not reflect human experience and universal truth. It stands as a mirror for men and reflects the values of a male-supremacist society' (p. 20).

Thompson's *Merchants of Culture* (Chapter 6 in this volume [2010]) is a sociological account of the development and infrastructure of the trade publishing sector in the United States and Britain, based on sales data and on extensive, albeit anonymised, interviews with publishers. He follows Bourdieu's framework and terminology for analysing the publishing industry, but he identifies further kinds of capital in operation: in addition to economic capital and symbolic capital, he lists human capital (staffing), social capital (networks) and intellectual capital (copyright). His introductory chapter, reproduced here, describes the publisher's role metaphorically as a 'value chain', in which each link represents one of the six main functions of the publisher, and each of these functions contributing specific value. Yet the links in the chain are fragile and vulnerable to change, which might cause them to be disintermediated. He raises the question, 'Given that the publishing chain is not rigid and that particular tasks or functions can be eclipsed by economic and technological change, what reason is there to believe that the role of the publisher itself might not be rendered redundant?' (p. 48).

The significant challenge that the digital environment presents to the cultural authority and function of the publisher is addressed by Michael Bhaskar in *The Content Machine: Towards a Theory of Publishing from the Printing Press to the Digital Network* (Chapter 7 in this volume [2013]). This analyses the potential of digitisation and the internet to render redundant the gatekeeping, editing and distribution roles of the publisher. The internet, in Bhaskar's view, fundamentally alters the practices and function of the publisher, offering a medium for individualism and democracy, but conversely as a vehicle for the concentration of digital media ownership by a handful of conglomerates in the West. Examining the key features of the network, he draws attention to two apparently opposing forces: that of centralisation and fragmentation. On the one hand the network enables technology giants to achieve unprecedented levels of power, influence and disruption, thus threatening and overturning existing models of communication and traditional agencies like publishers, but on the other hand it permits unprecedented levels of fragmentation and openness. These dual and competing effects of the network present new challenges to the publisher and create openings for new players: both the 'amateur' publisher and also new corporations.

These texts offer contrasting interpretations of the publisher's role during the twentieth and early twenty-first centuries and suggest various models and metaphors for explaining the functions of the publisher. Unwin's self-assurance about the cultural significance of the gentlemanly publisher, who balances commerce and culture, is succeeded by Spender's critique of the publisher as a patriarchal censor and gatekeeper. Bourdieu depicts the publisher as a key agent in the 'field of cultural production' and Genette portrays the publisher as the creator of the 'threshold' of a text. More recently, Thompson regards publishing as a series of links in the 'value chain', and questions whether the publisher is due to be 'eclipsed, marginalised, transformed or taken over by others', while Bhaskar depicts the publisher as a node in a digital network, who faces an 'existential challenge' in the contemporary networked environment. The position of the publisher in literature, culture and society – once assured – is increasingly deemed contentious, problematic and unstable.

SUGGESTED FURTHER READING

Feather, J., 2005. *A History of British Publishing*. London: Routledge.

Mumby, F. A., 1954 [1930]. *Publishing and Bookselling: A History from the Earliest Times to the Present Day*. London: Jonathan Cape.

Murray, S., 2007. 'Publishing studies: Critically mapping research in search of a discipline'. *Publishing Research Quarterly*, Winter, 3–25.

Rose, J. (ed.), 1991. *British Literary Publishing Houses, 1881–1965*. Detroit and London: Gale.

Spiers, J., 2011. *The Culture of the Publisher's Series*. Vols 1 and 2. Basingstoke: Palgrave Macmillan.

Sutherland, J., 1998. 'Publishing history: A hole at the centre of literary sociology'. *Critical Inquiry*, 14 (3), 574–589.

Unwin, S., 1926. *The Truth about Publishing*. London: Allen & Unwin.

2 The Trials of a Publisher

Stanley Unwin

It has been said, by whom I don't remember, that 'Everyone knows about the trials of an author because, as writing is his profession, he takes care that his troubles shall not be hidden. But the publisher's trials have usually to be borne in secret.'

There are those who would maintain that the whole process of publishing is one prolonged trial from the arrival of the disorderly manuscript, bearing neither name nor address, to the vexatious libel action that may unexpectedly follow the publication of the most innocent work. But I am not one of them; I am too conscious of the many compensations publishing has to offer.

In the past, probably the chief trial of a publisher was that the day he became one he ceased to be an ordinary human being. He found himself regarded at one moment as an unscrupulous rogue with Machiavellian cunning, and the next as a philanthropist with unlimited endowments behind him. The rapidity of the change from one role to the other was sometimes startling. In my youth railway companies, until they took to prosecuting people and publishing lists of convictions, were regarded as 'fair game'. Publishers sometimes appeared to be in that unhappy position. I remember one author frankly admitting to me that he regarded it as quite all right to do a publisher down. Publishers in fact sometimes seemed to be regarded as being of a pariah class, in dealing with whom truthfulness and common honesty were superfluous. No doubt that was at the back of the mind of the author who, in my Fisher Unwin days, typed two copies of his manuscript and sold the copyright in his work for cash to two different publishers. Fortunately I was the prompter in producing the money, so that when the unfortunate publishers compared notes after both had printed the book, T. Fisher Unwin was found to be the owner of the copyright and was spared the unpleasant job of prosecuting.

I sometimes used to think it was a pity that the late Herbert Jenkins, when he left his money to the RSPCA, did not add a proviso that, for the purposes of his legacy, a publisher was an animal. However, publishers *are* ordinary human beings, and fortunately today most authors recognize that fact and treat us accordingly. Nevertheless a publisher has to remember (and console himself with the knowledge) that almost everything he does will be considered wrong, and that the utmost publicity will be given to his every shortcoming; that as John Fox once wrote to Charles Scribner, a publisher is 'a man who is blamed if a book fails and ignored if it proves a success'. If he rejects a manuscript, he will be wrong in the author's eyes. If he accepts anything but those rare works of genius that may come his way but once in a blue moon, he will be wrong in the eyes of booksellers and critics. If he points out (correctly) that there is no probability of the sales of a particular book covering its printing bill – it is assumed not that there is anything wrong with the book or its subject, but that the publisher is mean and unenterprising. If, however, in a spirit of generosity, he publishes such books and finds his way to Carey Street, his creditors will be loud in their complaints. If he publishes a translation with the slightest blemish, he will be jumped on; but if he ventures on a mild protest when confronted with a translation too bad to be printable, he is apt to make an enemy for life. During the First World War I had just such a translation. It was so obviously, so palpably bad, that we had to have the work almost completely redone. It is our rule to give the translator's name, but in this instance we refused – I think quite rightly – to give the first translator the credit, or rather the unqualified credit, for the second translator's work. To do so would not only deceive the public, but might easily lead another publisher into the trouble we had experienced, because we ourselves had agreed to the author's choice of translator on the strength of a previous translation, which subsequent inquiry revealed was originally as bad as ours.

The translator was very angry, and found an ingenious way to vent her spleen. She persuaded a Scottish friend to sue us in Scotland for a debt of the predecessors of our predecessors, for which we were in no sense responsible, legally or morally. Some people doubtless understand Scottish law – I don't pretend to. Before our side of the matter was heard, the good lady had secured what is known as 'a writ of attachment', which prevented one of our biggest customers in Scotland from making any further payments to us till the matter was settled. We were advised that if we proposed to contest the claim it was essential to attend the court in person. With my colleagues and most of our staff away at the war, it simply couldn't be done. The amount involved was fortunately not considerable, so that it was simpler and cheaper to pay; but next time I shall go to Scotland.

Middlemen may be a great trial to a publisher for other reasons than is usually supposed. I am often accused of antipathy to literary agents, though I have some very good friends among them, because I have always maintained that they should be as open to criticism as publishers are, and have pointed out that just as there are good and bad publishers, there are good and bad agents.

My firm had gone to a great deal of trouble over a particular manuscript in which we were interested, and the author had recast it in accordance with our reader's detailed suggestions. At that stage a friend told the author that he ought to employ an agent, which he did. The book was shortly thereafter announced by another publisher. A year or two later the author returned to us, bemoaning the action of his agent – a well-known firm – because the publisher to whom the agent had transferred his work was now bankrupt. When we next had occasion to write to that particular agent, we mentioned, without giving reasons, that unfortunately we lacked confidence in his firm. It brought a strange letter from him the nature of which will be gathered from our reply:

'We have not accused you of the practice of "auctioning" books which you go out of your way to deny. But as you raise the question, it may interest you to know that I have at this moment on my desk a copy of a letter you wrote a few years back to one of your clients in which the following passage occurs:

'"On my report of the book, *supported of course by the fact that it is accepted by Allen & Unwin*, Messrs. —— are willing to publish it". ...

A subsequent letter reveals the fact that the publisher in question had not looked at the manuscript (over which we had gone to considerable trouble and expense) but had relied exclusively upon our judgment.

'The foregoing will perhaps explain our nervousness in negotiating with you.

'The result of the transfer to another firm of the book referred to in the correspondence proved most unfortunate for your client; but that aspect of the matter is not our business.'

A point which I think authors sometimes overlook is that almost inevitably and naturally agents have their special friends among publishers whom they tend, probably unconsciously, to think of first, whether or not they are necessarily the best suited for the particular book being offered. Moreover, some agents have no dealings at all with some publishers of repute and vice versa.

Whether as the author of *The Truth About Publishing*, or for some other reason I know not, but I am constantly asked for my advice about agents. Fortunately there are a few firms I have no hesitation in recommending.

Authors, even the most charming, are apt to suffer from illusions. One, harboured by most, is that it would be a disaster were their book not out in time for Christmas. Now unless it is a 'gift book' which no one would want to buy at any other time, this is often far from being the case. More books are issued in October and November than in any other months of the year, with the result that a smaller proportion are reviewed. Unless the books are published very early in the season they are too late for the Overseas Christmas season, which in some cases may be the more important. Furthermore, booksellers are confronted at that time with so many new books that they tend to be more discriminating and more cautious in their buying than at any other period except immediately before stocktaking. The publisher, whose sole aim is to sell his wares, is quite unprejudiced, and may be relied upon to give the best advice about the date of publication. The wise author defers to his publisher's judgment in such a question, but in this matter not all authors are wise. In a large proportion of cases, if a book cannot be published before the end of October it is best held over for publication in January or February – both excellent months, when people have Book Tokens to exchange.

Advertising can be a great trial. I wonder how many authors realize that probably nearly as much is spent to please or placate them as to sell their books. That peculiarly well-informed writer, Frank Swinnerton, has pointed out:[1]

'To authors it will come as incredible that advertising does not sell books. Yet that is the truth. *Advertising does not sell books.*' [His italics.]

The fact is that just as whipping will maintain, and even accelerate, the speed of a top that is already spinning, but will achieve nothing with one that is lying dormant on the ground, so advertising will maintain, and even accelerate, the sales of a book which is already being talked about, but will do little or nothing for one in which there is otherwise no interest. When we are told that a book has sold so well because it was advertised, it would almost certainly be true to say that it was extensively advertised because it was selling so well.

In the same way, many authors believe that their books would sell much better if they were on all the bookstalls, whereas the only books which justify that form of display are those that are very cheap, or for which there is already a demand, or certain to be a demand. A book will not sell merely because it is on a bookstall any more than it will sell merely because it is advertised. The secret is to get a book talked about. If that is achieved, sales, and probably bookstall display and advertising, will follow. But how is a publisher to convince an author of such unpalatable truths? We all admit that though you can take a horse to the water you cannot make it drink, but how many authors really believe that though a publisher can take his (or her) book to the booksellers he cannot make them buy? Fortunately most George Allen & Unwin authors in all such matters seem to be endowed with quite exceptional wisdom and unusual understanding.

Another illusion, seldom entertained by competent authors, is that the publisher's readers and others are waiting to plagiarize their work. I think it may be said that the more worthless the manuscript, the greater the fear of plagiarism. The author who tells you that he 'has solved the riddle of the universe', whose manuscript won't stand five minutes' investigation, is of course confident that his ideas are going to be stolen. We had one amusing incident with a manuscript of so-called verse which had inadvertently been included in another package. The authoress was confident that the person to whom the MS had accidentally been sent would appropriate her priceless 'poems' and started discussing the amount of damages she would claim; yet the recipient in returning them to us said she had no idea that anyone would have the effrontery to send a publisher such worthless rubbish.

If a competing book is offered to a publisher on a subject in which he has specialized, his own author, if consulted, would in many cases want him to decline the competing book without a moment's hesitation. If the book is definitely not so good as the one already published, the advice is of course sound, but what if the book is as good, or perhaps rather better? Again, most authors would want it turned down. But in that case they would probably be wrong. There are advantages in a publisher having all the best books on a subject in which he has specialized. In the hands of another publisher the second book would indeed be a competitor. If both are handled by the same firm each can be made to advertise the other and both will benefit. The extent to which books in the same category or class can be made to advertise each other is seldom realized by authors, and not always by publishers.

I dare not dwell upon the multifarious troubles connected with book production, but I cannot pass over the difficulties that may attend the most insignificant printer's error.

In a biography of a worthy gentleman which we published, mention was made of the fact that when he was ill, Lady Blank brought him flowers – gay ones. In the course of printing, the last 's' disappeared. Any other 's' would probably not have mattered, but the sentence now read 'Lady Blank brought him flowers – gay one'. Lady B., a most virtuous and respectable old lady, objected vehemently to being pilloried as a 'gay one'. The sale of the book had to be suspended until the offending page was reprinted.

The dispatch of review copies would seem to be a simple process, particularly if the list has been mutually agreed. Unfortunately one or two editors are apt to be a little reckless in assuring authors that they have not had their books. (I admit the authors brought it on themselves by asking.) One distinguished literary editor (now deceased) seemed to take a fiendish delight in doing so. The trouble is that even if in such a case you show the author the formal receipt for the book, you do not necessarily satisfy him. In one case, to please a most important client, I sent a duplicate copy addressed personally to that particular editor, and got his initials on the receipt, but when next the author met him he still maintained he had not got it.

It used to puzzle me why important books failed to be reviewed in the one journal in which they would arouse most interest. The explanation proved to be simple. The editor had told the literary editor that he would review it personally, but found himself too pressed to do it until it was too late.

Apart from the destination of the review copies, the English publisher knows that the number he sends out is likely to be regarded as wrong. Either the author will think him stingy, or the Authors' Society will regard him as reckless. The German publisher suffers under no such disability. The law regarding publishing fixes the percentage, and for that matter saves him many of the English publisher's tribulations. It is recognized over there that both the publisher and the author need protection.

The answers given by some editors to importunate authors reminds me of many instances where over-zealous booksellers' assistants have assured authors that there has been such a run on their books that they have sold out, and have been unable to get further supplies. Imagine what such an author thinks of his publisher when the latter is called upon to disillusion him, and explain that there has been no run on the book, that it has never been out of stock, that the bookseller in question has never used a single copy, and refuses to put even one into stock.

Not only authors can regard publishers as philanthropists. A large body of people delude themselves with the notion that publishers live by giving their wares away; and consider it rather a privilege to encounter a recipient for them. The extent to which books are 'cadged' is unbelievable, and it is often the wealthiest who are the worst offenders. We receive book-begging letters of some kind almost every day, and often from institutions and people who would never think of 'begging' for any other commodity.

The misuse of the telephone is a very serious trial. The 'phone contributes far more to the inefficiency than to the efficiency of a publishing office – thoughtless people ring up for information needing hours of research; editors inquire about rights in illustrations of books long out of print, when a moment's reflection would tell them that an immediate answer over the telephone was out of the question. Some people – I fear a growing number – suffer from telephone mania. When they have nothing definite to do they ring up someone on the telephone. Publishers are interesting people with no particular occupation – let's ring up a publisher.

According to one distinguished novelist a publisher ought to spend most of his time entertaining authors. To do so at lunch can be one of the most pleasant aspects of publishing, but to devote one's entire home life to it would indeed be a trial. It is a trial which some publishers seem to survive with equanimity if not to enjoy, but one that I have successfully avoided. I find most authors agree with me that some part at any rate of a publisher's evenings could not be better spent than in reading their manuscripts in the quiet of his home.

3 The Market of Symbolic Goods

Pierre Bourdieu

THE STRUCTURE AND FUNCTIONING OF THE FIELD OF RESTRICTED PRODUCTION

The system of production and circulation of symbolic goods is defined as the system of objective relations among different institutions, functionally defined by their role in the division of labour of production, reproduction and diffusion of symbolic goods. The field of production per se owes its own structure to the opposition between the *field of restricted production* as a system producing cultural goods objectively destined for a public of producers of cultural goods, and the *field of large-scale cultural production*, specifically organized with a view to the production of cultural goods destined for non-producers of cultural goods, 'the public at large'.

In contrast to the field of large-scale cultural production, which submits to the laws of competition for the conquest of the largest possible market, the field of restricted production tends to develop its own criteria for the evaluation of its products, thus achieving the truly cultural recognition accorded by the peer group whose members are both privileged clients and competitors. The field of restricted production can only become a system objectively producing for producers by breaking with non-culture-producing sections of the dominant class. This rupture could only be the inverse image, in the cultural sphere, of the relations that develop between the intellectual and the dominating sections of the dominant class in the economic and political sphere. From 1830 literary society isolated itself in an aura of indifference and rejection towards the buying and reading public, i.e. towards the 'bourgeois'. By an effect of circular causality, separation and isolation engender further separation and isolation, and cultural production develops a dynamic autonomy.

Freed from the censorship and auto-censorship consequent on direct confrontation with a public foreign to the profession, and encountering within the corps of producers itself a public at once of critics and accomplices, it tends to obey its own logic, that of the continual outbidding inherent to the dialectic of cultural distinction.

The autonomy of a field of restricted production can be measured by its power to define its own criteria for the production and evaluation of its products. This implies translation of all external determinations in conformity with its own principles of functioning. Thus, the more cultural producers form a closed field

17

of competition for cultural legitimacy, the more the internal demarcations appear irreducible to any external factors of economic, political or social differentiation.[1]

It is significant that the progress of the field of restricted production towards autonomy is marked by an increasingly distinct tendency of criticism to devote itself to the task, not of producing the instruments of appropriation – the more imperatively demanded by a work the further it separates itself from the public – but to provide a 'creative' interpretation for the benefit of the 'creators'. And so, tiny 'mutual admiration societies' grew up, closed in upon their own esotericism, as, simultaneously, signs of a new solidarity between artist and critic emerged. This new criticism, no longer feeling itself qualified to formulate peremptory verdicts, placed itself unconditionally at the service of the artist. It attempted scrupulously to decipher his intentions, while excluding the public of non-producers from the entire business, by attesting, through its 'inspired' readings, the intelligibility of works which were bound to remain unintelligible to those not sufficiently integrated into the producers' field.[2] Intellectuals and artists always look suspiciously – though not without a certain fascination – at dazzlingly successful works and authors, sometimes to the extent of seeing worldly failure as a guarantee of salvation in the hereafter: Among other reasons the interference of the 'general public' is such that it threatens the field's claims to a monopoly of cultural consecration. It follows that the gulf between the hierarchy of producers dependent on 'public success' (measured by volume of sales or fame outside the body of producers) and the hierarchy dependent upon recognition within the peer competitor group undoubtedly constitutes the best indicator of the autonomy of the field of restricted production.

No one has ever completely extracted all the implications of the fact that the writer, the artist, or even the scientist writes not only for a public, but for a public of equals who are also competitors. Few people depend, as much as artists and intellectuals do, for their self image upon the image others, and particularly other writers and artists, have of them.

'There are', writes Jean-Paul Sartre (1948: 98) 'qualities that we acquire uniquely through the judgements of others'. This is especially so for the quality of a writer, artist or scientist, which is so difficult to define because it exists only in, and through, the circular relations of reciprocal recognition among peers.[3] Any act of cultural production implies an affirmation of its claim to cultural legitimacy[4]: When different producers confront each other, it is still in the name of their claims to orthodoxy or, in Max Weber's terms, to the legitimate and monopolized use of a certain class of symbolic goods; when they are recognized, it is their claim to orthodoxy that is being recognized. As witnessed by the fact that oppositions express themselves in terms of reciprocal excommunication, the field of restricted production can never be dominated by one orthodoxy without continuously being dominated by the general question of orthodoxy itself, that is by the question of the criteria defining the legitimate exertion of a certain type of cultural practice. It follows that the degree of autonomy enjoyed by a field of restricted production is measurable by the degree to which it is capable of functioning as a specific market, generating a specifically cultural type of scarcity and value irreducible to the economic scarcity and value of the goods in question. To put it another way, the more the field is capable of functioning as a field of competition for cultural legitimacy, the more individual production must be orientated toward the search for culturally pertinent features endowed with value in the field's own economy. This confers properly cultural value on the producers by endowing them with marks of distinction (a speciality, a manner, a style) liable to be recognized as such within the historically available cultural taxonomies.

Consequently, it is a structural law, and not a fault in nature, that draws intellectuals and artists into the dialectic of cultural distinction – often confused with an all-out quest for any difference that might raise them out of anonymity and insignificance.[5] The same law also imposes limits within which the quest may be carried on legitimately. The brutality with which a strongly integrated intellectual or artistic community condemns any unorthodox attempt at distinction bears witness to the fact that the community can affirm the autonomy of the specifically cultural order only if it controls the dialectic of cultural distinction, continually liable to degenerate into an anomic quest for difference at any price.

It follows from all that has just been said, that the principles of differentiation regarded as most legitimate by an autonomous field are those which most completely express the specificity of a determinate type of practice. In the field of art, for example, stylistic and technical principles tend to become the privileged subject of debate among producers (or their interpreters). Apart from laying bare the desire to exclude those artists suspected of submitting to external demands, the affirmation of the primacy of the mode of representation over the object of representation is the most specific expression of the field's claim to wield and to impose the principles of a properly cultural legitimacy regarding both the production and the reception of an artwork.[6] Affirming the primacy of the saying over the thing said, sacrificing the 'subject' to the manner in which it is treated, constraining language in order to draw attention to language, all this comes down to an affirmation of the specificity and the irreplaceability of the product and producer. Delacroix (1923: 76) said, aptly, 'All subjects become good through the merits of their author. Oh! young artist, do you seek a subject? Everything is a subject; the subject is you yourself, your impression, your emotions before nature. You must look within yourself, and not around you'. The true subject of the work of art is nothing other than the specifically artistic manner in which the artist grasps the world, those infallible signs of his mastery of his art. Stylistic principles, in becoming the dominant subject of controversy among producers, are ever more rigorously perfected and fulfilled in works of art. At the same time, they are ever more systematically affirmed in the theoretical discourse, accompanying confrontation. Because the logic of cultural distinction leads producers to develop original modes of expression, the different types of restricted production (painting, music, novels, theatre, poetry, etc.) are destined to fulfil themselves in their most specific aspects – those least reducible to any other form of expression.

The circularity of the relations of cultural production and consumption resulting from the objectively closed nature of the field of restricted production, enables the development of symbolic production to take on the form of an almost *reflexive history*: The incessant clarification of the foundations of his work provoked by criticism or the work of others determines a decisive transformation of the relation between the producer and his work, which reacts, in turn, on the work itself.

Few works do not bear within them the imprint of the system of positions in relation to which their originality is defined; few works do not contain indications of the manner in which the author conceived the novelty of his undertaking or of what, in his own eyes, distinguished it from his contemporaries and competitors. The objectification achieved by criticism which elucidates the meaning inscribed in a work, instead of subjecting it to normative judgements, tends to play a determining role in this process by stressing the efforts of artists and writers to realize their idiosyncrasy. The parallel variations in critical interpretation, in the producer's discourse, and even in the structure of the work itself, bear witness to the recognition of critical discourse by the producer – both because he feels himself to be recognized through it, and because he recognizes himself within it. The public meaning of a work in relation to which the author must define himself, originates in the process of circulation and consumption, dominated by the objective relations between the institutions and agents implicated in the process. The social relations which produce this public meaning are determined by the relative position these agents occupy in the structure of the field of restricted production. These relations, e.g. between author and publisher, publisher and critic, author and critic, are revealed as the ensemble of relations attendant on the 'publication' of the work, that is, it's becoming a public object. In each of these relations, each of these agents engages not only his own image of other factors in the relationship (consecrated or exorcized author, avant-garde or traditional publisher, etc.) which depends on his relative position within the field, but also his image of the other factor's image of himself, i.e. of the social definition of his objective position in the field.

To appreciate the gulf separating experimental art, which originates in the field's own internal dialectic, from popular art forms, one might consider the evolutionary logic of literary language use. As this restricted language is produced in accordance with social relations, whose dominant feature is the quest for distinction, its use obeys what one might term 'the gratuitousness principle'. Its manipulation demands the almost reflexive knowledge of schemes of expression which are transmitted by an education explicitly aimed at inculcating the allegedly appropriate categories.

'Pure' poetry appears as the methodical application of a system of explicit principles which were at work, though only in a diffuse manner, in earlier writings. Its most specific effects, for example, derive from games of suspense and surprise, from the concerted betrayal of expectations, and from the gratifying frustration provoked by archaism, preciosity, lexicological or syntactic dissonances, the destruction of stereotyped sounds or meaning sequences, ready-made formulae, *idées reçues* and commonplaces. The recent history of music, whose evolution consists in the increasingly professionalized search for technical solutions to fundamentally technical problems, appears to be the culmination of a process of refinement which began the moment popular music became subject to the learned manipulation of professionals. But probably nowhere is this dynamic model of a field tending to closure more completely fulfilled than in the history of painting.

Having banished all narrative content with impressionism and recognizing only specifically pictorial principles, painting progressively repudiated all traces of naturalism and sensual hedonism. Painting was thus set on the road to an explicit employment of the most characteristically pictorial principles of painting, which was tantamount to the questioning of these principles and, hence, of painting itself.[7]

One needs only compare the functional logic of the field of restricted production with the laws governing both the circulation of symbolic goods and the production of the consumers to perceive that such an autonomously developing field, making no reference to external demands, tends to nullify the conditions for its acceptance outside the field. To the extent that its products require extremely scarce instruments of appropriation, they are bound to precede their market or to have no clients at all, apart from producers themselves. Consequently they tend to fulfil socially distinctive functions, at first, in conflicts between sections of the dominant class, and, eventually, in relations among social classes. By an effect of circular causality, the structural gap between supply and demand contributes to the artists' determination to steep themselves in the search for 'originality' (with its concomitant ideology of the misunderstood genius). This comes about, as Arnold Hauser has suggested,[8] by placing them in difficult economic circumstances, and, above all, by effectively ensuring the incommensurability of the specifically cultural value and economic value in a work.

There is one essential condition for this: One has to be in form, as a sportsman has to be in form to run a hundred metres or to play a football match'.

It is unlikely that all writers and artists whose works are objectively addressed to the 'mass public' have, at least at the outset of their career, quite so realistic and 'disenchanted' an image of their function. Nonetheless, they can hardly avoid applying to themselves the objective image of their work received from the field. This image expresses the opposition between the two modes of production as objectively revealed in the social quality of their public ('intellectual' or 'bourgeois', for example). The more a certain class of writers and artists are defined as beyond the bounds of the universe of legitimate art, the more they are inclined to defend the professional qualities of the worthy, entertaining technician, complete master of his technique and metier against the uncontrolled, disconcerting experiments of 'intellectual' art.

There is no doubt, moreover, that the emergence of large collective production units in the fields of radio, television, cinema and journalism as well as in scientific research, and the concomitant decline of the intellectual artisan in favour of the salaried worker, entail a transformation of the relationship between the producer and his work, This will be reflected in his own representation of his position and function in the social structure, and, consequently, of the political and the aesthetic ideologies he professes. Intellectual labour carried out collectively, within technically and socially differentiated production units, can no longer surround itself with the charismatic aura attaching to traditional independent production. The traditional cultural producer was a master of his means of production and invested only his *cultural* capital, which was likely to be perceived as a gift of grace. The demystification of intellectual and artistic activity consequent on the

transformation of the social conditions of production particularly affects intellectuals and artists engaged in large units of cultural production (radio, television,
journalism). These constitute a proletaroid intelligentsia forced to experience
the contradiction between aesthetic and political standpoints stemming from its
inferior position in the field of production and the objectively conservative functions of its activity.

POSITIONS AND POSITION-TAKINGS

The relationship maintained by producers of symbolic goods with other producers,
with the significations available within the cultural field and, consequently, with
their own work, depends very directly upon the position they occupy within the
field of production and circulation of symbolic goods. This, in turn, is related to the
specifically cultural hierarchy of degrees of consecration. Such a position implies an
objective definition of their practice and of the products resulting from it. Whether
they like it or not, whether they know it or not, this definition imposes itself on
them as a fact, determining their ideology and their practice, and its potency manifests itself never so clearly as in conduct aimed at transgressing it. For example,
it is the ensemble of determinations inscribed in their position which inclines
professional jazz or film critics to issue very divergent and incompatible judgments
destined to reach only restricted cliques of producers and little sects of devotees.
These critics tend to ape the learned, sententious tone, and the cult of erudition
characterizing academic criticism, and to seek theoretical, political or aesthetic
security in the obscurity of a borrowed language.[9]

As distinct from a solidly legitimate activity, an activity on the way to legitimization continually confronts its practitioners with the question of its own legitimacy.
In this way, photography – that middle-brow art – condemns its practitioners to
create a substitute for the sense of cultural legitimacy which is given to the priests
of all the legitimate arts. More generally, all those marginal cultural producers
whose position obliges them to conquer the cultural legitimacy unquestioningly
accorded to the consecrated professions expose themselves to redoubled suspicion
by the efforts they can hardly avoid making to challenge its principles. The ambivalent aggression they frequently display toward consecratory institutions, especially
the educational system, without being able to offer a counter-legitimacy, bears
witness to their desire for recognition and, consequently, to the recognition they
accord to the educational system.

All relations that a determinate category of intellectuals or artists may establish with any and all external social factors – whether economic (e.g. publishers,
dealers), political or cultural (consecrating authorities such as Academies) – are
mediated by the structure of the field. Thus, they depend upon the position occupied by the category in question within the hierarchy of cultural legitimacy.

The sociology of intellectual and artistic production thus acquires its specific
object in constructing the relatively autonomous system of relations of production
and circulation of symbolic goods. In doing this, it acquires the possibility of grasp-
ing the positional properties that any category of agents of cultural production

or diffusion owes to its place within the structure of the field. Consequently, it acquires the capacity to explain those characteristics which products, as position-takings, owe to the *position* of their producers within the system of social relations of production and circulation and to the corresponding position which they occupy within the system of *cultural positions objectively possible* within a given state of the field of production and circulation.

The position-takings constitutive of the cultural field do not all suggest themselves with the same probability to those occupying at a given moment a determinate position in this field. Conversely, a particular class of cultural position-takings is attached as a potentially to each of the positions in the field of production and circulation (that is, a particular bundle of problems and structures of resolution, themes and procedures, aesthetic and political positions, etc.). These can only be defined differentially, that is, in relation to the other constitutive cultural positions in the cultural field under consideration. 'Were I as glorious as Paul Bourget', Arthur Cravan (1966: 324) used to say, 'I'd present myself nightly in music-hall revues in nothing but a G-string, and I guarantee you I'd make a bundle'. This attempt to turn literary glory into a profitable undertaking only appears at first sight to be selfdestructive and comical because it assumes a desacralised and desacralising relationship with literary authority. And such a stance would be inconceivable for anyone other than a marginal artist, knowing and recognizing the principles of cultural legitimacy well enough to be able to place himself outside of the cultural law.[10] There is no position within the field of cultural production that does not call for a determinate type of position-taking (*prise de position*) and which does not exclude, simultaneously, an entire gamut of abstractly possible position-takings. This does not require that possible or excluded position-takings be explicitly prescribed or prohibited. But one should beware of taking as the basis of all practice the strategies half-consciously elaborated in reference to a never more than partial consciousness of structures. In this connection one might think, for example, of the knowledge of the present and future structure of the labour market that is mobilized at the moment of a change in orientation.

All relations among agents and institutions of diffusion or consecration are mediated by the field's structure. To the extent that the ever-ambiguous marks of recognition owe their specific form to the objective relations (perceived and interpreted as they are in accordance with the unconscious schemes of the habitus) they contribute to form the *subjective* representation which agents have of the *social* representation of their position within the hierarchy of consecrations. And this semi-conscious representation itself constitutes one of the mediations through which, by reference to the social representation of possible, probable or impossible position-takings the system of relatively unconscious strategies of the occupants of a given class of positions is defined.

It would be vain to claim to assess from among the determinants of practices, the impact of durable, generalized and transposable dispositions, the impact of the perception of this situation and of the intentional or semi-intentional strategies which arise in response to it. The least conscious dispositions, such as those constituting the primary class habitus, are themselves constituted through the internalisation of an objectively selected system of signs, indices and sanctions.

And these are nothing but the materialization, within objects, words or conducts, of a particular kind of objective structures. Such dispositions remain the basis upon which all the signs and indices characterizing very varied situations are selected and interpreted.

In order to gain some idea of the complex relations between unconscious dispositions and the experiences which they structure or, what amounts to the same, between the unconscious strategies engendered by habitus and strategies consciously produced in response to a situation designed in accordance with the schemes of the habitus, it will be necessary to analyse an example.

The manuscripts a publisher receives are the product of a kind of pre-selection by the authors themselves according to their representation of the publisher who is occupying a specific position within the space of publishers. The authors' representation of their publisher which may have oriented their production is itself a function of the objective relationship between the positions authors and publishers occupy in the field. The manuscripts are, moreover, coloured from the first by a series of determinations (e.g. 'interesting, but not very commercial', or 'not very commercial, but interesting'), stemming quasi-mechanically from the relationship between the author's position in the field of production (unknown young author, consecrated author, house author, etc.) and the publisher's position within the system of production and circulation ('commercial' publisher, consecrated or avant-garde). They usually bear the marks of the intermediary whereby they came to the publisher (editor of a series, reader, 'house author', etc.) and whose authority, once again, is a function of respective positions in the field. Because subjective intentions and unconscious dispositions contribute to the effectiveness of the objective structures to which they are adjusted, their interlacing tends to guide each agent to his 'natural niche' in the structure of the field. It will be understood, moreover, that publisher and author can only experience and interpret the pre-established harmony achieved and revealed by their meeting as a miracle of predestination: 'Are you happy to be published by Editions de Minuit?' 'If I had followed my instincts, I would have gone there straight away ... but I didn't dare; I thought they were too good for me ... So I first sent my manuscript to Publisher X. What I just said about X isn't very kind! They refused my book, and so I took it to Minuit anyway.' 'How do you get on with the publisher?' 'He began by telling me a lot of things I hoped had not shown, everything concerning time, coincidences'.[11]

The publisher's image of his 'vocation' combines the aesthetic relativism of the discoverer, conscious of having no other principle than that of defiance of all canonic principles, with the most complete faith in an absolute kind of 'flair'. This ultimate and often indefinable principle behind his choices finds itself continually strengthened and confirmed by his perception of the selective choices of authors and by the representations authors, critics, the public and other publishers have of his function within the division of intellectual labour.

The critic's situation is hardly any different: The works which he receives have undergone a process of pre-selection. They bear a supplementary mark, that of the publisher (and, sometimes, that of the author of a preface, an author or another critic). The value of this mark is a function, once more, of the structure of objective relations between the respective positions of author, publisher and critic.

It is also affected by the relationship of the critic to the predominant taxonomies in the critical world or in the field of restricted production (for example, the *nouveau roman*, 'objectal literature', etc.).

> 'Apart from the opening pages, which seem to be a more or less voluntary pastiche of the *nouveau roman*, *L'Auberge espagnole* tells a fantastic, though perfectly clear, story, whose development obeys the logic of dreams rather than reality' (Lalou: 1966).[12]

So the critic, suspecting the young novelist of having entered the hall of mirrors, enters there himself by describing what he takes for a reflection of the *nouveau roman*. Schönberg describes the same type of effect: 'On the occasion of a concert given by my pupils, a critic with a particularly fine ear defined a piece for string quartet whose harmony – as can be proved – was only a very slight development of Schubert's, as a product bearing signs of my influence'. Even if such errors of identification are not rare especially among the conservative critics, they may also bring profit to the 'innovators': On account of his position, a critic may find himself predisposed in favour of all kinds of avant-garde; accordingly he may act as an initiate, communicating the deciphered revelation back to the artist from whom he received it. The artist, in return, confirms the critic in his vocation, that of privileged interpreter, by confirming the accuracy of his decipherment.

On account of the specific nature of his interests, and of the structural ambiguity of his position as a trader objectively invested with some power of cultural consecration, the publisher is more strongly inclined than the other agents of production and diffusion to take the regularities objectively governing relations between agents into account in his conscious strategies. The selective discourse which he engages with the critic, who has been selected not merely because of his influence but also because of the affinities he may have with the work, and which may even go to the length of declared allegiance to the publisher and his entire list of publications, or to a certain category of authors, is an extremely subtle mixture, in which his own idea of the work combines with his idea of the idea the critic is likely to have, given the representation he has of the house's publications.

Hence, it is quite logical, and highly significant that what has become the name of a literary school (the *'nouveau roman'*), adopted by the authors themselves, should have begun as a pejorative label, accorded by a traditionalist critic to novels published by Editions de Minuit. Just as critics and public found themselves invited to seek the links that might unite works published under the same imprint, so authors were defined by this public definition of their works to the extent that they had to define themselves in relation to it. Moreover, confronted with the public's and the critics' image of them, they were encouraged to think of themselves as constituting more than simply a chance grouping. They became a school endowed with its own aesthetic programme, its eponymous ancestors, its accredited critics and spokesmen.

In short, the most personal judgments it is possible to make of a work, even of one's own work, are always collective judgments in the sense of position-takings referring to other position-takings through the intermediary of the objective relations between the positions of their authors within the field. Through the public meaning of the work, through the objective sanctions imposed by the symbolic market upon the producer's 'aspirations' and 'ambitions' and, in particular, through the degree of recognition and consecration it accords him, the entire structure of the field interposes itself between the producer and his work. This imposes a definition of his ambitions as either legitimate or illegitimate according to whether his position objectively implies, or denies, their fulfilment.

Because the very logic of the field condemns them to risk their cultural salvation in even the least of their position-takings and to watch, uncertainly, for the ever-ambiguous signs of an ever-suspended election, intellectuals and artists may experience a failure as a sign of election, or over-rapid or too brilliant success as a threat of damnation. They cannot ignore the value attributed to them, that is the position they are entitled to within the hierarchy of cultural legitimacy, as it is continually brought home by the signs of recognition or exclusion appearing in their relations with peers or with institutions of consecration.

For each position in the hierarchy of consecration there is a corresponding relationship – more or less ambitious or resigned – to the field of cultural practices which is, itself, hierarchized. An analysis of artistic or intellectual trajectories attests that those 'choices' most commonly imputed to 'vocation', such as choice of intellectual or artistic specialization – author rather than critic, poet rather than novelist – and, more profoundly, everything defining the manner in which one fulfils oneself in that 'chosen' speciality depend on the actual and potential position that the field attributes to the different categories of agents notably through the intermediary of the institutions of cultural consecration. It might be supposed that the laws governing intellectual or artistic 'vocations' are similar in principle to those governing scholastic 'choices', such as the 'choice' of faculty or discipline. Such a supposition would imply, for example, that the 'choice' of discipline be increasingly 'ambitious' (with respect to the reigning hierarchy in the university field) as one ascends towards those categories of students or teachers most highly consecrated, scholastically, and most favoured in terms of social origin. Again, it might be supposed that the greater the scholastic consecration, mediated by social origin, of a determinate category of teachers and researchers, the more abundant and ambitious would be their production.

Among the social factors determining the functional laws of any field of cultural production (literary, artistic or scientific), undoubtedly the most important is the hierarchic position of each discipline or specialization and the position of the different producers in the hierarchy peculiar to each subfield. The migrations of labour power which drive large sections of producers towards the currently most consecrated scientific discipline (or, elsewhere, artistic genre), and which are experienced as though 'inspired' by vocation or determined by some intellectual itinerary and often imputed to the effects of fashion, could be merely reconversions aimed at ensuring the best possible economic or symbolic return on a determinate kind of cultural capital. And the sensitivity necessary to sniff out these movements of the cultural value stock-exchange, the audacity requisite to abandoning well-worn paths for the most opportune seeming future once more depend on social factors, such as the nature of the capital possessed and scholastic and social origins with their attendant objective chances and aspira-tions.[13] Similarly, the interest which different categories of researchers manifest in different types of practice (for example, empirical research or theory) is also a composite function. It is dependent, first, on the ambitions which their formation and their scholastic success and, thus, their position in the discipline's hierarchy allows them to form by assuring them of reasonable chances of suc-cess. Secondly, it is a function of the objectively recognized hierarchy of the very different material and symbolic profits which particular practices or objects of study are in a position to procure.[14]

If the relations which make the cultural field into a field of (intellectual, artistic or scientific) position-takings only reveal their meaning and function in the light of the relations among cultural subjects who are holding specific positions in this field, it is because intellectual or artistic position-takings are also always semi-conscious strategies in a game in which the conquest of cultural legitimacy and of the concomitant power of legitimate symbolic violence is at stake. To claim to be able to discover the entire truth of the cultural field within that field is to transfer the objective relations between different positions in the field of cultural produc-tion into the heaven of logical and semiologic relations of opposition and homol-ogy. Moreover, it is to do away with the question of the relationship between this 'positional' field and the cultural field; in other words, it is to ignore the question of the dependence of the different systems of cultural position-takings constituting a given state of the cultural field upon the specifically cultural interests of different groups competing for cultural legitimacy. It is also to deprive oneself of the pos-sibility of determining what particular cultural position-takings owe to the social functions they fulfil in these groups' strategies.

Consequently, we can postulate that there is no cultural position-taking that cannot be submitted to a *double interpretation*: It can be related, on the one hand, to the realm of cultural position-takings constituent of the specifically cultural field; on the other hand, it can be interpreted as a consciously or unconsciously orientated strategy elaborated in regard to the field of allied or hostile positions.[15] Research starting from this hypothesis would doubtless find its surest landmarks in a methodical analysis of *privileged references*. These would be conceived, not as simple indices of information exchanges (in particular, implicit or explicit bor-rowings of words or ideas), but as so many landmarks circumscribing, within the common battlefield, the small network of privileged allies and adversaries proper to each category of producer.

'Citatology' nearly always ignores this question, implicitly treating references to an author as an index of recognition (of indebtedness or legitimacy). In point of fact this apparent function may nearly always be associated with such diverse func-tions as the manifestation of relations of allegiance or dependence, of strategies of affiliation, of annexation or of defence (this is the role, for example, of guarantee references, ostentatious references or alibi-references). We should mention, here, two 'citatologists' who have the merit of having posed a question systematically ignored: 'People quote another author for complex reasons – to confer meaning, authority or depth upon a statement, to demonstrate familiarity with other work in the same field and to avoid the appearance of plagiarising even ideas conceived independently. The quotation is aimed at readers of whom some, at least, are supposed to have some knowledge of the work quoted (there would be no point in quoting if this were not so) and to adhere to the norms concerning what may, and what may not, be attributed to it' (Cloyd and Bates 1964: 122). When it is not immediately explicit and direct (as in the case of polemical or deforming references), the strategic function of a reference may be apprehended in its modality – humble or sovereign, impeccably academic or sloppy, explicit or implicit and, in this case, unconscious, repressed (and betraying a strong relationship of ambivalence) or knowingly dissimulated (whether through tactical prudence, through a more or less visible and naive will to annexation – plagiarism – or through disdain). Strategic considerations may also stalk those quotations most directly orientated towards the functions commonly recognised as theirs' by 'citatology'. One just has to think of what might be termed an *a minima* reference, which consists in recognising a precise and clearly specified debt (by the full-length quotation of a sentence or an expression) in order to hide a far more global and more diffuse debt. (We should note, in passing, the existence of *a maxima* references, whose functions may vary from grateful homage to autovalorising annexation – when the contribution of the quoter to the thought quoted, which, in this case, must be prestigious, is fairly important and obvious.)

The construction of the system of relations between each of the categories of producers and competing, hostile, allied or neutral powers, which are to be destroyed, intimidated, cajoled, annexed or won over presumes a decisive rupture, first, with naive citatology as this does not go beyond any but the most phenomenal relationships; furthermore – and in particular – with that supremely naive representation of cultural production which takes only *explicit references* into account. How can we reduce Plato's presence in Aristotle's texts to explicit references alone, or that of Descartes in Leibniz's writings, of Hegel in those of Marx? We speak here more generally of those *privileged interlocutors* implicit in the writings of every producer, those masters whose thought structures he has internalized to the point where he no longer thinks except in them and through them, to the point where they have become intimate adversaries determining his thinking and imposing on him both the shape and the substance of conflict. Manifest conflicts dissimulate the *consensus* within the *dissensus* which defines the field of cultural battle in a given epoch, and which the educational system contributes to produce, by inculcating an uncontested hierarchy of themes and problems worthy of discussion. Given this, implicit references allow also to construct that intellectual space defined by a system of common references appearing so natural, so incontestable that they are never the object of conscious position-takings at all. However, it is in relation to this referential space that all the standpoints of the different categories of producers are differentially defined.

In addition to other possible functions, theories, methods and concepts in whatever realm are to be considered as strategies aimed at installing, restoring, strengthening, safe-guarding or upsetting a determinate structure of relationships of symbolic domination; that is, they constitute the means for obtaining or safe-guarding the monopoly of the legitimate mode of practising a – literary, artistic or scientific – activity.

How, for example, could one fail to see that 'epistemological couples' are nearly always covers for oppositions between different groups within the field? Such groups are led to transform interests associated with possession of a determinate type of scientific capital and with a determinate position within the scientific field, into epistemological choices. Is it not legitimate to suppose that there is a strategic intention (which may remain perfectly unconscious) lurking behind a theory of theory such as Merton's? Does one not better understand the *raison d'être* of works by the 'high methodologists', such as Lazarsfeld, as one realizes that these scholastic codifications of the rules of scientific practice are inseparable from the project of building a kind of intellectual papacy, replete with its international corps of vicars, regularly visited or gathered together in *concilium* and charged with the exercise of rigorous and constant control over common practice?

By ignoring the systems of social relations within which symbolic systems are produced and utilized, the strictly internal interpretation most frequently condemns itself to the gratuitousness of an arbitrary formalism: In point of fact, an appropriate construction of the object of analysis presupposes a sociological analysis of the social functions at the basis of the structure and functioning of any symbolic system. The semiologist, who claims to reveal the structure of a literary or artistic work through so-called strictly internal analysis exposes himself to a theoretical error by disregarding the social conditions underlying the production of the work and those determining its functioning.

A field of cultural production may have achieved virtually complete autonomy in relation to external forces and demands (as in the case of the purest sciences), while still remaining amenable to specifically sociological analysis. It is the job of sociology to establish the external conditions for a system of social relations of production, circulation and consumption necessary to the autonomous development of science or art; its task, moreover, is to determine those functional laws which characterize such a relatively autonomous field of social relations and which can also account for the structure of corresponding symbolic productions and its transformations. The principles of 'selection', objectively employed by the different groups of producers competing for cultural legitimacy are always defined within a system of social relations obedient to a specific logic. The symbolic standpoints are, moreover, functions of the interest-systems objectively attached to the position producers occupy in *special power relations*. These are the social relations of symbolic production, circulation and consumption.

As the field of restricted production closes in upon itself, and confirms itself as capable of organizing its production by reference to its own internal norms of perfection – excluding all social, or socially marked content from the work – the dynamic of competition for specifically cultural consecration becomes the exclusive principle of the production of works. Especially since the middle of the 19th century, the principle of change in art has come from within art itself, as though history were internal to the system and as if the development of forms of representation and expression were merely the product of the logical development of axiomatic systems specific to the various arts. To explain this, there is no need to hypostatize the laws of this evolution: If a relatively autonomous history of art and literature (or of science) exists, it is because the 'action of works upon works', of which Brunetière spoke, explains an ever increasing proportion of artistic or literary production. At the same time, the field as such explicates and systematizes specifically artistic principles of the production and the evaluation of the work of art. The relationship, moreover, which each category of producer enjoys with its own production is more and more exclusively determined by its relationship with the specifically artistic traditions and norms inherited from the past. The exact nature of the latter relationship is, again, a function of its position in the structure of the field of production.

True, cultural legitimacy appears to be the 'fundamental norm', to employ the language of Kelsen, of the field of restricted production. But this 'fundamental norm', as Jean Piaget (1950: 239) has noted, 'is nothing other than the abstract expression of the fact that society "recognizes" the normative value of this order'. It does this in such a way that it 'corresponds to the social reality of the exercise of some power and of the "recognition" of this power or of the system of rules emanating from it'. Thus, the relative autonomy of the field of restricted production authorizes the attempt to construct a 'pure' model of the objective relations defining it, and the interactions which develop within it. But one must remember that this formal construction is the product of the temporary bracketing-off of the field of restricted production (as a system of specific power relations) from the surrounding field of the power relations between classes. It would be futile to search for the ultimate foundation of this 'fundamental norm' within the field itself, since it resides in structures governed by powers other than the culturally legitimate; consequently, the functions objectively assigned to each category of producer and its products by its position in the field are always duplicated by the external functions objectively fulfilled through the accomplishment of its internal functions.

4 Paratexts: Thresholds of Interpretation

Gérard Genette

A literary work consists, entirely or essentially, of a text, defined (very minimally) as a more or less long sequence of verbal statements that are more or less endowed with significance. But this text is rarely presented in an unadorned state, unreinforced and unaccompanied by a certain number of verbal or other productions, such as an author's name, a title, a preface, illustrations. And although we do not always know whether these productions are to be regarded as belonging to the text, in any case they surround it and extend it, precisely in order to *present* it, in the usual sense of this verb but also in the strongest sense: to *make present*, to ensure the text's presence in the world, its 'reception' and consumption in the form (nowadays, at least) of a book. These accompanying productions, which vary in extent and appearance, constitute what I have called elsewhere the work's *paratext*,[1] in keeping with the sometimes ambiguous meaning of this prefix in French[2] (I mentioned adjectives like 'parafiscal' [a 'taxe parafiscale' is a special levy] or 'paramilitary'). For us, accordingly, the paratext is what enables a text to become a book and to be offered as such to its readers and, more generally, to the public. More than a boundary or a sealed border, the paratext is, rather, a *threshold*,[3] or – a word Borges used apropos of a preface – a 'vestibule' that offers the world at large the possibility of either stepping inside or turning back. It is an 'undefined zone'[4] between the inside and the outside, a zone without any hard and fast boundary on either the inward side (turned toward the text) or the outward side (turned toward the world's discourse about the text), an edge, or, as Philippe Lejeune put it, 'a fringe of the printed text which in reality controls one's whole reading of the text'.[5] Indeed, this fringe, always the conveyor of a commentary that is authorial or more or less legitimated by the author, constitutes a zone between text and off-text, a zone not only of transition but also of *transaction*: a privileged place of a pragmatics and a strategy, of an influence on the public, an influence that – whether well or poorly understood and achieved – is at the service of a better reception for the text and a more pertinent reading of it (more pertinent, of course, in the eyes of the author and his allies). To say that we will speak again of this influence is an understatement: all the rest of this book is about nothing else except its means, methods, and effects. To indicate what is at stake, we can ask one simple question as an example: limited to the text alone and without a guiding set of directions, how would we read Joyce's *Ulysses* if it were not entitled *Ulysses*?

The paratext, then, is empirically made up of a heterogeneous group of practices and discourses of all kinds and dating from all periods which I federate under the term 'paratext' in the name of a common interest, or a convergence of effects, that seems to me more important than their diversity of aspect. The table of contents of this book undoubtedly makes it unnecessary for me to list these practices and discourses here, except that one or two terms are provisionally obscure, and these I will soon define. As far as possible, my approach follows the order in which one usually meets the messages this study explores: the external presentation of a book – name of author, title, and the rest – just as it is offered to a docile reader, which certainly does not mean every reader. In this respect, my saving everything I call 'epitext' for the end is no doubt especially arbitrary because many future readers become acquainted with a book thanks to, for example, an interview with the author (if not a magazine review or a recommendation by word of mouth, neither of which, according to our conventions, generally belongs to the paratext, which is characterized by an authorial intention and assumption of responsibility); but the advantages of putting the epitext at the end will, I hope, turn out to be greater than the drawbacks. In addition, this overall arrangement is not so strict as to be especially coercive, and those who ordinarily read books by beginning at the end or in the middle will be able to apply the same method, if it is one, to this book, too.

Furthermore, the paratextual messages inventoried here (in a preliminary, condensed, and doubtless incomplete way) do not constitute a uniformly unvarying and systematic presence around a text: some books lack a preface, some authors resist being interviewed, and in some periods it was not obligatory to record an author's name or even a work's title. The ways and means of the paratext change continually, depending on period, culture, genre, author, work, and edition, with varying degrees of pressure, sometimes widely varying: it is an acknowledged fact that our 'media' age has seen the proliferation of a type of discourse around texts that was unknown in the classical world and *a fortiori* in antiquity and the Middle Ages, when texts often circulated in an almost raw condition, in the form of manuscripts devoid of any formula of presentation. I say an *almost* raw condition because the sole fact of transcription – but equally, of oral transmission – brings to the ideality of the text some degree of materialization, graphic or phonic, which, as we will see, may induce paratextual effects. In this sense, one may doubtless assert that a text[6] without a paratext does not exist and never has existed. Paradoxically, paratexts without texts do exist, if only by accident: there are certainly works – lost or aborted – about which we know nothing except their titles. (Some examples: numerous post-Homeric epics or classical Greek tragedies, or *La Morsure de l'épaule* [published in English as *The Shoulder Bite*], which Chrétien de Troyes takes credit for at the beginning of *Cligès*, or *La Bataille des Thermopyles*, which was one of Flaubert's abandoned projects and which we know nothing else about except that the word *cnémide* [greave] was not to have appeared in it.) These titles, standing alone, certainly provide food for thought, by which I mean they provide a little more than many a work that is everywhere available and can be read from start to finish. Finally, just as the presence of paratextual elements is not uniformly obligatory, so, too, the public and the reader are not unvaryingly and uniformly obligated: no one is required to read a preface (even if such freedom is not always opportune for the author), and as we will see, many notes are addressed only to *certain* readers.

The approach we will take in studying each of these elements, or rather each of these types of elements, is to consider a certain number of features that, in concert, allow us to define the status of a paratextual message, whatever it may be. These features basically describe a paratextual message's spatial, temporal, substantial, pragmatic, and functional characteristics. More concretely: defining a paratextual element consists of determining its location (the question *where?*); the date of its appearance and, if need be, its disappearance (*when?*); its mode of existence, verbal or other (*how?*); the characteristics of its situation of communication – its sender and addressee (*from whom? to whom?*); and the functions that its message aims to fulfill (*to do what?*). This questionnaire is a little simplistic, but because it almost entirely defines the method employed in the rest of this book, no doubt a few words of justification are in order at the outset.

A paratextual element, at least if it consists of a message that has taken on material form, necessarily has a *location* that can be situated in relation to the location of the text itself: around the text and either within the same volume or at a more respectful (or more prudent) distance. Within the same volume are such elements as the title or the preface and sometimes elements inserted into the interstices of the text, such as chapter titles or certain notes. I will give the name *peritext* to this first spatial category[7] – certainly the more typical one [...]. The distanced elements are all those messages that, at least originally, are located outside the book, generally with the help of the media (interviews, conversations) or under cover of private communications (letters, diaries, and others). This second category is what, for lack of a better word, I call *epitext* [...]. As must henceforth go without saying, peritext and epitext completely and entirely share the spatial field of the paratext. In other words, for those who are keen on formulae, *paratext = peritext + epitext*.[8]

The *temporal* situation of the paratext, too, can be defined in relation to that of the text. If we adopt as our point of reference the date of the text's appearance – that is, the date of its first, or original,[9] edition – then certain paratextual elements are of prior (public) production: for example, prospectuses, announcements of forthcoming publications, or elements that are connected to prepublication in a newspaper or magazine and will sometimes disappear with publication in book form, like the famous Homeric chapter-titles of *Ulysses*, whose official existence proved to be (if I may put it this way) entirely prenatal. These are therefore *prior* paratexts. Other paratextual elements – the most common ones – appear at the same time as the text: this is the *original* paratext. An example is the preface to Balzac's *Peau de chagrin*, a preface produced in 1831 along with the novel it introduces. Finally, other paratextual elements appear later than the text, perhaps thanks to a second edition (example: the preface to Zola's *Thérèse Raquin* – four months later) or to a more remote new edition (example: the preface to Chateaubriand's *Essai sur les révolutions* – twenty-nine years later). For reasons of function that I will elaborate on below, here we have grounds for differentiating between the merely *later* paratext (the Zola case just mentioned) and the *delayed* paratext (the Chateaubriand case). To designate elements that appear after the author's death, I – like everyone else – will use the term *posthumous*; to designate elements produced during the author's lifetime, I will adopt the neologism proposed by my good master Alphonse Allais: *anthu-mous* paratext.[10] But this last antithesis is applicable not solely to delayed elements; for a paratext can be at one and the same time original and posthumous, if it accompanies a text that is itself posthumous – as do the title and the (fallacious) genre indication of *La Vie de Henry Brulard, écrite par lui-même. Roman imité du Vicaire de Wakefield* [*The Life of Henry Brulard, written by himself. A novel in imitation of 'The Vicar of Wakefield'*].

If, then, a paratextual element may appear at any time, it may also disappear, definitively or not, by authorial decision or outside intervention or by virtue of the eroding effect of time. Many titles of the classical period have thus been shortened by posterity, even on the title pages of the most reliable modern editions; and all of Balzac's original prefaces were deliberately deleted in 1842 at the time his works were regrouped to form the whole known as *La Comédie humaine*. Such deletions, which are very common, determine the life span of paratextual elements. Some life spans are very short; to my knowledge, the record is held by the preface to *La Peau de chagrin* (one month). But I said above, 'may disappear *definitively or not*': an element that is deleted – for example, when a new edition comes out – can always reemerge upon publication of a still newer edition. Certain notes in Rousseau's *Nouvelle Héloïse*, absent from the second edition, lost no time returning, and the prefaces Balzac 'deleted' in 1842 are present today in all reliable editions. The duration of the paratext is often intermittent, therefore, and this intermittence, which I will speak of again, is very closely linked to the basically functional nature of the paratext.

The question of a paratextual element's *substantial* status will be settled, or eluded, here – as it often is in practice – by the fact that almost all the paratexts I consider will themselves be of a *textual*, or at least verbal, kind: titles, prefaces, interviews, all of them utterances that, varying greatly in scope, nonetheless share the linguistic status of the text. Most often, then, the paratext is itself a text: if it is still not *the* text, it is already *some* text. But we must at least bear in mind the paratextual value that may be vested in other types of manifestation: these may be iconic (illustrations), material (for example, everything that originates in the sometimes very significant typographical choices that go into the making of a book), or purely factual. By *factual* I mean the paratext that consists not of an explicit message (verbal or other) but of a fact whose existence alone, if known to the public, provides some commentary on the text and influences how the text is received. Two examples are the age or sex of the author. (How many works, from Rimbaud's to Sollers's, have owed part of their fame or success to the glamor of youth? And do we ever read 'a novel by a woman' exactly as we read 'a novel' plain and simple, that is, a novel by a man?) Another example is the date of the work: 'True admiration,' said Renan, 'is historical'; in any case, it is indisputable that historical awareness of the period in which a work was written is rarely immaterial to one's reading of that work.

I have just tossed together the most unsubtle and patently obvious characteristics of the factual paratext, but there are many others, some more trivial and others more basic. Examples of the more trivial are membership in an academy (or other exalted body) or receipt of a literary prize. Examples of the more basic (and these we will meet again) are the implicit contexts that surround a work and, to a greater or lesser degree, clarify or modify its significance. These implicit contexts may be authorial (the context formed around, for example, *Père Goriot* by the whole of *La Comédie humaine*), generic (the context formed around the same work [*Père Goriot*] and the same whole [*La Comédie humaine*] by the existence of the genre known as 'the novel'), historical (the context formed, for the same example, by the period known as 'the nineteenth century'), and so forth. I will not undertake here to specify the nature or gauge the weight of these facts of contextual affiliation, but we must at least remember that, in principle, every context serves as a paratext.

5 Gatekeeping

Lynne Spender

The values which a society holds and the institutions it creates are not an accident. They reflect the conscious and unconscious choices made by people in power and positions of authority. The way of life – and the quality of life – is directly or indirectly determined by the decisions which are made within the circles of the powerful.

There is nothing new about this understanding; be it nuclear weapons or the availability of creches, the disproportionate unemployment of blacks or the location of a new airport that is the explicit issue, there is widespread recognition that it is but a few who make the choices, even though it may be the many who feel the consequences. So it would be reassuring to know that those who enjoyed the privilege of decision-making were a 'representative' group, holding a range of values and priorities and able to appreciate the significance of their actions for all who are affected by them. Sleep would come easily at night if we were to know that the vast range of decisions which were being made – and which would impinge on our lives in myriad ways – were being undertaken in a fair and neutral manner, and embodied the needs and aspirations of all members of society.

But this is not the case. There is no reassurance. Since we have been keeping records we know that only half of humanity (and a segment of that half) has had any influence in the decision-making circles. The only values and priorities that have been reflected are those of the male. In each generation a group of privileged men, on the basis of their own experience and with the endorsement of other men, has had the right to decree the social values. It is not just a matter of whether there will be peace or war, mines or conservation areas, football pitches or child-minding facilities, that has been decided by men, but the more subtle – and some would say more insidious – *scheme* of values which would have us believe that war, or mines, or football pitches are sound and sensible ways of organizing society. What is considered significant, sane and suitable at the most basic level in our ordering of experience, has been decreed – and built upon – for centuries by a small band of men who have found it easy to accept that their ways are the right ways.

From government to education, from science to religion, from medicine to the media, it has been men who have been in command and given the orders; they have made the policy decisions and put them into practice through the organizations and institutions which they, as the dominant group, control.

This means that our culture, which we have been encouraged to see as *human* culture, is nothing other than a product of the understanding and beliefs of the dominant group – men! Regardless of their position in a male-determined hierarchy, women have never contributed to the making of our society in equal numbers and on the same terms as men. Even if tomorrow women were to comprise half the politicians, or business executives, or priests or scientists, what we have to keep in mind is that they would be coming into a system which men have devised for themselves, in which the values and the rules of the dominant group are already decreed, and into which the 'newcomers' would have to fit. For women to contribute to our value system, our social ideology and view of the world, on the same terms as men, women would have to be free to decree at least half the rules ... by which men would have to abide.

Because we have become aware of the extent to which women have been excluded from this process of forming our values and beliefs, and because we are beginning to appreciate the significance of this male monopoly, we are currently witnessing a demand for women to be included in the circle of the decision makers ... so that our society reflects the consciousness of both sexes. Yet we cannot confine the demand to the presence of women in *equal numbers*; if women are not *admitted on the same terms as men*, then men will be able to retain their dominance.

Our culture at the moment, far from representing the sum total of human experience, reflects the experience of men. What does not make sense to the dominant group therefore does not make sense; what is not a priority – or a problem – for men, is therefore not a priority or a problem. The 'social reality' which we inhabit, the view of the world into which we have all been initiated as members of society and which we are obliged to affirm, is one which takes as its standards, the standards of white, educated men. There are no 'alternative' standards which allow for the values and priorities of those who are not white, or male, for example; there is only one standard and those who display any departure from it are defined as 'not up to standard'. Our culture, ostensibly neutral and the outcome of human effort and consciousness, in reality embodies and encodes the values of the dominant group who have produced it:

> What is there – spoken, sung, written, made emblematic in art – and treated as general, universal, unrelated to a particular position or a particular sex as its source and standpoint, is in fact partial, limited, located in a particular position and permeated by special interests and concerns.
>
> (Dorothy Smith 1978: 283)

Not surprisingly there are many women who object to this arrangement. For over a decade (this time round) feminists have been setting out the implications – for both sexes – of a system of values and beliefs that promotes and applauds the interests of one half of humanity and denies and derides the interests of the other half. In doing so we have come to understand (as our foremothers did) that it is not a case of pointing out to men the error (and injustice) of their ways so that they can mend them, it is a case of depriving the dominant group of their power base. Many men do not want to give it up.

We have not been excluded by accident. The institutions that men have established have frequently been *based* on our exclusion and designed to create sexual inequality. In the eighteenth century, for example, men excluded women from education and were then able to argue that because women were not educated they could make no worthwhile contribution to the culture. In the nineteenth century men excluded women from the political arena and were then able to argue that because women had no head for politics, they could play no part in running society. We can see in the past how the institutions which men had set up for themselves were used to reinforce and maintain women's subordination. What we tend to forget is that the same process is at work in the present.

In 1969 Kate Millett introduced into the language the term 'sexual politics' to refer to 'power structured relationships, arrangements whereby one group of persons is controlled by another' (p. 23). She did us the service of alerting us – yet again, for women have perceived this before (see Spender 1982b) – to the *purposeful* nature of the arrangements in our society, where men have assumed power and control and have used it to keep women, as a group, without resources, and without access to both the public and private worlds that men have traditionally – and conveniently – enjoyed.

In 1973 Mary Daly raised the same issue in another way when she recognized the power that goes with the ability to 'name the world' – to decree what is real, what is reasonable, what is right. Women have not had access to that power. Men have been the 'producers' of the belief system and women the 'consumers'. Men's way of seeing themselves and the world has been the only commodity on sale; the raw material of women's lives has not been processed and is not therefore available for use.

It is not just that men's values are put forward, it is also that women's are discarded. And the longer men stay in power, and retain the right to determine what society sees as important, the longer women are 'outside' and are seen to be displaying their 'unfitness for public office' ... just as they did when they were outside education, and outside the political framework. When men decree what is significant and women disagree ... then what women want is seen as insignificant and a sign that they are not to be taken seriously, not to be admitted to the circles of power. It is a nice interlocking – and supremely convenient – arrangement for men.

Fortunately, however, there are many women who won't accept this brand of 'logic' of the dominant group, and who refuse to believe that the values women hold are 'silly' no matter what men may say. Elizabeth Janeway (1980), Adrienne Rich (1979), Dorothy Smith (1978) and Dale Spender (1981a, 1981b, 1982a, 1982b) have followed Kate Millett and Mary Daly and are among the many who have insisted that the reason male experience is granted more significance and authority in our society has little to do with the *quality* of male experience but much to do with the dominant group's desire to value itself ... and retain its power.

There have been numerous periods when women of the past have come together to forge their own meanings and understandings about male power, and the process has been revived over the last ten years as women have once more elaborated, refined and validated these insights in feminist networks and have extended their analysis of the establishment and maintenance of our male-dominated culture. One of the names that women have provided to describe the world from the position which women occupy is that of 'Gatekeeping'.

The 'gatekeepers' are the guardians of the culture. They are the ones who formulate the standards – and the justifications for those standards, the ones who pass judgment on what makes sense, what is credible. Gatekeepers are those, for example who can decree that the mind and body in our society are separate entities – regardless of the number of Indian mystics who suggest otherwise: they are the ones who can declare what constitutes a proper sexual relationship (in which nose-rubbing plays no part no matter how many members of the Eskimo or Maori community testify to its satisfactory nature, and in which the vaginal orgasm does play a part, no matter how many women express their incomprehension). The guardians of the culture have very considerable powers – among them the power to declare as right and proper arrangements which suit them.

Generally, the theory of gatekeeping suggests that the people who hold decision-making positions in our society actually select the information and ideas that will be allowed to pass through the 'gates' and be incorporated into our culture. Specifically, the theory draws attention to the fact that our patriarchal society is purposefully arranged so that men fill the decision-making positions and become the keepers of the gates. On the basis of their experience and their understandings, men can allow entry to the information and ideas that they find appropriate and they can reject any material that they find unsuitable or unimportant. Gatekeeping thus provides men with a mechanism to promote their own needs and interests at the expense of all others. In doing so, it effectively ensures the continuation of a male-supremacist culture.

Undoubtedly, 'gatekeeping' is a term that arises out of women's experience of the world. Women are aware that we, as a group, are often kept from filling policy and decision-making positions and thus from acquiring the authority associated with them. 'Gatekeeping' provides us with a linguistic tool to name the techniques used to arrange our exclusion. We know that the social organization of our culture has evolved with male experience as the central reference point and that female experience has been excluded or eclipsed. We can see how men, already in positions of power, perceive other men as the best candidates for other positions of power, for within a male frame of reference, only male experience is valued. From this point we can understand how the authority granted to men becomes genuine authority because it is perpetually associated with men. Women do not have and cannot acquire authority in the same way. There is no need for men to set up committees and conspire personally to exclude women. The process of gatekeeping achieves the same effect in an impersonal way that allows men to dissociate themselves from any form of discrimination. At the same time, it works to reinforce the already pervasive myth of male superiority by continually making positions associated with power available to men.

If we consider the institutions that play major roles in determining our traditions and our way of life, women's exclusion from the upper levels is patently obvious. The exclusion may be structural and explicit as it is in the church, or it may be the result of social expectations that encourage consideration of certain roles as appropriate only for men. In either case it is an *arranged* exclusion and reserves decision-making roles for men. In government, the law, education, commerce, religion, medicine and the arts, women are still considered exceptional if they manage to acquire and hold on to positions of power and authority. Women at the upper levels are rarely seen as representatives of their sex but as female versions of the males who should rightfully hold the positions.

Whether or not men understand its workings or appreciate its significance, gatekeeping serves to reinforce male authority and to perpetuate male dominance. Because men have decreed that their logic, their reason and their truths are *human* logic, reason and truth, they have only to be honourable men in order to discriminate against women and then disclaim the practice. Their denial of women's truths, far from constituting a conspiracy, is transformed into the logical and reasonable application of high standards and high motives in the execution of their duty.

Naturally, many are puzzled by female accusations of gatekeeping and the connotations of active and political intervention. The protests ring loudly and clearly. Of course they would appoint women to positions of authority – if only there were any qualified; of course they would address women's issues – if only they were important; of course they would study women poets – if only there were some good enough. In their view, such decisions have nothing to do with 'gatekeeping'. They are based on *reason* and are the result of rational processes which uphold society's standards.

What is rarely considered though, especially by men, is that such standards are male standards. They are based on the tradition formed 'as the circle of those present builds on the work of the past' and in our society 'the circle of men whose writing and talk was significant to each other extends backwards in time as far as our records reach. What men were doing was relevant to men, was written by men about men for men' (Smith 1978: 281). As the dominant group, men have been able to set their own standards and, through control of the organizational apparatus of society, to project and validate them as universal.

Out of these arrangements has emerged a social reality which automatically grants status and significance to men and their concerns. Available information from the past and the present provides justification for *all* of society to see men as the important group. Women, as members of a sub-dominant group, warrant less attention. Women's concerns are not regarded as major concerns and the information and ideas presented within society reflect this. In almost every situation where men and women both participate, men are given greater credibility and men's contributions are seen as having greater value. Because women are seen as less important than men, what women *say, do* and *think*, is considered less important than what men say, do and think. The end result is a whole way of life that reflects male dominance and continues to support it.

For example, when women talk, especially to each other, the assumption is that they 'gossip' and 'natter' and that what they say is of little consequence. Women themselves are frequently motivated to seek out 'male' conversation, not because they can participate in it – they are usually given few opportunities (Spender 1980b) – but because they will be judged more favourably through their association with men than with other women. While men are regarded as the important members of society, acceptance by them, on any terms, can be construed as providing a form of status and prestige. The fact that many 'female' conversations deal with socially defined female experiences such as the preparation of food and the raising of children, and that these may constitute an essential area of communication for the survival of the species, is not usually given substantial value because women themselves are not valued. It is 'women's talk' and as such, regardless of its subject, it is seen as irrelevant to the real business of life that is embodied in men's talk. Men's verbal interactions are not termed 'gossip' or 'old husbands' tales' – even when they are discussing their sexual conquests or reminiscing about their youth. Apart from the notion that their talk is assumed to be important because they are important, men have been in control of language and of naming their own activities (Spender 1980b). So while women 'chatter', 'natter', 'prattle' and 'nag', men 'discuss', 'debate' and 'analyse' with the inevitable outcome of reinforcing men's activities as significant and women's as unimportant, if not ridiculous. This is gatekeeping at its demonstrable best!

Regardless of the situation, interpretations and value judgments of women's and men's contributions consistently favour men. Even what women *do* is arranged to be less significant than what men do. The male-determined social structures that make men the obvious candidates to enter the public world of money, power and action also make women the obvious candidates to stay within the private world of family, home and personal relationships. What men do in the public world is called 'work' and consists of a range of occupations for which they are financially rewarded. These occupations are hierarchically structured and the higher the level reached, the more money, status and independence men can earn. But what women *do* in their private realm, performing nearly two-thirds of the world's work hours (UN Report 1980), is regarded as 'non-work' (Oakley 1974: 1). 'Non-work' involves no specific financial remuneration, no sickness or unemployment benefits, no pension and far from providing status and independence for women, forces them into direct dependence on a 'working' male. Production and reproduction in the home are not seen as comparable to the *real* business of production in which men are engaged. Certainly there is no correlation between women's increased productivity in the home and higher status or rates of pay. Indeed, as Ann Oakley explains it, the male concept of work as 'the expenditure of energy for financial gain, defines housework as the most inferior and marginal work of all' (Oakley 1974: 4). As in the case of women talking, the effects are to diminish the status of women and to make it easier to discount our opinions. The reluctance of many women to write 'Occupation: *Housewife*' is understandable when we realize that to do so is to label ourselves, in society's terms, as inferior beings.

Thus are women's words and actions devalued because they differ visibly from the words and actions of men. But even invisible processes are subjected to negative assessment when women are involved. Regardless of their effectiveness in problem-solving or their contribution to a broader understanding of issues and events, women's *thoughts* are generally regarded by society as irrational, illogical and emotional. And of course, to the men who have named the world and who have appropriated logic, rationality and objectivity as the labels for their own (subjective) thinking patterns, women's thoughts – when they are different from men's – are automatically regarded as *ir*rational and *il*logical. Who but an irrational person would claim otherwise?

Whatever women say, do or think, society has been conditioned to view women as inferior to men. The whole assessment of women's roles and their position in society is part of what Molly Haskell refers to as 'the big lie'. Haskell claims that, 'The big lie perpetrated on Western Society is the idea of women's inferiority, a lie so deeply ingrained in our social behaviour that merely to recognize it is to risk unraveling the entire fabric of civilization' (quoted in Trahey 1974: 61). It has been to prevent recognition of 'the big lie' that gatekeeping has evolved. Only by arranging for the exclusion of women from positions of power and from the registers of achievement can men ensure their own superiority and the privileges that accompany their superior status. It is not surprising that such great efforts have been expended in establishing a system of gatekeeping when it is understood that so much is at stake, for men.

From the time Aristotle stated in his seemingly 'logical' and dispassionate pronouncements that we should 'look upon the female state as being as it were a deformity, though one which occurs in the ordinary course of nature' (quoted in Rogers 1968: 37), there has been within our culture, both a source and support for a tradition of the disparagement of women. And it has been well utilized! For spurious reasons, including our smaller brain size and our loss of sense during menstruation, rationalizations for women's mental and physical inferiority have abounded. At the same time, evidence of male superiority – men's contributions to our culture, their 'better' understandings of the world and of women – have been deliberately promoted and presented as the truth.

The history that both women and men confront is men's history (Lewis 1981). Our science is seen as a peculiarly male phenomenon (Arditti 1980) and our sociology is the male study of males (Roberts 1981a). Psychology is the application of male standards to human behaviour (Chesler 1972; Miller 1977) and health care as we know it, is the result of the deliberate appropriation of its practice by men during the nineteenth century (Ehrenreich and English 1979). Religion, through careful editing and translating, presents us with a male deity (Spender 1980b; Stanton 1974) and our literary history has been shaped by the attitudes 'of white men towards non-whites and non-males' (Bernikow 1974). In fact, all of the knowledge presented in our society as legitimate has arisen from a 'male as superior' perspective. Through the controls that gatekeeping has offered exclusively to men, male knowledge has been projected as universally true.

The overall result has been that women have been rendered invisible by the recorded data available in our culture, except in the roles that have been chosen for them by men and in relation to men. In accordance with Judaeo-Christian tradition, women are portrayed as conforming to the prototype of the Virgin Mary – essentially virtuous and submissive – as men's wives, mothers, muses and supporters – or they are presented in the mould of Eve as seductive temptresses – essentially evil – and the cause of the downfall of many a good man. No other roles for women are projected as valid. The tradition of female autonomy and women's centuries-old struggle against male oppression have been conveniently concealed. As Adrienne Rich says,

> The entire history of women's struggle for self-determination has been muf-
> fled in silence over and over. One serious cultural obstacle encountered by any

feminist writer is that each feminist work has tended to be received as if it emerged from nowhere; as if each of us had lived, thought, and worked without any historical past or contextual present. This is one of the ways in which women's work and thinking has been made to seem sporadic, errant, orphaned of any tradition of its own.

(Rich 1979: 11)

In an extensive study of women's acknowledged and unacknowledged contributions to our culture, Dale Spender in *Women of Ideas* (1982a) has revealed the tremendous amount of women's knowledge that has been generated during the last few centuries and the tremendous efforts made by the establishment to minimize and discredit that knowledge. Spender's research proves unequivocally that gatekeeping has played a major role in preserving the inequality of the sexes in all aspects of life and to all men's advantage.

Thus the questions that we are now invited to ask about our cultural heritage are quite different from those we have asked in the past. Rather than trying to discover why there are no 'great' women artists (Nochlin 1977), we want to know who made up the notion of greatness and on what criteria it was established. Instead of asking why the long association between women and writing has produced so few 'great' women writers, we want to know why it was important to rank women's written words and to discriminate between the words of women and men. Whose interests, after all, have been served by differentiation on the basis of sex and by continually judging male contributions as 'greater' than women's? With this question in mind, we want to ask what may be an even more pertinent question, namely why *any* women writers, thinkers, scientists or artists have been included at all in the recording of our culture!

In other words the area of inquiry has shifted from assessing the creative work of women to recognizing the destructive work that men have done by acting as gatekeepers. Immediately we see the need to explore the techniques men have used to limit women's access to the public world and to eclipse women's contributions from our culture. Immediately we see the connections between the assessment and recording of achievement, and the processes and people involved in publishing.

For centuries the institution of publishing has been instrumental in determining *what will be made publicly known* and publishing has been the gate through which material has been obliged to pass in order to qualify for inclusion in our written records. Publishers have acted as guardians of the gate and private, written words have required their approval in order to be transformed into public, printed words. With the focus now on publishers as guardians, we realize that approval for women's actions and women's written words has not often been forthcoming – especially when those words and actions have challenged men's interests in a significant way.

Like other media industries, publishing has been and is still very much a 'man's world' (Strainchamps 1974). 'Women are concentrated in the lowest ranks ... and [there are] virtually none at the top' (West 1978: 6). Decisions in publishing are made by men and the processes involved in publishing are controlled by men. In the selection of people to fill policy-making positions and in the selection of material to be made publicly available, male consciousness is the reference point.

Men make the best candidates in the system that men have devised and thus become the gatekeepers.

But knowledge about gatekeeping techniques provides us with an opportunity to deconstruct the controls that men have been using within publishing. Research into *their* activities rather than our own cannot fail to expose their manipulation of public, printed words in order to promote their own view of the world and their associated positions of dominance. The bias and self-interest that have given us a published heritage of men's truths and an *unpublished heritage* of excluded and discarded women's truths now become glaringly obvious. It is becoming increasingly difficult to deny that the *unpublished heritage* exists, not because women's perceptions are less valid or truthful than men's, but because it has suited those in power to remove from public awareness any material that could threaten or challenge their authority and privileges. With the political nature of men's actions so named, the purposeful nature of our value system and social structures becomes quite clear. Within publishing, as elsewhere, men stand accused of subterfuge and gross intervention in the recording of our heritage and the creation of our social reality. It is an accusation for which there can be no 'rational' defence!

6 Merchants of Culture

John B. Thompson

THE PUBLISHING CHAIN

The publishing chain is both a *supply chain* and a *value chain*. It is a supply chain in the sense that it provides a series of organizational links by means of which a specific product – the book – is gradually produced and transmitted via distributors and retailers to an end user who purchases it. Figure 6.1 offers a simple visual representation of the book supply chain. The basic steps in the book supply chain are as follows. The author creates the content and supplies it to the publisher; in trade publishing this process is typically mediated by the agent, who acts as a filter selecting material and directing it to appropriate publishers. The publisher buys a bundle of rights from the agent and then carries out a range of functions – reading, editing, etc. – before delivering the final text or file to the printer, who prints and binds the books and delivers them to the distributor, which may be owned by the publisher or may be a third party. The distributor warehouses the stock and fulfils orders from both retailers and wholesalers, who in turn sell books to or fulfil orders from others – individual consumers in the case of retailers, and retailers and other institutions (such as libraries) in the case of wholesalers. The publisher's customers are not individual consumers or libraries but rather intermediary institutions in the supply chain – namely, the wholesalers and retailers. For most readers, the only point of contact they have with the book supply chain is when they walk into a bookstore to browse or buy a book, or when they browse the details of a book online, or when they check out a book from a library. For the most part they have no direct contact with publishers and know very little about them; their primary interest is in the book and the author, not in the publisher.

The publishing chain is also a *value chain* in the sense that each of the links purportedly adds some 'value' in the process. This notion is more complicated than it might at first seem, but the general idea is clear enough: each of the links performs

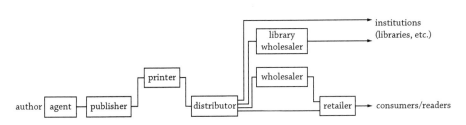

Figure 6.1   Book supply chain

a task or function which contributes something substantial to the overall task of producing the book and delivering it to the end user, and this contribution is something for which the publisher (or some other agent or organization in the chain) is willing to pay. In other words, each of the links 'adds value'. If the task or function is not contributing anything substantial, or if the publisher (or other agent) feels that it does not add enough value to justify the expense, then the publisher (or other agent) may decide to cut the link out of the chain – that is, to 'disintermediate' it. Technological change may also alter the functions performed by particular links in the chain. The functions of the typesetter, for example, have been radically transformed by the advent of computerization, and some typesetters have sought to take on new functions, such as marking up texts in specialized languages like XML, in order to protect their position (or to reposition themselves) in the value chain.

Figure 6.2 summarizes the principal tasks or functions in the publishing chain. This diagram is more elaborate than Figure 6.1 because each organization in the supply chain may carry out several functions (the agents or organizations that typically perform the various tasks or functions are indicated in brackets).

The starting point of the value chain is the creation, selection and acquisition of content – this is the domain where authors, agents and publishers interact. The interaction is much more complex than it might at first seem. Sometimes it is a simple linear process: the author writes a text, submits it to an agent who takes it on and then sells it to a publisher. But often it is much more complicated than this simple linear process would suggest: an agent, knowing what publishers are looking for, often works closely with his or her clients to help shape their book projects, especially in the area of non-fiction, and proposals may go through multiple drafts before the agent is willing to send them out, or a publisher may have an idea for a book and seek to commission an author to write it, and so on. It is not altogether unhelpful to think of agents and publishers as 'gatekeepers' of ideas, selecting those book projects they believe to be worthwhile from the large number of proposals and manuscripts that are submitted to them 'over the transom' by aspiring authors and rejecting those that don't come up to scratch.[1] But even in the world of

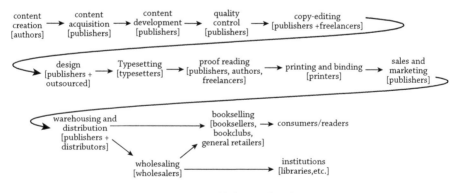

Figure 6.2   Publishing value chain

trade publishing, which probably concurs with this model more closely than other sectors of the publishing industry, the notion of the gatekeeper greatly oversimplifies the complex forms of interaction and negotiation between authors, agents and publishers that shape the creative process.

In trade publishing, both agents and publishers are involved in selecting content, working with authors to develop it and exercising some degree of quality control. The essential difference between the agent and the publisher is that they sit on opposite sides of the table in the market for content: the agent represents the interests of the author and is selecting and developing content with a view to selling it (or, more specifically, selling a bundle of rights to exploit it), whereas the publisher is selecting content with a view to buying it (or buying the bundle of rights) and then developing it for publication. The development of the content will commonly involve reading draft material and editing it (sometimes several times); it may also involve picture research, copyright clearance and various kinds of quality control. Many of the other functions in the publishing chain, such as copy-editing, text and jacket design, proofreading and indexing, will either be handled by specialized staff in-house or will be outsourced, depending on the publisher. Virtually all publishers today outsource typesetting, printing and binding to specialized typesetting firms and printers. Most publishers retain responsibility for sales and marketing, although some smaller publishers may buy in sales and distribution services from specialized firms or from other publishers who take on third-party clients. The sales reps sell to the booksellers, retailers and wholesalers (many smaller booksellers are supplied by wholesalers), and the booksellers and retailers stock the books, display them and seek to sell them to individual consumers/readers. Books are supplied to booksellers, retailers and wholesalers on a sale-or-return basis, so that unsold stock can be returned to the publisher for full credit.[2] The publisher employs a range of marketing and publicity strategies, from advertising and authors' tours to attempts to get authors on radio and television programmes and to get books reviewed in the national press, in an effort to bring books to the attention of readers and drive sales (or 'sell-through') in the bookstores, which is the only way of ensuring that books which have been notionally 'sold' into the retail network are not returned to the publisher.

Each task or function in the publishing chain exists largely by virtue of the fact that it makes some contribution, of varying degrees of significance, to the overall objective of producing and selling books. Some of these tasks (design, copy-editing, typesetting, etc.) are within the range of activities that could be done by a single publishing organization, although a publisher may decide to disaggregate the functions and contract them out in order to reduce costs and improve efficiency. Other tasks are rooted in activities that are quite distinct and that have, in historical terms, a more settled institutional differentiation. This differentiation may be characterized by harmonious relations between the agents and organizations involved, since all have something to gain from cooperation; but they can also be characterized by tension and conflict, since their interests do not always coincide. Moreover, particular positions within the chain are not necessarily fixed or permanent. Changes in working practices, economic developments and technological advances can all have a major impact on the publishing chain, as tasks that were previously commonplace or essential are bypassed or eclipsed.

Given that the publishing chain is not rigid and that particular tasks or functions can be eclipsed by economic and technological change, what reason is there to believe that the role of the publisher itself might not be rendered redundant? What are the core activities or functions of the publisher? Are these activities that could be phased out by new technologies, or that could be done by others? Could publishers themselves be disintermediated from the publishing chain? These questions have been raised often enough in recent years: in an age when anyone can post a text on the internet, who needs a publisher anymore? But the issues are more complicated than they might seem at first sight, and to address them properly we need to examine more carefully the key functions traditionally performed by the publisher and distinguish them from other activities that can be outsourced to freelancers or specialized firms. Figure 6.3 highlights six key functions of the publisher – it is by carrying out these tasks or functions that the publisher has traditionally made a distinctive contribution to the value creation process.

The first function is content acquisition and list-building. This is in many ways the key function of the publisher: to acquire and, indeed, help to create the content that will be turned into the books that comprise the publisher's list. The publisher acts not just as a filter or gatekeeper but in many cases plays an active role in creating or conceiving a project, or in seeing the potential of something and helping the author bring it to fruition. Some of the best publishers are those who are able to come up with good ideas for books and find the right authors to write them, or who are able to turn what might be a rather inchoate idea in the mind of an author into something special, or who are simply able to see potential where others see only dross. There is a real skill here that involves a blending together of intellectual creativity and marketing nous, and that distinguishes outstanding editors and publishers from those who are run of the mill.

The second function is financial investment and risk-taking. The publisher acts as the banker who makes resources available up front, both to pay advances to authors and agents and to cover the costs of acquisition, development and production. In the entire publishing chain it is only the publisher, in the last analysis, who takes the real financial risks – everyone else gets paid (assuming that the author has received an advance on royalties and that the publisher has paid the bills). If the book fails to sell, it is the publisher who writes down any unsold stock and

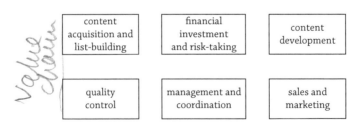

Figure 6.3 Key functions of the publisher

writes off any unearned advance. In the book publishing chain, the publisher is the creditor of last resort.

The third and fourth functions are content development and quality control. In some cases the content provided by an author is in excellent condition and needs very little input from the publisher, but in many areas of publishing this is the exception rather than the rule. Draft manuscripts are commonly revised and developed in the light of comments from editors and others. It is also the responsibility of the publisher to assess the quality of the text and to ensure that it meets certain standards. These standards will of course vary from one publisher to another and a variety of assessment procedures may be used, ranging from the judgement of in-house editors to evaluations by one or more external readers who are specialists in the field (although in trade publishing it is rare to go out of house). Quality control is important for the publisher because it is one of the key means by which they are able to build a distinctive profile and brand in the publishing field and thereby distinguish themselves from other houses.

The fifth function is what could be loosely described as management and coordination. This label describes a range of management activities that are an integral part of the publishing process, from the management of specific projects which may be exceptionally complex to the management of specific activities or phases in the life cycle of the book. For example, even if copy-editing is outsourced to freelancers, the freelancers must be given work and instructions, their terms of work must be agreed and they must be paid, and all of this requires management time and expertise; this is often handled by a dedicated in-house manuscript editor or desk editor. Similarly, even though typesetting, design and printing may be outsourced to specialized firms, the whole production process, from copy-edited manuscript to bound books, must be managed; this is usually done in-house by a production manager or controller. Decisions must be taken about prices and print runs, and stock must then be managed throughout the life cycle of the book. The copyright must also be managed through the sale of subsidiary rights (translations, reprints, serialization, etc.). All of these activities require a great deal of management time and expertise, and in most cases they are handled by in-house managers who have responsibility for specific sectors of the production and publishing process.

The sixth and final function is sales and marketing. I have bundled these activities together although they are in fact quite distinct. Marketing comprises a range of activities concerned with informing potential customers of the availability of a book and encouraging them to buy it. These activities include catalogue preparation and mailing, advertising, direct mail, sending out review copies and, more recently, various kinds of e-marketing. Most trade publishers also have a separate publicity manager and/or department whose task is to cultivate relations with the media and secure media coverage for a book – coverage that ranges from reviews, extracts and interviews in the printed press to radio and television appearances, book signings and author tours. Marketing and publicity have the same aim – namely, to make consumers/readers aware of books and persuade them to buy them; the only real difference is that the publisher pays for marketing, whereas publicity, if you can get it, is free. The task of the sales manager and the sales team is to call on the key accounts – which include the bookselling chains, independent booksellers, online booksellers, wholesalers and a variety of general retailers from supermarkets to warehouse stores – to inform them of the forthcoming books, solicit orders and manage the publisher's relations with their key customers, with the aim of ensuring that books are stocked and available in bookstores for consumers to browse and buy.

These various sales and marketing activities are concerned not simply to bring a product to the marketplace and let retailers and consumers know that it is available: they seek, more fundamentally, to *build a market* for the book. To publish in the sense of making a book *available to the public* is easy – and never easier than it is today, when texts posted online could be said to be 'published' in some sense. But to publish in the sense of making a book *known to the public*, visible to them and attracting a sufficient quantum of their attention to encourage them to buy the book and perhaps even to read it, is extremely difficult – and never more difficult than it is today, when the sheer volume of content available to consumers and readers is enough to drown out even the most determined and well-resourced marketing effort. Good publishers – as one former publisher aptly put it – are market-makers in a world where it is attention, not content, that is scarce.

These six key functions of the publisher define the principal respects in which publishing firms 'add value'. Whether these are functions that will always be performed by traditional publishing firms, or whether, in the changing information environment brought about by digitization and the internet, at least some of these functions will be eclipsed, marginalized, transformed or taken over by others, are questions to which there are, at this point in time, no clear answers. But before speculating about the imminent disintermediation of publishing firms, one would be well advised to reflect carefully on the functions actually performed by publishers in the cultural economy of the book, on which functions will continue to require fulfilment in the future and, if they do, on who will perform them and how.

7 The Digital Context and Challenge

Michael Bhaskar

A sense that the written word is seeing the greatest transformation since Gutenberg is, despite becoming a cliché, not unwarranted. Not only are books and publishing experiencing the most profound transition since the dawn of the press but our entire communications paradigm is witnessing arguably the greatest change in history. Moreover we are still in the early phases of digital technology. Over the coming decades it will undoubtedly evolve in unexpected ways. To paraphrase Zhou Enlai on the French Revolution, even by the end of the present century it will be too soon to tell regarding the digital revolution. The impact has been felt across sectors and publishing is no exception. Such technologies beg the questions what is a book and what does publishing it mean?

In response has been the ballooning of what author Ewan Morrison (2012) calls a 'speculative meta-practice',[1] a series of discussions across conferences, blogs, email lists, seminars, industry consortia, newspapers and consultations, and indeed in books like this, dissecting the emergence of digital publishing in minute detail. Every move by publishers, retailers, start-ups and technology firms has been closely scrutinised. For a number of years the joke was that the best way to make money in digital publishing was to host a conference. In such changeable conditions adding to this debate in long form is doomed. In the space of a week, for example, the iPad transformed digital tablets from a small niche to a mainstream product pursued by all major technology manufacturers. My intention is therefore to avoid speculative meta-practice as much possible, moving beyond immediate concerns. Using contemporary examples, I seek to pick out the underlying trends and tendencies, those truly transformational factors and the deep patterns driving the challenge set by digital publishing.

Most visibly, the digital revolution has manifested itself for book publishers in terms of ebooks. As Thompson (2005, 2010) has pointed out, the ebook is only the culmination of changes in the publishing workflow since the 1980s – books only become print at a late stage in the publication process. Most of the actual work on them already takes place in digital formats. Nonetheless ebooks have exercised publishers a great deal. Yet they are neither the most interesting nor the most challenging part of the digital transition. Significant effort ensures ebook behaviour mirrors print. The standard business model for ebooks is, like print, based on unit sales, while the standard workflow, and indeed product, echo those of print books. The only difference is an ebook's immateriality. Nonetheless, moving to the 1s and 0s of binary code caused a host of problems, despite, in many ways, not being such a momentous shift after all.[2]

Desktop publishing's (DTP) early entrance proves digitisation and dematerialisation alone are incapable of disrupting publishing. Rather, the growth of digital *networks* is key. The sociologist Manuel Castells has written extensively on the rise of a 'network society' where changing social formations and advancing digital technology create new cultural forms. The network society is fundamentally altering our communications, creating 'mass self-communication' and convergence, the phenomenon of all media merging in one digital system. The impact of this integration could hardly be more profound. Network topology creates an informational economy, shrinking geographic coordinates, changing patterns of productivity and work, a media and society very different to that of the mid-twentieth century. Networks are about connections, data transferral, linkages, paths and webs of contact. Digital networks represent a vast increase in the capabilities of networks generally and we are still absorbing their consequences.

We can't make straightforward distinctions between media forms, technological environments and social structures. Today, this means sketching the consequences not just of a digital age but more importantly, a network age. An ebook without a network, without a distribution channel, is scarcely more radical than a printed book. An ebook on the open web has a near infinite capacity to be copied and shared, instantaneously, around the world. The difference is stark. As Castells puts it, 'The emergence of a new electronic communication system characterized by its global reach, its integration of all communication media, and its potential interactivity is changing and will change forever our culture' (Castells 2010: 357). He implies the network does not only reshape the distribution of content; it reshapes content – and us – as well.

To understand the digital challenge we need to uncover the relevant network effects emerging from the Internet (whose name says it all: the network of networks) and ask how they up-end publishing. This chapter looks at the architecture of the network as a means of understanding the real problems of digital: disintermediation and a destabilised copyright. Publishers have hitherto worried about operational problems including digital supply chains, new product creation, commercial terms, contracts, new staff, IT infrastructure and web marketing. They have played down the other two. By and large the initial confusion around digital publishing has abated. Operational factors have been controlled, clear growth strategies laid out, worries managed.

Eventually the network will start to tell. If publishing was existentially challenged before digital, then that challenge just got bigger. At its heart lies a deceptively simple and unthreatening question:

If anyone can be a publisher, what makes you a publisher in the first place?

NETWORK EFFECTS

Discussions of the Internet have to deal with both its relative newness and constantly developing nature. First, the browser-based web was heralded as the future; a decade later the same web was declared dead thanks to growing non-web data traffic and a new generation of browser-bypassing connected devices

(Anderson and Wolf 2010). Conclusions are at best interim. Network effect is used here in the broadest sense, to include all kinds of properties of digital networks. Of course, publishing and indeed any human endeavour have always relied on networks – of people, capital, goods and knowledge – but traits of digital networks are particularly marked. We have a twin movement of centralisation and fragmentation, centrifugal and centripetal forces working through a shared architecture, each an effect of it, each feeding into and driving the other. Everything on the Internet shares this pattern of centralisation and fragmentation, not just publishing or media.

Centralisation

In the early days of the Internet, the so-called 'California Ideology' imbued the technology with a sense of utopian promise: it would herald an opening and levelling where great visionaries would craft new democratic and libertarian social and aesthetic forms. Yet centralisation has increased. Just a few websites and device manufacturers dominate the landscape of digital culture. Far from being unpredictable, it is a feature of the network embodied in the notion of the 'Highlander Principle' (taken from the film's tagline 'There can only be one'). There can only be one tablet, search engine, online store and social network. One service occupies a space to the exclusion of all others, thereby becoming enormously powerful in key verticals. There is some competition, but digital big business displays a remarkable degree of centralisation.

Google has an estimated 67 per cent market share for global online search enquiries.[3] Despite seeing significant inroads from its rival Apple and the rise of smartphones and tablets, Microsoft still has nearly 90 per cent of the market for operating systems. Facebook is double the size of the next 14 social networks put together.[4] Even after an aggressive push from other OEMs Apple still has 57.6 per cent of the global tablet market as of 2012[5] while between them Apple and Google have a near duopoly on smartphone operating systems. Amazon has around 70 per cent of the global ebook market and in many territories enjoys overwhelming superiority in online bookselling, just as for many years Apple's iTunes utterly dominated music downloads. The *New York Times* has reported on how tech firms marry hardware and software to create seamlessly locked experiences in emulation of Apple's integrated approach.[6] Lines of ownership and market share are not clear cut, but there is nonetheless an obvious pattern of centralisation whereby mega-nodes become the prime brokers of the network. The tendency is towards monopolistic or oligopolistic dominance in a vertical.

Each actor in this West Coast drama has a clear incentive to promote centralisation – on their products and services. Despite the Internet's openness digital technology centralises. Lock-in occurs everywhere. Think of the QWERTY keyboard, one interface decision enshrined as essential despite the possibility of better alternatives. Philosopher and computer scientist Jaron Lanier (2011) gives the example of the MIDI musical encoding, the *de facto* standard for all digital music. He asks, is this the best encoding, is it desirable all our music takes one form? It hardly matters as we're already locked in. Our systems are designed to play this and only this format. Lock-in makes life easy, but means you can't get out. The phenomenon relies on path dependence, whereby past decisions condition future options. If computers and behaviour require a QWERTY keyboard then we can't easily change, just as if we already have an Amazon account it's much easier to continue purchasing from Amazon than start with a new retailer. Lanier (2011) points out that although digital technology offers almost unlimited creative potential it also allows lock-in to spread faster and more fully than ever before.

Studying the mathematics of network topology is currently in vogue and we are beginning to better understand the deep ramifications of network design. One means by which networks centralise is through their ability to add value through centralisation. The most famous explanation is Metcalfe's Law, originally applied to the telephone network. It states the value of a network is proportional to the square of the number of users on the network. In essence, the more people on a network the more valuable it becomes. Immediately we see why Facebook is so much bigger than its rivals – your friends are more likely to be there and so its utility increases. Centralisation helps centraliser and user. Metcalfe's Law has been joined by Reed's Law and Beckstrom's Law, which look at networks in terms of the value added to each interaction on the network provided by the network. Common to them all is the sense that utility and network size are connected. Beyond a certain point networks will inherently and exponentially increase as value accrual is dispersed among the network, incentivising those outside to join. Strong mathematical frameworks have been established to demonstrate this as an inherent feature of all networks, although significant debates remain. An associated feature is the 'bandwagon effect' – the more people to have done something the more people do it in future.[7] The more iPhones out there the more people buy iPhones. The logic of conformity takes over when things have happened before or reach scale.

Legal scholar Jonathan Zittrain (2008) sees these powerful network effects as having a further driver in the form of rogue elements on the Internet pushing users into closed but protective systems. Both the Internet and the original PC are 'generative' technologies, which is to say, technologies allowing third parties to build on them without prejudice. They encourage diversity and supersede closed proprietary online services like Minitel or Compuserve by being more usable, adaptable and capable. However with the spread of malware and cybercrime, the web's open architecture becomes a liability: the web has 'tightly coupled networks of data flows that can pass both the latest world news and the latest PC attacks in adjoining data packets' (Zittrain 2008: 56). Most users aren't interested in a system's generativity so much as their security. So-called 'tethered appliances' that are umbilically linked to a centralised service, and so closed from new, unapproved applications, have grown in response. Even web 2.0 services like Facebook are tethered insofar as ultimate control remains with the platform, not the user. Tablets, smartphones and family-oriented gaming devices all accelerate the trend, threatening many beneficial features of our emergent digital ecosystem. As people gravitate, for better or worse,[8] to closed and tethered systems it only increases lock-in and centralisation on those systems.

To go with the Highlander Principle, and what Zittrain (2008) has called the 'Fort Knox Problem', we have the Wu Cycle. Tim Wu (2011), another legal scholar, proposes a gestalt running through the commercial patterns of communications technology over the last 150 years: 'the Cycle'. Communications technologies start decentralised and idealistic before quickly becoming dominated by monopolistic corporations. 'Without exception,' he writes, 'the brave new technologies of the twentieth century – free use of which was originally encouraged, for the sake of further invention and individual expression – eventually evolved into the "old media" giants of the twenty-first, through which the flow and nature of content would be strictly controlled for reasons of commerce' (Wu 2011: 6). AT&T is a classic example, built by the great industrialist Theodore Vail into a vast telecoms monopoly by beating off powerful incumbents.[9] The 'Bell System' was more ideology than company, fusing technology, service, draconian usage restrictions and monopolistic economics. Similar patterns are discernible in the history of film, with its Vail equivalents like Adolph Zukor at Paramount ('the Napoleon of Motion Pictures') who invented the studio system, and radio, where David Sarnoff turned the Radio Corporation of America into a corporate behemoth smothering the once burgeoning field of amateur radio. At one stage just three networks dominated US television: NBC, CBS and ABC. In their heyday, like the BBC in Britain, they represented an extraordinary concentration of communication power. The process is not unidirectional and periods of openness follow extreme monopolies. We could, though, have reached a similar oligopolistic juncture for consumer digital technology. The Randian figures of Vail, Zukor and Sarnoff have their obvious counterparts in the likes of Jobs, Gates and Zuckerberg. All the major players focus on the 'master switch' of the Internet, aiming to be the superpower, the AT&T, of the digital age. History may not repeat itself. If Wu (2011) is right though, and the cycle keeps turning, we are looking at loss of openness and a further increase in centralisation.[10]

For those of us who like to believe in an open Internet encouraging diversity and offering new avenues for expression, this litany of technological and commercial binds makes depressing reading. Faults of old media are replicated and, worse, hugely concentrated as centralisation breeds centralisation. This is not to say one company will dominate, or to deny the enormous variances in culture, practices and aims between organisations as mutually incompatible as Apple and Google. New forces will emerge and become dominant themselves, before also succumbing to bad luck or bad management. Rather I merely note how one key aspect of communications networks is the tendency to centralise on a very limited number of platforms, whose owners accrue all the power and benefit of that centralisation. Luckily, this isn't the last word.

Fragmentation

Despite centripetal tendencies, the Internet and the web, thanks to the vision of its creators, remain open. Moreover, access is growing. Anyone with rudimentary skills and basic access can create websites. Even tethered services like Facebook are built with a high degree of openness compared with media outlets of the past. The profusion of websites and content is dizzying, a gushing fountain of data comprising trillions of web pages, hours of video footage uploaded to YouTube every minute, hundreds of billions of photos. Millions of blogs. A numberless blizzard of tweets, status updates and Foursquare check-ins. More content than ever before, far more, is now created and disseminated. Basic production and distribution are reduced to a fraction of their former costs. Understood from this angle, the centralisation of the web is actually a response to extreme fragmentation: Google indexes and organises what otherwise would be an impossible chaos of information. Many giants of modern technology are relatively young companies; Apple and Microsoft started in the 1970s; Amazon and Google in the 1990s; while Facebook began in 2004, reaching a valuation of above $100 billion dollars in just eight years, indicating the climate is not one of total ossification. Hope always remains for the agile start-up to make a difference.

Media once had a series of gatekeepers, whose blessing and permission controlled access to audiences. When everyone can communicate to everyone that breaks down. Compared to the media environment of the postwar years we live in an era of super-abundance. Overwhelming complexity and fragmentary content production are barely held together by the forces of centralisation. 'User generated content', now familiar to the point of banality, is part of the picture, as are new organisations and the still-expanding old media order keen to carve their place at the table of digital culture.

Yet another legal theorist, Yochai Benkler (2006), authored the canonical theory of fragmentation in his landmark study, *The Wealth of Networks*. Benkler (2006) looks at how the 'industrial information economy' evolves into a 'networked information economy' where non-market forms of 'social production' have a much greater role than when high capital constraints kept individuals and non-market actors from reaching large audiences. Benkler argues:

> the networked environment makes possible a new modality of organizing production: radically decentralized, collaborative, and nonproprietary; based on sharing resources and outputs among widely distributed, loosely connected individuals who cooperate with each other without relying on either market signals or managerial commands.
>
> (Benkler 2006: 60)

This works in an opposite move to centralisation, the effects of which Benkler (2006) regards as exaggerated. A hub-and-spoke system, with producers on the rim sending works to the centre, is replaced by a decentred architecture where everyone is a node, and power is distributed and the multiple connections are made in two-way communications channels. This is the essence of the networked information environment, a world of 'commons-based peer production' very much outside the mass-market, proprietary, professional and copyright-driven worlds of traditional media.

Michael Hart's Project Gutenberg is a classic example of social production. Relying on a huge army of volunteers to scan, proofread, error correct and convert to multiple formats its vast archive of titles, the labour is free, the results openly shared. Other examples of commons-based peer production are well publicised, especially open source software like the Linux operating system and, of course, Wikipedia. Information and communication are, Benkler (2006) argues, fundamental to humans and societies, so it is no surprise to see radical results when they shift. Where inputs were tightly controlled they are now open and widely accessible. Where outputs were high-cost restricted goods they are now, again, open and widely accessible. In such an innovation-friendly context, the problems engendered by fragmentation – information overload, polarisation of discourse, the splintering of content origination – will be solved. The very openness of the networked information economy generates answers without replicating the problems of big old media gatekeepers. No other communications mechanism has grown like the Internet. By working against the centralised capital structures of traditional media, it expanded and transformed the spread of culture and information. Far from centralisation fever, the Internet represents the greatest cultural democratisation in history.

Some implications for publishing have been teased out by fellow travellers in the movement against restrictive copyright, theorist Clay Shirky (2002) and novelist Cory Doctorow (2011). Writing about the growth of blogs in 2002, Shirky hit upon a particularly telling phrase to describe the then-recent activity: 'the mass amateurisation of publishing'. Suddenly barriers to entry, those choke points on supply in the physical world, were removed. Everyone, in theory, could be a publisher when steep entry costs were replaced with simple access. Cue hundreds of millions of blogs. This is 'a technological change whose ramifications are mainly cultural' (Shirky 2002). Doctorow made a similar point in the *Guardian* newspaper:

> The Internet has created a large number of new kinds of publishers who act to connect works and audiences. These essentially group into search engines, then bloggers, curators, and tweeters, and finally suggestion algorithms (such as Amazon's 'people who bought this also bought...' recommendations; Reddit's human voting system; Netflix's suggestion system).
>
> (Doctorow 2011)

The Internet means not just a 'mass amateurisation of publishing' but a mass amateurisation of all one-to-many communications and cultural practice in a global fission of media control.

In summary, digital environments have two seemingly opposed tendencies, powerful dynamics of centralisation and fragmentation. Seeing them as acting in conflict, however, is entirely wrong. They are part of the same pattern. Without key nodes the digital realm would be a maddening Borgesian labyrinth; without fragmentation it would be totalitarian, monopolistic and monolithic. The centre and the periphery evolve so drivers pushing towards centralisation complement and enable those moving towards fragmentation. Put simply, the network does both, and we can't see one without the other. Just as Google's indexing brings a measure of discoverability to the web's cacophony, so proprietary app stores offer discovery and delivery platforms to an ever-growing wave of software. This patterning has deep philosophical roots. Deleuze and Guattari, for example, saw the process as one with lineage stretching throughout the history of thought.[11] For Castells, 'networks have become the predominant organizational form for every domain of human activity' (Castells 1997: xliv), and certainly this problematic of centralisation and fragmentation vexes publishing. After all, no publisher can control these processes. The contours of this new networked environment, described as 'a possibility factory' (Kelly 1999: 46), are the real existential challenge for publishers.

Part Two
Authorship

The nature and practice of authorship have been central to recent debates in literary studies. Contemporary cultural and literary criticism has disturbed the romantic idea of the author as the source of meaning of the text, while book historians pay close attention to the interdependence of the author, as a player within a complex network of value in the production, reception and circulation of a writer's work. Addressing the relationship between theories of authorship and its contemporary practice, the selected texts in this section focus on the rapidly changing status of authorship during the twentieth and twenty-first centuries, in response to ideological, technical and social changes, and evaluate the way that the author is constructed by and for commerce. They reflect on the business imperatives governing the practice of authorship: the impact of corporatisation and publishers' marketing strategies on an author's career; the pressures of literary celebrity; the asymmetrical power relations operating between authors, publishers and literary agents; and the transformative impact of digital media.

The early twentieth century saw rapid changes in the profession of author-ship, as a result of transformations in commercial, technical and legal practices. Literary agents came to wield more power in the literary marketplace, and new opportunities opened up for selling subsidiary rights, for example through maga-zine serialisation, hardback publication, book clubs, paperback sales, abridged or digest publication, movie rights, television rights, translation rights and drama rights (West 1989: 145). Mary Ann Gillies (Chapter 8 [2007]) considers how the rise of the literary agent fundamentally changed the relationship between author and editor in the early twentieth century, as agents gave authors a much stronger bargaining position and their rights were defended in a new way. Not surprisingly, the transition provoked opposition and resistance in the publishing industry. With reference to A. P. Watt's role in defining the role of the literary agent at the end of the nineteenth century, and to the work of J. B. Pinker and Curtis Brown in the early twentieth century, Gillies charts the 'new power nexus' that emerged between authors, agents and publishers (p. 64).

The excerpts by Juliet Gardiner (Chapter 10 [2000]) and Joe Moran (Chapter 9 [2000]) reflect on the practice of authorship in the literary marketplace in the late twentieth century, in relation to postmodern theories of authorship. Moran considers how the contemporary literary marketplace undermines the notion of authorship as an individualistic activity, and argues that 'the creation of the author as a "personality" by a vast network of cultural and economic practices ... cuts to the heart of the paradoxical nature of celebrity culture as a whole, which promotes individualism at the same time as it undermines it' (pp. 69–70). In his view, literary celebrity functions by reifying individuals and allowing them to be used by capitalist society as 'ideal social types, as focal points for the desires and longing of audiences' (p. 68). Gardiner's essay also addresses the phenomenon of the 'author brand' in late twentieth-century publishing and bookselling. With reference to the lavish promotional campaign for Martin Amis's *The Information*, she examines the problematic role of the author 'in the circulation and reception of the meaning of the text' (p. 72), and investigates the paratextual strategies adopted by his publisher. She notes that book marketing and promotional tactics, which rely on the author brand to sell books, are in marked contrast with trends in literary theory that de-centre the author as the source of a text's meaning, most influentially in Foucault's 'What Is an Author' and Barthes 'The Death of the Author', both first published in 1967. Identifying a general shift in the publishing industry from 'author production to author promotion' Gardiner considers that whereas once the industry operated with two distinct circuits of acclaim of 'high' and 'low' culture, increasingly works of literary fiction as well as popular fiction are expected to be fast sellers. To achieve this, the author has to have an instantly recognisable brand, which involves their involvement in an endless cycle of publicity, while also maintaining an illusion of being 'unbeholden to the fickle vagaries of the marketplace' (p. 77).

The transformation of the role of the author by digital technology is discussed by George Landow in his chapter 'Reconfiguring the Author' from his seminal work *Hypertext: The Convergence of Contemporary Critical Theory and Technology* (Chapter 12 [2006]). He maintains that the malleable and alterable nature of digital text, both textually and typographically, has led to a convergence of the functions of the reader and writer and a reduction in the writer's autonomy and authority over the text. Readers, however, are more active and reflective about the choices they make in reading, and can assimilate and accumulate texts to become authors themselves. The concept of a stable literary canon is thereby challenged, because every experience of reading is individualised. Landow argues that hypertext epitomises the theories of postmodern critics in relation to the de-centred and unstable author, despite the fact that their theoretical speculations preceded the advent of digital text and the internet. He reflects on the new opportunities for authors to bypass publishers, and claims that the distinction between professional authors and amateurs is gradually becoming less relevant. Although the self-publishing model has conventionally been disparaged as vanity publishing, Landow draws attention to its advantages, claiming that the costs have fallen so low that it is affordable to almost everyone; it is an effective form of author promotion; it offers the potential for high sales due to word-of-mouth advertising; and it also opens up opportunities for non-commercial publishing.

Laura Dietz (Chapter 11 [2015]) reviews how the career of the author is being transformed in the digital age, and how authors achieve recognition when their work is published digitally. She poses a series of questions: what or who confers legitimacy to the author in the contemporary digital publishing environment? Does it depend on the reputation of the publisher's imprint, the terms of payment to the author, or the size of the advance? What is the importance of a digital presence for a writer's career, both in terms of e-book publishing and digital promotion? Although acknowledging that these questions cannot yet fully be answered while the industry is still in such a state of transition, Dietz suggests that contemporary writers are in a quandary, for while on the one hand digital disruption places their careers in jeopardy, on the other hand authors who are resistant to change run the risk of being marginalised.

The role of the author has substantially changed since the early twentieth century, and these essays reflect on the fundamental alterations in authorship as a profession and in the power relations between the writer and publisher during the twentieth and twenty-first centuries. The introduction of the literary agent as an intermediary resulted in new divisions of responsibility between authors and publishers, while the corporatisation of the industry and changes in publishers' marketing practices have led to increased pressures on authors to engage in publicity activities, and to the creation of a culture of literary celebrity. No longer simply the creator of a literary text, the author is now heavily involved with, and invested in, the various stages of literary production, marketing and promotion. Moreover, recent digital transformations have opened up new possibilities for authors, providing greater opportunities for autonomy, self-promotion and self-publishing while also increasing the demands made upon them, and undermining their opportunities for financial reward.

SUGGESTED FURTHER READING

Barthes, R., 1967/1997. 'The death of the author', in S. Heath (ed.), *Image Music Text*. London: Fontana.

Burke, S., 1995. *Authorship: From Plato to the Postmodern: A Reader*. Edinburgh: Edinburgh University Press.

Foucault, M., 1980. 'What is an author?', in J.V. Harari (ed.), *Textual Strategies: Perspectives in Post-Structuralist Criticism*. London: Methuen, 141–60.

Gardiner, J., 2000. 'Recuperating the author: Consuming fictions of the 1990s'. *The Papers of the Bibliographical Society of America,* 94 (2), 255–274.

West, J.L.W., 1989. *American Authors and the Literary Marketplace since 1900*. Philadelphia: University of Pennsylvania Press.

8 Agents and the Field of Print Culture

Mary Ann Gillies

Agents and the Transformation of the Literary Marketplace

Watt may not have invented the role of literary agent, but he certainly played a central part in defining and refining it. By the turn of the century, other agents had begun to challenge his supremacy – notably J.B. Pinker and Curtis Brown. But for almost twenty years, from the late 1870s through the late 1890s, Watt dominated, setting the standard against which his competitors and successors were measured. His activities altered how publishing businesses operated and how literature was produced. This, in turn, transformed the literary marketplace. His influence is both direct and subtle.

The direct influence can be seen by the ways that Watt, and the other agents who came to occupy prominent positions, prompted a radical shift in the balance of power in publishing. Agents undermined publishers' traditionally dominant position by forcing them to expose their activities to public scrutiny – public in the sense of authors and agents. They helped authors to empower themselves – by assisting them in their fights for better financial terms and more control over their literary property. Watt served as publisher for the first twelve issues of the Society of Authors' journal – the *Author* – in which many debates about authors' ownership of their work and reform of copyright legislation appeared. He also sold advertising space for the journal. In both capacities, he was directly involved in the authors' fight for greater control of their work.[1] But perhaps the best evidence of the extent of Watt's growing influence can be found in the virulence of the responses from the party who apparently had most to lose – the publisher.

In the last twenty-five years of the nineteenth century, it was common-place for publishers to point out the decline in literary quality that they saw as a consequence of the expanded marketplace and the ongoing commercialization of literature. Many held the agent largely responsible for this. The most celebrated dispute between publishers and agents is that which occurred in 1905 between the American publisher Henry Holt and the London-based agent Albert Curtis Brown. Because Holt's views are similar to those of many of Britain's powerful publishers, at least initially, and because the exchange with Curtis Brown so fully elaborates the concerns of both sides, their exchange is worth looking at in some detail.

Holt laments the transformations brought about by the increasing sums of money paid to authors and the competition engendered by writers who hawked their wares in the marketplace. He places the blame for the situation squarely at the door of the literary agent. He allows that there might be 'a justification for a person so unbusinesslike as the author generally is, supplementing himself with a business adviser to look over contracts and royalty statements – a sort of lawyer and auditor.' But he goes on to say that 'in carrying his functions farther, the agent has been the parent of most serious abuses,' and 'a very serious detriment to literature and a leech on the author, sucking blood entirely out of proportion to his later services; and has already begun to defeat himself.'[2] Such strong sentiments are surely incited by his real fear, not only for the condition of literature, but also, and more importantly, for the condition of publishers.

In his response to Holt, Curtis Brown presents a different assessment of the situation:

> Now it used to be considered good form for the author to know little or nothing about market rates, and to take whatever he could manage to get from his publisher without resorting to any systematic use of competition. When the agent came along and began to prove by expert knowledge of market prices that in many cases the author had not received as much as his work was worth in the open market, it was only human nature for that author's publisher to call the agent a villain.[3]

Brown's reasonable claim is that agents make the playing field level:

> The wise literary agent of to-day and of the future will act for the author on a policy of competition, it is true, but competition carefully tempered by regard for the value of friendly relations between author and publisher. The best arrangement between author and publisher is the one of closest touch on the literary side of the work, leaving the commercial side to be arranged between publisher and agent, on the basis of the value of the author's work in the open market.[4]

Implicit in Brown's remarks is the belief that the resulting redistribution of power among publisher, agent, and author will lead to a system that works better for all parties. While this is certainly open to argument, it is evident that just such a power-sharing relationship evolved. Despite their best efforts, publishers had no way to stop the rise of agents, for if they refused to deal with Watt or other agents, they risked cutting themselves off from a large number of writers and thus jeopardizing their firms' futures. Once Watt was firmly established, a new power nexus became inevitable.

Watt's activities also had a subtler, but equally significant, impact on the shape of literary culture that lasted well into the twentieth century. When one looks at Watt's client list – either the one supplied in his own advertisements or the list of contributors to the various volumes of *Letters to A.P. Watt* – a number of observations may be made.[5] First, Watt's clients were individuals who had proven themselves in the literary marketplace, as judged by the sales of their works. In many cases, they were also authors who had attained a measure of critical success, either in the form of favourable reviews from well-placed critics or in the accumulation of symbolic capital. Knighthoods were awarded to Watt's clients Walter Besant, Arthur Conan Doyle, and Rider Haggard, for instance, while Rudyard Kipling won a Nobel Prize for literature in 1907.

Second, it is clear that Watt did not typically expend energy or capital in the nurturing of unproven talent. He preferred to approach writers once they had established themselves. The way in which Rudyard Kipling became Watt's client provides a typical example. Harry Ricketts, one of Kipling's biographers, notes that within months of Kipling's return to London in 1889, 'he had become a phenom- enon,' whose work had provoked 'a wide range of expectations ... even before his arrival in London.'[6] And Martin Seymour-Smith, another Kipling biographer, says that when Kipling arrived in London in October of 1899, he 'really was a rising young author.' Shortly after his arrival, despite what Seymour-Smith calls Kipling's 'general rule about the literary world coming to him,' Kipling 'called on Andrew Lang, who took him to the Savile club, where he would have soon met Hardy, Sir Walter Besant ... Haggard, Gosse, James, the literary historian George Saintsbury, and many others.'[7] Clearly, Kipling was moving in the sort of circles that would draw Watt's attention to him, and it was only a matter of time before the two met. In fact, within months of his arrival, Walter Besant introduced Kipling to 'the liter- ary agent A.P. Watt, whom he employed until his death.'[8] While there is no doubt that Watt played a central role in Kipling's career from the time he took him on as a client (a fact Kipling acknowledged when he remarked to Olive Schreiner about Watt that 'he is very kind and nice and does everything for you except – writing your book')[9] – it is nonetheless the case that Kipling was already well launched in his career when he became Watt's client. Similar stories could be told about other Watt clients. Besant, who became a client of Watt's in 1884, had enjoyed a success- ful career as a novelist dating back to his collaboration with James Rice in the early 1870s;[10] Rider Haggard's *King Solomon's Mines* (1885) had attracted widespread critical attention, and within the year he signed on to Watt's agency;[11] and Arthur Conan Doyle, who joined Watt's stable of clients in 1890, had carved out a modest reputation for himself as a historical novelist and had already published the first of his Sherlock Holmes tales – 'A Study in Scarlet' and 'The Sign of Four.'[12]

Third, because Watt's clients were usually already successful, their works tended to reflect the prevailing literary tastes of the time. Granted, those tastes were becoming ever more diverse, as evidenced by the fact that George MacDonald, Rudyard Kipling, Marie Corelli, and Arthur Conan Doyle were all represented by Watt. However, Watt's clients were not often at the vanguard of literary experi- mentalism that later became associated with modernism (with the notable excep- tions of W.B. Yeats and August Strindberg, for example), in large measure because such works had yet to capture sufficient attention from readers or critics to bring their authors the cultural or economic capital that would have drawn Watt's atten- tion to them.[13]

The results of what might well be characterized as Watt's conservative approach were far-reaching. Because his was the leading agency of the era, a new writer's career could be given an enormous boost if he or she were added to Watt's client list. Joining Watt meant that all the contacts and experience of the firm were brought into play on the writer's behalf: doors were opened and opportunities provided that the writer struggling on his or her own might not have had. The obvious catch here was that the writer's work had to be the sort that Watt felt his agency could sell. Those whose works could not be slotted into an existing market niche were unlikely to be taken up by Watt. And as a result, they were more likely to have a difficult time finding a publisher willing to take a chance on their work, since as the twentieth century dawned publishers were relying more on Watt, and other agents, to provide them with marketable literature.[14] With as large a client base as he had, Watt might have been able to champion a new writer, knowing that he would benefit little from his actions in the short term, but also knowing that his other clients generated enough income to keep him solvent. If the new writer did catch on, not only would Watt's investment be returned, but also other clients might well be attracted to Watt, who might further exploit the market created by the demand for this new kind of writing. However, Watt's business model had little room for championing of new writers, a fact that would have consequences both for the profession of agenting and for print culture in general.

Ironically, Watt's conservative business practices proved beneficial to print culture for two reasons. First, the clients he represented continued to produce literature that met the demands of large segments of the reading public. Watt was adept at assessing what certain kinds of readers wanted and his firm continued to seek out writers who could supply them with the material they wanted even when many well-placed literary critics were beginning to champion the experiments of modernist writers. Second, as the literary marketplace evolved to accommodate new readers and writers from differing backgrounds, Watt's tendency to stick with established writers and markets meant that other literary agents emerged to assist new writers in taking advantage of the market's rapid expansion. As these new agents, such as Pinker, staked out turf in the broad print culture field, they challenged not only Watt's position as the preeminent literary agent, but also his ways of doing business. Thus because Watt was slow to change, his rivals provided an alternative that not only serviced an important emerging coterie of authors and publishers, but also enabled literary agency to adapt to meet the needs of the rapidly evolving print culture field.

9 Disembodied Images: Authors, Authorship and Celebrity

Joe Moran

The notions of authorship formulated within the academy and outside it have radically diverged in recent years – while academic criticism has formulated theories about the death, disappearance or absence of the author, this figure still seems to be very much alive in non-academic culture. This chapter discusses literary celebrity in relation to some of these apparently conflicting notions of authorship, examining theoretical perspectives in relation to the actual effects of the literary marketplace and the way that authors themselves have responded to the phenomenon of celebrity. It begins by examining how the transformation of authors into media images connects with the efforts within academic literary criticism to question the figure of the author as the authoritative originator of texts and to view individualistic notions of authorship instead as culturally and historically determined. It then goes on to examine a number of texts in which authors have dealt with these issues, which tend to pivot similarly around questions of authorial intention and agency. If the main contention of anti-intentionalist textual criticism is that a text 'is not the author's (it is detached from the author at birth and goes about the world beyond his power to intend about it or control it)',[1] a similar case might be made for the way in which celebrity has impacted on the work and public personality of authors. The academy's scepticism about the figure of the author thus has more similarities than might at first be apparent with celebrity's appropriation of the authorial personality.

THE DEATH OF THE AUTHOR?

Several critics have already pointed to the irony that the kinds of publicity about authors [...] seemed to emerge at roughly the same time as academic criticism was becoming increasingly suspicious of essentialist notions of the individual author. Malcolm Bradbury, for example, suggests that we now live 'in two ages at once: the age of the author hyped and promoted, studied and celebrated; the age of the author denied and eliminated, desubjected and airbrushed from writing'.[2] Others have drawn attention to the transformation of literary critics and philosophers who have proclaimed the death of the author-subject into media celebrities, even suggesting that this represents a kind of bad faith on their part. Peter Washington, for example, argues that the most enthusiastic sponsor of the 'death of the author',

Roland Barthes, 'brought to theory a journalist's sense of publicity and a decorator's eye for effect ... how appropriate that the author of the Author's Death should be a narcissist whose only subject is himself!'[3]

In fact, though, the irony would not have been lost on Barthes himself: the kind of 'anti-authorial' criticism with which he is associated is actually useful to this discussion in pointing to the ways in which the figure of the author can function as a vehicle for ideologies which promote the autonomy and singularity of the individual subject, and which attribute value and authority to certain texts (and authors) but not others. Barthes urges the death of the author as a project for literary criticism precisely because, he says, 'the image of literature to be found in ordinary culture is tyrannically centred on the author, his person, his life, his tastes, his passions'. He aims to show that the privileged figure of the author is a modern invention, the product of bourgeois society's discovery of 'the prestige of the individual'.[4] Barthes's demystification of *Le Figaro's* lionization of André Gide in *Mythologies*, for example, points to 'the glamorous status which bourgeois society liberally grants its spiritual representatives (so long as they remain harmless)'.[5]

Similarly, Michel Foucault's essay, 'What is an Author?' traces the conditions by which contemporary literary discourse has come to be dominated by 'the sovereignty of the author' back to the seventeenth and eighteenth centuries, when literary texts began to be attached to the name of a single author as part of their transformation into legally reinforced, marketable cultural properties. According to Foucault, 'in our culture, the name of an author is a variable that accompanies only certain texts to the exclusion of others ... the function of an author is to characterize the existence, circulation, and operation of certain discourses within a society'.[6] Both Barthes and Foucault, then, are criticizing not so much the common-sense notion that individual authors write texts, but the kinds of mystical associations which cluster around them in capitalist societies, naturalizing them as the only authoritative source of textual meaning and as a locus of power and authority within a culture.

As I have attempted to show [...], this is precisely how literary celebrity functions, reformulating authorship within the literary marketplace and using it as the repository of all kinds of conflicting cultural meanings and values. The same might be said, in fact, for celebrity culture in general, which reifies individuals and allows them to be used by capitalist society in a variety of ways – as market stimuli, as representations of ideal social types, as focal points for the desires and longings of audiences, and so on. This emphasis in Barthes's and Foucault's work on the social construction of the individual thus has similarities with the theories of the Frankfurt School of cultural criticism, which deal more generally with the way in which capitalism has valorized a particular form of individualism, making 'the peculiarity of the self ... a monopoly commodity determined by society'. In particular, Adorno and Horkheimer attack the American culture industries for producing a star system of 'pseudo individuality ... a shallow cult of leading personalities'.[7] In his essay, 'The Work of Art in the Age of Mechanical Reproduction', Walter Benjamin similarly comments that the Hollywood film industry responds to the shrivelling of the aura with an artificial build-up of the 'personality' outside the studio. The cult of the movie star, fostered by the money of the film industry, preserves not the unique aura of the person but the 'spell of the personality', the phony spell of a commodity.[8]

It is not difficult to see how early studies of stardom by Boorstin and others were influenced by the Frankfurt School critics in their definition of the celebrity as devoid of depth or individuality, a 'human pseudo-event'.

Both Jane Gaines and Celia Lury have looked more specifically at these developments in the culture industries in relation to contemporary authorship. Gaines explores the shift in emphasis in American law from questions of copyright (ownership of a product by its author) to trademark (ownership of an image by a corporation) as protection for cultural products, pointing out that the 'legal displacement of the author', a product of the growing power of corporations to control the production of literature and culture, is 'roughly contemporaneous with what postmodern theory has diagnosed as the eclipse of the author by his or her own text'.[9] Lury also examines the repositioning of intellectual property rights from copyright to trademark law and argues that this is a response to the increasing importance, in Benjamin's terms, of 'exhibition value' over 'cult value'. As Lury explains it,

> the cultural producer's protected position as originator has been undermined by the commercial exploitation of the possibilities of replication offered by the technologies of culture ... The development of market relations can thus be seen to have been a factor in both the emergence and the decline of the author-function as a form of asymmetry in cultural reproduction.[10]

Lury suggests that entrepreneurial capitalism created the individual author with the consolidation of copyright law in the eighteenth century, reinforcing this ideologically with the invention of a romantic notion of an 'author-god', but that monopoly capitalism is now threatening to destroy this figure with its promiscuous exploitation of new markets. This is true, up to a point: in the areas of popular culture that Lury and Gaines examine – films, broadcast media, commercials, comics – the 'author-function' is indeed becoming less important as large corporations increasingly control the output of the entertainment industry. In the literary sphere, however, the figure of the author (as we have seen, a complex synergy of 'cult value' and 'exhibition value') is still very much alive. Within this sphere, a more pressing problem is that the name of the author herself can become merely an image, either used to market a literary product directly or as a kind of freefloating signifier within contemporary culture. Although the most extreme example of this is provided by the celebrities who opportunistically adorn the dustjackets of novels ghost-written by other people, this is only one of the many ways in which an author's name can be used for promotional effect.

There is a danger, then, that the anti-individualizing effects of the literary marketplace – the creation of the author as a 'personality' by a vast network of cultural and economic practices – will actually threaten the whole notion of authorship as an individualistic activity, taking away agency from the author at the same time as it apparently celebrates that author's autonomy as a 'star author'. The author becomes gradually less in control not only of her work but also of her image and how it circulates, at the same time as the machinery of celebrity asserts what literary critics call 'the intentional fallacy', which assumes that she is wholly in control of it. This cuts to the heart of the paradoxical nature of celebrity culture as a whole, which promotes individualism at the same time as it undermines it, being founded on what Leo Braudy calls 'a public rhetoric of individualism that offsets an increasingly pervasive web of institutional and corporate relations', with celebrity being seen as 'the only way out of increasingly complex political and economic dependence on others … in a more crowded, corporate and collective world'.[11] As Stuart Ewen has written:

> It is this objectification of the person that, most probably, explains much of the turmoil and grief, the identity crisis that often accompanies stardom. Perhaps celebrities, too, become uncomfortable in their own skins as they, in the eyes of others, become frozen images; as their faces and bodies and mannerisms become icons; always the personage, never the person. It is difficult to be a disembodied image.[12]

10 'What is an Author?' Contemporary Publishing Discourse and the Author Figure

Juliet Gardiner

On 20 May 1995 an enigmatic poster started appearing in London bus shelters, on the escalator of London underground stations and on the tube train itself. For four weeks Londoners – and those living in other large urban conurbations in Britain – were supposedly intrigued and tantalised by a turquoise poster with a single 'i' on it. The deconstruction of advertising semiotics has become a necessary quotidian proficiency in the conditions of late capitalism, interpolating the consumer into the construction of product appeal. Increasingly over previous decades advertisements have become not communicators of product information, but referents of allusion and intertextuality that presuppose a complex matrix of consumer subjectivities and identities. It is often only possible to be certain that an advertisement for cigarettes *is* an advertisement for cigarettes by counter indices, by reading the health warning legend along the bottom.

The recognition denies the need for any possible information content in the advertisement since it is the signification of an aestheticised – albeit ironised – life style that *is* the information.[1] The aesthetic, for example, of Absolut vodka advertisements where a bottle shape assumes a variety of hot cultural references (a Damien Hirst 'medical' construction, a painting by the winner of the 1998 Turner Prize, Chris Ofili, a New York skyscraper, a Hümmel tschotskey, etc.) privileges the knowing consumer and creates a cognitive intimacy in a world of large-scale commodity production. But this trope is predicated on a number of assumptions, the most obvious of which is that persons viewing the advertisement will be able to decode the sign and thus recognize the product to which it refers, and it is by this act of recognition that the consumer inscribes value to the product that he or she is mutely appealed to purchase.

But the 'i' poster was not a coded advertisement for a well-known product whose identity, like Absolut, Silk Cut or Benson & Hedges, was already fixed in the mind of the consumer. It, too, was a tease but one which when explicated may well have remained a tease for the majority of those who might have puzzled over it. The 'i' stood for information and the poster campaign was mounted to announce the publication in paperback of Martin Amis's (then) most recent novel *The Information* which was itself something of a tease since it is never entirely clear from this book what the Information of the title *is* other than the ultimate information: namely that we are mortal.

So what might this initiative suggest about literary production in Britain today, and in particular how might it be possible to read the significance of a £100,000 promotional campaign for one book as mobilising notions of the author-function in current publishing discourse when the name of the author is the most elusive – indeed for the most part the absent – signature in this particular campaign?

Since Foucault's query 'What is an Author'[2] and Barthes' pronouncement of 'The Death of the Author'[3] in 1967 both, in crude simplification, decentring the author as the source of meaning of the text and constituting the reader as the agent in the construction of that meaning, the trace of the author has remained problematic and, to an extent, untheorised. Usurped as the creator of meaning at the moment of composition, how does the author source the meaning of the text in use? What function does he or she play in the circulation and reception of the meaning of the text? In other words, if, in Foucault's formulation 'the function of the author is to characterize the existence, circulation, and operation of certain discourses within society,'[4] can an analysis of the representation of the author in a particular instance play a part in disentangling any of those 'certain' discourses? How might the study of the identification of a hoped-for market for a particular author, and the promotion of that author to target that market, illuminate the promotional practices of contemporary publishing as one of the 'site[s] of the struggles for monopoly of the power to consecrate, in which the value of works of art and belief in that value are continuously generated'?

The relationship of the author to his or her text is represented on publication by the author's 'parenting' of the text through the belated introduction into English law of a Moral Rights clause in the 1988 Copyright, Designs and Patents Act which asserts the 'patrimony' of the author and thus his or her inalienable right (except by waiver that is) as the guarantor of the integrity of the text. This peritextual[5] indication is situated on the copyright verso and embeds the author with the publisher(s) and printer as those responsible for the book of which the text-as-written-by-the-author is part. However, whilst this account of the *production* of a book locates the author as part of a nexus (though a collaboration that produces the material object since reference to the collaboration involved in the production of the text for publication – editing – and of its circulation, is absent here), the *promotion* of the book (the various mechanisms by which it eventually reaches the end user, the reader) foregrounds only the author. In this regard the Romantic definition of the author as stand-alone source of meaning and authority, becomes conflated with a more overlooked root of the word author, the Latin, 'agere' to act or perform. The author not only writes the text, increasingly in various ways she or he speaks it, circulating its meaning through media interviews, reviews, business reports and so-called news items, in 'personal appearances,' at readings and literary events.

The context for this is the political economy of the infotainment industry, a marathon of which publishing, with various degrees of reluctance and ineptitude, has become a part. The conglomeratisation of publishers into large, international, multi-imprint aggregates themselves frequently but a media arm of a corporation with film, television, telecom, broadcast and computer interests, has led to rationalisation. Not a rationalisation of books published – since in 1996 the number of new books and new editions published in the UK topped 100,000 for the first time ever – but of the promotional effort expended on certain titles to ensure that of that 100,000, or of the 200–300 novels offered to booksellers on average each month, this select number stand a chance of becoming candidates for the best selling list. In publishing and bookselling, new technologies which have considerably reduced production costs have conversely restricted reception opportunities through tighter stock control and monitoring in book shops and libraries, and have insisted on a concentration of promotional strategies.

The change in patterns of book selling has been paralleled by the growth of specialist chain book shops, most notably Waterstone's or Borders. In 1998 a holding company was formed by which Waterstone's was extracted from W.H. Smith and merged with Dillons (giving the group a marketing share of 20.2 percent) and the U.S. giant, Borders, acquired Books etc., and opened their first mega store in London's Oxford Street. Waterstones opened its largest shop yet with 28,000 sq. feet of selling space in Sauciehall Street Glasgow, stocking 150,000 individual titles (60,000 is the norm), and this trend towards the in-city book mega store (on an admittedly UK scale) is continued with the extension of Dillons flagship shop in Gower Street (but renamed – or as the book trade calls it 'rebadged' – Waterstone's), another superstore this time in Leeds, and the 'biggest bookshop in the world' – a claim disputed by Barnes & Noble[6] – when Waterstone's moved into the shop that was Simpsons of Piccadilly in autumn 1999, premises that provides 54,000 ft. of selling space housing 300,000 titles and a million books.

These shops are in prime locations adjacent to such retail outlets as Next, Our Price or The Body Shop. They invite customers in with a variety of devices – long opening hours that exceed the usual working day and the working week and suggest that book buying can be a part of the almost round the clock culture of shopping, now a socio-cultural activity like cinema visiting. They stage readings and other events that carry the message of the book shop as place of entertainment, as do the *café latte* bars that are such a characteristic of U.S. book buying and are beginning to penetrate the British market.[7] The design of these book shops connive at the impression of consumer power and a parallel lack of didacticism, there is a democracy of choice about the wares displayed. Gone are the intimidating narrow, shelf-lined shops where it was necessary to know what you were looking for in order to find it; now the proliferation of 'front tables' with their suggestion of a plenitude of choice and the invitation to pick up and browse books on whim is crucial to booksellers and to publishers since it is on these altars that books, displayed front out, take their chance of success. Front table displays are carefully monitored: books that don't move are relegated. Six weeks is the absolute maximum opportunity that books have to get established, either from a front table site, or from an author dump bin that the publisher has persuaded the bookseller to assemble, where 12 or 24 copies of the same book (or the newly-published hardback of the particular author and the new paperback edition of the previous hardback by the same author) are displayed face out. Once a book is shelved spine out, its selling curve dips alarmingly unless it is already well established.

Increasingly centralised buying – 'Swindonisation' as it's still known in the UK trade since Swindon is where the HQ and buying offices of W.H. Smith, the chain that used to own Waterstone's and is still a major player in the book market, are situated – the growth of wholesale chains with their pre-selected lists that have already filtered out a large number of titles, the increase in direct telephone order-ing to major wholesalers who now employ their own sales staff, factors which signal the demise of the publisher's represent active who toted round individual copies of publisher's titles seeking orders, and efficient stock control regulated by such devices as EPOS (electronic point of sale) mean that it is an ungenerous market both to get books into the book shops in respectable numbers, and to keep them there for long enough to establish a selling presence.

Thus, the selling of a book has happened long before it reaches the bookshop: in order to persuade shops to subscribe in acceptable numbers to a title, publisher's marketing departments need to be able to point to a high profile promotional budget that will give a book pre-publication visibility, and that means author vis-ibility since an author can be the subject of interviews or profiles and a participant in a variety of events that will mobilize interest across a far wider field than can a two-column book review in the quality press which is all that a book alone can achieve.

The collapse of the Net Book Agreement (NBA) in autumn 1995 and its final juridical interment in the spring of 1997, has exacerbated this trend – that is, that discounting means that booksellers necessarily concentrate on a limited number of high profile books and aim to sell sufficient volume to cover the cost of discount-ing. And these loss leaders that are intended to bring customers into the shops will have to be recognizable products – that is, books by authors whose names are instantly recognizable. The author name functions as a sign but promotional strat-egies differentiate and complicate the meaning of that sign.

The author in his or her designation as a brand name has become a sign of the event of commodification and this sign informs the whole process of publication. As recently as five years ago UK publishers had sales departments and publicity assistants. The two have been merged as Marketing which can no longer be seen as something that happens to a book after it is written. Marketing is constitutive *of* its writing not only in the sense of formulaic writing, but also a book's representa-tion. 'Robert, you are a brand name,' trumpeted the publisher at Random House in an *Omnibus* profile to the author of *Fatherland*, Robert Harris, when the publisher had gone to Harris' home to show him the jacket of his next book *Enigma* – a book of which Harris confessed he had at that moment 'written considerably less than a quarter.'[8]

The tradition of publishing houses was that the author/editor relation was what bound a successful author to the house: the editor was a necessary midwife to the author's prose. It was the author/editor bond that acted as a book's collateral when contracts were negotiated. With the increasing aggregation of publishers and rationalizing of their lists and concomitant downsizing of their staff, that continu-ity can no longer be counted on; in today's climate the legendary Maxwell Perkins would probably have had four jobs in the last four years and now be working from home, euphemistically 'project managing.'

The current outcry in Britain and the U.S. about declining editorial standards is partly an attack on a liberal educational philosophy and practice that supposedly privileges creativity, innovation and cultural plurality over the teaching of grammar and spelling and the study of canonical texts, represented as a defence of the English language; it is also a sober understanding of what the logic of late capitalism has wrought on the publishing process and how the author function has been reconfigured. Authors are represented now not as an investment of time – editorial time – but as an investment of capital both in justification of paying high advances and in negotiating two or three, or even, in the case of authors such as Peter Ackroyd, five-or more-book contracts by publishers determined to retain authors in whom they are investing considerable sums of money by purchasing their future productive capacity. Pete Ayrton, owner of the small British experimental list, *Serpent's Tail*, evidencing what he calls, borrowing from the French, '*mediatique*,' 'presents well on chat shows,' points to the fact that whereas once a publisher seeking a rights deal at Frankfurt would press a synopsis or sample chapter on an interested fellow publisher, they are now as likely to produce a photograph of the author.[9]

What this shift in emphasis from author production to author promotion has done is to make transparent the dynamics of authorship and acclaim and challenge not only the Romantic view of the author but the other discourses, legal and academic among them, that reinforce it. It *was* possible to discuss the circuits of acclaim of high and low culture as if they operated according to a different set of principles, as if the fields of restricted production and that of mass production, to employ Bourdieu's formulation,[10] were binary in their operation. Low culture was seen as unproblematically part of the marketplace – indeed, created for it, defined by it. The formulaic, predictable nature of a Catherine Cookson, a Jeffrey Archer, a Dick Francis were out in the marketplace from the mid 80s relying not on reviews which such books did not get – unless they were ironic – but on a direct address to the reader through promotional posters and book shop signings at which customers queued up to buy books and have the author sign them. The performative role was linked to an appropriate location – Dick Francis on the racecourse and Jeffrey Archer in Harrods, Princess Michael of Kent in Hatchards of Piccadilly – the imprimatur was fixed. The name on the cover that already signed authorship was thus resigned – or assigned – in a spectated act that served a double function both of customizing the book in terms of the direct, unmediated address to the purchaser, and in locking the book into its reception (signed books cannot be returned by booksellers so in this loop of commodification the sign of the author increases the value of the book both to the reader *and* to the author).

It has become a commonplace for publishers to assert that their competitors are not now other publishers with competing books, as was the perception a decade ago,[11] but manufacturers of other leisure products – videos, audio books, CD ROMs – and that these have thus set an agendum for marketing that publishers fail to emulate at their peril. These imperatives map Bourdieu's field of mass production for mass market paperbacks, but how do they address the phenomenon of the literary author, operating in a field in which books are consecrated or valorised to an extent by the fact that the author is unvalued in the wider marketplace?

The literary author's expectation was for steady sales that built on acclaim and reputation, as each book was successively evaluated on individual merit and became part of the *oeuvre*; such books backlisted so that an author's value could be measured (literally) by the volume of space his or her books took up on a book shop shelf. It was a simulacrum of the closed community of an educated élite where acclaim was by word of mouth – a fiction still perpetuated today. But in the environment of fast turnover this was deemed not to be possible: the only way that a work of fiction can become a best seller and then a backlist item, is to become a fast seller. The increasing competition for space, linked to the extension of the marketplace since the collapse of the NBA, means that the brand has to be instantly recognisable. In some cases, of course, the publisher serves as the branding device. In the case of Oxford University Press, for example, the authority acquired by OUP's academic monograph and reference publishing has 'authorised' the Press's ventures into the trade reference sector – the *Oxford Companion to English Literature*, the *Oxford Book of Ghost Stories*, the *Oxford Book of Frets and Discontents* for example, but in the case of most trade books, the publisher is unknown to, or rather ignored by, the majority of purchasers and readers of books.[12] Rather 'customer loyalty' has to be cultivated through the author, the author is the brand, it is the author who has to be recognisable and built in as product recognition. If the representation of the author has been re-configured, so has his or her work. He or she has become a unitary sign for all the processes of publishing, and they in turn represent him or her. Thus, the promotable fiction author who spends, say, a year writing a novel, will now spend considerably *more* than a year promoting it in a round of press, radio and television interviews, bookshop readings, and other events on publication – a circuit that is replicated whenever and wherever across the globe the book is subsequently published. Furthermore, he or she will be interpolated into a circuit of promotion as part of the culture industry reinforcing his or her status by reviewing other authors of perceived comparable status, sitting on panels to award prizes to other authors, teaching creative writing workshops to would-be authors at the 'writer's centres' that have sprung up all over Britain and on a Greek island, taking part in the circuit of literary festivals that now proliferate in the UK – Hay-on-Wye, Cheltenham and Edinburgh, to name only the largest. He or she may well also be offered to write a monthly column in, say, *Esquire* or *GQ*[13] or *Prospect* or a weekly one in the *Independent* or a regular one in the London *Evening Standard*[14] which has nothing to do with books and will certainly be invited to appear on chat shows on radio and tv and talk about nothing to do with his or her latest book, indeed nothing to do with books at all. The voracious growth of talk show radio and television, the explosion of new magazines, the proliferation of local radio stations and cable tv has created an insatiable void for people to fill with talk, a need for the articulate celebrity. The author is still 'author of' but has come to represent an accretion of cultural capital of which his or her books form an increasingly small part.

If branding is a device used to locate a product within an identifiable market sector then the question of how that sector is identified becomes critical. In media production – newspapers, magazines, commercial radio and television – where production economics are a fusion of sales and advertising revenue, market research is undertaken to provide advertisers with a profile of readers, since consumption is constituted as a social practice and therefore individual consumer identities aggregate around a 'lifestyle' that can be targeted with products that can be seen to be cognate to – indeed constitutive of – that identity.

Trade books[15] – as CDs and videos – are cultural products with a one-way income stream: purchase. They lack seriality and yet hope to develop a loyal following to ensure returns on – increasingly high – investment. In a market where price difference is marginal,[16] and use not a relevant category, product differentiation is based on a largely unresearched reading of the market for cultural goods that has absorbed the concept of a lifestyle, or a psychographics profile dissecting a mass market.[17]

This differentiation is problematic to manage when economic factors require a mass product sale, whereas cultural factors insist that only by masking the diffusion with an appearance of exclusivity can this be achieved. Since the factors that make such a market sector cohere are rhetorical rather than quantifiable, in order to utilise its potential it is necessary to presume and address its existence – to 'brand' the market sector to be targeted as well as branding the product – the book. In this exercise the representation of the author function is crucial in masking the transformed relation of authorship to the market. Once the system of patronage had declined and expanding educational opportunities and technological developments in the last quarter of the nineteenth-century firmly linked the livelihood of the author to the operation of the market. However in the case of the non-mass market author it had been possible for him or her to shelter under an ideological cover of the 'transcendent' author who happens to sell but whose value is represented as being largely due to the fact that he or she is *unbeholden* to the fickle vagaries of the marketplace. With the competitive economic demands of the post 1980s expansion and aggregation of publishers and book selling outlets, the so-perceived literary author has been required to achieve a high profile in the marketplace in ways that do not compromise his or her 'value' by being associated with an 'unknowing' mass market.

11 Who Are You Calling an Author? Changing Definitions of Career Legitimacy for Novelists in the Digital Era

Laura Dietz

Cory Arcangel is not a novelist. 'Fiction' is the word on the spine of his latest art project, but even that is a reach. The project is a book of retweets, published by Penguin in 2014, harvested from his feed of anything at all containing the words 'working on my novel'. His decision to call the result a 'novel'[1] is pure provocation: it bears no resemblance to the books his tweeters intended to write. Bound together, one per page, these hundred-some reports of not-working – because whatever one was doing the moment before or the moment after, the tweet itself is not novel-generating activity – are to the artist 'about the act of creation and the gap between the different ways we express our-selves today'.[2] Reviewers see something darker. What is 'funny, sad and oddly touching' in the eyes of the *Guardian*[3] is 'an aggregate of delusion, narcissism, procrastination, boredom, self-congratulation, confusion – every stumbling block, in other words, between here and art' to the *Paris Review*.[4] The artist strains to explain that the project is not, in fact, out to ridicule its subjects, but ridicule is how it strikes these observers. What makes it 'touching' – not just 'delusion' but affecting, pathetic delusion – is the reviewers' certainty that these tweeters who declare themselves writers are not writers, and never will be until they can close the app and get to work.

Publishing is an industry transformed by digital delivery.[5] As literary culture remakes itself to embrace books without pages and authors without editors, the definition of 'published', and by extension 'published author', is changing. In the absence of firmly agreed standards, emerging authors rely on 20th century industry practices to categorise others, and define themselves, as 'genuine writers' or 'pitiable aspirants' – while operating in 21st century marketplaces and intellec-tual communities. Authors are obliged, for income or book-selling publicity or sim-ply to participate in literary culture and debate, to write in formats (the blog, the tweet, the Instagram post, the Facebook status update, the digital original) that prominent voices in the literary establishment – like those above – call illegitimate.

This chapter will analyse the ways in which luminaries of the old regime, stars of self-publishing, and emerging players attack, co-opt, remake, and rehabilitate 'below-board' formats in their authorship of their own 'authorship'. As more of us write in public, while fewer are blessed by the legitimising hand of traditional publishing, negotiating that shifting boundary is emerging as a key component of the modern literary career.

WHO MINTS AN AUTHOR?

Writing is an art and a profession. Qualification as an author requires certification in both spheres. None of the key approaches for defining a writer as 'artist' – human capital, census definition, creative industries, creative environment, or subjectivist – is without controversy, or without grey areas.[6] To define 'professional' is to confront a similar series of loopholes. To be professional is to be paid for one's work, unless one is not paid, like a poet published in esteemed journals but never compensated except in author's copies,[7] or one is paid in the wrong way, corrupted by grants and bursaries and academic jobs (identified as a scourge of art by Nobel judge Horace Engdahl, whose prize money is presumably an exception),[8] or one is paid by the wrong people, like the 4.8 million purchasers who made Barbara Freethy a *New York Times* bestseller, but through Amazon rather than a traditional publishing house.[9] 'Whether one is considered a writer depends first and foremost on publications, not on diplomas or other formal criteria. A writer is not so much someone who writes, but someone who is recognised as such.'[10] A 'real writer' writes real things. Realness – legitimacy – is bound up in the shared and shifting understanding of what counts as publication.

There is nothing unique about literature's dilemma of definition. Publishers are confronting the same revolutions in 'dominant logics'[11] and rituals of inclusion and certification[12] seen in other creative industries, from film to music to photography. Digital distribution and marketing have called into question who should play the old roles of editor, publicist and bookseller – and whether some of those roles are obsolete. Steve Coll notes that

'Jeff Bezos's conceit is that Amazon is merely an instrument of an inevitable digital disruption in the book industry, that the company is clearing away the rust and cobwebs created by inefficient analog-era 'gatekeepers' – i.e., editors, diverse small publishers, independent bookstores, and the writers this system has long supported.'[13] Successful recent antitrust cases against the 'Big Five' of Penguin Random House, Macmillan, HarperCollins, Hachette and Simon & Schuster (or the 'Big Six' before the 2013 Penguin/Random House merger) present publishers as the enemies of readers, working in concert not to bring the best new literature to market, but to keep prices for literature unnaturally high.[14] The gatekeeper, however, is not dead. Behind fears for readers – that we will drown in dross – and for jobbing authors – that we will starve – is a deeper assumption, that selectivity and exclusivity are necessary, that literature should maintain hierarchy for its own sake. As Anand and Jones point out, 'theorists such as Goode (1978), Becker (1982) and Caves (2001) have argued that unequal distribution of prestige is critical to productive activity in any creative field.'[15] Young Turks argue for different gatekeepers rather than no gatekeepers, because the real terror of levelling is not that everything will be legitimate, but that nothing will be. Just as writers need 'real books' to be authors, readers need authors if there are to be 'real books' to read: 'When Sade was not considered an author, what was the status of his papers? Simply rolls of paper onto which he ceaselessly uncoiled his fantasies during his imprisonment.'[16] The size and citizenship of the country of the chosen is debatable, but its borders will be bounded, indeed defined, by the wall of ineligibles; the precise criteria only visible in close examination of the almost-chosen, the barely-illegitimate, the nearly-good.

The case studies here focus on novelists, grounding discussion in the field of trade publishing, rather than the fields of (for example) scholarly press or literary magazine publishing, which sometimes release long-form fiction but have their own logics and ways of assigning value.[17] The tools and techniques these novelists pioneer, however, can easily be employed by poets, essayists, short story writers, biographers, memorists, or any writer for whom the label 'real book' is desirable.

THE ALMOST-CHOSEN AND THE NEARLY-GOOD

Emerging writers seeking to clear that wall of ineligbles and land safely in the country of the chosen contend not only with the realistic possibility of self-publishing (when fan fiction superstars and Kindle Original bestsellers are courted, not disdained, by traditional publishing houses) but with a publishing establishment trimming back the familiar signifiers of respectability. Some of the old measures of a publisher's investment in a given title – the launch party, the national book tour, even the hardcover release – are in retreat, reserved for a smaller and smaller core of authors. As PEN/Faulkner Award winner Ann Patchett says, 'the process is simply too expensive, and too emotionally damaging, to replicate the kinds of tours I lived through in the early nineties.'[18] Blog tours, Skype call-ins and 'virtual launch parties' quietly take the place of the costlier forbears. Industry insiders adapt, accepting that an absence of (some) old signifiers does not necessarily doom a new title.

The signal difference between a 'proper' book contract and a shady one is the advance. However tiny, an advance-on-royalties represents an inarguable commitment: the publisher is not borrowing, or sharing, or waiting to see; he has bought rights for publication and paid cash that cannot, with very rare exceptions relating to breach of contract, be reclaimed. He must now sell copies if he is to make a return on his investment. Money flows in one direction only, from publisher to author, and the publisher has assumed a measurable financial risk.

Even the advance, however, is under negotiation. 'Profit-sharing' imprints like Macmillan New Writing (Macmillan) and Hydra (Random House) present authors with a very different proposal. The promise of a more generous royalty is counterbalanced by the elimination of up-front payment to the author. The original terms of the science fiction, fantasy and horror-focussed Hydra, and its stablemates Alibi (crime), Loveswept (romance) and Flirt ('new adult'), were even more dramatic: that some largely unspecified editorial, production and marketing costs could be directly charged to the author. The prospect of reverse payment, of an author owing his publisher not a commissioned manuscript, but cash,[19] is reminiscent of the vilified vanity press.[20] Response to the Hydra model from the Science Fiction and Fantasy Writers of America (SFWA) was swift and fierce. The leverage applied by SFWA was not just bad publicity. The SFWA's public letter to Hydra warned that this 'outrageous and egregious' attempt to 'shift to the author costs customarily borne by the publisher', on top of 'predatory' efforts to sign naive new authors on terms 'beyond the pale of standard publishing practices', would lead to delisting as a qualifying market. In other words, new writers who had published only through Hydra (or, if the terms spread to other imprints, to the whole of Random House) would not be eligible for membership in their writers' organisation: they would not, by definition, be real authors.[21]

Random House altered its terms. In the face of a challenge not only to its 'reputation ... as an equitable partner for writers' but to its legitimacy, submission guidelines now offer the parallel option of 'a more traditional publishing arrangement' on the 'advance plus royalty model'.[22] A modified profit-sharing option, with no up-front costs to the author, remains.[23] Even for authors choosing the advance plus royalty model, credibility is uncertain. Though the phenomenon of the Big Five digital-only author is still new, and readers have not yet formed firm opinions, focus group respondents in 2014 were skeptical, and assigned lower status to such titles.[24] It is now possible to be a 'Penguin Random House author' without ever receiving a payment from Penguin Random House, or even a stack of author's copies one might lug to festival tables or resell on the sly. One's author copy is a file, with the same Digital Rights Management as the one for sale on Amazon: unloanable, unsellable, and as splendidly private as a lined pocket diary. It is a file on one's computer, as it was before the contract was signed.

The buffer zone around mainstream publishing, that no-man's-land of demi-respectability, has spread, but in both directions. New forms of public writing have stretched the outskirts, but the borders of the city of literature itself have also been pulled back. Corporate consolidation has reduced the number of major publishing companies to which one can sell a novel.[25] The lower typical production cost of an e-book is balanced by a lower typical price point.[26] Though the profit margins of the top 60 publishing companies have grown,[27] revenues have dropped slightly, and the overall volume of book sales has remained broadly steady.[28] While the slice accorded to self-publishers and digital-only editions has grown, the pie has remained the same size. The 'traditional slice', that safe territory free of any taint – those books/novels that tick every box of 20th century publishing respectability – has shrunk.

If there is risk associated with untried forms, why not delay? The pragmatic response to digital disruption would seem to be conservatism, waiting for the results of first adopter experiments before publishing in new venues. Yet flight to traditional forms carries its own risks. Modern bookselling requires promotion, and publishers increasingly require that such promotion include digital presence for authors.[29] A writer's pre-existing 'platform' forms a large part of the decision to publish in the first place.[30] Blogging is not enough: where once an author might be able to get away with essay-like long form posts – material that emulated, and was sometimes repurposed as, traditional personal essays or magazine features – Tracy van Straaten, vice-president of trade book publicity at Scholastic says '"we now talk about the complete social media footprint of something in the educator space, the consumer space, the author space, the bookseller space .... The collective conversation is immensely important"'.[31] Even for authors whose stature allows them to dictate their own terms, resistance to digital presence may be read not as principled, but as risible: witness the response to Jonathan Franzen, 'accused of irrelevance and cane-shaking'[32] for his criticisms of Salman Rushdie's Twitter use. Writers too conservative to participate, and to participate on industry terms, may find themselves too conservative to be published.

12 Reconfiguring the Author

George Landow

EROSION OF THE SELF

Like contemporary critical theory, hypertext reconfigures – rewrites – the author in several obvious ways. First of all, the figure of the hypertext author approaches, even if it does not merge with, that of the reader; the functions of reader and writer become more deeply entwined with each other than ever before.[1] This transformation and near merging of roles is but the latest stage in the convergence of what had once been two very different activities. Although today we assume that anyone who reads can also write, historians of reading point out that for millennia many people capable of reading could not even sign their own names. Today when we consider reading and writing, we probably think of them as serial processes or as procedures carried out intermittently by the same person: first one reads, then one writes, and then one reads some more. Hypertext, which creates an active, even intrusive reader, carries this convergence of activities one step closer to completion; but in so doing, it infringes on the power of the writer, removing some of it and granting it to the reader. These shifts in the relations of author and reader do not, however, imply that hypertext automatically makes readers into authors or co-authors – except, that is, in hypertext environments that give readers the ability to add links and texts to what they read.[2]

One clear sign of such transference of authorial power appears in the reader's abilities to choose his or her way through the metatext, to annotate text written by others, and to create links between documents written by others. Read-write hypertext like Intermedia or Weblogs that accept comments do not permit the active reader to change the text produced by another person, but it does narrow the phenomenological distance that separates individual documents from one another in the worlds of print and manuscript. In reducing the autonomy of the text, hypertext reduces the autonomy of the author. In the words of Michael Heim, 'as the authoritativeness of text diminishes, so too does the recognition of the private self of the creative author' (Heim 1987: 221). Granted, much of that so-called autonomy had been illusory and existed as little more than the difficulty that readers had in perceiving connections between documents. Nonetheless, hypertext – which I am here taking as the convergence of poststructuralist conceptions of textuality and electronic embodiments of it – does do away with certain aspects of the authoritativeness and autonomy of the text, and in so doing it does reconceive the figure and function of authorship. One powerful instance of the way hypermedia environments diminish the author's control over his or her own text appears in the way so-called open systems permit readers to insert links into a lexia written by someone else. Portal Maximizer, for example, permits overlaying one author's Web documents with another author's links, although the original document remains unchanged.[3]

William R. Paulson, who examines literature from the vantage point of information theory, arrives at much the same position when he argues that 'to characterize texts as artificially and imperfectly autonomous is not to eliminate the role of the author but to deny the reader's or critic's submission to any instance of authority. This perspective leaves room neither for authorial mastery of a communicative object nor for the authority of a textual coherence so complete that the reader's (infinite) task would be merely to receive its rich and multilayered meaning.' Beginning from the position of information theory, Paulson finds that in 'literary communication,' as in all communication, 'there is an irreducible element of noise,' and therefore 'the reader's task does not end with reception, for reception is inherently flawed. What literature solicits of the reader is not simply receptive but the active, independent, autonomous construction of meaning' (Paulson 1988: 139). Finding no reason to exile the author from the text, Paulson nonetheless ends up by assigning to the reader a small portion of the power that, in earlier views, had been the prerogative of the writer.

Hypertext and contemporary theory reconceive the author in a second way. As we shall observe when we examine the notion of collaborative writing, both agree in configuring the author of the text as a text. As Barthes explains in his famous exposition of the idea, 'this "I" which approaches the text is already itself a plurality of other texts, of codes which are infinite' (Barthes 1974: 10). Barthes's point, which should seem both familiar and unexceptional to anyone who has encountered Joyce's weaving of Gerty McDowell out of the texts of her class and culture, appears much clearer and more obvious from the vantage point of intertextuality. In this case, as in others at which we have already looked, contemporary theory proposes and hypertext disposes; or, to be less theologically aphoristic, hypertext embodies many of the ideas and attitudes proposed by Barthes, Derrida, Foucault, and others.

One of the most important of these ideas involves treating the self of author and reader not simply as (print) text but as a hypertext. For all these authors the self takes the form of a decentered (or centerless) network of codes that, on another level, also serves as a node within another centerless network. Jean-François Lyotard, for example, rejects nineteenth-century Romantic paradigms of an islanded self in favor of a model of the self as a node in an information network: 'A self does not amount to much,' he assures us with fashionable nonchalance, 'but no self is an island; each exists in a fabric of relations that is now more complex and mobile than ever before. Young or old, man or woman, rich or poor, a person is always located at "nodal points" of specific communication circuits, however tiny these may be. Or better: one is always located at a post through which various kinds of messages pass' (Lyotard 1984: 15). Lyotard's analogy becomes even stronger if one realizes that by 'post' he most likely means the modern European post office, which is a telecommunications center containing telephones and other networked devices.

Some theorists find the idea of participating in a network to be demeaning and depressing, particularly since contemporary conceptions of textuality deemphasize autonomy in favor of participation. Before succumbing to posthumanist depression, however, one should place Foucault's statements about 'the author's disappearance' in the context of recent discussions of machine intelligence (Foucault 1977: 119). According to Heinz Pagels, machines capable of complex intellectual processing will 'put an end to much discussion about the mind-body problem, because it will be very hard not to attribute a conscious mind to them without failing to do so for more human beings. Gradually the popular view will become that consciousness is simply "what happens" when electronic components are put together the right way' (Pagels 1989: 92). Pagels's thoughts on the eventual electronic solution to the mind-body problem recall Foucault's discussion of 'the singular relationship that holds between an author and a text [as] the manner in which a text apparently points to this figure who is outside and precedes it' (Foucault 1977: 115). This point of view makes apparent that literature generates precisely such appearance of a self, and that, moreover, we have long read a self 'out' of texts as evidence that a unified self exists 'behind' or 'within' or 'implicit in' it. The problem for anyone who yearns to retain older conceptions of authorship or the author function lies in the fact that radical changes in textuality produce radical changes in the author figure derived from that textuality. Lack of textual autonomy, like lack of textual centeredness, immediately reverberates through conceptions of authorship as well. Similarly, the unboundedness of the new textuality disperses the author as well. Foucault opens this side of the question when he raises what, in another context, might be a standard problem in a graduate course on the methodology of scholarship:

> If we wish to publish the complete works of Nietzsche, for example, where do we draw the line? Certainly, everything must be published, but can we agree on what 'everything' means? We will, of course, include everything that Nietzsche himself published, along with the drafts of his works, his plans for aphorisms, his marginalia; notations and corrections. But what if, in a notebook filled with aphorisms, we find a reference, a reminder of an appointment, an address, or a laundry bill, should this be included in his works? Why not? ... If some have found it convenient to bypass the individuality of the writer or his status as an author to concentrate on a work, they have failed to appreciate the equally problematic nature of the word 'work' and the unity it designates. (p. 119)

Within the context of Foucault's discussion of 'the author's disappearance' (p. 119), the illimitable plenitude of Nietzsche's oeuvre demonstrates that there's more than one way to kill an author. One can destroy (what we mean by) the author, which includes the notion of sole authorship, by removing the autonomy of text. One can also achieve the same end by decentering text or by transforming text into a network. Finally, one can remove limits on textuality, permitting it to expand, until Nietzsche, the edifying philosopher, becomes equally the author of *The Gay Science* and laundry lists and other such trivia – as indeed he was. Such illimitable plenitude has truly 'transformed' the author, or at least the older conception of him, into 'a victim of his own writing' (p. 117).

Fears about the death of the author, whether in complaint or celebration, derive from Claude Lévi-Strauss, whose mythological works demonstrated for a generation of critics that works of powerful imagination take form without an author. In *The Raw and the Cooked* (1964), for example, where he showed, 'not how men think in myths, but how myths operate in men's minds without their being aware of the fact,' he also suggests 'it would perhaps be better to go still further and, disregarding the thinking subject completely, proceed as if the thinking process were taking place in the myths, in the reflection upon themselves and their interrelation' (Lévi-Strauss 1969: 12).[4] Lévi-Strauss's presentation of mythological thought as a complex system of transformations without a center turns it into a networked text – not surprising, since the network serves as one of the main paradigms of synchronous structure.[5] Edward Said claims that the 'two principal forces that have eroded the authority of the human subject in contemporary reflection are, on the one hand, the host of problems that arise in defining the subject's authenticity and, on the other, the development of disciplines like linguistics and ethnology that dramatize the subject's anomalous and unprivileged, even untenable, position in thought' (Said 1985: 293). One may add to this observation that these disciplines' network paradigms also contribute importantly to this sense of the attenuated, depleted, eroding, or even vanishing subject.

Some authors, such as Said and Heim, derive the erosion of the thinking subject directly from electronic information technology. Said, for example, claims it is quite possible to argue 'that the proliferation of information (and what is still more remarkable, a proliferation of the hardware for disseminating and preserving this information) has hopelessly diminished the role apparently played by the individual' (p. 51).[6] Michael Heim, who believes loss of authorial power to be implicit in all electronic text, complains: 'Fragments, reused material, the trails and intricate pathways of "hypertext," as Ted Nelson terms it, all these advance the disintegration of the centering voice of contemplative thought. The arbitrariness and availability of database searching decreases the felt sense of an authorial control over what is written' (Heim 1987: 220). A database search, in other words, permits the active reader to enter the author's text at any point and not at the point the author chose as the beginning. Of course, as long as we have had indices, scholarly readers have dipped into specialist publications before or (shame!) instead of reading them through from beginning to end. In fact, studies of the way specialists read periodicals in their areas of expertise confirm that the linear model of reading is often little more than a pious fiction for many expert readers (McKnight, Richardson, and Dillon 1988).

Although Heim here mentions hypertext in relation to the erosion of authorial prerogative, the chief problem, he argues elsewhere, lies in the way 'digital writing turns the private solitude of reflective reading and writing into a public network where the personal symbolic framework needed for original authorship is threatened by linkage with the total textuality of human expressions' (Heim 1987: 215). Unlike most writers on hypertext, he finds participation in a network a matter for worry rather than celebration, but he describes the same world they do, though with a strange combination of prophecy and myopia. Heim, who sees this loss of authorial control in terms of a corollary loss of privacy, argues that 'anyone writing on a fully equipped computer is, in a sense, directly linked with the totality of symbolic expressions – more so and essentially so than in any previous writing element' (p. 215). Pointing out that word processing redefines the related notions of publishing, making public, and privacy, Heim argues that anyone who writes with a word processor cannot escape the electronic network: 'Digital writing, because it consists of electronic signals, puts one willy-nilly on a network where everything is constantly published. Privacy becomes an increasingly fragile notion. Word processing manifests a world in which the public itself and its publicity have become omnivorous; to make public has therefore a different meaning than ever before' (p. 215). Although in 1987 Heim much exaggerated the loss of privacy inherent in writing with word-processing software per se, he turns out, as Weblog diaries prove, to have been prescient. When he wrote, most people did not in fact do most of their writing on networks, but the Internet changes everything: e-mail and personal blogs blur the boundaries between public and private.[7] Although Heim may possibly overstate the case for universal loss of privacy – the results are not in yet – he has accurately presented both some implications of hypertext for writers and the reactions against them by the print author accustomed to the fiction of the autonomous text.

The third form of reconfiguration of self and author shared by theory and hypertext concerns the decentered self, an obvious corollary to the network paradigm. As Said points out, major contemporary theorists reject 'the human subject as grounding center for human knowledge. Derrida, Foucault, and Deleuze ... have spoken of contemporary knowledge (*savoir*) as decentered; Deleuze's formulation is that knowledge, insofar as it is intelligible, is apprehensible in terms of *nomadic centers*, provisional structures that are never permanent, always straying from one set of information to another' (Said 1985: 376). These three contemporary thinkers advance a conceptualization of thought best understood, like their views of text, in an electronic, virtual, hypertextual environment.

Before mourning too readily for this vanished or much diminished self, we would do well to remind ourselves that, although Western thought long held such notions of the unitary self in a privileged position, texts from Homer to Freud have steadily argued the contrary position. Divine or demonic possession, inspiration, humors, moods, dreams, the unconscious – all these devices that serve to explain how human beings act better, worse, or just different from their usual behavior argue against the unitary conception of the self so central to moral, criminal, and copyright law. The editor of the Soncino edition of the Hebrew Bible reminds us that

Balaam's personality is an old enigma, which has baffled the skill of commentators ... He is represented in Scripture as at the same time heathen sorcerer, true Prophet, and the perverter who suggested a peculiarly abhorrent means of bringing about the ruin of Israel. Because of these fundamental contradictions in character, Bible Critics assume, that the Scriptural account of Balaam is a combination of two or three varying traditions belonging to different periods ... Such a view betrays a slight knowledge of the fearful complexity of the mind and soul of man. It is only in the realm of Fable that men and women display, as it were in a single flash of light, some one aspect of human nature. It is otherwise in real life. (668)

Given such long observed multiplicities of the self, we are forced to realize that notions of the unitary author or self cannot authenticate the unity of a text.[8] The instance of Balaam also reminds us that we have access to him only in Scriptures and that it is the biblical text, after all, which figures the unwilling prophet as a fractured self.

Part Three
Readership and the Literary Marketplace

The chapters in this part address the processes and multiple spaces of reading, both public and private. They focus on the literary marketplace in Britain and America in the twentieth century, and seek to define and categorise readership, and to analyse the institutional contexts in which literature is consumed. They explore the impact of changes in society that affected reading practices and patterns of book borrowing and ownership, and review the various ways in which publishers have attempted to reach new readers.

The first two chapters testify to widespread concerns in the early twentieth century about the impact of the 'mass market' on books and publishing, with respect to publishers' negotiation between culture and commerce, their approach to readers and their provision of reading materials for them. Queenie Leavis's 1932 study of the contemporary British reading public states that while 'it's safe to say that everyone does read, book buying is a minority activity and the majority of the public are borrowers of books' (Chapter 13 in this volume). She depicts a reading public stratified by social class, and is particularly disparaging of the reading choices of the 'poorest class' for whom 'the reading habit is now often a form of the drug habit'. The modern publishing industry in her view produces standardised products for maximum profit. Leavis's compartmentalisation of readership into different 'brows' – 'highbrow', 'middlebrow' and 'lowbrow' – has been widely criticised: it is deemed 'anachronistic' by Claire Squires (2007: 44), while John Sutherland (1981: 8) regards Leavis's study as 'suffused with pessimism, or at best a depressed sense that whatever hope there is lies in the resistant power of "an armed and conscious minority"'. Nevertheless, this early example of what was later termed 'literary sociology' provides a pivotal analysis of the relationship between social class and readership in the interwar period.

The second extract (Chapter 14) is from a speech first delivered in 1929 by Geoffrey Faber, founder of Faber & Faber, to the Associated Booksellers of Great Britain and Ireland, in which he reflects on the state of bookselling and the book trade in Britain, and on the ongoing tension between commerce and culture in the trade. He raises concerns about the effects of mechanisation and standardisation of the business on readers, and claims that the book trade has 'followed the line of least resistance and fed the people with mush'. Faber makes a case for books being exceptional cultural objects:

> books are the life-blood of civilized humanity. ... Without books, there could be no accumulation of knowledge, no free circulation of thought, no

communication between the ages, no hope of solving the problems with which humanity is confronted, and no relief from their increasing pressure.

The book trade is described as the 'midwife of literature', an agent that offers a vital, behind-the-scenes, service to the author in bringing their work into existence. Faber avoids the simple categorisation of literature favoured by Q. D. Leavis, arguing that readers like himself combine reading 'highbrow' with 'lowbrow' literature, but he expresses similar anxieties about the debasing impact of commerce on culture, and challenges bookshops to 'diminish the deplorable mass of mechanical rubbish which clogs bookshops and disfigures bookstalls all over the country'. He argues for a balance: for books which generate a profit while also 'leading the mulish British Public a step or two further than it thinks it wants to go' and managing 'to raise the standard of public taste'.

The rise of mass-produced fiction and the middlebrow in America in the early twentieth century is the subject of Chapter 15, excerpted from Janice Radway's *A Feeling for Books: The Book-of-the-Month Club, Literary Taste and Middle-Class Desire* (1997), which employs an innovative range of research methodologies, including memoir, institutional history, ethnography and cultural theory. The Book-of-the-Month Club encapsulated modes of mass literary production that were lamented by the likes of Faber (1934) and Leavis (1932), but Radway provides a sympathetic history of the way that the club's publisher, Harry Scherman, navigated the tensions between economic and cultural capital in this operation, and how he 'introduced into the literary field marketing strategies that had been widely used in other industries', in so doing provoking widespread criticism. Radway argues that the book club challenged 'the character and function of the literary field as a unique public space', by foregrounding 'the connections between culture and the market' and attempting 'to obliterate the distinction between those who were cultured and those who were not'. Its main impact, in her view, was to create a new literary space, the 'middlebrow', which was a 'permeable space between regions and forces otherwise kept conceptually distinct'.

Allen Lane's Penguin Books enterprise shared many features with the American Book-of-the-Month Club. He was a leading figure in the commercialisation of British publishing and was considered by many contemporaries to have a degenerative effect on the book trade. Clive Bloom, in this extract (Chapter 16) from *Bestsellers: Popular Fiction Since 1900* (2002), assesses the impact of the paperback revolution in Britain, and the controversy it aroused. Bloom charts how, notwithstanding criticism, the trend for paperbacks spread in the United Kingdom and America and created a new readership for books.

These studies of readership focus on the shifts that occurred in reading and the literary marketplace in the first half of the twentieth century in response to commercial and technological changes. They reveal a persistent anxiety on the part of scholars and publishers regarding the negative impact of these changes on the reading public: from concerns about the impact of 'big business' on 'mulish' readers to disquiet about the debasing impact of the paperback and the bestseller.

SUGGESTED FURTHER READING

Barber, K., 2006. *The Anthropology of Texts, Persons and Publics*. Cambridge: Cambridge University Press.
Delany, P., 2002. *Literature, Money and the Market: From Trollope to Amis*. Basingstoke: Palgrave Macmillan.
Hartley, J., 2001. *Reading Groups*. Oxford: Oxford University Press.
Miller, L., 2006. *Reluctant Capitalists: Bookselling and the Culture of Consumption*. Chicago: University of Chicago Press.
Towheed, S., R. Crone and K. Halsey (eds), 2010. *The History of Reading*. London: Routledge.

13 The Book Market

Q. D. Leavis

In twentieth-century England not only everyone can read, but it is safe to add that everyone does read. Though the Report on Public Libraries (1927) states that not more than 11 per cent of the population make use of the public library books, yet the number of Sunday newspapers sold will correct any false impression these figures may give. On the day of leisure even the poorest households take a news-paper, though it may be of a different type from that favoured by the educated. A Sunday morning walk through any residential district will reveal the head of the family 'reading the paper' in each front window; in the poorest quarters the *News of the World* is read on the doorstep or in bed; the weekly perusal of the *Observer* or the *Sunday Times*, which give a large proportion of their contents to book-reviews and publishers' advertisements, is in many cases the only time that even the best-intentioned businessman or schoolmaster can spare for his literary education.

The *Advertiser's ABC* for 1929 gives the total net sales of eight of the chief Sunday papers alone as nearly ten millions, and there exist others nearly as popular for which figures are not available. If one remembers that a newspaper is usually assumed to be read by five people, and that the entire population of Great Britain is forty-three millions, it seems reasonable to conclude the existence of an inveterate general reading habit. The more interesting question, What do they read? cannot be answered without first indicating where and how the reading matter is obtained.

The striking peculiarity of the situation is that while, as demonstrated above, the entire population above the school age has acquired reading habits, shops existing solely to sell books are rare outside the university towns of Oxford, Cambridge, and Edinburgh, certain parts of London and a few big cities. Serious book-buying has not increased in proportion to literacy;[1] the bulk of the public does not buy many books[2] but borrows or hires them, in the former case from the not very satisfactory municipal or endowed libraries, in the latter from subscription libraries of various kinds. The investigation made in 1924 into the stocks and issues of urban libraries revealed that while they had 63 per cent of non-fiction works on an average to 37 per cent of fiction, only 22 per cent of non-fiction was issued in comparison with 78 per cent of fiction, while the county libraries, which stocked 38 per cent of non-fiction to 62 per cent of fiction, issued only 25 per cent non-fiction.[3] This, considering that the 11 per cent minority which takes advantage of its right to borrow books from the public libraries is probably the more enterprising section of the poorer reading public, shows convincingly enough the supremacy of fiction and the neglect of serious reading which characterize the age.

The fiction shelves of a public library commonly contain the classics and hardy popular novels of the past, representative works of all the most popular contemporary novelists, and (more rarely) the 'literary' novels of the age,* but seldom what is considered by the critical minority to be the significant work in fiction – the novels of D. H. Lawrence, Virginia Woolf, James Joyce, T. F. Powys, and E. M. Forster. Apart from the fact that three out of the five are held by the majority to be indecent,[4] a fact suggestive in itself, four out of the five would convey very little, if anything, to the merely literate. A librarian who has made the experiment of putting 'good' fiction into his library will report that no one would take out *South Wind* or *The Garden Party*, whereas, if he were to put two hundred more copies of Edgar Wallace's detective stories on the shelves, they would all be gone the same day. Attached to the public library is a reading-room, where a number of people can always be seen looking through the newspapers, periodicals, and magazines provided.

The public library, then, is the chief source for the poorer class of reading-matter in book form. For those who can afford an annual subscription the Times Book Club and Mudie's Library exist in London (and send out boxes of books to their country clients), Messrs W. H. Smith's bookstalls provide handy circulating libraries at railway termini and junctions, while in every town of any size Messrs Boots, the multiple chemists, run similar libraries at very low rates. At these libraries, for the lowest payment (it need not be more than half a guinea a year), the subscriber may borrow such novels and works of history, biography, travel, essays, etc., as the library chooses to provide for him, while for a larger payment he may order what he wishes (except that by three of these firms a strict moral censorship is enforced). No figures are available,[5] and no information forthcoming from these libraries on application, but as a result of spending many hours at different branches of each and at different times of the day, the writer was able to conclude that the proportion of 'guaranteed' or 'on demand' subscriptions is not very great; that is, that in general those who are enterprising and affluent enough to subscribe to a circulating library are prepared to have their reading determined for them. And 'reading' in this case means fiction.[6] It is not an exaggeration to say that for most people 'a book' means a novel. This becomes apparent if one watches the process of selection, in which the assistant is generally consulted in some such formula as 'Another book like this one, please,' or 'Can you recommend me a nice book?' The assistant glances at the novel held out and produces another novel which is accepted without question. She may ask 'Have you read this?' and the answer will be 'I can't remember, but I'll take it.' Where criticism is offered, it almost invariably betrays a complete ignorance of values, e.g. a common complaint: 'I can't read Conrad, sea-stories bore me,' or alternatively: 'I like Conrad because I'm so fond of stories about the sea.' In the better districts the subscribers bring lists of novels they have copied out from the newspaper advertisements or reviews.

---

* By 'literary novels' is meant those contemporary novels which the general public accepts as 'literature'. It will be discussed at length in Chapter 3, of this part, but I will anticipate for the reader's convenience by stating here that it includes the works of Willa Cather, Thornton Wilder, John Galsworthy, and David Garnett, among others.

Undoubtedly there are subscribers who use the circulating libraries to supplement and direct their book-buying. But no one who has made a point of frequenting London and provincial branches of the book-clubs for the past few years can avoid concluding that the book-borrowing public has acquired the reading habit while somehow failing to exercise any critical intelligence about its reading. It is significant that the proportion of fiction to non-fiction borrowed is overwhelmingly great, that women rather than men change the books (that is, determine the family reading), and that many subscribers call daily to change their novels. This, along with the information volunteered by a public librarian that many take out two or three novels by Edgar Wallace a week, and the only other books they borrow are 'Sapper's' or other 'thrillers', suggests that the reading habit is now often a form of the drug habit. In suburban side-streets and even village shops it is common to find a stock of worn and greasy novels let out at 2d. or 3d. a volume; and it is surprising that a clientele drawn from the poorest class can afford to change the books several times a week, or even daily; but so strong is the reading habit that they do.

An article in the *Publishers' Circular** called 'Pushing a Lending Library' shows the kind of fiction in demand at such places. It was apparently a small suburban circulating library, which charged 3d. a week. Its regular advertisement was:

BOOKS!

Good Selection by

'Sapper'	Edgar Wallace
Sax Rohmer	William Le Queux
Zane Grey	Margaret Pedler
E. M. Dell	Margaret Peterson
May Christie	Kathlyn Rhodes

Olive Wadsley

These were the regular authors advertised, with the addition of Rider Haggard, Ruby M. Ayres, and Oppenheim, and the advertisement is reported as being highly successful. (It will be noticed that by the heading 'Books' is meant novels.)

In the case of such tuppenny dram-shops the choice of reading is determined in effect by the supply, which is the shopkeeper's attempt to provide attractive reading, but even in the great subscription libraries the client is as passive. The writer of 'a *bona-fide* experience' relates in the *Manchester Evening News*† how when he went into Mudie's to change a novel for his wife the assistant produced 'a detective story by J. S. Fletcher and a romantic adventure by W. J. Locke', explaining that 'if a woman is taken up with a house all day, she doesn't want tales about married

* 6 August 1927.
† 22 February 1926.

problems or misunderstood wives – she knows enough about these already; she can't be bothered with dialect after a day's work, and historical novels aren't alive enough. What she enjoys is something that is possible but outside her own experience – you see if I'm not right.' The writer adds 'And she was.'

The effect of all this upon taste will be examined later on in this study; the effects on the book market are thus described by Mr Stanley Unwin the publisher in his important work, *The Truth About Publishing*:

> Circulating libraries are amongst the biggest buyers upon whom the town traveller calls, and here we enter upon a very thorny subject. There are some publishers who defend the circulating libraries; some who would like to see them abolished root and branch. In so far as they promptly and efficiently sup-ply the public with the particular books for which the public asks, it is difficult to see that serious objection can be reasonably taken to them; but unfortunately the conditions here laid down are applicable only to what is known as 'guaran-teed subscriptions', and, although I have no statistics before me, I imagine that guaranteed subscribers form a tiny minority. There is no certainty that what other subscribers ask for they will be given ...

> The present system tends to assist the circulation of indifferent and bad books, and to retard the circulation of really good books, especially those by writers who have not yet established reputations ... There is one circulating library that makes a boast of the extent to which it can force its subscribers to take what is given them, which means, in that particular case, what the library can buy cheapest ... The remedy for all this is not necessarily the abolition of circulating libraries (the circulating-library habit has become far too engrained in England for that), but the educating of the public to see that they get the books they ask for and not substitutes ... I feel strongly that any form of subscription other than a guaranteed subscription is pernicious.

Without going here into the question of what Mr Unwin means by the terms 'bad books' and 'really good books', one can at least point out that the provision of novels by the commercial libraries for their subscribers means a provision for the widest common level of taste, since it pays better to buy (at a substantial discount) three hundred copies of one novel that everyone will be willing to read than a few each of a hundred different books that will not circulate throughout the clientele. Any book-seller if asked why people don't buy books will inevitably reply that the circulating libraries are responsible – 'look at France, where the only way to read a book is to buy it, and haven't book-sales increased in France three- or four-fold since the war?' But though the facts are correct, the explanation is inadequate. The English public will not pay for books as freely as it pays for clothes and entrance to the cinema, but it does buy the work of the journalist – magazines (at a shilling or more a month), and any number of newspapers to a family. The French buy books because France has an educated public,[7] the English buy journals and periodicals.

Scattered liberally throughout every district, even the poorest, are newsagents' shops whose function is to supply the neighbourhood's reading; these explain the absence of bookshops. An analysis of the stock of typical newsagents[8] yielded the following representative list:

1. Periodicals. ((A) after a title signifies American.)
   (*a*) Daily and weekly newspapers in great variety.[9]
   (*b*) A few cultural weeklies of different levels, ranging from the *New Statesman and Nation* (neither obtainable unless ordered) to *John o' London's*, which contains literary gossip, and articles about books and authors by popular writers.[10] In between comes such a paper as *Everyman* or the *Week-End Review*, that sets out to tell its readers which books they will like, or the *Listener*, published by the B.B.C.
   (*c*) Weekly humorous papers such as *Punch* (based on the middle-class prejudices) and the *Humorist* (lower class).
   (*d*) Seven or eight luxurious shilling illustrated news magazines with a *Punch* orientation,[11] e.g. the *Taller, Sphere, Sketch, Sporting and Dramatic, Bystander*.
   (*e*) An occasional representative of the literary periodicals (see below).
   (*f*) More than a score of substantial story magazines, 6d. or 1s. monthly – e.g. the *Strand, Happy, Hush Magazine, Nash's, Wide World* ('The Magazine for Men'), *True Story, World Stories of Thrills and Adventure*, and several devoted to detective stories, one at least, *Black Mask*, American.
   (*g*) Women's magazines – i.e. magazines containing stories as in class (*f*) but specially designed for a feminine public by means of articles on home-furnishing, housekeeping, clothes, cookery, and beauty, with a heavy cargo of advertisements.
   Twelve of these are stocked regularly – e.g. representative titles are *Modern Woman* ('It specializes in the *personal touch*'), *Good Housekeeping* (A), *Ideal Home, Delineator* (A), *Woman and Beauty*, the most popular of all being American. These frequently boast of supplying 'first-class fiction'.
   (*h*) Nine film magazines – not technical but filled with fiction and articles of film interest, and film publicity designed to create 'film-fans'. Of these nine, seven are American, with such names as *Motion Picture Classics* (A) ('The Magazine with a Personality'), *Screen Romances* (A), *Screen Play Secrets* (A), *Screenland* (A) ('America's Smartest Screen Magazine'), the *Motion Picture* (A), the *Picturegoer*.
   A newsagent, asked of this section 'And do they sell?' replied 'Vastly.' Perhaps here should be mentioned *College Humour* (A), an American magazine devoted to articles, stories, and jokes on college life.
   (*i*) 2d. weekly papers in magazine form containing the crudest marketable fiction – e.g. *London Novels* ('Was He Her Husband?'), *Love Stories* ('Only a Painted Doll'), *Peg's Paper, Eve's Own* – at least a dozen.
2. A large stock of 6d., 9d., and 1s. paper novels[12] (by popular writers such as Oppenheim, Edgar Wallace, Baroness Orczy).
3. Benn's Sixpenny Library (light educational pamphlets).
4. A selection of Benn's Sixpenny *Augustan Poets*.
5. A row or two of Nelson's 1s. 6d. Classics and a few more of 2s. popular novels.
6. An assortment of children's books, dictionaries and cookery books.
7. A number of sixpenny novels published by the Readers' Library and the Novel Library.

The proportions may vary slightly – class 5 may be absent, or it may swell in an affluent district to include more expensive popular novels and such safe 7s. 6d. or even half-guinea works as the Forsyte volumes, *The Good Companions*, *The Week-End Book*, the latest P. G. Wodehouse and Ethel M. Dell, or classes 3 and 4 may not be represented. But nevertheless the significant facts emerge, that books are not generally bought but magazines are, that of these there is an enormous steady sale at all levels and prices, although there is not enough demand for serious papers to make it worth the newsagents' while to stock them on chance,[13] and that what Mr Oliver Madox Hueffer found in his recent investigation of a poor South London suburb is largely true of the book market all over the country:

> Literature was confined to chemists' or to drapers' shops and devoted chiefly to fiction and the cheaper magazines. The few free public libraries strove, not unworthily, to cater for more serious readers, but lack of funds prevented the acquisition of new works to any useful extent and their contents were too miscellaneous to be of great value to the student.*

Moreover, certain reading habits have been formed and stabilized by the kind of matter provided by the magazine and the manner of its presentation. These will be discussed in Part II, but some indication of the general trend will be found in the popularity of women's and film magazines, especially those published in America and consequently in an idiom hitherto foreign to the English periodical.

Another point to be made here is that classes (*a*), (*c*), (*d*), (*f*), (*g*), and (*h*) contain at least as much advertisement as letterpress, and when the cost of printing and illustrating the paper and the rates of payment to writers and staff are considered, it becomes evident that the price which the retailer pays for the paper or magazine is a good deal less than the cost of production. That is to say, the periodical is virtually dependent upon the advertiser,[14] so that its policy is to consider the advertisers' interests above, all, and (since it only pays to advertise where sales are greatest) to sacrifice everything to a large circulation. The effects of this principle will be made plain in Part II.

There is one other agent whose influence upon the book market must not be overlooked. If the Times Book Club and Mudie's serve the upper middle class and Boots' the lower middle class, while the newsagent's represents the bookshop for most people, there is the bookshop of the working class to consider. Where multiple stores have a branch there is usually to be found a bazaar of the American firm, Messrs Woolworth; here for 3d. or 6d. nearly everything necessary to existence may be bought, including literature. It is all fiction, and of three kinds. There is a counter for 2d., 3d., and 6d. paper novels by Gene Stratton Porter and the English equivalents. There is another labelled 'Yank Magazines: Interesting Reading', where American magazines are remaindered at 3d., and of these there is presumably a steady sale, as the stock changes frequently. There is, moreover, a brisk trade done in the Readers' Library and similar 6d. cheap editions, first introduced to the public

---

Some of the English (1930), by Oliver Madox Hueffer, p. 291.

by these stores. The Foreword to each volume explains the object of the series in these terms:

> The READERS' LIBRARY is intended to bring the best-known novels of the world within the reach of the millions, by presenting at the lowest possible price per copy, in convenient size, on excellent paper, with beautiful and durable binding, a long series of the stories, copyright and non-copyright, which every one has heard of and could desire to read.

> Nothing of the kind has ever before been possible, even in the days when book production has been least expensive.[15] To render it possible now it will be necessary that each volume should have a sale of hundreds of thousands of copies, and that many volumes of the series should in due course find their way into nearly every home, however humble, in the British Empire.

> The publishers have the utmost confidence that this end will be achieved, for already, in less than five years that these books have been on the market, upwards of fifty million copies have been sold in Great Britain alone.

> The novels of the READERS' LIBRARY will be selected by one of the most distinguished of living men of letters,[16] and a short biographical and bibliographical note on the author and his works will be appended to each volume.

The editor started off by choosing the popular classics (*Uncle Tom's Cabin*, *The Last Days of Pompeii*, *Pilgrim's Progress*, *Westward Ho!*, etc.) and writing a critical introduction to each; but soon a new principle became apparent: whenever a super-film was released – *Love* (film-version of *Anna Karenina*), *Ben Hur*, *His Lady* (film of *Manon Lescaut*), *The Man Who Laughs* (film-version of *L'Homme Qui Rit*) – 'the book of the film' was published too (and advertised as such on the dust-cover, with photogravures from the film inside). This sold so well that the next stage was to produce an eponymous book of the film or play, when none existed, put together by a hack. These, with thrillers and very popular novelettes, now hold the field and acknowledge the frank commercialization of a series which was hailed warmly on its appearance in 1924 by statesmen and bishops. The distinguished man of letters descended in his introductions from critic to apologist, then to a champion of popular taste;[17] last of all he contented himself with a few facts about author and story.

The latest stage is the appearance of the Readers' Library Film Edition with this Foreword:

> The Readers' Library Film Edition has been instituted to meet a real modern demand. Interest in a film is by no means exhausted merely by seeing it. The two arts, or forms of expression, the picture and the written word in book form, react one on the other ... In a word, the filmgoer wishes also to read the book of the film, and the reader to see the picture.

To meet this undeniable call for literature associated with the film, it would not be enough to produce books of inferior quality ... *Publication will coincide with the appearance of each new and important film.* *

The distinguished man of letters has been dropped in favour of the American film-producer, a change all the easier since the 'talkie' furnishes ready-made dialogue. The introductory paragraph is now significantly directed away from literature, and the appeal to the reader is focused on the film-star:

'The Rogue Song', based on the popular romantic musical comedy 'Gipsy Love', is one of the most colourful achievements of the talking screen. The story makes a gripping novel, and Mr Val Lewton's style has captured all the melody and romance of the film, which has for its star Lawrence Tibbett, America's greatest baritone ... This heart-throbbing romance of a gypsy bandit's love for a beautiful princess forms one of the most delightful film novels we have yet published.

There appears to be money in 'literature associated with the film', for the Novel Library ('For Fiction Lovers') has similarly gone over to the talkies. Starting, like the Leisure Library Ltd and the Detective Story Club Ltd,† as a close imitation of the Readers' Library, it has stopped publishing Wells and Galsworthy for the masses and now produces the book of the talkie.

Welcome Danger is introduced to the public in the language of the talkies – 'Know Harold Lloyd? Sure. Seen him in "College Days" and "Safety Last"? Sure. Well, you haven't laughed until you've seen him in "Welcome Danger" – the funniest thing he's done yet. And you'll be tickled to death when you read the book, for in it you get right close up to Harold,' etc.

The effect of the increasing control by Big Business – in which it would hardly be unreasonable, on the strength of the evidence above, to include the film inter-ests – is to destroy among the masses a desire to read anything which by the widest stretch could be included in the classification 'literature', and to substitute some-thing which is best described by the title-page of a specimen:

'The Girl from China'
novelized by Karen Brown.
Adapted from
John Cotton's
DRIFTING
Universal Picture
starring MARY NOLAN.

---

* The italics are mine.
† All three are sold along with the Readers' Library.

A selection of the Readers' Library is now sold by most newsagents, but the chief sale of these libraries is still at the bazaars. Here, while passing from counter to counter to buy cheap crockery, strings of beads, lamp-shades, and toffee, toys, soap, and flower-bulbs, and under the stimulus of 6d. gramophone records filling the air with 'Headin' for Hollywood' and 'Love Never Dies', the customer is beguiled into patronizing literature. If it is a country town, the bazaar is packed on market-day with the country folk who come in once a week to do their shopping, so that Woolworth literature supplies the county with reading;* if it is a city, the housewives of the district make their regular tour on Saturdays, though a constant stream passes along the counters handling the goods throughout the week. So paper-covered novels by Nat Gould, Charles Garvice and Joseph Hocking,[18] P. C. Wren, Sabatini and Phillips Oppenheim; American magazines – *Ranch Romances* ('Love Stories of the Real West'), *Far-West Stories*, *Love Romances* ('Gripping clean love stories'), *The Popular Magazine* ('America's Best and Brightest Fiction Magazine'), *Marriage Stories*, *Detective Classics*, *Black Mask* ('Detective Fiction'), *Gangster Stories* ('A Magazine of Racketeers and Gun Molls'); and sixpenny books – *Harem Love* ('by Joan Conquest, author of *Desert Love*'), *Officer* ('An Underworld Thriller by Hulbert Footner'), *The King of Kings* (the story of the super-film of Christianity); all go home in the shopping baskets.

---

* 'Before I conclude this letter, I cannot help observing that the sale of books in general has increased prodigiously within the last twenty years. According to the best estimate I have been able to make, I suppose that more than four times the number of books are sold now than were sold twenty years since. The poorest sort of farmers, and even the poor country people in general, who before that period spent their winter evenings in relating stories of witches, ghosts, hobgoblins, &c. now shorten the winter nights by hearing their sons and daughters read tales, romances, &c., and on entering their houses you may see Tom Jones, Roderick Random, and other entertaining books stuck up on their bacon racks, &c. If *John* goes to town with a load of hay, he is charged to be sure not to forget to bring home "Peregrine Pickle's Adventures"; and when *Dolly* is sent to market to sell her eggs, she is commissioned to purchase "The history of Pamela Andrews".' – *Memoirs of the first forty-five years of The Life of James Lackington, Bookseller*, written by himself, 2nd ed. 1792, p. 386.

14 A Publisher Looks at Booksellers

Geoffrey Faber

In the beginning of their business lives, then, the men who are attracted to the book trade in both of its great branches – bookselling and publishing – are naturally, for the most part, men who love books. There are exceptions. There are publishers and booksellers who would really be a great deal happier if they kept a pair of scales on the counter and sold the stuff by weight. But we will not bother at present about grocers who have taken the wrong turning. We, here, are a society of *book* men. We are in, or connected with, the book trade because we love books, and though we are under the regrettable necessity of making money out of them, and though the more money we so make the better pleased we are, we would most of us rather be making a moderate competence out of books than a fortune (shall I say?) out of soap.

I think it is worth while to emphasize this truism rather strongly, because it is sometimes scoffed at. I have heard it suggested that it is a mere irrelevant piece of sentiment. You know the kind of robust cynicism. Business is business, and books are mere articles of merchandise like any other. What do their contents or their appearance matter, as long as people will buy them? A man of this sort said contemptuously to me the other day, when I had been so unwise as to bring the word 'literature' into the conversation: 'Do you think I'm in the book trade for my health?' When I replied that I couldn't think of any other reason why he should be in it, he was quite unable to take my real meaning.

Now is it really so absurd that a business man should care about the objects of his business? Surely his whole life would be the dreariest of farces if he didn't care about them, and care about them intensely – even passionately. Surely the odds would otherwise be against his even being successful. Why should publishers and booksellers be less interested in the things they make and sell than wireless manu-facturers and distributors, or cloth-makers and tailors, or the motor car trade? Indeed they are not. But there is a tendency to admit, with a rueful smile: 'Of course, we would rather fill our list – or our shop, as the case may be – with really good stuff; but after all, business is business....' Is there anybody in this room – I don't exclude myself – who can deny that he has on occasion, and probably on more occasions than he cares to admit even to himself, argued with his conscience in that kind of way? If you ask me, what the devil his conscience has to do with his business, I answer that it has everything to do with it. The cardinal fallacy of our industrial civilization is just this current cant of 'business is business', mean-ing simply the neglect of conscience in business, the attempt to divorce business

102

from the ordinary values of life; because the result is, and must be, that business itself ceases to be worth being really busy about. And applying this to the book trade, I venture to say that one at least of the reasons why the book trade is in the feeble condition it is, relatively to the still very great wealth of our country, our high wages, the spread of education and the large size of the population, is that it has, with the honourable exceptions of which we all know, followed the line of least resistance and fed the people with mush.

Of all trades ours can be least excused from the consequences of its actions, because the article in which we deal is undeniably by far the most important article of commerce in the world. When we say that we love books, what do we really mean by that easy phrase? We can hardly mean that we just have a childish fondness for a number of pieces of paper between two boards. Some of us would be inclined to say that we meant beautiful books – books lovely to handle and look at – works of art in themselves, quite apart from their contents. That is not an attitude I want to decry, though it runs easily into excesses. Yet the tangible and visible book is not the real book. The real book – to borrow a metaphor from religion – is the soul incarnate in all this print and paper. I do not like a book whose body is too handsome for its soul, or a book (to change the metaphor) too big for its boots. No. The claim which books make upon our regard is of a different, a more compelling, nature. Whether we realize it or not, books are the life-blood of civilized humanity. Without books, science, history, philosophy, the drama, the novel, could not exist at all; even poetry could never have got beyond the stage of minstrels' lays; while religion and law would be the mysterious property of privileged castes of priests and lawyers. Without books, there could be no accumulation of knowledge, no free circulation of thought, no communication between the ages, no hope of solving the problems with which humanity is confronted, and no relief from their increasing pressure. And, it is true to say, on the kind of opportunities which we publishers and booksellers are able to offer to the writers of books depends the kind of books which come to be written. That, at any rate, is the point of view from which I speak; and anybody to whom it seems like highfalutin nonsense will no doubt think the rest of what I have to say nonsense too.

But let me add two qualifications. The first is this. However exalted a view we may take of literature, and of the functions of the book trade as the midwife of literature, we must not lose our common sense or our sense of humour. The world is an imperfect place, and literature shares its imperfections. I don't spend all my spare time reading Plato, Shakespeare and Dante. I spend a good deal of it reading Mr. Edgar Wallace. I am not for a moment suggesting that the book trade should traffic in nothing but artistic and learned masterpieces. What I do say is this: let us unashamedly take an interest in the quality of the books we produce and sell, let us do our best to produce and sell books that are good in their own kind, and diminish the deplorable mass of mechanical rubbish which clogs bookshops and disfigures bookstalls all over the country; and let us do what we can to give the best – the really best – a better chance than it now has of holding its head above the flood of mediocrity.

My second qualification is this: publishing and bookselling are both forms of business. They must make profits; if they don't they must cease to exist. They must therefore take account of what the public wants. To expect either the publishers or the booksellers to concentrate on highbrow books would be silly. There is a mean in all things.

It is precisely the achievement of the proper balance between these various considerations which gives to publishing – at any rate to the sort of publishing which interests me – its worth-while character. The thing is not easy. I want to help to raise the standard of public taste; but it would be fatal folly to outrun the standard of public taste too fast and too far. It is necessary to be constantly readjusting one's judgment to the facts; to take risks where the risks are intrinsically worth taking; to abandon or postpone a cherished scheme which would cost too much in the face of public indifference. It is remarkable how the facts *will* change – both in a good and in a bad direction. It is certainly an essential part of the equipment of a publisher who is up to his job to be able to take such changes into account before they occur. Perhaps the most remarkable recent instance of a big change intelligently anticipated by publishers is provided by those two great war books – *Sergeant Grischa* and *All Quiet on the Western Front*. It is tempting to say that no sensible publisher would have turned the latter book down. But I believe it was, in effect, turned down, in America, by two big publishing houses. Which shows that it is always easy to be wise after the event.

However, I am digressing. The point is that, while most of us publishers – all of us, in fact, who are worth our salt – do continually take risks in the interests of good books, do try to keep our judgment alert and elastic, and do aim at leading the mulish British Public a step or two further than it thinks it wants to go, it is only a relatively small proportion of booksellers who exercise corresponding virtues on their side of the fence.

The publisher takes too many and too dangerous risks; the bookseller must take his risk too. But there are occasions when it is reasonable for a bookseller to ask that the publisher shall 'see him safe'; and if a bookseller wrote to me in such terms as these I should be strongly disposed to do all I could to help him to sell the book he asked for.[1]

The trouble is that very few booksellers would take such pains over a single book. The book trade is increasingly a prey to standardization. The big fashionable sellers have it too much their own way; the taste of the public is more and more sheeplike. Why bother over the exceptional books? There is no immediately obvious answer, if all that matters is a quick turnover. But, if *literature* matters, there is a very serious answer. I confess that the rise of book clubs and book societies, and the increasing monopoly of the mass-sellers, fill me with foreboding for the future of English letters. The cultivated aristocracy whose patronage made the English literature of the great ages has gone long since; and even the educated, reasonably leisured, middle class, with plenty of money to spend on decent books and some inclination to spend it, which maintained, the Victorian age, has all but gone too. Do not forget that a very substantial part of bookselling, and of publishing too, in this country consists in selling the masterpieces produced under those vanished or vanishing conditions. Literature now is in the hands of the mob; and the mob is stampeded. It moves in a mass, this way or that, and all its thinking is done for it. For those who will hit the taste of the masses the reward is very large. Hence an ever growing temptation to write for the herd, to publish for the herd, to buy for and sell to the herd.[2] I do not question the sincerity or the excellence of the choices which the Book Society makes; nor do I deny the obvious fact that it is in the Book Society's power to lift an unknown writer of talent or genius out of obscurity into something like fame. Nevertheless the influence of such organizations is, to my mind, on balance, an unfortunate one, because it saps, as other influences everywhere are sapping, the roots of honest individual judgment. The whole nation reads to order. Books are, increasingly, written to order. Unless a whole-hearted effort is made to counteract these tendencies, the life may be squeezed out of English literature in a very few generations.

book club

rise of community of modernsleen as
killing creativity

15 The Scandal of the Middlebrow: The Professional-Managerial Class and the Exercise of Authority in the Literary Field

Janice Radway

CONFLICTING MODES OF LITERARY PRODUCTION

It should be clear by now that Harry Scherman's Book-of-the-Month Club did not intervene in the publishing business alone. Through its establishment of a committee of experts and its claim to send out the best book every month to its subscribers, the club additionally disrupted the established structures of literary practice and authority. Indeed, this latter maneuver generated the most intense attacks on the book club and its imitators, widening what had at first been only a trade war. Furthermore, it intensified the ongoing debate about the consequences of mass-produced standardization, especially within the literary field itself.

In creating his selling machine Scherman introduced into the literary field marketing strategies that had been widely used in other industries. Like those who sold Quaker oats and Pearline soap, he marketed books under the sign of the Book-of-the-Month Club in order to convince potential subscribers that his wares were reliable. By creating the brand name of the Book-of-the-Month Club, he committed himself to the promotion of products supposedly uniform in quality and to the suggestion that consumers themselves were fundamentally the same.[1] To make such a claim, however, in a society whose national identity was still intimately connected to its celebration of American individualism was highly problematic. It proved especially so for Scherman because he was working in an industry where products were still generated by a mode of production constitutively defined by valorization of an independent, autonomous creator.

By 1926 the general mode of production in the United States had been thoroughly transformed by the accumulated economies of speed and by the methodical reorganization of manufacture, distribution, and consumption into a single integrated and incorporated system. The literary mode of production, though, was still characterized by profound conflicts and contradictions.[2] Large sections of the publishing industry continued to be modeled after the imperatives of a mode of production in which individual authors with unique talents and training produced singular objects characterized by stylistic particularities and distinctive concerns. These individuals offered their products rather than their labor to publishing houses. Publication, in this view, was conceptualized as a linear process of natural issue and intellectual property transmission.

Other sections of the industry, however, had adopted the logic of modern mass production. They had installed corporate creation and managed distribution at the center of their enterprises in order to increase the flow of commodities for the market. Within this system, publication was conceived of as an endless process of circulation and cultural recycling, a reformulation and ever-widening distribution of previously existing material. Predictably, these operations were tarred with powerful epithets and dismissed as entertainment by champions of the author and the mode of production of which he was perhaps the defining element.[3] The category of the lowbrow was understood to include all standardized cultural objects that were generated through a corporately organized mode of production, including moving pictures, radio programs, and pulp novels. The space of the middlebrow was occupied by products that supposedly hid the same machine-tooled uniformity behind the self-consciously worked mask of culture. The evaluative geography of the high, the low, and the middle, it would seem, was mobilized specifically at this moment to control the temporal ascendancy of new, highly threatening productive forces.

To explain why resistance to some aspects of consumerist modernization persisted in the literary field is no easy matter. In effect, a mode of literary production lived on as residual cultural form, that is, as a form organized and developed at an earlier historical moment but surviving virtually intact into a rapidly changing present.[4] Generally, those associated with this particular mode of production claimed for themselves oppositional status; they cast themselves as the heroic resistance to a decline in the nature and the position of the literary, which they attributed to the appearance of collective production and mass distribution. In an effort to explore the sources and characteristics of this resistance, I look more closely at some additional objections leveled at the proprietors of middlebrow culture. My aim is to clarify the nature of the threat these new forms of production posed to a certain understanding of the literary field as well as to beliefs about the function that field performed in the larger social formation. Although a complex set of social and material factors surely contributed to the perpetuation of familiar relations between the kinds of authors, publishers, and readers that had come to characterize trade book publishing, it seems clear that the longevity of the system as a whole must be attributable in some fundamental way to the continuing ideological power of a particular understanding of print culture and the role of authorship and individual creation within it. Through a detailed investigation of the next stage in the book club debates, this chapter will attempt to specify in greater detail why these new distribution agencies seemed to pose such a threat to cherished ideas about the character and function of the literary field as a unique public space. [...]

THE STRUGGLE TO DEFINE THE POSITION OF THE LITERARY FIELD

At issue, as we have seen, was the nature of the social relationship to be forged between newly visible and apparently alien cultural consumers on one hand and the new, integrated, corporate agencies for literary and cultural production on the other. Some, such as Harry Scherman and Henry Seidel Canby, argued that these profit-minded agencies could be harnessed to the project of educating people otherwise excluded from access to specialized knowledge. They envisioned, in effect, an alliance between the forces of capital and a new group of literary professionals who would direct these agencies in dispassionate, disinterested fashion for the benefit of all. Scherman and Canby used the language of democracy to argue that they were extending culture to those who might not otherwise have access to it. Others, such as Stuart Chase and Waldo Frank, were profoundly skeptical that such an alliance might work in the service of anyone but the corporate owners themselves. They argued, in opposition, that to remain uncorrupted, expertise would need to persist as wholly independent and autonomous. In fact it would need to remain the prerogative of individuals if it was to preserve a space for critique.

It is important to acknowledge in this context, then, that some of the opposition to both standardization generally and the book clubs specifically was elaborated as part of an emerging anticapitalist critique among professional-managerial workers in the literary field. In fact many of Scherman's critics objected to the clubs as an intrusion or penetration by the market into what they conceptualized as a previously free, uncolonized, natural domain, the domain of transcendent literature, culture, and art. Their objection to Harry Scherman's resolute materialization of culture as one more commodity among others grew in part out of their belief that artistic creation had the power to transcend the merely quotidian and the mundane and therefore could stand as the basis of a moral, ethical, and even political critique of the instrumentalism and utilitarianism embodied in capitalism. Setting their sights on their profession's capacity to identify works of high literary merit, which they believed transcended the specific conditions of their making, they were appalled by people like Scherman who failed to maintain the distinction between the material and the transcendent, the economic and the cultural. In criticizing new cultural middlemen such as Scherman, many participants in this debate about the autonomy of literature and art were implicitly making claims about the superiority of the literary field as an intrinsically oppositional space, as a public space set apart, beyond, or outside the market. Thus they portrayed it as the rightful home of the revolutionary avant-garde, a poetic cadre with the special expertise and sensibility to remake the world into a nobler, more humane, truly lettered place.

It bears repeating here that the criticisms of the Book-of-the-Month Club tended to link Scherman's failure to maintain categorical distinctions and to preserve the true purity of the literary with the simple existence of his advisory apparatus alone. The focal point of debate was the judges' position within a commercial, profit-minded organization. What was at issue was whether the process of book evaluation and recommendation should be organized in so instrumental a fashion in the first place or linked so closely to bookselling. The book club critics argued that reading ought to be guided by the more traditional and supposedly less coercive forms of expert advice offered by friends, neighborhood bookstore clerks, and, it must be said, 'impartial' literary reviewers. The point to be made here is that these were the opinions of people laboring as reviewers, that is, as writers in a reconfigured literary field transformed by the appearance, first, of book review pages in metropolitan daily newspapers and, then, by the appearance of the weekly newspaper book review sections and magazines such as *The Saturday Review of Literature*. In fact, reviewing itself had been undergoing a process of professionalization for a number of years prior to the appearance of the Book-of-the-Month Club as the needs and demands of this new kind of periodical made it increasingly possible for individuals to make a salaried living exclusively as cultural commentators, columnists, and book reviewers. The debate over the advisory apparatus at the book clubs, then, can be understood as an intragroup struggle among similar but differently placed members of one section of the professional-managerial class, that fraction charged with oversight of the literary field.

Positioned as competitors by virtue of the different organizations they labored for, participants in the book club wars argued over their proper location and allegiance as key figures in the field, as arbiters who were instrumental not only in defining the idea of the literary and in identifying examples of it but also in producing belief in the value of such work in the first place.[5] Scherman's critics in fact occupied virtually the same position he did in the developing literary economy. They dispensed advice and opinions about cultural goods available on the market. However, their location within newspapers and highbrow magazines, which displaced and disguised their own institutional relationship to the advertisers and corporate owners that increasingly made their existence and social reach possible, enabled these reviewers to claim that they operated as individuals in an even more disinterested, civic fashion than did Scherman's judges.

It is evident, then, that the critics of the book clubs were alarmed by the implications of a direct connection between literary reviewers and an organization interested in selling books. They were concerned lest the quest for corporate profit infect the otherwise disinterested search for the literary. However, they did not recognize their own definition of the literary or their desire to associate themselves with it as a similarly interested endeavor. They did not see their defense of the literary, tucked away as it was between the lines of their criticism of the Book-of-the-Month Club, as an argument on behalf of their own authority and their right to control the larger literary field itself. It seems clear, though, that their criticism was driven at least in part by their unconscious concern that the club's power as an organization would enable it to usurp their role as cultural mediators, as arbiters of literary value and excellence. At stake, finally, in their quarrel with the book clubs was not only the question of who would control the literary field but also who or what would define the nature of the relationship between the field itself and the forces of capital so clearly involved in its transformation. In quarreling about the proper location and allegiances of those whose writings would establish the ground on which particular judgments were to be made, they were in fact debating what the proper role and function of literature, information, and culture ought to be in a twentieth-century world of commodities, capitalism, and consumption.

In the end the Ehrenreichs' analysis of the structural location of the professional-managerial class enables us to see that these debates about the book clubs, reviewing, and the position and function of expert literary advice were in fact a struggle to resolve the ambiguity and ambivalence of the literary professional's position between capital and labor. Especially at issue in the intrafield dispute was the question of where literary critics, advisers, and judges should labor and in whose service. Could a highly trained professor and literary critic like Henry Canby labor for a profit-minded organization like the Book-of-the-Month Club and still manage to recommend books that exhibited literary excellence rather than commercial possibility? Or, by surrendering his own disinterested concern for the public good to the corporation's desire to reach more readers, would he thereby foster the thorough commodification and devaluation of the public sphere? Equally at issue was the question of whether reviewing was to be conceived of as a process that facilitated bookselling, thereby augmenting an important capitalist industry, or whether it was an independent, consumer-oriented activity designed to serve the needs of aspiring readers. Or was it to be understood more abstractly and even more autonomously as a disinterested, almost sacred calling entered by those who saw themselves striving selflessly to realize the noblest human values through the identification of the larger culture's finest artistic creations?

Scherman and Canby, of course, argued that they extended culture's reach to new audiences, and thus they stressed the service-minded character of their business and pegged all of their operations to perceived reader demand. In opposition, their critics remained wary of the tastes of alien audiences whom they concretized and demonized as 'the masses,' and they suggested that critics ought not pander to them but should, rather, protect the literary by becoming its legitimate custodians. The debate about the appropriateness of the actions of the Book-of-the-Month Club judges was, finally, a debate about whether the professional book expert should be thought of as a salesmen and promoter, as a teacher and pedagogue, as a kind of cultural apostle with a special relationship to the divine activity of creation, or, more properly, as a leader in a politicized and redemptive avant-garde.

Most of Scherman's critics, of course, took up some version of the latter two positions, defending the supposedly superior status of the literary as a source of human knowledge. They maintained that their true allegiance was neither to the capitalists who employed them nor to the worker-readers they hoped to address but rather to the abstract principles constituting the literary field as a special space, a true outside, a place beyond the market and free from its instrumentalism and utilitarianism. They accordingly envisioned a role for themselves either as conservators of a revered cultural tradition, as missionaries in the service of a literature made sacred by virtue of its preservation of humane values in the face of capitalist reification and commodification, or they construed themselves as revolutionaries in the service of an alternate world yet to be born. In either case they positioned themselves clearly in opposition to the bankers, advertisers, and corporate owners who employed them or paid them through the aegis of a distant publisher.

Yet it must be said as well that in casting themselves always as independent critics capable of perceiving the truth and value inherent in real literary art, they equivocated about the source of their capacity to detect literary excellence when they saw it. They were never clear about whether it was their technical training, which might itself be extended to others, or some sort of inherent moral superiority that enabled them to see and to evaluate in a way different from the lay reader. As a consequence, their claim to authority over the literary field tended to be staked on their difference, on their distinction and distance from those who could not perceive as they did. Ironically, then, for many of them, disdain, disgust, and contempt characterized the attitude they adopted toward the population they supposedly hoped to reach with their efforts at enlightenment and education. Unable or unwilling to approach readers whose tastes and preferences differed so obviously from their own, they abandoned any who could not already attend to their trained commentary. Ever disdainful of popularizations, book chat, and book news, they deserted those readers who were on a quest after culture. They left them to the devices of other literary professionals whose orientation, for whatever reason, was more tolerant, less obsessed with the fate of literature conceived in a narrow sense, and more open to the search for books that could perform multiple functions for diverse readers. In a sense many of the Book-of-the-Month Club's critics took up an oppositional stance toward capitalism and the culture industry it funded, but they did so as members of an aristocracy of taste.

Additionally, in repeatedly foregrounding their status as individuals, the book club critics refused to recognize their position within a particular class or class fraction, that is, as part of a group of people with shared interests and investments. In effect they were indulging in a strategy that Stuart Blumin has identified as characteristic of the middle class more generally, the class, he suggests, that always insists that it is not a class. Blumin is referring to the phenomenon of the middle class's ideological privileging of individualism, its claim that an individual's social status and position is a function of his or her hard work, determination, and initiative rather than of any particular structural location within the economy. The book club critics' refusal to recognize the investments behind their own statements about literature and the state of cultural production was thus a highly characteristic move, the very act that enabled them to misrecognize the way they were implicated in the commercial system of production they so wanted to criticize. By insisting on their status as rational individuals and by characterizing their criticism as the disinterested search for the inherently and universally good, they refused to recognize their work as a defense of their own privilege, just as they refused to acknowledge that they were in fact trying to persuade others to adopt their particular values and views. In effect the book club critics ignored the way they themselves were embedded in the commercial system, and as a consequence they were able to maintain the illusory view of themselves as somehow special, different, outside, and beyond the market.

It might be said in summary, then, that most of the book club criticism was driven by deep suspicion about the corporations and class that owned and directed the productive forces in the United States, including the major newspapers and magazines that paid the salaries of the reviewers and critics who developed the critique in the first place. Consequently they labored industriously to establish their own distance from capital by insisting on the categorical difference between the economic and the cultural, between the market and art, and between out-and-out advertising and their own, supposedly disinterested advisory activity. Yet they could not identify easily with the larger population they were supposedly attempting to inform and to guide, in part because their own social position and identity depended on their ability as a group to legitimate their special expertise and therefore their cultural authority. That authority was therefore dependent in a crucial way on the differences between the critics and those they were asked to advise and to address. The assertion of that difference often realized itself in the form of moral superiority that thereby prevented many of them from thinking seriously about why they wanted to address and educate others in the first place. Accordingly they demonized not only those who lacked their cultural competence and refined taste, the mass-produced, consuming automatons supposedly tied to the book clubs, but also institutions like the Book-of-the-Month Club itself to which such individuals supposedly turned in order to acquire, the critics argued, a counterfeit version of the authentic cultural knowledge only they themselves could provide. It is not hard to understand, then, why middlebrow operations like the Book-of-the-Month Club looked so scandalous. They were threatening to the extent that they foregrounded the connections between culture and the market and to the extent that they threatened to obliterate the distinction between those who were cultured and those who were not.

What was most scandalous, finally, about the Book-of-the-Month Club was not simply its proximity to lowbrow culture. In fact, nearly all of its critics admitted it was nowhere near as degraded as radio or the movies. Rather, what was troubling was its failure to maintain the fences cordoning off culture from commerce, the sacred from the profane, and the low from the high. The Book-of-the-Month Club was threatening because it seemed to create a permeable space between regions and forces otherwise kept conceptually distinct, a space that had to be mapped consequently as the middle ground – as the middlebrow – in order to keep it under control. Crucially, the club exposed the fact that the middle ground existed potentially as a colonizable space that was being surveyed and occupied by new cultural authorities deeply involved with the activity of promoting the distribution, circulation, and hence production of cultural goods. Their interests and tastes, therefore, understandably looked very different and highly threatening to those attempting to maintain their distance and that of the literary field itself from the material forces controlling and structuring its operation. In representing these new authorities as dictators and policemen, the critics of the book clubs sought to mobilize in opposition an older vision of a political community of autonomous readers and independent cultural shareholders, each of whom singularly but unfailingly would manage to confirm the hegemony of rationality, liberalism, discretion, and taste.

16 How the British Read

Clive Bloom

THE PAPERBACK

Paperback production seemed to threaten traditional publishing methods, seemed indeed to be a revolution not merely in publishing but in culture itself. The paperback revolution put publishing firmly within an industrial and commercial setting, yet 'serious' culture and 'serious' literature, in particular, were seen by many critics and publishers alike as antithetical to mass society. Thus the widening of the book market was not merely a commercial but also a *moral* decision. Critics such as Q. D. Leavis spilt much ink on worrying whether the increase in the market had actually diminished quality – commercial crassness overtaking and overwhelming artistic merit in the search for quick profits. Gentlemen publishers were obliged to take care of business and had no choice but to look for increasing markets. (Their status was always problematic: gentlemen and tradesmen, as Harold Macmillan was considered by his prospective aristocratic parents-in-law.) Geoffrey Faber, for instance, could easily equate the *restriction* of the market with a retention of artistic quality; by 1934 he was arguing that,

> The market is glutted. General publishing is therefore fast degenerating into a gambling competition for potential bestsellers. This is a profoundly unsatisfactory state of affairs which may have – will have – very evil effects on the future of English letters....But in so far as over-production is a cause of the evil, we have the remedy in our own hands. We have only to agree to reduce our output in order to restore the book trade to a healthy condition.[1]

Such a refrain was repeated throughout the century and especially at times of *falling* sales, as in the 1970s. Could, therefore, a wider *quality* market be found, outside that which already existed and which would not end up 'fast degenerating' but would retain its 'healthy condition' in terms both of sales and of moral quality? The appearance and the marketing of paperbacks would provide important answers.

The paperback revolution is usually credited to Allen Lane whose Penguin imprint was launched through F. W. Woolworth stores on 30 July 1935.

> Penguins needed the most aggressive and Americanised of the multiple stores to break into the market. They needed mass sales, above the bestseller threshold (13,000–17,000 was the initial break-even range); Lane calculated that he would need an annual volume sale of 2 million. And they exploited a new, technologically transformed kind of book, the mass-market paperback, a

phenomenon Mrs Leavis does not anticipate in *Fiction and the Reading Public*. No-one would maintain that Penguin Books have aggravated the cultural condition. Yet Penguins could not have succeeded without the vulgar '3d and 6d' store which represented for the Leavises in 1933 some of 'the worst effects of mass-production and standardisation'.[2]

Lane and his brothers had a simple and clear vision: middle-brow titles, produced in clearly designed packaging (which included an innovative logo), colour coded for making choosing easier, paper-bound and mass produced – the list itself dependent upon successful backlist authors augmented with carefully chosen lesser names whose books would be protected and promoted by their place within a recognisable series. As one critic put it, these titles aimed at 'description or expression of knowledge in understandable terms' for a middle-brow readership who would, perhaps, usually borrow books from a library rather than purchase them.[3] By being sold through large general retailers such books 'lost' a certain prestige but gained a wide and paying readership who would now buy on impulse whilst looking for other goods, or actively seek out a good read at a 'reasonable' price. Books by Ernest Hemingway, André Maurois, Compton Mackenzie, Dorothy L. Sayers, and Agatha Christie (July 1935) were followed by those of Liam O'Flaherty, Norman Douglas, Dashiell Hammett, Louise Bromfield, Victoria Sackville West and Samuel Butler (October 1935). Although eclectic, the books reflected a higher seriousness, even in the choice of thrillers. This all harked back to the moral and educational purposes of nineteenth-century publishers who realised that cheaper books did not need to mean diminishment of standards.

The mainstream paperback augmented rather than replaced hardback books and even the most recalcitrant hardback publisher soon understood the possibilities opened up by paperback reprints. Nevertheless, paperback publishing caused a problem for traditional competition. In March 1957 Gollancz attempted an experiment in which certain titles were simultaneously published in cloth and paper cover versions. In March 1957 Macmillan experimented with a paperback series destined for 'the intelligent man's library'. Michael Joseph launched a hybrid, neither hardback nor paperback. Influenced by the 'new spirit' of the Festival of Britain, the Mermaid Series sold at 4s 6d and was meant to bring 'colour' to the book industry.

Yet, from being vilified as the destroyer of the book trade and the enemy of culture, Lane's Penguins were soon acknowledged as the saving grace of bookselling and a vital new innovation in the dissemination of cultural values. The style was soon copied by American publishers such as Dell, and imprints such as Ace, Signet and Gold Medal Books. In Britain, Hodder and Stoughton repackaged their yellow-back popular titles and re-released them in paperback versions, thus creating new readerships for E. Phillips Oppenheim, Sidney Horler, Edgar Wallace and Sax Rohmer. There were obvious copycat publications too, such as the Toucan novel series produced by Stanley Paul during the 1940s. By the mid-1950s Penguin had sold 4 million copies of current titles (including Paul Brickell's *The Dambusters*, 1951; 1954). The 1960s completed this pattern of growth and paperback ascendancy.

Part Four
Censorship and Print Culture

The publication of transgressive materials has been regulated over the centuries by both explicit and implicit forms of censorship. This has taken on many different guises, and the texts in this section examine the complex relationship between publishers and censorship, with particular attention to its specific manifestations: market censorship, obscenity censorship, political and religious censorship. These studies shed light on how prohibitions and constraints are imposed upon publishers and readers and how such sanctions have been accepted, contested and resisted.

Sue Curry Jansen in *Censorship: The Knot that binds Power and Knowledge* (1991) regards censorship as omnipresent and universal rather than restricted to specific institutional acts of prohibition and repression. Drawing on Michel Foucault's theories of censorship (1976, 1977), she argues that the exercise of governmental power and authority is decentralised and takes place through discourse. While critics have conventionally focused on 'regulative censorship', or overt forms of communication control, Jansen maintains that attention should instead be focused on 'constitutive censorship': the fundamental taboos and social conventions that operate at the most basic level of discourse. Claiming that the operations of the censor are hidden in contemporary society, she describes the way in which 'market censorship' operates in contemporary America, and how the conglomerated publishing industry uses market research to carry out pre-publication censorship of any publications that might fail to guarantee high profit margins.

Market censorship is also the subject of Lewis A. Coser's seminal analysis of the American publishing industry (1975), in which he defines publishers as 'modern gatekeepers of ideas', with the power to 'make decisions as to what is let "in" and what is kept "out"' (p. 126). Coser analyses the extent to which commercial constraints influence the editorial decision-making process. Writing at a time before the advent of rapid conglomeration and centralisation, he characterises the publishing industry as a cottage or craft industry, highly autonomous and reliant not on the state but almost wholly on the vagaries of the marketplace. In this context, the publishing decision is complex, involving commercial considerations, concern with the amplification of the publisher's image and prestige, and also an enduring sense that the publisher is engaged in a 'high cultural mission' (p. 128). Coser argues that publishers, 'pushed and pulled by contradictory expectations' of commerce and culture, 'find it hard to develop a clear-cut sense of professional identity' (p. 129). He also observes that 'gatekeeping' describes not only the publishing decision in itself but also the extent to which books and publications are promoted and marketed; this factor determines to a great extent which will see the light of day, and which ones will sink without a trace.

How obscenity legislation was imposed, subverted, challenged and overturned over the course of the twentieth century, and in diverse geographical context, is explored by Alistair McCleery in his assessment of 'The Trials and Travels of *Lady Chatterley's Lover*' (2013). He draws attention to the close link between profit and pornography, and the delicate balancing act that D. H. Lawrence and his publishers faced in reconciling pecuniary and literary motivations in their publishing decisions, for example with respect to the 1928 Florence edition and 1930 Paris edition of the novel, as well as the Penguin edition of 1960, which was a resounding commercial success. The trial and acquittal of this notorious edition under the new Obscene Publications Act marked a major landmark case in British cultural history: the episode is widely thought to signify a major societal shift from Victorian conservatism to modern liberalisation. However, McCleery problematises this simple interpretation, comparing the London-based trial of the book with its subsequent trials in Scotland, Canada, New Zealand, Australia, India, South Africa and China, and discerning a pattern of wide-scale liberalism in the metropolitan centres and conservatism in the provincial peripheries.

Archie L. Dick's chapter 'Combating Censorship and Making Space for Books', from *The Hidden History of South Africa's Reading Cultures* (2012), focuses on the intense interest of South Africa's apartheid government and security police in the control of books, and also draws attention to the dysfunction of these censorship forces; the numerous and ingenious ways in which political activists and prisoners managed to subvert control of their reading. He examines how religious books, and in particular the Bible, were read and employed by prisoners during solitary confinement, for 'personal, profane, and political purposes' (p. 146), and also to the ways that regulations surrounding reading in prison libraries and individual cells were widely undermined. Ultimately, Dick concludes that books provided an important example of how political prisoners ultimately 'resisted and defeated apartheid censorship' (p. 150).

These studies of books and censorship illuminate the complex relationship between the author, the legislature, the publisher and the reader. They challenge simplistic models and theorisations, with examples of censorship that was both generative and restrictive, examples of publishers that colluded with the state and also those that challenged or defied censorship legislation, and instances of readers who followed authorised practices and those who adopted resistant and subversive reading strategies.

SUGGESTED FURTHER READING

Heath, D., 2009. 'Obscenity, censorship, and modernity,' in S. Eliot and J. Rose (eds), *A Companion to the History of the Book*. Oxford: Wiley-Blackwell, 508–519.

Rose, J., 2001. *The Holocaust and the Book: Destruction and Preservation*. Amherst: University of Massachusetts Press.

Travis, A., 2000. *Bound and Gagged: A Secret History of Obscenity in Britain*. London: Profile.

17 The Censor's New Clothes

Sue Curry Jansen

I

The Cense of Censorship

The *Oxford English Dictionary* offers two definitions of censor:

1. The title of two magistrates in Ancient Rome, who drew up the register or census of the citizens, etc., and had the responsibility of the supervision of public morals.

2. An official in some countries whose duty it is to inspect all books, journals, dramatic pieces, etc., before publication, to insure that they shall contain nothing immoral, heretical, or offensive to government.

The *OED* notes that the word, 'censor,' derives from the root *cense*: from the Latin *censure* – to estimate, rate, assess, be of opinion, judge, reckon.

In Ancient Rome the responsibilities of the census-taker and the censor were closely aligned. The census-taker counted and classified people. The censor assessed and classified the products of the people's minds: ideas and their surrogates, books. The entitlement of the *Index Librorum Prohibitorum* indicates that the offices of papal censorship were similarly conceived.

Like the census, *censorship* is a form of surveillance: a mechanism for gathering intelligence that the powerful can use to tighten control over people or ideas that threaten to disrupt established systems of order.[1]

Prior censorship controlled by state or religious authorities remains the norm in many parts of the world. Western Liberals consider such surveillance regressive and label regimes that practice it totalitarian or authoritarian.

II

Censors Without Stamps

Lawyers have assumed custody of the term, 'censorship,' in contemporary Liberal societies. Cut away from the fabric of history, the term has lost much of its resonance. Current Anglo-American usages of the term conceive of censorship narrowly as a monopoly power of the state which is exercised in Liberal societies only under extraordinary circumstances, e.g. in wartime and other temporary emergencies, to control extreme sexual lasciviousness, and to make possible prosecutions for libel and slander on behalf of private citizens. This configuration discourages inquiry into the most serious forms of censorship operating in Liberal societies today: censorships routinely undertaken by state bureaucracies in the name of 'national security' and censorships routinely sanctioned by the 'profit principle.' By reducing dialogues on censorship to litigations involving publishers' claims to profits, the Anglo-American legal community has removed a powerful emancipatory concept from the vocabulary of the people.

Liberal perspectives on censorship had their genesis in the Enlightenment. They were emancipatory, even revolutionary, within a context in which the Church and Crown held exclusive monopolies over public channels for the distribution of knowledge: pulpit, politics, press and pedagogy. Liberalism defended the rights of individuals against the encroachment of powerful institutions. But the platform that secured liberty for Diderot and Company has proven too narrow to accommodate critics of intelligence agencies and corporate conglomerates. Liberalism has now become an administrative stance. Under the cover of tolerance (pluralism), modern Liberalism protects the political and economic interests of a plurality of powerful elites. The absence of an adequate vocabulary of resistance makes it very difficult to describe effectively Cato's new clothes. It permits the corporate-state to use the language of liberty to deny liberty.

In contemporary Liberal societies, census-takers continue to wear official badges and are still entrusted to count and classify people. But their methods are remarkably archaic, even primitive, when compared with the sophisticated technology of surveillance developed by market researchers, corporate demographers, pollsters, credit investigators, bill collectors, tax assessors, and police agents. In Liberal societies, censors seldom wear badges. Yet they have developed systems for counting and classifying people's ideas that are far more comprehensive and invasive than the most Draconian measures envisioned by Roman censors or Spanish inquisitors.

Liberalism did not eliminate censorship. It forced censors underground. It eliminated the warrant for censorship but not the need for it. It secularized the mana of control from fealty to realty. The marketplace, not the priest or feudal lord, became the ultimate arbiter of Liberal power-knowledge. The immediate effect of this secularizing process was to radically democratize the criteria for classifying people and ideas. For a time, it also democratized profit-making opportunities and made it possible for industrious tradesmen of humble origins, like Ben Franklin, to accumulate sizable holdings. The transition from entrepreneurial to corporate capitalism, however, inverted the terms of the bargain once more. The emergence of the corporate state skewed the social arrangements of mass production to concentrate power and profits in the hands of a nascent industrial elite. In short, liberalism separated Church from State but sanctioned the union of state and commerce.

Under the new cosmology of the corporate state, success became, in the words of Andy Warhol, 'what sells.' Or, more accurately, what is sold!

In attempting to rationalize their marketing strategies, corporate decision-makers, like the censors of Rome, assume the mantle of mediators of public morals (as well as managers of private profits). Those who control the productive process determine 'what is to be mass produced in the cultural area and what will not be produced.'[2] These *market censors* decide what ideas will gain entry into 'the marketplace of ideas' and what ideas will not. They inspect books, journals, dramatic pieces, etc., before publication, to ensure that they contain nothing that seriously challenges the basis of the existence of the corporate state. That is, *they decide what cultural products are likely to ensure a healthy profit margin.* And most of the time the products that survive the prior censorship of marketing research – the books, news, scripts, games, coupons, programmed learning modules, syllabi, styles, visuals, advertisements, party platforms, etc. – incorporate ideology and values that celebrate the corporate state and vilify its critics.[3]

III

Socially Structured Silences of Liberalism

Those who historically have been denied full access to the privileges of Liberalism – members of the lower classes, women, blacks, radicals, homosexuals, foreigners, etc. – have provided the most compelling testaments against abuses by the corporate state. But grievances filed by the walking wounded do not project healthy sales profiles. They seldom make the papers. Even authors of the caliber of Ralph Ellison and Richard Wright could only cross the profit line that bars publication in America by addressing their narratives of black oppression to whites rather than to other blacks.

The most comprehensive critique of capitalism was, of course, put forth by Karl Marx. The confrontational style and the revolutionary program empowered by the nineteenth-century journalist's indictment of 'the material censorship' of Liberalism invited both the excesses of overzealous followers and the stern repressions by authorities. Marx responded to the excesses of his followers by complaining that he was 'not a Marxist!' But Marx's complaint could not contain 'Marxism' or its opposition, and the spiraling escalation of excesses resulted in marginalization of the Marxist critique in most of the West and its near eclipse in the United States. Similarly, the institutionalization of excess – including installation of state censorship by triumphant Marxist-Leninist regimes – led to the suppression of Critical Marxism within Soviet bloc nations, as well as to the legitimization of official repression of Communist Party activities in Liberal societies.[4] The sensational slogans invoked by the corporate state to justify its retreat from the principles of democratic tolerance – Labor Insurrection, Commie Plots, The Red Menace, the Yellow Peril, etc. – not only made the papers, they made the headlines!

Exiles from enemy regimes have posed a special problem for corporate Liberalism. They are news. Good news! They generate healthy sales profiles and superb ideology. They offer compelling testaments of the genuine dangers inherent in all systems of statist control.

But exiles are dissidents. They play by a different set of rules. Their emancipatory dreams carry the imprimatur of alien systems of power-knowledge. Therefore they cannot always be relied on to measure success by what sells. Aleksandr

Solzhenitsyn was not the first Russian dissident outraged by the 'moral bank-ruptcy' of Western materialism. The great nineteenth-century humanist Aleksandr Herzen abandoned his homeland in protest against Czarist censorship, but later expressed profound disillusionment with the extremely narrow limits of permission imposed on freedom of expression by market censorship in the West.

IV

Liberal Critical Traditions

The established canons of Liberal aesthetics and literary criticism do offer some modest precedents for protest against the imperatives of commercialism. These precedents, however, are frankly elitist. Embracing the nineteenth-century cult of genius, they celebrate the heroism of the lonely artist who defends the integrity of his/her work against the coarse demands of a philistine patron: industrial capitalism. But they ignore the plight of ordinary people who are cut off from the generative powers of creativity by conditions of cultural production in industrial societies.

There are two main currents within this tradition of Liberal criticism. The first is a souvenir of pre-industrial aristocratic pastoral humanism. It bears the imprimatur of the romantic rebellion against the demon-god, Progress. Baudelaire's definition of Progress expresses the angst of the Romantic reaction against the advance of industrialism: 'the progressive privation of the spirit, the progressive domination of matter.'[5]

The second critical precedent is a distinct artifact of the class system of Liberal societies. It posits a dichotomy between 'high culture' (authentic culture) and 'mass culture' ('schlock'). This dichotomy places the blame for the blighted condition of most of the arts in the twentieth century on consumers not producers. It rationalizes the elitism of art for the few on the grounds that the many (cum 'masses') have abysmal taste. It deflects attention away from the fact that 'mass culture' is produced for the people, not by the people. It papers over the dirty little secret that 'mass culture' is manufactured by elites to make money and to inhibit the development of authentic cultures of resistance among members of the underprivileged classes of Liberal societies. It robs language of its integrity and critical resilience by anthropomorphizing the social arrangements of production: by using the term 'mass' to refer to people rather than the conditions of production (mass production) under which they must work.

In America, complaints about the distortion of 'serious art' by commercial considerations have generally combined the elitism of the old humanism with the new hubris of cultural materialism. Melville's complaint – 'Dollars damn me ... What I feel most moved to write, that is banned, it will not pay' – typifies the convention of aesthetic classism in American literary criticism.[6]

This aesthetic classism fails to provide an effective platform for cultural criticism because it can say nothing about the epochal changes in the deep structure of power-knowledge brought about by the mass production of culture. It cannot address the profound implications of the collapse of the perennial schism in

Western cognitive structures which had always separated official versions of reality from folk constructions: a dualism that prospered even under the rule of the medieval church. As Mikhail Bakhtin points out, in the Middle Ages and in the early modern period, 'an immense world of forms and manifestations of laughter opposed the official and serious tone of medieval ecclesiastical and feudal culture.'[7] With the transformation to mass-produced culture, however, laughter, carnival, profanity, rebellion, contact with forbidden worlds, even criticism itself became synthetic commodities mediated by corporate-controlled communication networks.

In sum, Liberal critical traditions deflect attention away from serious analysis of the new technology of power-knowledge which has brought the laughter of the powerless under the discipline of the powerful.

V

Mass Production and the Production of Knowledge in Liberal Societies

The myopia of Liberal criticism reflects a larger failure in the scope of the democratic vision that empowered the political covenants of the Enlightenment: the fact that free speech guarantees have never applied to the social organization of production in industrial societies. When American wage-earners enter the factory gate or close the office door, they effectively surrender their rights to free assembly, free speech, and democratic decision-making. Although the only form of 'prior censorship' formally legitimated by the U.S. Supreme Court applies to government employees (specifically, employees and former employees of intelligence agencies), David W. Ewing maintains that as far as free speech is concerned 'people in government agencies fare a little better than people in tightly controlled private corporations.'[8] Academe is a workplace: a major center for the production and distribution of knowledge in industrial cultures. In *The Higher Learning in America* (1918), Thorstein Veblen documented the fact that from the beginning market censorship has skewed the foundations of academic culture in America.[9]

Mass production requires centralized control systems. If democracy is to survive, citizens of industrial societies must discover, recover, or reclaim the emancipatory vocabulary necessary to articulate and enforce effective strategies for controlling the controllers. We must sharpen the critical edges of terms like liberty, democracy, enlightenment, public opinion, and censorship.

VI

Changing Models of Censorship

Freud contended that it is a mark of the advance of civilization when men are no longer burned – merely their books.[10] But many men and women were burned before this fateful advance to civilization occurred. In *The Fear of the Word:*

Censorship and Sex (1974), Eli Oboler reconstructs a detailed picture of the clumsy apparatus of un-Enlightened surveillance in post-Reformation Switzerland:

> Suppose you are living in Geneva, Switzerland, in the year 1553. You can expect a minister and an elder to visit you and your family once a year, and these men will question you about the most intimate details of your way of living. You may not frequent taverns or dance or sing 'indecent or irreligious' songs. You are cautioned against excesses in entertainment, extravagance in living, and immodesty in dress.

> The law even specifies how many different items can be served at one meal, and which colors and what quality of clothing you may wear. If you are a woman and wear jewelry or lace or frilly hats, you will certainly be admonished by the ruling clergy; you know that a neighbor was put to jail for 'arranging her hair to an immoral height.' Books which are considered wrong in religious tenets or tending toward immorality are not available to you. You may not attend any theatrical performances; as a matter of fact none is to be found in Geneva at this time ... Your children must have names to be found in the Bible. If you write books disagreeing with Calvin, you will not have to retract your opinions, but will have to throw all available copies of your writing into the fire with your own hands.

> You may feel that your child is disrespectful – but you don't dare report this to authorities, even if he happens to hit you; the child next door was actually beheaded for striking his parents. If you serve more than three courses at any meal, even at a wedding or other banquet or feast occasion, watch out for the ecclesiastical police ... If you visit a Geneva inn, you will not be permitted to sit up after nine o'clock at night, unless you are known to be a spy by profession ... The ruler of Geneva during the mid-decades of the sixteenth century, John Calvin, is probably the epitome of all censors ... When Calvin set up a theocracy in Geneva ... it naturally included a very strong censorship, perhaps the strongest religiously-motivated censorship of all time, even stronger than that of the Roman Catholic Inquisition.[11]

If the Calvinist ethos cultivated the groundings for the development of mercantile capitalism, its mode of surveillance proved much too cumbersome to control the large and heterogeneous workforce necessary to keep the wheels of industrial capitalism turning. The imperatives of mechanized production required a radical reformulation of humankind's temporal rhythms. The installation of Big Ben in the center of London symbolized the new mechanized conception of time. In 'Time, Work-Discipline, and Industrial Capitalism,' E.P. Thompson systematically explores the ways in which early factory workers were disciplined into internalizing a vision of time which no longer relied on the categories of sun or season.[12] Thompson maintains that this discipline – this resocialization – was marked by widespread resistance and conflict which brought about massive social unrest and violent class conflict.

VII

The Science of Panoptics

Jeremy Bentham's *Panopticon* (1843) exemplified the new technology of Enlightened censorship. The Panopticon offered a model for centralized control which could circumvent open (visible) conflicts between the masses and moral agents. Architecturally the Panopticon serves equally well as a model for a prison, factory, school, or asylum. Within the Panopticon, small individual cells are arranged in a circle so that inmates, workers, students, or patients are under constant observation by moral authorities – guards, managers, teachers, or physicians. The cells isolate those enclosed within the Panopticon from one another. Moreover the lighting system combines with a series of louvered blinds to prevent inmates from seeing the observer. Several famous penitentiaries are literal copies of Bentham's plan. Richard Sennett points out that,

> This design was the purest application of the principle that the people in command should always be in a position to oversee, anticipate, and discipline the movements of those in their charge. In such a setting for moral reform, the factory foreman or prison official acquires far more power than the natural parent, and nurturance is replaced by one-sided control: the subject is influenced but cannot approach or influence those who are taking care of him or her.[13]

In his novel *Falconer*, John Cheever uses the Panopticon as a symbol of modernity. Foucault maintains that Panopticonism is the paradigm of Liberal authority.[14]

Panopticonism provides a working model for agents of subterranean censorship. It is technically superior to all previous forms of censorship because it secures its mechanisms of control within the epistemological foundations of the social order it empowers. Metaphorically, the Panopticon describes the architecture of the modern bureaucracy, corporation, spy network, system of mass marketing, and mass education. It also describes the circuitry which makes possible radio, television, computers, and global satellite systems: the Electronic Panopticon which replaces Bentham's louvered blinds with neatly concealed matrices of wires, transistors, and silicon chips. So that today nearly every citizen of an enlightened society is wired to the Tower and yet remains only marginally aware of the attachment.

Electronics revolutionized the science of Panoptics. Discipline is no longer limited to the penitentiary, factory, school, asylum, or military regiment. It now penetrates (and erodes) the privacy of the home so that even the physical arrangement of furniture in the typical American living or 'family room' comes to resemble the lay-out of Bentham's Panopticon. Chairs are no longer arranged to facilitate conversation among people in the room but rather to provide optimal viewing of the signals transmitted from the Tower to the receiver that each citizen eagerly places in his or her home. From infancy it is now possible for a citizen of the corporate state to absorb the prevailing code of domination in a painless and entertaining way.[15] From infancy many children are taught that the message from the Tower is more important than anything they might have to say by parents who routinely tell them: 'Be quiet! I want to hear this!'

The Electronic Panopticon has brought about far more radical modifications in human temporal rhythms than those required by the mechanization of production. And it has done so without any significant resistance! Moreover, the Electronic Panopticon does not need to isolate physically those enclosed within its cells. It achieves the same effect by limiting opportunities for meaningful interpersonal relations: relations built upon conversation, listening, privacy, intimacy, and a shared sense of community. In short, it not only eliminates the power to resist, but also the desire to resist. For even if we turn the switch off there is nothing left to fill the void. Like characters in a Samuel Beckett play, we discover that the only thing we have to say is that we have nothing to say.

Moreover, during the early morning hours when that switch is finally turned 'off' in most American homes, other hardware in the technology of the Electronic Panopticon remains 'on': computer storage systems which contain information about the birth, death, marital status, monetary transactions, as well as the educational, work, military, and criminal records of virtually every American citizen; electronic surveillance systems which unobtrusively video-tape the movements of citizens in retail outlets, hotel lobbies, banks, airports, and border crossings; and polygraph apparatus which not only permits employers to monitor the credentials, reputations, and public assertions of prospective employees but also their thoughts. Once the wires are in place, the Electronic Panopticon works automatically. Only minimal supervision from the Tower is required. Official and quasi-official control is exercised through licensing, regulation, and broadcasting codes and standards, but the decisive controls are the controls that are built into the marketing system itself.

John Calvin's representatives made their inspections once a year. The Electronic Panopticon exerts its discipline twenty-four hours a day. And, with the installation of an international network of communications satellites, it now has the power necessary to extend its reach throughout the globe.[16]

Under Panoptic discipline no ecclesiastical police force is needed to inspect your table or measure the height of your coiffure. And no cop is needed to bust your head to get you to work on time. Ham-handed tactics can be abandoned. *This is an advance*. It is better to burn books rather than authors, and to change heads rather than break them.

But minds changed, cultivated, or colonized to facilitate the purposes, priorities, and plans of distant elites are not free minds. Panoptic control systems do not satisfactorily resolve the contradictions of freedom and control. They betray the egalitarian promises of the Enlightenment and place arbitrary constraints on human autonomy. They render the controller, warden, or censor invisible and thereby permit him/her to operate outside of the rules of participatory democracy. Moreover, they endow the cense of censorship with a 'phantom objectivity' which makes it extremely resistant to criticism.[17]

VIII

Exposing the Wiring

state which carries out its routine operations behind closed doors is not a
cy. Enlightenment which requires the cover of darkness is not real enlight-
ensors who call themselves by other names are still censors.

orship is ever justified in a democracy, it is only when its groundings are
public scrutiny. Liberal critical traditions have discouraged us from asking fundamental epistemological questions about the relationship of power and
knowledge.

The essential question is not, 'Is there censorship?' but rather 'What kind of
censorship?' Posing this question is not an affirmation of darkness but an invitation to enlightenment. To expand the boundaries of human freedom, we must first
identify them.

18 Publishers as Gatekeepers of Ideas

Lewis A. Coser

Relations between producers of ideas and their consuming publics or audiences are typically mediated through social mechanisms that provide institutional channels for the flow of ideas. These channels, in turn, are controlled by organizations or persons who operate the sluicegates; they are gatekeepers of ideas inasmuch as they are empowered to make decisions as to what is let 'in' and what is kept 'out.' Understanding the function of gatekeeping and analyzing the factors that determine the gatekeepers' decisions will hence give major clues about the ways in which cultural products are selected for distribution.[1]

A great variety of persons and institutions have exercised gatekeeping functions in the world of ideas at different historical periods and in different cultural constellations. The Catholic clergy manned major gates in medieval times and, to a lesser degree, in the postmedieval period. Educational institutions, academies and learned societies, salons, coffee houses, learned journals, the daily press, the modern mass media and many other institutions have occupied central positions which allowed them to select among intellectual products, sifting the chaff from the wheat, and making authoritative decisions as to which intellectual products deserved sponsorship for wider distribution and which were to be kept out of circulation.[2] While these institutions typically gave the accolade of approval to some intellectual creations while denying passage to others, still other institutions, such as censorship, functioned mainly as watchdogs of the spirit, attempting to keep out products that might perturb a given state of cultural affairs or a given distribution of power.[3]

One centrally important group of modern gatekeepers of ideas that deserves to be explored is the publishing industry. Even though one could argue that, in the age of modern electronic media, publishing no longer occupies the near-monopolistic position in the realm of culture that it once enjoyed, it seems obvious – Marshall McLuhan not-withstanding – that the men and women who control access to the medium that Gutenberg invented are still in a position to channel the flow of ideas and control a central, though by no means the only, medium for ideas.

Three major structural conditions help shape the character of the publishing industry in America: (1) the industry is highly decentralized; (2) it operates in a market that is extremely uncertain and unpredictable; and (3) its internal organization is characterized by a predominance of craft over bureaucratic features.

Perhaps the most important aspect of the publishing industry in America is that it is highly decentralized. In contrast to the state of affairs in Russia and other state socialist societies, where a very few decision makers in the state-operated publishing houses function as central gatekeepers, decision making in the American publishing industry is dispersed. It resides in a great number of autono- mous firms. American books are published by about 1,000 houses. Some of these firms, to be sure, are much larger than others; 200 firms do about 85 percent of the business, yet neither monopoly nor oligopoly characterizes the industry. Moreover, 'for every publisher who has sold out to a conglomerate, there is an editor who has set himself up as a publisher.'[4] Publishing is in fact – and I say this only semi- facetiously – a cottage industry with a $3 billion turnover.

An almost equally important aspect of the industry is the fact that, again in contrast to Russia or China, it depends almost exclusively on the market for books. Even though the government or private organizations such as foundations may subsidize a book, the bulk of the output of publishing houses is sold on the free market as a commodity. However, as distinguished from other commodities, books face a most uncertain market due to unpredictability and rapid shifts in consumer preferences. While about 27,000 new titles are issued annually, the probability of any one's appearing in a given bookstore is only 10 percent;[5] the probability of any one's bringing in a profit is very much lower. Moreover, book publishing is one of the few major industries that finances practically no market research to overcome its built-in uncertainty in market chances.[6]

Finally, book publishing resembles the construction industry in that most of its units are organized along craft rather than bureaucratic lines.[7] Even lower level personnel are given professional status and are rarely associated with any firm over long periods of time. Although executives may tamper with the final product, lower level personnel 'are *delegated* the responsibility of producing marketable creations, with little or no interference from the front office beyond the setting of budgetary limits. Due to widespread uncertainty over the precise ingredients of a best-seller formula, administrators are forced to trust the professional judgment of their employees. Close supervision in the production sector is impeded by ignorance of relations between cause and effect.'[8]

These three structural characteristics shape the operation of the industry and lend to its distinctiveness. They account in particular for the dispersal and decen- tralization of decision making between, as well as within, individual firms, and they make for the fact that many or most decisions, far from being regulated by bureaucratic routines, are highly idiosyncratic. For these reasons, it would seem that the study of decision making in the industry must be prepared to account for such decisions in relatively individualistic terms rather than in terms of the highly structured role expectancies that govern decision making in bureaucratic organizations.

To these three characteristics must be added a fourth which, though perhaps of decreasing importance at the present time, still helps shape at least a sector of the industry: the notion on the part of many key personnel that they are engaged in a gentlemanly calling, a high cultural mission which should not be tainted by purely commercial considerations.

Under these conditions, the decision as to whether to publish a book is based on multiple factors, only one of which is an estimate of prospective sales, although this is the single aspect that has been dealt with in some detail in the pertinent literature.[9] Sales appeal, especially under the conditions of high market uncertainty mentioned above, is not likely to be the only consideration. Certain publishers see themselves as serving a vital function in the world of ideas and will hence attempt to attract distinguished authors or promising newcomers, even if commercial prospects are not very enticing. The self-image of publishers or editorial directors thus plays a certain part in their decisions. This self-image, in turn, depends on the reference group they have chosen for themselves. For some, the feedback coming from the listing of their stock on the exchange, or the stock of the conglomerate to which they belong, is a decisive consideration; for others, it may be the opinion of certain reviewers in elite publications; for still others, it may be their standing in the social world of New York or Boston celebrities.

It stands to reason that such points of reference are not chosen at will, but depend at least in part on structural characteristics. An editor or a firm that is part of a conglomerate is less likely to be moved by considerations of intellectual or social prestige than is the publisher of a small and privately owned house. Editors of university presses are more likely to be attentive to the standards and tastes of their local faculty and to the university's quest for recognition than to pure market considerations,[10] even though they may stress their commercial successes when comparing their own standing to that of other university editors.

The tradition of a particular house will also influence editorial decisions. Even though there are houses that seem ready to publish anything that is at all salable, there are others that will only publish what is in tune with the established tradition of the house.[11] Alfred A. Knopf prides himself on his distinguished record in publishing European novels and works of historiographic scholarship and will not publish works that, for example, Grove Press markets with enthusiasm. Certain textbook houses seem mainly interested in texts that have academic distinction, whereas others may find it easy to accept a text that caters to current fads and fashions.

To be sure, financial considerations are an important factor in the majority of cases, but given the uncertainties of the market and the fickleness of the public, it is much easier in publishing to defend idiosyncratic decisions than in organizational environments where precise profit-and-loss considerations standardize decision making. Furthermore, in an industry that lacks market research and where it is accepted that very few products will be profitable, idiosyncratic judgments influenced by noncommercial considerations have a much greater chance of being accepted than in more bureaucratized organizations.

In addition, structural considerations, especially the size of the firm, play a determining role. It stands to reason that a large house can afford to experiment with a number of titles, even in one specialized area, without the assurance that all will do well – as long as at least one is likely to be a success. Smaller houses, in contrast, must exercise greater care to avoid being saddled with too many failures. For this reason, contrary to the current conceit that makes a virtue of small size, larger houses may often be more inclined to innovation. On the other hand, smaller houses, more particularly newcomers, may have to be more alert to new trends in the hope of undercutting the larger and more traditional houses by introducing authors or fields not yet preempted by their big competitors.[12]

Decision makers in the publishing industry, as opposed to those in more bureaucratized settings, face a variety of pressures to live up to differing standards. Pushed and pulled by contradictory expectations, with some of their role partners stressing profitability while others insist on the facilitation of cultural contributions, they find it hard to gain a stable resting point. While a few may opt unambiguously for one set of performance standards, most are continually torn between several and hence find it hard to develop a clearcut sense of professional identity.

The decision to publish a book is, of course, only the first step. The subsequent fate of a manuscript will depend on the actions of a number of persons on different levels of the publishing house. Editors, editorial assistants, copy editors, sales directors and salesmen all have a role in shaping and polishing the work and in bringing it to the attention of its intended audience. For these persons also, self-image and reference groups are a major motivating factor. In addition, previous education and career aspirations are likely to have considerable influence.

A college editor who has been promoted to that position after a number of years on the road, and with a B.A. in English from a large state university, is likely to approach his work with a different frame of mind than an editor fresh from Amherst who aspires to make a mark in the world of ideas by becoming a new Maxwell Perkins. A copy editor just out of Vassar and attracted by the prestige and glamour of Madison Avenue is likely to differ considerably from an older house-editor who has been in the business for a long time and who derives major satisfactions from the regard received within the organization. Depending on their backgrounds, career aspirations, self-images and reference groups, publicity directors may differ in that some will be elated by favorable notices in *Publishers Weekly* while others will be satisfied only with major reviews in the *American Historical Review* or the *New York Review of Books*. Most salesmen today are fairly uninvolved with the books they sell, but there are still quite a few who love books and who are likely to make special efforts to push those they find personally attractive.

Certain persons within the hierarchy of a publishing house are likely to be attracted by the glamour of dealing with authors. They may enjoy the reflected status derived from such associations. Salesmen often regale prospective customers with stories about the foibles of famous authors they have known. Editors sometimes boast of their close involvement in the personal lives of 'their' authors. Often, one suspects, company-paid lunches between editors and authors serve to boost the editors' self-image at least as much as they lubricate the contact between author or prospective author and the publishing house.

A symbiotic, as well as ambivalent, relationship is likely to prevail between editor and author. The editor's career depends on the success of authors, and close contact between them is likely to create positive bonds; yet the editor is also the representative of his firm and must attempt to secure the best possible terms from the firm's point of view. Editors, like foremen in a factory or sergeants in the army, are likely to suffer from a high degree of structurally induced uncertainty and ambiguity.

One aspect of the craftlike organization of the publishing industry is the very high turnover rate among editors.[13] Unlike most incumbents of bureaucratic organizations, who tend to look for career opportunities and upward mobility within the company, editors tend to move from company to company in rather rapid succession. This rapid shifting of jobs may have quite dysfunctional consequences for authors inasmuch as they may have worked closely with an editor, only to realize shortly before the publication of their work that he has left the firm. His successor, who was not involved in the preparatory stages of the book's production, may evince little interest in it and hence not push it as aggressively as his predecessor might have. Moreover, the new editor is likely to have brought some authors from the previous firm and to pay them more attention than those newly inherited. In these ways the complicated network of particularistic relations between authors and editors runs counter to the universalistic contractual relations between the firm and its authors.

The editor and copy editor are supposed to help the author make his manuscript more readable and more attractive to prospective readers. This is bound to create tension. Authors often feel that editors sacrifice finer points of scholarship or refinement of style to sales appeal, while editors tend to think that authors are idiosyncratic and esoteric in their style and manner of presentation, and that they exclude themselves from effective communication with all but a very small fraction of the prospective reading public. Many a battle in the editorial office between author and editor is fought over salability versus scholarship or artistic merit, and communicability versus precision. Here again, let it be noted that much will depend on the self-image and career aspirations of the editor, as well as the traditions of the firm. Moreover, such battles are likely to have different outcomes at McGraw-Hill than at the Harvard University Press.

The publishing of books and their distribution may have consequences, both for specific authors and for the wider intellectual community, that have often gone unrecognized. A few examples are given below.

The decision to publish or not to publish a book may have a major impact on the subsequent career of an author. Many scholarly authors, for example, are fairly young persons still in the process of establishing their academic careers. For them, the publication of a book may make the difference between moving up the academic ladder and receiving tenure and moving to a less desirable or prestigious department. In such cases the decision of an editor to accept or reject a book, or to reshape it, may have considerable consequences. The editor of the Columbia University Press, for example, may in some instances have as much influence on a tenure decision as the judgment of the author's academic superiors and peers.

Book salesmen are much more than salesmen or informal talent scouts. They serve as communication links between the center of intellectual life and its periphery. They help academics in smaller departments and in the hinterland keep up with what is going on in the field. They provide information on academic trends, who is 'in' and who is 'out,' what new fashions have made their appearance, and what new subfields are in the ascendancy. They relay the gossip which is so essential in creating a sense of common identity between the outer and the inner circles of a discipline. Gossip networks serve to tie academics together. The salesman as a conveyor of gossip helps counteract the ever-present danger of a kind of class war between the 'ins' and the 'outs.'

In the same way, salesmen in non-academic fields serve as vital links between bookstores and publishing firms, between the center and the periphery.[14] Not only must bookstore owners be informed about trends and fashions in the big centers to keep their customers abreast, but they also need information to avoid stocking books that will not move. Salesmen serve, to a certain extent, as functional equivalents of market research. Most bookstores operate on exceedingly narrow margins. A busy bookstore may gross $100,000 a year, which means that the owner must have an inventory of 8,000 to 10,000 books worth $30,000 to $35,000, though net profits before taxes are likely to come to only some $15,000 or $16,000. Under these conditions, even small mistakes may break a store; therefore, given the high degree of uncertainty, accurate information provided by the salesman is at a premium. While in more predictable markets the salesman's status is low indeed, the book-salesman's status is high precisely because he still performs informational functions that most of his colleagues in other lines ceased to perform in the late nineteenth century.[15]

Still another aspect of the craftlike organization of the publishing industry and the high uncertainty of its market comes to the fore in advertising. Since many thousands of books are issued each year, large scale national advertising for all of them is clearly impossible. 'The advertising problem … is thus wholly different from that of the advertiser of a single brand that remains in sale indefinitely.'[16] Publishers therefore concentrate national advertising on only a few books which they judge to have high sales potential. Normally a publisher spends only 10 percent of projected sales revenue on advertisement, but under such conditions the dangers of engaging in self-fulfilling prophecies loom large, so that books which might have reached wider audiences do not, in fact, because initial promotion efforts were insufficient.[17]

On the other hand, it also happens that books which had been neglected by the publishing house suddenly 'take off' for reasons that remain mysterious to everyone concerned; such books receive additional advertisement and promotion only after they have made their way in the market.[18] The publishers of Charles Reich's *The Greening of America*, for example, were unaware that they had a best seller on their hands and initially printed only a few thousand copies, which they launched on a modest advertising budget. When Stanley Elkin's monograph, *Slavery*, was published in 1959, it was thought reasonable that the hardcover edition should number 2,500 copies. Since its appearance in paperback in 1963, it has steadily sold approximately 30,000 copies a year. When the new translations of *The Complete Greek Tragedies*, edited by David Grene and Richmond Lattimore, first appeared, only 2,000 copies were printed of each volume. In the past 12 years, the cumulative sales of a variety of editions have come to more than a million copies.[19]

In an industry faced with high degrees of market insecurity and unpredictability and where capital investment for each book is relatively low, it appears a rational organizational response to follow a shotgun principle, scattering many shots in the hope that at least a few hit the target. 'Under these conditions,' Paul M. Hirsch remarked, 'it apparently is more efficient to produce many "failures" for each success than to sponsor fewer items and pretest each on a massive scale to increase media coverage and consumer sales.'[20] However, such an approach to promotion is profoundly upsetting to authors or potential authors.[21] It is likely that the high rate at which authors move from one house to another is influenced not only by quarrels over rights and royalties, but also largely by complaints concerning insufficient promotion. This is especially so since promotion is meant not only to reach the book buyer directly, but also to motivate booksellers and jobbers to stock the book and to influence book review editors, librarians, and buyers for book clubs or paperback reprint houses.

Happily, the time has passed when historians of ideas conceived of ideas as the product of a kind of immaculate conception, untainted by the circumstances, the context and the time of birth. Ever since the pioneering efforts of Karl Mannheim,[22] Max Scheler,[23] Florian Znaniecki,[24] Theodor Geiger,[25] and their successors, a great deal has been done to elucidate the connections between ideas and the social context in which they arise and are received. A variety of institutional settings and gatekeepers of ideas have been described and analyzed.[26] Curiously enough, no major sociological study of the modern publishing industry is available,[27] though there are fine historical studies of that industry.[28] This article, which is a first step in that direction, is to be followed up by a book-length study. What is needed, *inter alia*, is a role analysis and an organizational analysis of the publishing industry, as well as an attempt to unravel the many threads that link publishing to the environment of producers and consumers of ideas.

19 The Trials and Travels of *Lady Chatterley's Lover*

Alistair McCleery

LADY CHATTERLEY'S LOVER

D. H. Lawrence wrote three versions of his novel in response to the operations of the publishing marketplace. Frieda Lawrence recalled: 'He wrote practically the whole novel three times, the third version is the published one, but my favorite [sic] was the first draught [sic].'[1] Richard Aldington has pinpointed a rival work whose success Lawrence wished to emulate in that third version: 'From the beginning I have wondered if D. H. Lawrence were not a little hopeful to cash in on the pornographic market of *Ulysses*, especially as his royalties were declining rapidly.'[2] If Lawrence's motivation in recasting his original novella through its more sexually explicit second and third versions was to make money, then the 'grey market', consisting of literary fiction bought in expectation of pornography, could be very profitable without the risk of the author necessarily losing status or credibility. *Lady Chatterley's Lover* could remain the purchase of the intellectual avant-garde as well as seekers of mere sexual titillation – what Lawrence himself called 'the "improper" public'.[3] The avant-garde, as both creators and audience, can be defined in terms of minority challenges to majority culture. In the case of *Lady Chatterley's Lover*, those challenges were both sexual and – in a manner inextricably linked to that – aesthetic. Indeed, the interlocking of the sexually daring and aesthetically adventurous was characteristic of Modernism.[4] However, in challenging the mainstream view of how explicit a writer could be in sexual matters, Lawrence was also aligning himself, however unwillingly, with those writers who did it solely for financial gain by writing for the pornography market.

If Lawrence's motivation was more than pecuniary (and being only human he probably had mixed motives), then he created a dilemma for himself: how to maintain the artistic integrity of his work – and the different versions surely indicate that such integrity was not absolute – without being condemned as the author of a 'dirty book'. Far from resolving this dilemma, Lawrence used a familiar stratagem of the pornographer – the limited edition – to optimise and protect his financial interests, both in Florence in 1928 and again in Paris in 1930. He justified himself, shortly after publication of the Florentine edition, in writing to Edward Dahlberg: 'As for writing pariah literature, a man has to write what is in him and what he can write and better by far have genuine pariah literature than sentimentalities on a "higher" level.'[5] However, Lawrence's choice of Pino Orioli as publisher of the limited edition of *Lady Chatterley's Lover* in Florence in 1928 was, in following the example set by Norman Douglas, as well as the precedent of Joyce, a method both of maximising his income from the novel and, in its exclusiveness, of hiding from prosecution for obscenity.[6]

The 1930 edition of *Lady Chatterley's Lover* was published in Paris. That simple sentence conceals a wealth of associations. To readers of this book, it possibly evokes images of the rue de l'Odéon, Beach and Joyce, standing outside or sitting inside the bookshop, and a ferment of literary activity among the lost generation in exile. To contemporaries, however, 'published in Paris' would have aroused an expectation of something saucy, something naughty, something titillating, and something illegal. The first volume of Frank Harris's *My Life and Loves*, the complete autobiography, where 'complete' signalled unexpurgated, was also published in Paris as were what Donald Thomas has called 'shabbier contemporaries'.[7] The irony in this situation lies in Lawrence's undertaking of the Paris edition as a response to pirates who had also realised the commercial value of the novel within the pornographic market and, standing outside the law anyway, did not need to justify it in terms of its aesthetic value as 'genuine pariah literature' rather than the somehow inauthentic. The illegal market represented the greater one, particularly in the USA where the vigilance of the Customs and Post Office prevented ready import from Florence or Paris. Lawrence believed that it was 'useless to mail copies to America'.[8] Yet that market, stimulated by the increasing reputation of the novel as a 'dirty book', a reputation itself enhanced by the official seizures, remained to be satisfied by pirates.

Samuel Roth published the first pirated version of *Lady Chatterley's Lover* in the USA in 1928.[9] The book was reset rather than photographed; this enabled Roth to exercise some prissiness in the editing of the text in the sure knowledge that no purchaser would ever complain about less raciness than expected. For example, the line – 'she threaded two pink campions in the bush of red-gold hair above his penis. "There!" she said. "Charming! Charming!"' – was cut altogether. None of this mattered as the reputation of the novel ensured its illicit sales. That reputation drove the sale not only of counterfeit editions but also of other versions, of which Roth notably published two. D. H. Lawrence's *Lady Chatterley's Husbands; an anonymous sequel to the celebrated novel, Lady Chatterley's Lover* (New York: William Faro, 1931) reads like a poor Harlequin romance: it is badly written, much of it filler between erotic passages, of which there are very few. *Lady Chatterley's Friends; a new sequal [sic] to Lady Chatterley's lover and Lady Chatterley's husbands* (New York: William Faro, 1932) begins precisely where the previous sequel ended and retains the flavour of a poor romance. These novels, in their titular reference to the D. H. Lawrence 'classic', hid their nature, and market, behind the camouflage of literary standing.

The first trade edition (that is, not limited) of *Lady Chatterley's Lover* was published in 1933 by the Odyssey Press and authorised by Frieda Lawrence.[10] Like other titles produced by its publisher (the Albatross Press), it was not for sale in, or to be introduced into, the UK or the USA, where the Customs authorities would have seized it anyway. This added to any anticipated titillation from the book itself the thrill of smuggling it on the liner from Le Havre to New York or the ferry from Calais to Dover.[11] For the fainter of heart, Lawrence's expurgated version continued to be available: despite the reluctance of Secker, his London publisher, to handle even that.[12] The expurgated novel was also accessible in numerous translations before the Second World War, including a Japanese version, translated by Ito Sei, from 1935. The English-language unexpurgated version circulated in Japan from the 1930s in the Odyssey Press edition, satisfying both a Japanese desire for the modern and European and, for those with the requisite language skills, an undoubted prurience.[13] Before any trial of the novel took place anywhere in the world, its status and nature had been already prejudged: as emblematic of the modern, for one market, or as a subversive work of pornography for another.

THE TRIALS BEFORE 1960

The first trial of *Lady Chatterley's Lover* took place in Japan.[14] In 1949 the small literary publishing house, Oyama shoten, undertook Ito Sei's translation of the unexpurgated version as the first in a planned series of Lawrence's works. The decision that *Lady Chatterley's Lover* should be the first represented a commercial judgement based on the novel's pre-existing reputation and consequent sales that could provide the publicity and funding for the rest of the series. It would be disingenuous to suggest that profit had not been part of decision to publish: the novel was both a cultural product and a commodity whose low price was intended to make it accessible to a volume market. The translation appeared in two volumes in 1950; from mid-April to late June the first volume sold 80,029 copies and the second 69,545.[15] Japan at this point was still under American Occupation and, under the administration of Roosevelt 'New Dealers', had been moving towards a greater liberalisation of its society, culture and economy. Yet this sense of modernising change, that may have encouraged Oyama shoten to believe that legal publication of an unexpurgated *Lady Chatterley's Lover* was now possible, suffered a sudden shock with the outbreak of the Korean War on 25 June 1950. The USA now needed a stable Japan as a base for its operations and this entailed a restoration of power to traditional authorities. On 26 June 1950, police seized copies of the book under Article 175 of the Criminal Code and then put the translator and the publisher on trial. The Occupation administration decided not to intervene, that this was one area of Japanese life where the Japanese could exercise independent authority.[16] The guilty verdict was never really in doubt; this trial was not to be a significant milestone on the journey to a more open society. The perceived need to create a conservative bulwark against Communist subversion of society led, as it did in Québec a decade later, to cultural illiberalism. While the Japanese trial of the novel became, as it did elsewhere, an illustration of a post-war struggle between the progressive and the conservative, in the context of the early years of the 1950s, the latter held power.

The first American edition of the unexpurgated version was published in May 1959 by the Grove Press under Barney Rosset. To link the Grove Press to Oyama shoten as a small, literary publishing house would be to sacrifice absolute truthfulness for symmetry. The Grove Press did have a high reputation as a publisher of avant-garde literary works from William Burroughs and others of the

Beat Generation to Samuel Beckett, Pablo Neruda and Octavio Paz from overseas. Yet the challenge to the aesthetic values of the establishment by the counterculture also entailed a challenge to its moral certainties. While this yoking of the aesthetically adventurous and the sexually daring was described above as characteristic of Modernism in Lawrence's writing of *Lady Chatterley's Lover*, or of Joyce's writing of *Ulysses*, it obviously cannot be restricted to one period alone. So *Lady Chatterley's Lover*, despite being first published in 1928, becomes emblematic in 1959 (and beyond) of the assertion of a new form of modernity. The Grove Press's reputation in the marketplace reflects that of the novel itself, both literary and pornographic, and, like Oyama shoten, the commercial success attendant upon catering to both markets must have been a factor in Rosset's decision to publish a work in which he had no rights. Immediate and successful prosecution by the US Post Office followed its publication. In July 1959 an appeal by Grove to the Federal District Court against the Post Office's ban on sending the book through the mails brought a favourable verdict from Judge Frederick Bryan: 'A work of literature published and distributed through normal channels by a reputable publisher stands on quite a different footing from hard core pornography furtively sold for the purpose of profiting by the titillation of the dirty-minded.'[17] However, it would be naïve to think that the pre-existing reputation of the novel was now effaced by being published in literary packaging. The US market was now open not only to Grove but to any other publisher as well and many poured in: Pocket Books, Dell, Pyramid and the New American Library (the only one to hold the rights from the Lawrence Estate).

There had been evidence of a thaw in UK official attitudes before the Penguin paperback publication of *Lady Chatterley's Lover* in 1960. In the case of *The Philanderer* by Stanley Kauffmann, prosecuted and acquitted in 1954, the trial judge emphasised that the tendency to deprave and corrupt had to be seen in a contemporary context. Books had to be judged, and obscenity defined, by the standards operating then rather than in the past.[18] In 1959, *Lolita*, published by Weidenfeld and Nicolson, had not been prosecuted. That decision had been taken at a meeting between the Home Secretary, the Attorney General, and the Director of Public Prosecutions at which only the Attorney General dissented from the decision. He was overruled partly because a new statute was making its way through the parliamentary process that would itself reform the treatment of banned books. The 1959 Obscene Publications Act grew out of a reaction to the disproportionate propensity to prosecution pompously exhibited by successive Conservative Home Secretaries, particularly Sir David Maxwell-Fyfe. The 1959 Act altered the framework of obscenity trials so that literary merit, the common good, could be taken into account and attested to by expert witnesses. It contained a new definition of obscenity including a stress upon the work as a whole (rather than selected passages) and a significant qualifier – 'having regard to all relevant circumstances' – in terms of the book's availability. However, two negative changes were introduced: the work no longer had to be sold, with most often the police acting as bogus customers or agents provocateurs, but merely likely to be sold; and the right to trial by jury was discretionary.[19] That there was a trial in the UK in 1960 of *Lady Chatterley's Lover* was not, in other words, a foregone conclusion. As C. H. Rolph points out in his introduction to the transcript of the trial: 'The decision to prosecute was a great surprise to many in the world of publishing, and of the law'.

The trial of Penguin Books in 1960 helped to clarify the status of the novel, to test the operation of the new Obscene Publications Act, and to settle the question whether the manner of publication – in this case, sold in volume at a relatively low price – in addition to the nature of the book was relevant to its legal status. Penguin possessed a strong pre-existing brand as 'a reputable publisher'. The company had already issued in 1949 a set of ten of Lawrence's novels and other writings to mark the twentieth anniversary of his death. In addition, *Sons and Lovers* and *The Rainbow* had long been Penguin paperbacks, 'both complete and unexpurgated' – as their listing in the Penguin promotional material described them. At the trial Allen Lane suggested that he had considered publication in 1950 but that the earlier context for such a publication was extremely difficult. (He may even have been aware of the Tokyo trial as two Japanese writers reported on it to a meeting of International PEN held in Edinburgh in 1952.) The publication of *Lady Chatterley's Lover* in 1960 was therefore presented as a natural, even essential supplement to the Penguin catalogue.

It is not the intention here to offer a detailed account of the trial and Penguin's victory. However, one of the points the Penguin team was most concerned about, in preparing for the trial, was a possible suggestion that the major motive behind the publication of the novel was profit. Two defences were prepared.[20] Firstly, if the motive had been sales, then Penguin could at any point have produced successfully the expurgated version of the novel. New American Library had sold 1,500,000 copies of this in the USA; the edition published by Ace Books in April 1958 sold 230,000 copies in the UK during 1959.[21] Secondly, Penguin was publishing *Lady Chatterley's Lover*, as Lane had first intended, as part of a uniform collected works rather than an exceptional issue undertaken purely to generate profit and, indeed, the novel would appear at the same price as all the others, 3/6d, where extra profit could be easily accrued by charging 5s.[22]

Yet the calculated risk involved in defending the principle of publication brought commercial success. Penguin sold 2,000,000 copies of *Lady Chatterley's Lover* in the six weeks up to Christmas 1960. A further 1,339,631 copies were sold in 1961. Penguin Books became a public company in April 1961 and the press linked the share issue with the trial of *Lady Chatterley's Lover* by referring to the shares as 'Chatterleys'. The offer for sale of 750,000 of the company's 2,500,000 4s shares at 12s each (the remainder was held by family trusts) was oversubscribed. 150,000 people applied and 3,450 were successful in a ballot for 200 shares each. Penguin employees were given preferential treatment for the balance of 60,000 shares. At the close of the first day of trading, the shares were being bought and sold for 17s, a premium of 5s each, and the value of Allen Lane's stake in the company rose to £1,147,500.

On the other hand, the 1960 trial is less often portrayed as a commercial break-through than as the starting point of the liberalisation of western societies throughout the 1960s. For the cultural historian, the lifting of the ban on *Lady Chatterley's Lover* has marked a boundary between the repressive 1950s and the liberated 1960s, an instance of the 'immense freeing or unbinding of social energies' that Fredric Jameson argued to be characteristic of the latter decade.[23] The 'end of the Chatterley ban', in this reading, represents a new zeitgeist in the English-speaking world – with swinging London at its centre. The perceived liberation of the 1960s is hypostatised in the novel, as cultural artefact, but the novel is also a market commodity. Resistance to the distribution of the latter is overcome by an appeal to the former. Yet such resistance persisted, particularly if the verdict was regarded as specifically metropolitan, that is, London-centred. For example, the novel could not be sold in Scotland as the jurisdiction of the trial court covered only England and Wales.

Penguin advised booksellers in Scotland to hold on to their stock but some of them put it on sale on 10 November 1960. Other copies were being 'smuggled' in from England to be sold at 10s each. Penguin held its collective breath against the possibility of a member of the Scottish public making an individual complaint to the Procurator Fiscal. A ruling from the Lord Advocate would be more likely to be favourable if no complaints had been received. Alexander McBain, a Chartered Accountant in Glasgow, attempted in December 1960 to raise a Bill of Criminal Letters in the Court of Session (Scotland's highest indigenous court before a case would go to the UK House of Lords) against John Menzies for selling the 'obscene' novel *Lady Chatterley's Lover*. He wrote to the Director of Public Prosecutions in London, Maurice Crump, asking for information: 'certain copulatory and etymological statistics'; and an explanation of the lack of reference at the London trial to Lawrence's *The Man Who Died* – revealing in that the religious basis of his fight. His request was rather patronisingly dismissed by Civil Service and Government and his legal action failed.[24]

However, his attempt to overturn the Penguin verdict, at least as far as Scotland was concerned, was indicative of a wider resistance to both the publication of the novel and the swinging sixties. In this light, the 1960 trial in London was the beginning of a slow process rather than an overnight revolution. Indeed, the further trial of Alexander Trocchi's *Cain's Book* in 1964 in Sheffield showed that the process had not yet reached south Yorkshire. Magistrates there had judged the novel, first published in the UK by John Calder in 1963 after the American edition from the Grove Press, obscene within the terms of the Obscene Publications Act (1959) and ordered the book's destruction. Despite the precedent of *Lady Chatterley's Lover*, and the same line of defence, including the calling of expert witnesses, the novel was effectively banned. The provincial verdict in Yorkshire was upheld by the Lord Chief Justice and two of his judicial colleagues on appeal to the Queen's Bench. The significance of their verdict lies in two factors: the extension of the definition of obscenity beyond sexual matters to encompass a wider range of opportunities to offend and corrupt; and the clarification that the defence of 'public good' on the basis of literary merit was not absolute.[25] The case gave a new lease of life to the use of obscenity charges against literary works where it could be argued that illegal behaviour or behaviour detrimental to social norms was being promoted. It challenged that metropolitan complacency engendered by earlier official acquiescence in the *Lady Chatterley's Lover*'s judgement and the solidarity of the literary community in the successful outcome of the Penguin trial.

THE TRAVELS AFTER 1960

That challenge was also made in Canada where the tension between metropolis and periphery was accentuated by the federal form of government. The Federal Government in Ottawa had amended the national Criminal Code in 1959 to exempt any worthy literary works otherwise dubbed obscene by reason of specific passages. The Grove Press, New American Library (NAL) and other editions of *Lady Chatterley's Lover* leaked through a porous border from April 1959: by the time the Penguin edition was licensed for sale in the UK in November 1960, 1,250,000 copies of the NAL unexpurgated version and 2,200,000 copies of the NAL expurgated version alone had been sold in Canada.[26] The exception to this rosy picture of cultural openness and commercial success was the Province of Québec, more conservative, more Catholic, than its fellow members of the Dominion of Canada. Copies of the NAL unexpurgated edition were seized in Québec as obscene material in November 1959. Unusually – compared to other jurisdictions – neither the publisher nor the bookseller were liable to prosecution, only the book itself. Judge Fontaine of the Court of the Sessions of the Peace, sitting in Montreal on 10 June 1960, ordered these books to be forfeited as being obscene.[27] He did not believe that literary merit was an issue in the case; he asserted that a work of literary merit could be obscene and listed the passages from *Lady Chatterley's Lover* that illustrated this in his judgement. An appeal against the verdict was heard and rejected by three judges sitting in the Québec Court of Appeal in April 1961. They followed the earlier court in acknowledging the literary merit of the novel but also in regarding it as irrelevant to the question of obscenity.

The Canadian Supreme Court found against the ban in 1962 and the novel, in both NAL and Penguin editions, returned to retailers' shelves where they were willing to stock it. The Court had split 5:4 in favour of the appeal: the dissenters included Chief Justice Kerwin and two judges from Québec.[28] The debate crystallised between those who gave precedence to the amended Federal Criminal Code and those who prioritised community standards where the definition of those standards depended mainly on the provincial origin of the judges. However, the narrow margin of victory was sufficient. Importantly, it set a precedent against which the actions of Customs authorities could be measured (after all, the editions on trial were all imports, whether from the UK or the USA). Customs departments, in whatever country, possessed quite draconian powers to seize and destroy imported publications. Many in Commonwealth countries took their lead from the UK Customs Consolidation Act of 1876. They operated quite autonomously; they did not need to read any material seized; and there was no questioning or appeal of their judgements unless the importer could afford to risk the costs of the trial in addition to the cost of the books impounded. However, the decision of the Supreme Court in Canada changed the attitudes of the Customs service there; from this point onwards, officers by and large ignored text-only items to focus on publications containing photographs or other illustrations.

Lady Chatterley's Lover, in both the Heinemann hardback and the Penguin paperback unexpurgated editions, were judged by New Zealand Customs as indecent and prohibited for import. The establishment of an Indecent Publications Tribunal (IPT) in 1964 provided the opportunity to appeal against the book's status. A successful appeal would bring the additional benefit of possibly freeing import into Australia where Penguin could exploit the larger market. In the event, the IPT did find the novel not indecent (on a 3:2 split) in April 1965. The Wellington government hesitated over a possible appeal before deciding to let sleeping dogs lie and Penguins enter the country legally.[29] This did indeed set a precedent for Australia, a commonwealth member that represented a larger market than New Zealand. Federal Customs and Excise lifted the pre-existing ban on the import into Australia of *Lady Chatterley's Lover* on 19 May 1965 (although a prosecution was still pending by the Attorney-General of Victoria of Rolph's The Trial of Lady Chatterley after the Vice Squad in Melbourne had found copies for sale locally).

If the more conservative state of Victoria, the Québec of Australia, persisted in legal obstructions to the novel, then the books would all be diverted to Sydney (New South Wales). Under Victorian law – no pun intended – literary merit could not be offered as defence nor did the novel have to be considered as a whole: the two novel features of the 1959 UK Obscene Publications Act that had affected the outcome of the trial there. The Magistrate in Melbourne would simply have to identify the presence of certain words in the book to have sufficient grounds to find it obscene and its sale banned. The Heinemann hardback edition had been on sale in Melbourne as it was seen to have a more restricted, less vulnerable market. However, in the context of the advance publicity concerning the Penguin launch, a sergeant from the Melbourne vice squad bought a copy of the Heinemann *Lady Chatterley's Lover* on 3 September from a local bookshop.[30] The reporting of this purchase was sufficient to paralyse the city's booksellers. Although they had ordered 25,000 copies in total of the Penguin paperback, none of them dared to sell it until some clarity over the official attitude was forthcoming. Until one of them offered the book for sale, then the State officials had no need to clarify their attitude and allowing that attitude to be questioned in court.[31] A similar form of police-prompted self-censorship had earlier operated in Victoria in the case of Mary McCarthy's The Group – to the disquiet of the book trade and public alike. Given that prior fiasco involving McCarthy's novel, the authorities curbed the zeal of the police and the Penguin paperback edition of *Lady Chatterley's Lover* eventually went on sale throughout Australia.[32] The pattern persisted: the trials and banning in India in 1960, the eventual unbanning in South Africa in 1980, the unbanning and then banning in China in 1986–89 ... [33]

CONCLUSION

Lady Chatterley's Lover became the particular focus of these trials in a way few other novels did. Its twin reputation, as a work of Modernist daring and as a work of sexual explicitness, provided the rationale for both its defence and its prosecution. That reputation also ensured that it has remained one of the best known, if not best read, books of the twentieth century whose very scarcity stimulated demand. Unlike Joyce's *Ulysses*, the other Modernist novel with which it is often paired, *Lady Chatterley's Lover* can be accessible to a general readership. The ease with which inferior versions and sequels were made that owed much to popular romance indicates the original's relationship with the latter, however distant. The language of *Lady Chatterley's Lover* was blunt (too blunt for Roth) but not arcane. Unlike again Joyce's *Ulysses*, the novel had the potential for large sales to that general readership if authorities could be persuaded to licence its publication. The accounts of its initial publication in a number of countries reveal the opportunism of small independent publishers seeking to make a lot of money while not compromising the integrity of their literary brand. Their size, and the sense of less to lose if taken to court, and much to gain in terms of publicity both for their edition of the novel and for their own role as champions of artistic freedom, underpinned their decision to run the risk of defeat. By their actions they prepared the way for the Penguin trial and the subsequent attempts to ensure that the commercial success in the UK (and USA as far as the NAL was concerned) was repeated throughout the English-speaking world. Their actions in publishing the unexpurgated novel also challenged government, legislature and judiciary in those countries to define the 'public good' in terms of literary works and exposed the struggle states had in reconciling community standards when the views of their metropolitan centres were at odds with those of their provincial peripheries. *Lady Chatterley's Lover* became emblematic of the new in its perennial conflict with the old – in different cultures, at different times. Its history also demonstrates that the relationship between authors, publishers and state is an ongoing process of redefinition with no absolute right of literature to protection from the law (or vigilantes).

20 Combating Censorship and Making Space for Books

Archie L. Dick

At two a.m. one morning in 1963 the apartheid security police banged on Ronnie Kasrils's door.[1] A series of raids on the homes of political activists followed the sabotage of Durban's power supply. Just a few hours earlier he had been reading about Pip's attempt to help Abel Magwitch escape from the authorities, in Dickens's *Great Expectations*. News from Mr Walpole not to go home alerted Pip to imminent danger. Kasrils hid beneath the floorboards before his wife Eleanor opened to the police, and he escaped a few hours later. Whether Pip's experience put Kasrils on his guard, helping him avoid detection, is uncertain. What is certain is that reading *Great Expectations* in the privacy of his home on the night of a raid meant much to him.[2] Eleanor also understood the value of special book spaces. She used Grigg's bookstore, where she worked, to receive and pass documents from underground couriers to the ANC leadership in Durban and Johannesburg. There were passwords and special signs, like carrying a copy of *Time* magazine. The courier would ask her, 'Do you have Olive Schreiner's *Cry the Beloved Country?*' and she would reply, 'That's by Alan Paton. Olive Schreiner wrote *Story of an African Farm*, my favourite South African novel.' 'Well, let me take both books' would be the rejoinder to confirm a genuine contact, and the transfer of secret documents took place.[3]

Books and book spaces featured in police raids, political trials, solitary confinement, and imprisonment during apartheid. Books 'condemned' political activists to jails, but as prisoners they used books to subvert the worst designs of incarceration and censorship. What books meant to readers changed in the spaces of homes, courtrooms, prison libraries, and prison cells. Readers made, unmade, and remade the meanings of books in different book spaces. Security policemen saw and read book titles as grounds for arresting activists during raids on their homes. Prosecutors interpreted books in courtrooms as evidence of crimes against the state during political trials. Prison authorities considered books and libraries as tools for remorse and rehabilitation, and political prisoners thought of them as 'sanity savers.'[4]

RAIDS

About eighty thousand people were detained without trial between 1960 and 1990, but there were probably many more political prisoners in South Africa in that period.[5] In 1978 alone there were 440 convicted political prisoners, mostly from the African National Congress (ANC) and Pan Africanist Congress (PAC). Of these, 400 were on Robben Island and the rest were in Pretoria Local, Pretoria Central, Kroonstad, and other prisons.[6] In many instances, the possession of banned or suspicious material led to detention and imprisonment. Security police kept meticulous notebooks to record political meetings, producing lists of books seized during raids of the homes and offices of hundreds of political activists around the country. About eighteen thousand pages of documents of all kinds were confiscated and presented at the infamous Treason Trial that lasted from 1957 to 1961.[7] The trial produced a huge archive or library of reading material resulting from the raids. An archives inventory reveals some idea of the amount and range of the documents.[8]

Books like James Aldridge's *The Diplomat*, Richard Wright's *Native Son*, and even Anna Sewell's *Black Beauty* were seized, as Treason trialist Lionel Forman discovered when he was arrested at home in December 1956.[9] The security police looked especially for 'suspicious' titles that could be used during trials. Amid much excitement, a copy of Claude Lightfoot's *Black Power and Liberation: A Communist View* was found during Winnie Madikizela-Mandela's arrest in 1969.[10] In a raid at Joe Slovo's home, Stendhal's *The Red and the Black* was seized. The book's title 'combined the two most subversive factors in South African officialdom's struggle equation.'[11] This was the third copy of the book that he had lost in as many raids. Sometimes, anything 'with a red cover' was regarded as suspicious.[12] Albie Sachs's issue of *Fighting Talk*, seized during his arrest in 1963, was probably taken simply because of its title.[13]

Even innocuous titles like Conrad Lorenz's *Aggression* – a book about fish – raised policemen's eyebrows when they arrested Quentin Jacobsen in 1971. They eventually confiscated Walter Kaufmann's *Existentialism from Dostoyevsky to Sartre*, Herbert Marcuse's *One-Dimensional Man*, William Powell's *The Anarchist Cookbook*, the *US Army Manual on Sabotage*, and Jacobsen's telephone directory.[14] A copy of Otto Kuusinen's *Fundamentals of Marxism-Leninism* secreted inside a brown paper cover labelled *Fundamentals of English Syntax* was seized during Jean Middleton's arrest. At her trial it was used to show that political activists were cunning and dangerous.[15] The journalist and activist Zubeida Jaffer was charged after forty-two days in detention for possessing three banned books, which included Franz Fanon's *Wretched of the Earth*.[16] Book raids were meticulously organized invasions of the bookshelves and other spaces that books inhabited in private homes.

Captain A.P. Van Niekerk supervised a thorough and efficient raid on Carl Niehaus's home on 12 February 1982. Five of his security policemen spent just over ninety minutes sifting through books and documents, compiling a list of sixty-one items. They looked for politically incriminating evidence of what Carl and his partner Johanna Lourens were reading or distributing, seizing five placards, a bag of pamphlets, and *No to Bantustans* stickers in a refrigerator on the veranda.[17] Materials were found in different rooms in desk drawers, filing cabinets, and on telephone tables and the floor. On the list also were Edward Roux's *Black Man's Struggle*, Kwame Nkrumah's *Revolutionary Path*, and several parcels of typed notes and a metal basket containing documents. Niehaus and Captain Van Niekerk signed the completed list. The instruments for political education in the liberation struggle were weapons to foment revolution in the eyes of the state. The confiscated books reappeared in courtrooms as damning evidence led by the prosecution, and they were never returned to their owners.

TRIALS

Just one year after the Congress of the People adopted the Freedom Charter at Kliptown in Soweto, 156 people representing a complete cross-section of South African society were arrested, charged with high treason, but later acquitted.[18] Prosecutors at the Treason Trial read the books (evidence of reading) simplistically as evidence of treason. The state's 'star witness,' Andrew Murray, a professor of philosophy at the University of Cape Town and an expert on communist doctrine, passed judgment willy-nilly. He opened books and condemned them with terse phrases like 'Straight from the shoulder of Communism,' or 'Contains Communist matter,' or 'Communist Propaganda.'[19] Even the catering notices 'Soup with meat' and 'Soup without meat' taken from the kitchen of the Congress of the People were submitted as evidence of possibly disguised communist slogans. Lionel Forman secretly co-authored an account of proceedings during the trial itself. He recalled that excerpts from the documents were read to the court in the solemn tone normally reserved for 'Show the jury the murder weapon.'[20] Ironically, political prisoners in the holding cells below the magistrate's court read and autographed copies of Forman's banned book about the Treason Trial.[21]

Other political trials also produced lists of books with the names and signatures of security policemen and political activists, dates and times of raids, as well as titles of the books. The Rivonia Trial of 1963 to 1964 presented as evidence Nelson Mandela's booklet *How to Be a Good Communist*, inspired by Liu Shao Chi and rewritten for an African audience, and *Born of the People* – a first-hand account of the guerilla uprising in the Philippines ghost-written by William Pomeroy. The prosecution also presented Mandela's study notes of these books. The apartheid state was obsessed with documenting what its citizens were reading and how they were reading. Typically, state lawyers tried to show connections between the books of the accused and their political activities, as happened in the case of Robert Resha and his copy of *The History of the Communist Party of the Soviet Union* by B.N. Ponomarev and A. Rothstein.[22] The prosecutors in Quentin Jacobsen's trial also tried to show such links. Jill Ogilvie, an unassuming reference librarian of the Johannesburg Public Library subpoenaed to court during the trial, read out a list of titles available in the library similar to those found in Jacobsen's possession.[23] The charges against Jacobsen were subsequently withdrawn because members of the public could also have read those books.

In their selection of 'suspicious' titles as evidence, security policemen and state prosecutors overlooked titles that actually guided political action. Fikile Bam was a member of the Yu Chi Chan Club, which was started to study guerilla warfare. Bam and the Club read Deneys Reitz's *Commando: A Boer Journal of the Boer War* as a source for planning their strategy. Yet at his trial this book was ignored, and prosecutors focused instead on books by Mao Tse Tung and Che Guevara.[24] Works of popular fiction were also read for political strategy, but security policemen and prosecutors ignored them because of their innocuous titles. Omar Badsha, who was detained several times in the 1960s, read chapter 14 of John Steinbeck's *Grapes of Wrath*, just as his political mentors had done at Congress Party Schools in the 1930s.[25] The chapter deals with serious protest themes such as organizing the poor, and the 'voice of the grassroots.'

Lawyers defending political activists, on the other hand, were more concerned that their clients should enjoy light reading during the trials. They advised and often insisted on avoiding serious books. Attorney George Bizos discouraged Jacobsen from reading philosophy or any 'heavy stuff' while he was awaiting trial in order to keep him 'as normal as possible.'[26] One of Ahmed Kathrada's lawyers told him not to read Dostoyevsky before the Rivonia trial.[27] Courtroom actors therefore interpreted books differently. State prosecutors saw them as evidence that helped to make the charges against political activists stick. Defence lawyers believed that books either relaxed or tensed up trialists. Accused activists saw their confiscated books as badges of defiance against the state and as instruments of liberation.

THE BIBLE IN SOLITARY CONFINEMENT

Section 17 of the ninety-day detention act of 1963 prohibited writing and reading in detention and solitary confinement.[28] The Bible was usually the only reading material supplied so that detainees would reflect 'on the harm done to society and to fulfil the Nationalist government's Christian duty.'[29] Detainees with other religious convictions were sometimes given their own holy books. Abdulla Haron, for example, kissed and placed the Koran on his prayer mat on the day he died in detention.[30] Fatima Meer, also a Muslim, was mistakenly given the Ramayana (a Hindu epic poem), which she found 'fascinating reading.'[31] Another Muslim, Ahmed Kathrada, was only allowed a Bible during his detention in 1963 but said 'it was a great help.'[32] Zubeida Jaffer read the Arabic-English Koran from 'cover to cover' during her second detention, expecting to be released when she had finished this task – and she was![33]

But access to holy books was often maliciously manipulated. Feziwe Bookholane's Bible was confiscated during her solitary confinement at Klerksdorp Prison. Instead, she played Scrabble with little pieces of toilet paper to prevent losing her mind.[34] Methodist priest Stanley Mogoba was given a Xhosa-language Bible while in isolation, which ironically he used to learn that language.[35] Reverend Frank Chikane was refused a Bible because a warder said 'it makes you a terrorist' and was eventually given an Afrikaans-language version.[36] Tshenuwani Simon Farisani, who was dean of the Evangelical Lutheran Church, was told that he was 'always reading the wrong verses of the Bible,' and was regularly denied one.[37] Michael Dingake was refused a Bible because it could get him 'expelled from the Communist Party.'[38] Emma Mashinini was refused a Bible, on the other hand, because she was a communist, but she later received one from her husband and another as a gift from Bishop Desmond Tutu.[39]

Bible taunts often became torture. Raymond Suttner's 'bible' (works of Marx, Engels, and Lenin) weighed down his outstretched arms while in a crouching position. On another occasion he was forced to read his 'bible' while lying flat on a table with just his head raised.[40] The uncertainty of detention led to disciplined, frugal, and unusual reading of the Bible. Albie Sachs read for fifteen minutes in the morning and an hour before supper.[41] James Kantor rationed himself to only ten pages per day.[42] Farisani read aloud from the book of Isaiah during his arrest, Susan Jobson read Ecclesiastes and Song of Songs 'out loud and in appropriate tones,' and Gonville ffrench-Beytagh chanted the Psalms, canticles, and prayers from the Book of Common Prayer.[43] The Bible was also read intensively to stave off madness and for inspiration. Neville Alexander read the authorized version many times, and Rusty Bernstein read it 'twice end to end.'[44] Raymond Mhlaba read it 'from front to back' during his six months of solitary confinement, and Winnie Madikizela-Mandela read it 'from cover to cover' during one of her periods of detention. It sometimes gave her a 'wonderful feeling of peace and tranquility' and at other times 'it was nothing but meaningless words.'[45] On the other hand, the words of the Bible inspired revolutionary thoughts in Jama Matakata. He saw 'Jesus as a freedom fighter who came to set captives free.'[46]

The Bible as a material artefact was also a useful resource for political prisoners. At Port Elizabeth Prison, Harold Strachan helped to make a set of dominoes from the thicker back page of the Bible. More irreverent was the use of the Old Testament for the purpose of masturbation, or 'vir draadtrekdoeleindes.'[47] Some prisoners would smoke the 'actual text of the Bible' even if it earned offenders six days without food. When they received two packets of Boxer tobacco and flint from a warder at Leeuwkop Prison, Indres Naidoo and fellow detainees used pages of the Gideon Bible and shavings from a war-issue toothbrush to make six long *zolls*. The thin leaves made excellent smoking paper. 'For the next three to four glorious days,' Naidoo gloats, 'the Bible became slimmer and slimmer,' providing less and less reading matter for one of his religious comrades.[48] Prison authorities allowed the Bible and other holy books in solitary confinement to promote penitence and rehabilitation. Political prisoners read them for personal, profane, and political purposes.

PRISON LIBRARIES

Prison authorities and political prisoners organized libraries. Prison regulation number 109(3) of 1965 required the establishment and maintenance of a properly organized library for all prisoners, containing literature of constructive and educational value.[49] The Department of Prisons allowed all books that were not banned by the state's Censorship Board to achieve its rehabilitation ideals. Another regulation enabled the prison commanding officer to prohibit reading matter of an overwhelmingly stimulating and sexual nature, stimulating photographs, and anything

that might promote unrest among prisoners.[50] For political prisoners, censor officers had also to apply all the 'B-orders,' which stated that 'politics and news from
outside was strictly forbidden.'[51] The library in the General Section of the Robben
Island prison became operational at the end of 1965. Under the supervision of a
warder, it was organized and run by Stanley Mogoba, Canzibe Rosebury Ngxiki,
and Dikgang Moseneke because of their educational backgrounds. They arranged
boxes of books brought from other prisons into divisions like Novels, Poetry,
Drama, History, Geography, Politics, and Science.

Mogoba drew on his experience in a high school library to start an accession register, and books were given numbers and entered on cards for borrowing purposes.
Soon afterwards, Mogoba was put into isolation with Achmed Cassiem and Sedick
Isaacs for trying to smuggle an article on prison conditions to the *Cape Times*
newspaper, and for participating in a hunger strike. Ironically, he says, the 'librarian now had nothing to read.'[52] Ngxiki suffered the same fate when he used his
freedom as librarian to spread the word of the impending hunger strike from cell
to cell. He never returned to the library.[53] Dikgang Moseneke and Klaas Mashishi
continued the library work. In the Segregation Section of Robben Island prison
that housed senior political prisoners, a common law convict brought around a
list from which titles could be selected. There were only about thirty books for the
sixty-five prisoners in the Segregation Section at the time, which was not enough
to go around. The convict contrived to quarrel with the political prisoners and they
were deprived of library books.[54]

Matters improved when Ahmed Kathrada began to run a tiny Segregation
Section library, assisted later by Sbu Ndebele and Khela Shubane. A bookshop in
Cape Town that closed down donated mostly romances by Daphne Du Maurier
and classics by Charles Dickens.[55] By June 1978 there were a few hundred
books in the Segregation Section.[56] Kathrada used his position as librarian to
communicate news and to educate General Section political prisoners when he
delivered, collected, and took stock of library books. Prison authorities wanted
prison libraries instead to educate and re-educate prisoners to reach higher
spiritual, educational, and social levels on their release.[57] In the 1960s, this
'rehabilitatory zeal' shaped the classification guide for library books at Pretoria
Central Prison into 'Educational' and 'Fiction.' Prisoners were allowed one
'Educational' and one 'Fictional' work. Of the bizarre classification subdivisions,
Hugh Lewin says:

> Educ/Lit and Educ/Hist ... happily catered for all of Dickens but only half of
> Jane Austen: *Northanger Abbey* made it as Educ/Lit, *Persuasion* could only make
> Fic/Romance; Tolstoy's *Tales* reached Educ/Lit, *Anna Karenina* only Fic/Rom;
> Graves got only to Fic/Hist with *Claudius the God*, while Sterne made it to Educ/
> Hist with *Tristram Shandy*.[58]

Lewin was not surprised when he once got a collection of children's ghost sto-
ries and a 'dreadful' Cecil Roberts but on other occasions received the whole of
John Galsworthy's *Forsyte Saga*, and E.M. Remarque's *All Quiet on the Western
Front*. When he queried a book by Edwin Spender instead of the poet Stephen

Spender as he had requested, the prison 'librarian' asked if Edwin Spender would not do since after all it was still Spender. His order from a university tutor's lists for Dostoyevsky's *Brothers Karamazov* was refused in spite of his having earlier read the prison library's copy of Dostoyevsky's *Possessed*.[59] An even stranger book arrangement later was chief warder Du Preez's catalogue of purchased books. Over time the books could not be traced: most were filed under 'T' since so many titles started with the definite article 'The.' Du Preez's catalogue also described Shakespeare's *The Tempest* as science fiction, and the entry for *Romeo and Juliet* appeared as 'author anonymous.'[60] Library services only improved when political prisoners themselves obtained degrees in librarianship through the correspondence University of South Africa (Unisa), and managed the libraries.

Sedick Isaacs ran Robben Island's General Section library and Ahmed Kathrada headed the Special Section library and the Pollsmoor Maximum Prison library as qualified librarians in the 1970s and 1980s.[61] Miss Katharine Haslam of the University of Cape Town Library sent Isaacs boxes of books after he requested material for the prison library. One box included Karl Marx's *Das Kapital*, which the prison censor vetting the books considered to be acceptable because it was a book 'about money.' The supply of communist and anti-communist literature from Miss Haslam allowed Sedick to develop a balanced library collection.[62] A popularity poll that he took identified *National Geographic* as the most popular magazine among Robben Island political prisoners in the 1970s.[63] The library space, on the other hand, was divided. Prisoners implemented a form of censorship when anti-communists stole the communist books and communists stole the anti-communist books from the prison library as a way of propagating their views. Ironically, unexpected cell raids by prison guards restored all the books to the library, which Sedick used as an open space for debate and discussion.

At Kathrada's B Section prison library in Pollsmoor Maximum Prison, the censorship tug-of-war was between prisoners and authorities. Censor officers 'took away' a number of fiction and non-fiction books in the mid-1980s. Sergeant Brand removed H. Bloom's *Transvaal Episode* and André Brink's *Looking on Darkness* on 28 May and 12 November 1984 respectively, and Charles van Onselen's two studies on the history of the Witwatersrand – *New Babylon* and *New Nineveh* – were 'taken back' on 9 July 1984. A prison official returned Menán du Plessis's *State of Fear* on 21 May 1985.[64] This book deals with the states of emergency in South Africa, and it is unclear whether the official had taken it to read it or whether he banned it for a while. Kathrada maintained an impressive list of films in his library that he copied out of the Cape Provincial catalogue of films.[65] The films were used for ninety-minute viewing programs, and the titles ranged from *China: The Social Revolution*, to *The Private World of Lewis Carroll*, to *Making Michael Jackson's Thriller*. Librarians and prisoners therefore undermined state rehabilitation and censorship policies in prison libraries. The community and censorship ethos of prison libraries faded, however, as prison authorities began to allow political prisoners to keep books in their cells.

PRISON CELLS

Sudden prison transfers, unannounced raids, and the reversal of privileges could bedevil reading, but during stable periods books played significant roles in the privacy and décor of prisoners' cells. Books created a relaxed atmosphere in which private reading occurred in relative comfort. Fatima Meer's colour painting of her prison cell shows the self-constructed bookshelves with a few books, newspapers, magazines, and flowers. It depicts not so much a cramped segregation cell as a personal reading space in a forbidding locale.[66] In this space she prepared the sociology lectures that she would present after her release. Here she enjoyed perusing the Indian weeklies the *Leader* and the *Graphic*, and indulged herself with the 'light reading' that her husband Ismael insisted on, such as Edith Wharton's *Old New York* and *QB VII*, and *Art of Africa*.[67]

A photograph of Nelson Mandela's cell also shows a private reading space and books reflecting his taste and interests. The photograph was prepared, however, as a piece of apartheid propaganda for a special visit by inspectors and journalists to Robben Island in 1977.[68] Pictures of neat rows of books on bookshelves belie the chaos of unexpected raids and the suspension of reading privileges that characterized everyday prison life. But reading facilities improved following pressure from the International Committee of the Red Cross. Prison authorities lowered the stand-up desks that jutted out from walls at chest level, and they provided three-legged stools for reading.[69] When prison authorities announced the end of manual labour in early 1977, Mandela ordered books on gardening and horticulture. The photograph shows some tomatoes he grew, and a snapshot of Winnie Mandela. The reading space accommodated his bookshelves and the range of books that he collected. In addition to works of economics, law, political science, and religion, he read all the unbanned novels of Nadine Gordimer, Steinbeck's *Grapes of Wrath*, and Tolstoy's *War and Peace*.[70]

Denis Goldberg's prison cell was a study carrel, even a laboratory space for experimenting with information retrieval techniques. This explains Goldberg's detailed Unisa examination answers, which included footnotes identifying authors, titles, and publishers of books he read. He numbered the pages of the examination answer books and then made cross-references back and forth across pages, and even across examination questions. Goldberg could do this because he had constructed a sophisticated index in the form of a makeshift filing cabinet, based on the bibliographies and reading lists in the Unisa study guides as sources for index entries. The files consisted of little cards made of cardboard paper on which the entries were written; they were then punched in the middle. These cards were held together by wires with the tops of toothpaste tubes as screws on each end. The cards remained intact even during security raids of his cell by burly prison guards.[71]

Albie Sachs personalized his Wynberg cell in 1963 with the piece of graffiti: 'Jail is for the birds.'[72] For Sachs, books in prison were precious. 'By means of the pages which I hold in my hands,' he explains, 'I am restored to mental activity and, above all, I resume my position as a member of humanity.' He wanted to read 'books alive with people' instead of books of philosophy, or politics or criticism.[73] His cell was a secret treasure chest that hid prized reading 'finds.' Hidden under his mattress was a crumpled double leaf of newspaper sodden with beetroot juice, fish oil, and vinegar that he had scooped up without the prison guards noticing during an exercise run. He says: 'For one whole glorious week I dipped into my treasure, each day carefully restoring it to its hiding place.'[74] The toilet flushed away the evidence, and on one occasion he put his arm down it to shred the paper with his nails when it blocked the outlet pipe.

Sachs hid books in places around the cell that would last for a couple of months in an emergency. He hid Robert Graves's *Greek Myths* and the Bishop of Woolwich's *Honest to God* just in case he needed to ration his reading and contemplate life and death and 'why the world is.'[75] He enjoyed a thick book as a gourmet enjoys a thick steak, and considered anything less than five hundred pages to be a short story. He preferred long books like Miguel de Cervantes's *Don Quixote*, Thomas Mann's *Buddenbrooks*, Irving Stone's *The Agony and the Ecstasy*, and James Michener's *Hawaii*, But he also read shorter novels like Nathaniel Hawthorne's *The Scarlet Letter* and S.G. Colette's *Claudine at School* and the works of 'Durrell, Henry James, Proust, George Eliot, Racine, Melville, Moss Hart, Mary Renault, Jan Rabie, Venter, C.P. Snow and Lampedusa.' Sachs sums up his personal reading space as follows: 'Stone walls do not a prison make … if you have company or books.'[76]

CONCLUSION

The physical spaces that books occupy shape their meanings, and the meanings change as the spaces change. Books inhabit private, public, and emotional spaces. They nestled in special nooks and disguised themselves in brown paper in the homes of political activists; they stood as sterile exhibits on courtroom tables; they sat on prison library bookshelves; they hid or brandished themselves in prison cells. These book spaces were violated, censured, sanctified, shared, and treasured. Political prisoners pressed a whole lot of living out of the books they read. They resumed their private and social lives, and reassessed their political convictions. Knowing what, how, and where they read teaches us how they resisted and defeated apartheid censorship.

Part Five
Books, Propaganda and War

How the state controls print culture in times of war and how complicit the publishing industry has been in enforcing censorship and supporting government propaganda in wartime are the key questions examined in this section. With particular reference to British and American publishing from 1914 to 1918 and 1939 to 1945, the selected texts question the author's, publisher's and reader's role in wartime and the constraints place on the circulation of ideas and information, in the face of the often conflicting imperatives of 'country, conscience and commerce' (Potter 2007).

The role of British writers in writing government propaganda during the First World War is reviewed by Peter Buitenhuis in *The Great War of Words: Literature as Propaganda 1914–1918* (1987). This extract describes how prominent British authors were enlisted by Charles Masterman into writing government propaganda at the outset of the First World War. Wellington House was the initial site of the British government's propaganda agency, established by Masterman to counter German propaganda overseas, especially in neutral nations such as the United States. Enlisted writers included H. G. Wells, Arthur Conan Doyle, John Buchan and Ford Madox Ford. Buitenhuis explains how covert propaganda efforts were rapidly organised, with the 'complete support of the British writing establishment' (p. 160). Elsewhere in the book, Buitenhuis assesses the arrangements made between commercial publishers and Wellington House, whereby publishers – including Hodder and Stoughton, Methuen, Blackwood and Sons, John Murray, T. Fisher Unwin, Darling and Son, Macmillan and Thomas Nelson and Sons – were paid five guineas and five shillings to publish government wartime propaganda covertly, using their own imprint.

Jane Potter provides further insights into this covert relationship between commercial publishers and the state during the First World War, in her chapter 'For Country, Conscience and Commerce: Publishers and Publishing, 1914–18' (2007). She depicts a publishing industry struggling for survival on account of paper shortages, rising production costs, and loss of staff to the armed forces. While certain firms only just managed to keep going during this period, others adapted more nimbly to the new conditions and managed to keep their businesses afloat by satisfying the public's taste for war-related titles. Potter also addresses the conundrum of why publishers took part in the Wellington House propaganda exercise, in particular those like William Heinemann and Stanley Unwin, who were pacifists. According to Potter, such collusion with the state was not simply a matter of opportunism or profiteering, as contended by Buitenhuis, but was ultimately more a matter of conscience and a sense of public duty, instilled in particular by their own personal experiences of wartime loss.

The relationship between the British publishing industry and the state during the Second World War is addressed by Valerie Holman in *Print for Victory: Book Publishing in England 1939–1945* (2008). This book documents the book trade's response to wartime regulations, restrictions and censorship laws, and this extract focuses on the means by which the book trade was supported by the Ministry of Information, on account of the 'cultural and symbolic value' of the book, and because it was regarded as 'an effective means of boosting morale and discreetly spreading propaganda' (p. 167). Adopting similar practices to those of Wellington House in the First World War, there is evidence of the government using independent firms to translate and publish their own titles covertly, and then financially supporting them by purchasing thousands of copies of the published works.

During the Second World War, Penguin Books received particular support from the government and fared better than many of its competitors in terms of its paper rationing allowance. The company became closely associated with the war effort, partly as a result of the Penguin Specials series, which was established in 1937 to explain and clarify political developments in Europe for the British reader. Penguin then established the Armed forces Book Club in 1942, with the aim to supply books to men and women serving abroad. Joe Pearson (1996) explains how Penguin Books was granted a near monopoly of paperback publishing for British troops, in association with the Workers' Educational Association. As paper rationing was tightened after 1941, however, the focus shifted to the recycling of paperbacks, and book donation schemes through the Red Cross. These factors served to place Penguin Books at the forefront of the British war effort, as well as at the leading edge of British publishing.

John Hench's chapter, 'The American Publisher's Series Goes to War, 1942–1946' (2011), reviews the creation, publication and reading of American propaganda in the form of book series that were designed both for the American forces and to counter German propaganda in 'overrun and aggressor nations' (p. 177). Hench evaluates the significance of a number of publishers' series: the Armed Series Editions that were produced in their millions and distributed to US forces across the globe; the Fighting Forces Series that were published for US military personnel; the Overseas Editions and Transatlantic Editions that were published for European and Asian citizens after the defeat of the Axis power; and the Bücherreihe Neue Welt series for German prisoners of war based in the United States. Although government-sponsored publications, they were issued by non-government entities to disguise the origins of the books. Hench assesses the remaining traces of evidence of the ways that these books were read, and how wartime reading communities developed around these book series. Although difficult to ascertain the 'propaganda benefits' deriving from these series, he maintains that these books indisputably helped 'develop a new generation of book readers and buyers' as well as 'fuelling the post-war paperback boom' (p. 183).

These historical studies demonstrate the close controls over print culture imposed by the state in times of war, through propaganda publishing initiatives, through legislation and through indirect methods like paper restrictions. There is repeated evidence that authors and publishers worked closely with the state in the enforcement of censorship and the production of wartime propaganda. The effectiveness of this printed propaganda in educating and influencing readers is, however, less certain.

SUGGESTED FURTHER READING

Anghelescu, Hermina G. B. and M. Poulain (eds), 2001. *Books, Libraries, Reading and Publishing in the Cold War*. Washington, DC: Library of Congress, Center for the Book.

Hammond, M. and T., Shafquat (eds), 2007. *Publishing in the First World War: Essays in Book History*. Basingstoke: Palgrave Macmillan.

Hench, J., 2010. *Books as Weapons: Propaganda, Publishing and the Battle for Global Markets in the Era of World War II*. Ithaca, NY: Cornell University Press.

Laugesen, A., 2010. 'Books for the world: American book programs in the developing world, 1948–1968,' in G. Barnhisel and C. Turner (eds), *Pressing the Fight: Print, Propaganda and the Cold War*. Amherst: University of Massachusetts Press, 126–132.

Trott, V., 2017. *Publishers, Readers and the Great War: Literature and Memory since 1918*. London: Bloomsbury Academic.

21 Setting up the Propaganda Machine

Peter Buitenhuis

The Liberal government led by Herbert Asquith was, with the notable exceptions of Lord Haldane and Winston Churchill, totally unprepared for the outbreak of war.[1] The German government, on the other hand, had not only anticipated the need for armies and supplies, but also prepared for psychological warfare. There was a German propaganda agency in place in the United States that began to distribute leaflets in many cities and to passengers arriving on transatlantic liners at the outbreak of war.

Lloyd George was told about this activity after an August Sunday luncheon at a golf club (where so many matters of the Asquith government seem to have been decided). He realized at once that German actions had to be countered and that the United States and other neutral nations had to be persuaded to share Britain's view of the war. He turned to his cabinet colleague, C. F. G. Masterman, and said: 'Will you look into it, Charlie, and see what can be done.'[2] In this casual manner, he launched one of England's most significant war efforts.

Charles Masterman was a brilliant and remarkable individual who has not yet been accorded his proper place in history [...]. In 1903 he had been appointed the literary editor of the *Daily Chronicle* and in that capacity had come to know many of England's leading literary men. He attracted many of them as contributors and appointed Hilaire Belloc and John Masefield to his staff. He entered Parliament in 1906 at the age of thirty-one and immediately embarked on a successful career, exciting attention as a prospect for the premiership. Shortly before the war, Prime Minister Asquith appointed him Chancellor of the Duchy of Lancaster. At that time, newly appointed cabinet ministers had to resign their seats in the House of Commons and run for re-election before they could take up their cabinet posts. When he did so, Masterman narrowly lost his seat, and so in February 1915, he had to resign from the government. Before then he had done much of the gruelling work of formulating and putting into effect Britain's first national health insurance scheme. In view of this, he was appointed to head the National Health Insurance Commission. Although not the most effective politician, he was a fine administrator, a devoted public servant, a successful author, and a widely read man. These qualities made a strong appeal to his long-time friend, Ford Madox Hueffer, who may have used some of these elements of character in Tietjens of *Parade's End*. Late in August 1914, the cabinet sanctioned Masterman's job as head of the War Propaganda Bureau. Because his work was to be kept highly secret, it made sense to place it in Masterman's existing office at Wellington House, Buckingham Gate.

In *British Propaganda during the First World War, 1914–1918*, M. L. Sanders and Philip M. Taylor have described in detail how Masterman organized the work there. Wellington House was used as a cover until the Bureau became the Department and later on the Ministry of Information and had to find more spacious quarters.[3]

Masterman's first instinct was to turn to the writers of England for help. He sent out a call for many of England's major writers to attend a secret meeting. On the afternoon of 2 September 1914, they gathered in the conference room. Around the table sat William Archer, Sir James M. Barrie, Arnold Bennett, A. C. Benson, R. H. Benson, Robert Bridges, Hall Caine, G. K. Chesterton, Sir Arthur Conan Doyle, John Galsworthy, Thomas Hardy, Anthony Hope Hawkins, Maurice Hewlett, W. J. Locke, E. V. Lucas, J. W. Mackail, John Masefield, A. E. W. Mason, Gilbert Murray, Sir Henry Newbolt, Sir Gilbert Parker, Sir Owen Seaman, George Trevelyan, H. G. Wells, Israel Zangwill, and assorted government officials. Rudyard Kipling and Sir Arthur Quiller Couch were unable to come but sent messages offering their services.[4] Even without them it was probably the most important gathering of creative and academic writers ever assembled for an official purpose in the history of English letters.

They were all well-known writers at the time, but the passing years have dimmed the reputation of some of them. William Archer was probably the best-known London drama critic of the period, the man most responsible for introducing the plays of Ibsen to the English stage. A. C. Benson was a famous Eton master, novelist, critic, and biographer of his father, the Archbishop of Canterbury. R. H. Benson, another son of the archbishop, became a noted Catholic author and a monsignor as well as a novelist. Robert Bridges was the current poet laureate and also a critic of some note. Sir Hall Caine, former secretary to D. G. Rossetti, wrote a large number of enormously popular novels and was perhaps the leading romanticist of the day. Maurice Hewlett, the historical novelist, was best known for his *The Forest Lovers*, but he was also a poet and essayist. W. J. Locke was secretary of the Royal Institute of British Architects and a popular novelist. E. V. Lucas, assistant editor of *Punch*, was the author of many books of satire, humour, and travel and wrote a fine biography of Charles Lamb. J. W. Mackail, classicist and literary critic, was Professor of Poetry at Oxford from 1906 to 1911. Sir Henry Newbolt was popularly known for his patriotic and imperialistic poems, and he was also a naval historian. Sir Owen Seaman, the editor of *Punch*, was a literary parodist and poet. George Trevelyan was one of the most famous historians of the period, and Israel Zangwill, probably the best-known Zionist of his time, a journalist and dramatist.

Unfortunately, no minutes have survived of that Wellington House meeting, if any were kept. All we have are glimpses from writers' letters and journals; Thomas Hardy recalled in a letter written much later to Anthony Hope 'that memorable afternoon in September, 1914, the yellow sun shining in upon our confused deliberations in a melancholy manner that I shall never forget.'[5] And Arnold Bennett laconically noted in his diary: 'Masterman in the chair. Zangwill talked a great deal too much. The sense was talked by Wells and Chesterton. Rather disappointed in Gilbert Murray, but I like the look of little R. H. Benson. Masterman directed pretty well, and Claud Schuster and the Foreign Office representative were not bad. Thomas Hardy was all right. Barrie introduced himself to me. Scotch accent; sardonic canniness.'[6] Whatever was said, the writers all pledged themselves to assist the war effort in any way they could, and the recruiting parade was over.

It was a remarkable success and began the march of writers to join the government service that continued throughout the war. William Archer, Anthony Hope, Sir Gilbert Parker, G. H. Mair, and Gilbert Murray joined the staff at Wellington House at the outset; Arnold Toynbee, Lewis Namier, John Masefield, John Buchan, Ian Hay, and Hugh Walpole joined later on. Arnold Bennett and H. G. Wells signed up in 1918. Most of the others, wrote propaganda pieces at the direct request of the government. One of those who did not was Thomas Hardy.[7]

All the writers present at the conference readily agreed to the utmost secrecy, and it was not until J. D. Squires published his story of British propaganda in the First World War in 1935 that it became known that many writers had been used by the government. Unfortunately, it is not easy to reconstruct exactly how the writers were used, since most of the records of Wellington House and the successive Department and Ministry of Information were scattered and destroyed at war's end. A commentator on British official propaganda, Ivor Nicholson, wrote in 1931 that an authoritative history of the subject could never be provided because the three men who could have written it, Masterman himself, G. H. Mair, the journalist and literary critic, and Sir James Headlam-Morley of the Foreign Office, were by that time already dead.[8] This is a great pity since this untold story would have been one of the most significant in the multifarious history of the Great War. But from Nicholson's own account, from references to the subject in other books and articles,[9] and from the files of Wellington House and the successive Department and Ministry of Information that were declassified by the Foreign Office (some as late as 1972), at least part of the story can be pieced together. In one of those files released to the Public Record Office in 1972 is a short history of British propaganda during the 1914–18 war made for the Foreign Office by H. O. Lee when it became necessary to re-institute propaganda at the outbreak of the Second World War. Lee related how the existence of a publishing operation at Wellington House was kept secret and how the work was distributed under the imprint of commercial publishing houses.[10]

In a parliamentary enquiry into the activities of Wellington House in November 1917, H. T. Sherringham, in charge of publications, testified that the agency got commercial houses to print their material in England and paid five guineas for the use of their imprint. He added that some authors received royalties for books published and distributed free by Wellington House. During the same enquiry Masterman testified that Wellington House guaranteed the purchase of a number of copies of pamphlets and books from publishers at a previously agreed price. It became clear to the parliamentary committee, somewhat to their surprise, that the books were used for propaganda purposes at home as well as abroad.[11] Some of the publishing houses used most often by Wellington House were Hodder and Stoughton, Methuen, Blackwood and Sons, John Murray, T. Fisher Unwin, Darling and Son, Macmillan, and Thomas Nelson and Sons.

For a time, unofficial organizations also swelled the chorus of Allied propaganda. Cate Haste has described some of them in *Keep the Home Fires Burning*. The first in the field was the Central Committee for National Patriotic

Associations, formed in the latter part of August 1914. The prime minister, H. H. Asquith, became the honorary president, and the vice-presidents were the Earl of Rosebery and Arthur Balfour. It organized the efforts of some writers, journalists, and politicians to lecture and write pamphlets upon the causes of the war and to justify England's role in the struggle. The committee organized patriotic clubs and rallies throughout Britain and set up subcommittees for various parts of the Empire and for neutral nations. The central committee co-ordinated the activities of groups such as 'The Fight for Right Movement,' founded by Sir Francis Younghusband, which numbered in its ranks such writers as Sir Edmund Gosse, John Buchan, Thomas Hardy, Sir Henry Newbolt, and Gilbert Murray. The Oxford Faculty of Modern History organized a group of historians to write pamphlets, published by the university press, which were also distributed by the central committee.[12]

The invasion of Belgium and the consequent flood of refugees into England was a direct cause of the founding of other patriotic and charity organizations, including the Belgian Relief Fund and the National Relief Committee in Belgium. Many of these groups converted the cause of charity into propaganda work. A favourite method of raising money for these funds was to publish literary anthologies selling for high prices to which many noted writers donated articles, poems, or stories.

The Allies and their enemies, the Central Powers, both recognized that the United States, the richest and most powerful of the neutral nations, had the power to tip the balance of the war, and both concentrated their propaganda efforts there. Great Britain had an enormous advantage in this respect from the start since a common heritage and a common language provided a firm ground for persuasion. But there was a large number of German immigrants and descendants in the United States and a strong reservoir of sympathy for that country, especially among the academics, many of whom had received their graduate training in Germany. However, most German propaganda was crude and inept, and it soon alienated potential support.

Even though many people in the United States were predisposed towards the Allied cause, the task of the Allied propagandists called for discretion and subtlety. It was important not to appear to infringe upon American neutrality; it was equally important not to give ammunition to the strong isolationist element, let alone the pro-German groups. For some time, no attempt was made to bring the United States into the war on the side of the Allies. The major goal of British propaganda in the first two years was to maintain a benevolent neutrality on the part of the United States to ensure the availability of loans and the shipment of foodstuffs and, later, war material. The first, and probably the most effective, of the agents in charge of this work was Sir Gilbert Parker, who was appointed in November 1914 and remained in charge until late in 1916. One of his chief assistants was Arnold Toynbee. Parker was a Canadian by birth and a popular romantic novelist by profession. As a young writer, he had travelled extensively in the United States before marrying a rich New Yorker. He then moved to England, where he became domiciled in 1890. Following one of his own major fictional themes, the young man from the provinces made good in the capital of the empire. He was elected to

Parliament in 1900 and knighted in 1902 for his services to Canada as a writer. He served as M.P. for Gravesend from 1900 to 1919 [...].[13]

Although his romantic imagination was an undoubted asset for his work as a writer of propaganda, Parker's main task was to ensure proper distribution of propaganda material in the United States. In a secret report to the cabinet dated June 1915, Parker described how he set about the work. He made a careful analysis of American press opinion and of the temper of the universities. Then, with the help of *Who's Who*, he prepared a gigantic, categorized mailing list of people in the professions, the church, the press, and the universities who were in the best position to influence public opinion.[14] By December 1914, Wellington House had received from Parker a complete file on the people to whom propaganda should be sent and some indication of what kind of information they should receive. Parker's own connection with propaganda was concealed. Books and pamphlets were sent out not under the name of Wellington House but ostensibly by 'friends' or interested parties to their opposite numbers in the United States. This material, it was claimed in a later enquiry, 'fans out ... in the shape of editorials, reviews, lectures, addresses, speeches, sermons, and so forth to audiences all over the States. ... It is quite undisputable that it has had a powerful shaping influence upon the American mind in regard to all the issues of the war.'[15]

In his part of the report to cabinet, Masterman claimed that Parker had built up an informal organization of thirteen thousand influential people in the United States who were distributing British propaganda. The Carnegie Fund for International Peace, headed by Nicholas Murray Butler, was a particularly useful source of assistance. American presses were also commissioned to publish books and pamphlets from Wellington House, and Parker's lists were made available to them. Parker had excellent working relationships with the senior reporters of the *New York Times* and the *Chicago Daily News*, and he used them for the dissemination of advantageous news and the suppression of bad. British authors, at the instigation of Masterman, had already announced their support of the war in an Authors' Manifesto which appeared in the *New York Times* on 18 September 1914. This was signed by all those present at the Wellington House meeting of 4 September, plus Granville Barker, A. C. Bradley, Laurence Binyon, Rider Haggard, Jerome K. Jerome, Henry Arthur Jones, Eden Philpots, Arthur Pinero, May Sinclair, Sir Gilbert Parker, and others – a total of fifty-four authors. This manifesto was reprinted on a full page of the Sunday supplement of the *New York Times* on 18 October, with the authors' signatures in facsimile – an impressive and apparently spontaneous demonstration of British authors' solidarity [...]. Parker followed this up by arranging a series of interviews and articles by prominent authors in the American press. These included Thomas Hardy, who, although he refused to write any propaganda, did consent to an interview, Arthur Conan Doyle, Henry James, Arnold Bennett, H. G. Wells, G. K. Chesterton, George Trevelyan, Mrs. Humphry Ward, and Israel Zangwill.

A considerable number of American professors volunteered to aid British propaganda efforts. The chief of these was Dr. Charles W. Eliot, former president of Harvard, who became one of the most active and zealous in the Allied cause. Other public figures, like Theodore Roosevelt and Joseph Choate, former ambassador to the Court of St. James, were subtly integrated into the British propaganda effort. 'In fact,' Parker concludes in his secret 1915 report to the cabinet, 'we have an organisation extraordinarily widespread in the United States, but which does not know it is an organisation. It is worked entirely by personal association and inspired by voluntary effort, which has grown more enthusiastic and pronounced with the passage of time. ... Finally, it should be noticed that no attack has been made upon us in any quarter of the United States, and that in the eyes of the American people the quiet and subterranean nature of our work has the appearance of a purely private patriotism and enterprise.'[16] Parker recapitulates some of this material in his next report to the cabinet in February 1916 and adds, tantalizingly, 'By these and other ways (some of a too confidential nature to be placed on paper) we are endeavouring by every various channel to make the two peoples understand each other's point of view ... and to stimulate and thank [sic] a large body of people upon a course favourable to the Allies.'[17]

Given the total lack of preparation for psychological war in Britain, it is remarkable how quickly and effectively the propaganda efforts were organized. Starting from scratch, Masterman had put together an office, engaged staff, and set out the main lines of propaganda production and distribution by the end of 1914. There is no doubt that the main reasons why he was so successful in this complex task was that he had the complete support of the British writing establishment. Without their skills and their quick action, he would have had little to show by the year's end. It is the object of succeeding chapters to show how these skills were put to the task of winning the war.

22 For Country, Conscience and Commerce: Publishers and Publishing, 1914–18

Jane Potter

Just days after the start of the war in Iraq in March 2003, the *Today Programme* on BBC Radio 4 aired a short segment by the journalist Mike Thompson entitled 'War Books', which highlighted the scramble by publishers for soldiers' memoirs.[1] Hodder & Stoughton's representative asserted that 'everybody will want to read about [the war in Iraq]'. Macmillan was touting its potential blockbuster, entitled *Task Force Dagger* about the hunt for Osama bin Laden. When the Macmillan editorial director was questioned as to whether the book was more fiction than fact, embellished with thrilling action in order to make it sell, she replied, 'None of us is a charity. It's not a philanthropic life.' (A comment she immediately followed with, 'Oh my God, I am going to get fired!') Her counterpart at the American firm Simon & Schuster admitted that 'the bloodier this war turns out to be, the more books it's likely to sell.'

This attitude is a far cry from that of publishers in the First World War, as the actions and reactions, both personal and professional, of those of 1914–18 show. Of course the idea of war as a literary commodity is not irrelevant to a study of the Great War book trade, for despite the differences in time and intent of these distinct conflicts, it is an apt concern for both. The bloody conflict that was the Great War did sell books, and although publishers in the First World War were also not charities, as they kept their eyes on the market in order to decide the kind and the volume of war books they would publish, theirs was a commitment not only to commerce – to profit – but also to country and their own consciences. It was a commitment borne not just out of practical necessity: general trade difficulties were coupled with individual personal sacrifice and grief. The house histories of various firms provide insights into the enormous challenges with which publishers were confronted on the outbreak of war in 1914. As F.A. Mumby has noted, the Great War 'shook the book trade, like everything else, to its foundations'.[2] The *Times Literary Supplement* is an invaluable indicator of the contemporary concerns of the trade. Its editorial for December 1914 analysed the situation after three months of war and asserted with relief that the worst fears had not materialised. Whilst the total number of books published was over 800 less than in the previous year of peace, the main slump in numbers 'occurred during the critical months of suspense in the first phase of the war, August and September. Afterwards the recovery was remarkable.'[3] Hopeful that the trade could maintain an even keel,

by August 1915 at the first anniversary of the outbreak of war, the TLS reported
that fiction continued 'to hold its own surprisingly well'. More novels than ever
before were being published because, the periodical opined, after a year of fighting,
'people are turning with relief from the war news to fiction especially to the more
popular novelists.'[4]

Fears that the demand for books would plummet were unfounded. The public
need for reading material, both on the subject of and as a diversion from the war,
was enormous. Those on active service, whether in the trenches or convalescing
in hospital, were an especially captive audience: 'The demand for the novelist who
could dispel the boredom of war was limitless.'[5] [...] [Yet] paper shortages, production costs, and the loss of staff to the Forces all caused anxiety about their commercial futures. [...] Like everyone else in the country, publishers had to grapple
with the enormous practical implications of the War. J.M. Dent, who founded
his eponymous firm in 1888 was by 1917 genuinely concerned that despite the
fact that 'everybody is doing his very best here' the War would force him to 'shut
down'.[6] An able workforce and materials such as leather for binding were increasingly difficult to secure. The outbreak of war brought Dent's Everyman series of
classics almost to a standstill. Established in 1906, the 700th volume of the projected 1,000 had been published in 1914, but the final volume was not published
until 1956. With war inflation forcing both the production and purchase price up,
the gold leaf that was a characteristic feature of the books was replaced by imitation gold: 'war had literally taken the glitter from the Everyman's Library, just as
it had tarnished everything else.'[7]

The Collins brothers also found that rising production costs and shortage of
paper caused them to stop production of their own series of classics, The Nation's
Library. Yet despite the loss of printers, binders, compositors, and other skilled
tradesmen, the firm did manage to devise up-to-date schoolbooks and produce a
large number of Bibles for men in the services. It also tailored its children's fiction
to reflect new 'heroic characters': 'It was hardly surprising that elderly peace-time
dowagers like Juliette the Mail Carrier yielded place to Hunting the U-Boats,
With Beatty in the North Sea and 'Midst Shot and Shell in Flanders'.[8] The Collins
brothers themselves had, from the outset of war, 'a clear view of their duty'.[9]
They enlisted along with 275 of their employees and William Collins IV's Ayrshire
home, Grey Gables, was run as a hospital. The directors contributed an equal sum
for every £1 raised at home to supply comforts to the Collins employees on active
service.

Edward Arnold was also committed to the welfare of his staff and promised all
who 'joined the services that he would find them a job after the war – "even if it
was window-cleaning"'.[10] It was not an easy promise to make. His firm's output
of titles shows the practical effects of wartime shortages and privations. In 1913,
his firm published 98 titles, but this number fell in 1914 to 51. A steady decline
is noted in 1915 with 45 titles published but the following year the number drops
dramatically to 28. The miniscule recovery in 1917 of 29 titles is eclipsed in 1918
by the lowest output since 1890 of 16 titles. Fiction on the Arnold list suffered
particularly with only one title being published in 1916, nine in 1917 and none in

1918, but 'Arnold showed a good publisher's awareness of the war and its implications and published about 30 books on various aspects of the [conflict]'.[11] These
included *The Zeppelin Raid in West Norfolk*, *A Surgeon in Belgium*, *Medical Diseases of
War* and *Struggle in the Air*.

Equally evocative titles helped to maintain William Heinemann's list: they
included *Fighting in Flanders* (E. Alexander Powell 1914), *Outwitting the Hun*
(Lieut. Pat O'Brien 1918), *On Active Service* (Major G.P.A. Phillips 1914), *War
Nursing* (Charles Richet 1918), *The Schemes of the Kaiser* (Madame Adam 1917)
and *From Dartmouth to the Dardanelles* (W.B.C.W. Forester 1916). Yet he also published the work of those writers who are now associated with a canon of disillu-
sioned or anti-war literature: Enid Bagnold, *A Diary without Dates* (1918), Robert
Graves, *Fairies and Fusiliers* (1917), and Siegfried Sassoon, *The Old Huntsman
and Other Poems* (1917) and *The Counter-Attack and Other Poems* (1918). [...]
Heinemann's trade colleagues at Hodder & Stoughton seem to have best weath-
ered the economic, practical, and indeed, ideological storms of the War. From
the outbreak in 1914, the firm's director, Ernest Hodder Williams, and its editor
and literary advisor, Sir William Robertson Nicoll, both believed 'their task was
to preserve unity and boost morale on the home front: it was a prerequisite of
victory [and] they dedicated their minds and energy wholly to the common task
with the high spirit of crusaders.'[12] This stemmed in part, no doubt, from the fact
that both men (Non-Conformist in religion, Liberal in politics) had close personal
ties to the corridors of power. Not only were many Hodder & Stoughton authors
members of Asquith's cabinet (among them, Churchill, Haldane, and Grey), but
the partners were exceptionally well informed about the progress of events': Nicoll
was actually 'given early information that Lloyd George would replace Asquith as
Prime Minister.'[13]

Like other firms, Hodder & Stoughton adapted their output to cater to and
anticipate public interest. They swiftly organised a War Book Department that
produced some of the most profitable and popular books of the War. Hodder &
Stoughton raised enormous amounts for charity with Princess Mary's Gift Book
(1914), which sold 600,000 copies in two years, and King Albert's Book (1914).
In May 1915 it announced in its periodical The Bookman that it would donate
25 per cent of its profits accrued during Booksellers Week to the Red Cross. And,
during that organisation's fund-raising drive the following year, the firm handed
over three pence in every shilling spent on their books. Hodder & Stoughton's
charitable activities did not diminish their commercial success, as the firm
'became increasingly identified with reading for entertainment.'[14] Although John
Attenborough has asserted that the firm's profits were 'deliberately reduced since
large sections of the ... list were devoted to the war charities', writers such as John
Buchan, Ian Hay, 'Sapper' (Herman Cyril McNeile), Ruby M. Ayres, and Berta Ruck
helped to assure both the firm's survival and its brand recognition amongst the
reading public.[15]

Whilst many firms drew on their long-respected reputations, business experience, and cache of dedicated authors to meet the onerous demands of wartime
publishing, it is remarkable that the newly-established firm of George Allen &

Unwin survived the first year of the war, let alone its duration. Having taken control of the bankrupt firm of George Allen on an extremely inauspicious date, 4 August 1914, the young, entrepreneurial Stanley Unwin found that the value of his assets was immediately reduced by about a third, old stock was rendered unsaleable, and sales of many of the standard publications were reduced by as much as 70 per cent. The rising cost of production and the price of paper, which dogged established firms like Heinemann and Dent, threatened to destroy completely the investment Unwin had just made.[16]

The practical problems of War were made even more difficult by Unwin's personal stance. He was from the outset a committed pacifist. To Unwin the War was avoidable, unnecessary, and 'stupid'.[17] [...] Given Unwin's outspokenness on the policies associated with the War, particularly in terms of the books he published, it is perhaps surprising that he was among a group of publishers who gave significant support to the government's propaganda work being undertaken at Wellington House. As Peter Buitenhuis has shown, the government decided early on in the War that Britain required an organisation to counter German propaganda abroad and to convince the neutral nations of the righteousness of Britain's cause. Charles Masterman was chosen as the head of operations and on 2 September 1914, literary figures met to pledge their support for the War, drafting and signing an 'Authors' Manifesto'. Henry Newbolt, Arthur Conan Doyle, Mrs Humphry Ward, May Sinclair, and H.G. Wells were among those who put their signatures to the document that claimed Britain had to join the War or face dishonour. It was printed in the New York Times on 18 September and in the London Times the following month.

Masterman and his colleagues pledged only to disseminate information that was accurate and expressed with measured argument. Sober-sounding documents such as Why We are at War: Great Britain's Case by Members of the Oxford Modern History Faculty (1914) and 'Carry On': British Women's Work in War Time (1917) were the order of the day. Mass distribution was to be avoided and a government imprint absent from all texts; it was felt that the reputable public figures and distinguished scholars writing for a government bureau were more likely to be taken seriously if it did not appear they were working for an official agency. To this end Wellington House pamphlets and books were distributed by mainstream publishers. Secrecy was further maintained by having the Stationery Office act as the official purchasing agent and A.S. Watt, the literary agent, carry out negotiations with the publishers on Wellington House's behalf. Steamship companies, labour organisations and peace societies, the Central Committee for Patriotic Organisations and even the Religious Tract Society all helped to distribute this material. Masterman acknowledged that there would be objections to such covert methods, but he was determined that the literature get 'into the hands of those who will read it' and not 'to thrust it or force it upon those who resent its gifts, or who will merely treat it as waste paper.'[18]

Wellington House transactions with publishers fell into two categories. The first was the purchase of books already on the open market and independent of initial Government backing. One example is Ernest Hodder Williams's memoir of R.J. Davis entitled One Young Man(1917), 'the simple story of a clerk that enlisted in

1914, fought on the western front for nearly two years, was severely wounded at the Battle of the Somme, and is now on his way back to his desk.' Wellington House purchased 776 copies of this book from Hodder & Stoughton for distribution. The second type of transaction entailed the 'purchase' – or what could be more accurately termed commissioning – of books for which there was a need but which 'would not appear [...] if some support were not forthcoming for them.'[19] In this case each publisher was paid five guineas for the use of his imprint and £5 towards the cost of advertising, the '5/5/- arrangement', as it was called. The Schedule of Wellington House Literature, now in the Imperial War Museum (though strictly confidential at the time) shows exactly who these publishers were and what they produced. Hodder & Stoughton published (or provided at 'the lowest terms') the most material for the bureau, over 130 pamphlets and books, evidence of how Williams and Nicoll were indeed 'very close to the central direction of the war'.[20] The books included Arthur Conan Doyle's The German War, Ford Madox Hueffer's When Blood is their Argument, J'Accuse by A. German, and The Front Line by C.E. Montague with drawings by Muirhead Bone. E.F. Benson authored Deutschland Über Allah (1917) that exposed 'Prussianism in Turkey'.

[...] Stanley Unwin's firm, despite all his outward protest against the War, was associated with 13 Wellington House documents, including The Allies' Prospects of Victory, Dangerous Optimism, The Pan-German Programme, and Three Aspects of the Russian Revolution. Of this last text in particular Wellington House ordered – through the Stationery Office – 200 copies from Unwin. It is not surprising that Hodder & Stoughton published so many tracts for the government – its other novels and memoirs are stridently patriotic, independently of any official sanction. But Stanley Unwin's involvement with Wellington House raises a number of questions. How can one be both a patriot and speak out against the government in time of war? How can one be a businessman and still follow the call of conscience? How did Unwin, himself a pacifist, justify his complicity and cooperation? [...] Patriots first or publishers? Patriots, all of these men would have argued. But if we compare the radically different outlook of publishers today, as evidenced from the Iraq war, could we argue that these Great War publishers were merely deluding themselves – and their reader-customers – as to their true motive, which was profit? We could argue this point, but we would be wrong. At the heart of the debate is the fact that the motives of publishers in 1914–18 were different. And these motives stemmed from quite a distinct difference of experience than that faced by those present at the London Book Fair in 2003. It is the personal sacrifices faced by publishers in the Great War that sets them apart and helps us to understand the actions they took and the attitudes they held about the all-encompassing conflict. J.M. Dent's professional troubles could not compare to his grief as a father, something he would have shared with his fellow citizens from all walks of life. Two of his youngest sons, who both entered the firm in 1913, joined up soon after the outbreak. One was killed at Neuve Chapelle, the other at Gallipoli. [...] Indeed, 'death was busy' among the book trade between 1914 and 1918.[21] [...] Despite the efforts of the Publishers' Association, publishing was not classified as a trade of national importance whose employees could be exempted from military service; 'both in the initial enthusiasm for voluntary recruitment in 1914–15,' writes John Feather, 'and in the later conscription to the forces, many good and essential men were lost.'[22] [...] The specific upheavals of 1914–18 therefore ranged from the grief of those who lost a son or other family member on the battlefields, through the concomitant sadness of the firms that suffered huge loss of staff on those same battlefields, to the sacrifices of those publishers who were themselves on active service. Those at home were also faced with practical pressures and personal anxieties as well as the ever-present and very real threat of Zeppelin raids. Unlike recent conflicts in Bosnia, Serbia, Afghanistan, and Iraq, which seem so far removed for the vast majority of the British – and American – populations, the Great War affected everyone. Publishers were close to the conflict in every sense. It was inextricably part of their professional *and* their personal lives. If they themselves did not suffer the loss of a family member, they certainly experienced the loss of members of their staff and knew friends who were bereaved, sometimes more than once. The lists of casualties in the papers and the sight of wounded on the streets escaped no-one's attention. This was truly total war. Publishers in the Great War remained businessmen – the profitability of their companies and how the War might help or hinder them could never have been far from their minds. Commerce and profit were important to keep going. But there was also a commitment to the individual conscience, to a sense of public duty, whether it be whole-heartedly in support of the war effort or more censorious about it. This does not absolve them of publishing what may have been half-truths, hyperbolic sentiments or scare-mongering stories either in their work for Wellington House or in those books and pamphlets arising from their own initiative. But it does go some way to understanding how and why so many acted as they did. [...] The fundamental difference between early 21st-century publishers and their counterparts of 1914–18 – the intertwining of country, conscience and commerce – was, above all, ensured by the roll call of the dead.

23 Publishing and the State: 'Books of Propaganda Value'

Valerie Holman

On 30 May 1940 the MoI had written to the Ministry of Supply and the Treasury spelling out its own paper requirements, but also arguing that book publishers should receive preferential treatment: 'The Ministry [had] reason to fear that if publishers were placed on a par with other non-official users of paper, the effect would be a disproportionate check on the production of books.'[1] It was their value for purposes of public morale and long-term propaganda that prompted this apparently generous gesture. According to the accompanying notes, 'It has been understood that the Ministry will have to charge to its allocation all independent publications to which it gives its support, and in some cases these may be very heavy.' This explains why 'paper is more vitally important to the Ministry of Information than to any other Department'. There were two ways in which the book trade might receive MoI 'support': 'Paper used for publications printed by outside publishers of which the Ministry buys the whole or part for its own purposes; and paper used for books and pamphlets printed by outside publishers and sold through commercial channels with the encouragement or at the instigation of the Ministry', a category under which at that time the MoI was asking the Ministry of Supply for 620 tons of paper. Publishers were still fighting for survival, yet there was no doubt within the MoI that books had cultural and symbolic value, nor that they were an effective means of boosting morale and discreetly spreading propaganda.

A chart recording the MoI's monthly consumption of paper from June 1940 to July 1941 shows that it was directed to a wide variety of externally-produced publications, including Oxford Pamphlets on World Affairs and war-related pamphlets from Macmillan and Longmans; foreign editions of *Picture Post* (fifty thousand copies in Portuguese); and periodicals such as *La France Libre* on a regular basis. Individual titles included *The Freedom We Defend* (25 tons in August 1940) and Puffin books (six tons in February 1941). An anonymous handwritten note to the Deputy Director General pointed out that 'Anyone who attempts to impose a real paper ration on the Ministry will at once come up against the objection – not altogether unfounded – that he is preventing the War Divisions from doing their job. This is the crux of the whole matter.'[2]

In the exchanges about paper consumption which took place between the Ministry of Supply and the Ministry of Information in January 1942, it was revealed that the MoI's quarterly allocation for September–November had been 440 tons, but 872 tons had been consumed. Of this, 62.5 tons had been allocated to book publishers – who had used only a third of this amount. 'The failure to reach the estimate was due to the caution used in drawing on this pool while the scheme for using 250 tons per annum to influence the policy of private publishers is still in its opening stages.'[3] The MoI now had a special reserve (250 tons) from which it could contribute up to 50 per cent of the paper needed for a book judged to be of propaganda value, and published commercially. As this revealing comment suggests, paper could be very persuasive: publishers had to produce books to survive, and if their own quota of paper was exhausted, then additional supplies from an external source, albeit for a specific title, might prove decisive. The MoI played a significant role in the wartime book trade as enabler and distributor, but through paper allocations from its special reserve it helped steer publishers towards producing one type of book at the expense of another. There was though, considerable sensitivity to censorship within the Ministry, the MoI casuistically exonerating itself as follows: 'The relation of printed matter to the furtherance of the war effort is not only not a censorship in any invidious sense but a conservation, but also it is in tune with the new but popular taste for austerity and it is a means of intensifying the essential prosecution of the War.'[4]

Books supported by the MoI were not straightforward propaganda: such publications would too closely have resembled those emanating from National Socialist Germany. Instead, they tended to highlight certain positive features of British history, culture, achievement or sensibility. Two examples, each published in 1942 and subsequently reprinted or translated, serve to illustrate the way in which the MoI acquired or encouraged particular texts with an underlying message to which it was sympathetic. There were in essence three readerships for such books: neutral countries yet to be persuaded to the Allied cause; Americans hovering on the brink of isolationism (until the bombing of Pearl Harbor at the end of 1941); and countries currently occupied by the enemy for whom Britain needed to be portrayed as an exemplar of democracy with a leading role to play in the future of Europe.

Andrew Butler was the official Ruin Recorder for the Royal Borough of Chelsea, who also belonged to a team of architects who had formed a voluntary protection service in response to an appeal from the Surveyor to the Fabric of St Paul's Cathedral. *Recording Ruin* is a diary of his early wartime activities, its style and anecdotes by turn affectionate, engaging, touching or humorous. Vividly conjuring up the strangeness of the world he now inhabits, he is clearly under the spell of those official war artists deputed to depict the aftermath of the Blitz, describing a church with its roof blown off as 'an ugly building but quite picturesque as a ruin, all red and scorched inside. Today's black sky helped it to look a little like one of Piper's modern paintings of fire and desolation.'[5] With a sharp eye for incongruities thrown up by the indiscriminate results of German aerial attack, in a recently-bombed mansion he sees a large clock disembowelled by a toppled statue, and the chaos crowned by a broken jar of marmalade. As a counterpoint to the destruction of property and life he witnesses at first hand, phrases such as 'it's a dull war in London', or 'nothing much is happening. One just goes on' convey the stoical resistance and refusal to be cowed that was just the face the MoI wished Britain to present to the rest of the world.

Where Butler showed the strength of the individual human spirit and nature of British pluck, Ernest Barker, Professor of Political Science at Cambridge, focused on Government, Community and the State in *Britain and the British People*. In 1940 OUP had launched a series called 'The World Today', starting with D.W. Brogan's *USA*. At the end of 1941, when a companion volume on Great Britain was needed for distribution in America (also to be translated into Spanish, Portuguese and French), Humphrey Milford of OUP set out the project in a letter to Barker: 'It ought to "sell" England as a democracy that works and that is not so far behind the times as many Americans believe us to be. I think a fair amount of space ought to be given to the social services and emphasis laid on the initiative that we have shown in that and many other fields. That is much more important than a description of the countryside.'[6] It would be 'a very great contribution to the war effort' and 'The Government would buy large quantities and will be eager to translate and distribute.' At first Barker refused on the basis that whatever he wrote would be voted too high-brow, and suggested J.B. Priestley in his stead but, won over by Milford's persuasive charm, he eventually capitulated. Published in 1942, the book went out of print only in 1964. The first two impressions amounted to 15,000 copies with a further 17,000 printed in 1944, eventually reaching a total of 44,000, but 'sales of the Oxford edition were very small compared with the total of the translations'.[7] This is borne out by an MoI chart showing the progress of books being printed in foreign languages by outside firms. On 21 July 1944 the job of printing 13,500 copies of *Britain and the British People* in Dutch was put in hand, but it was not passed for press until the following May, with an estimated delivery date of August 1945, the same delivery date given for 47,200 copies of the French edition which had also been put in hand a year before, on 25 August 1944: the day France was liberated. Despite the backlog, in June 1945, when quantities were adjusted after the end of the war in Europe, the MoI ordered French translations of an additional 27,000 copies for France, 10,000 for Belgium, 1900 for the colonies, and 5000 for Canada.[8]

A series was even more effective than an individual title, and none more so than Britain in Pictures, the brainchild of Hilda Matheson.[9] She was invited to become the first Director of the Joint Broadcasting Committee (eventually placed under the aegis of the BBC rather than either the MoI or the Foreign Office) which was in effect two organisations: one overt, whose remit was to broadcast to the UK and friendly countries, and one covert, which meant that Matheson reported to Section D of M16 dealing with the spread of information to enemy countries. Hilda Matheson died in October 1940 before seeing her publishing project realised, but it proved a very visible tribute to her initiative. The original editorial committee had comprised W.J. Turner (poet, musician, journalist and the JBC's Musical Director) who became the General Editor of the series after her death, and Dorothy Wellesley, later Duchess of Wellington, whose home 'Penns in the Rocks' was the original imprint for early volumes, and a drawing of whose temple to Yeats in the grounds features as a publisher's device on the title-page of each volume.[10]

Britain in Pictures was published by William Collins in association with Adprint, a company founded in 1937 by Wolfgang Foges, responsible for the concept of King Penguins, and largely staffed by Austrian refugees including Walter Neurath, the future founder of Thames and Hudson. Adprint sold itself as a book-packaging company but, having no paper quota itself, had to use paper from another publishing firm such as Collins, for whom it would produce illustrated books in photogravure.[11] Launched in March 1941, the series had a distinctive format and texts commissioned from many of Britain's best-known contemporary authors, including Graham Greene (who wrote *British Dramatists* on a boat bound for West Africa), George Orwell (*The English People*) and John Betjeman (*English Cities and Small Towns*). Each volume sold for 3s. 6d. and contained reproductions of English art from manuscripts to contemporary paintings and drawings, creating a sense of historical continuity and promoting the work of officially sponsored war artists. Rose Macaulay's *Life Among the English*, for example, includes drawings by both Henry Moore and Anthony Gross. Of the twenty illustrations, twelve were in black and white and eight in colour, reproduced photographically according to a special Adprint process already used to good effect in the first King Penguins. The editor, W.J. Turner, admitted at the launch that 'my chief interest in this series of books is not so much their undoubted usefulness as propaganda among neutrals … as their possible stimulus to ourselves.'[12] From the start, they were also seen as collectables and attractive Christmas gifts, promoted on the front cover of *The Bookseller* on New Year's Day 1942 – and again on the series' first birthday, by which time total sales had exceeded 181,000 despite a one shilling price rise. On the fourth occasion when Britain in Pictures featured on *The Bookseller*'s front cover, it was described as 'a large and comprehensive scheme, forming a highly important contribution to the national war effort'.[13] By the end of 1943 over sixty volumes had been published and sales had exceeded half a million.

Although apparently a commercial enterprise, in effect the series both originated in and was supported by the MoI, which bought a substantial number of copies and selectively translated those it felt appropriate to distribute as positive propaganda for Britain. Initially, five books were translated into French, each published in an edition of 10,000: *British Rebels and Reformers, British Trades Unions, The Government of Britain, English Social Services* and *Life Among the English*. The most successful volume in the UK was James Fisher's *Birds of Britain* (total sales reached 84,000), closely followed by books on flowers and wildlife, but selections for foreign markets indicate that a less pastoral and more political (i.e. democratic) image of Britain was being officially promoted overseas.[14]

Behind the scenes, though, Britain in Pictures was not an unmitigated triumph. Authors, agents and publishers were all deeply unhappy about the form of contract in use, and matters came to a head in June 1943. At that time, the contract between W.J. Turner (general editor) and the author stipulated that the author would receive £50 but had to assign copyright to the general editor who, by another contract, re-assigned it to Adprint. Given that the first edition of each volume was now being issued in a print-run of eighteen thousand, the Society of Authors calculated that, had royalties been paid even at the low rate of five per cent, each author would have earned £200.

William Collins, anxious to dispel any myths about the profitability of the enterprise so far, stated that from December 1939 to December 1942 the

Editorial Committee (which by 1943 was W.J. Turner alone) had received £3326 and paid out £1700 to authors. In 1940–41, Adprint had made a loss of £1500; in 1941–42 it made a profit of £1760. Adprint now willingly agreed to pay royalties, and even suggested that authors should receive 50 per cent of any monies made from the exploitation of foreign rights, but the firm remained adamant that it should retain copyright. William Collins himself was mystified by such intransigence, adding that his own firm 'would never think of taking the copyright in an author's work in return for an outright payment'. He was also concerned that if retrospective royalties were to be paid, Turner would be substantially out of pocket.[15]

What had begun as a propaganda scheme was, by September 1943, a more or less commercial venture. Collins paid the producers, Adprint, a fixed sum for a specified number of copies of each book and took the entire English edition. It was Collins who supplied most of the paper, with a small amount coming from the Government. According to the Society of Authors' minutes:

Although it might seem on the face of it that a great deal of money was being made on the series, in fact Messrs Collins made less out of Britain in Pictures books than out of any other books which they published. They made only six per cent in the case of sales of Britain in Pictures volumes in this country and they made a loss in the case of all copies sold in New Zealand, Australia and South Africa, copies in these countries having to be sold to booksellers at 2s. 6d. a copy. Mr Collins said that the cost of colour work was tremendous and that a great deal of money certainly went in the payment by Adprint to the colour experts and photographers engaged.[16]

To which, unsurprisingly, the Management Committee of the Society of Authors protested that this was at the expense of those who provided the texts.

Two months and many meetings later, Collins and Foges of Adprint were prepared to revise the contract with their contributors: the £50 outright payment would now cover only the first 20,000 copies of each title, and above that, there would be a pro rata payment; each contributor would be paid 75 per cent of the profits from translation rights, and Turner had agreed that in future he would take a licence rather than copyright. By a majority vote, the Society of Authors refused to accept this without modification, and threatened Adprint and Collins with stringent sanctions if they would not make yet further changes.[17] Interestingly, the Society felt its hand had been weakened by the passivity of literary agents: only A.D. Peters had protested at authors having to forfeit their copyright. For all members of the Committee this was a test case, but for different issues: Charles Morgan saw Britain in Pictures as the thin end of a wedge which might result in 'publishers returning to the evil practice whereby authors were treated as hacks and paid an outright sum for their work without any share in the proceeds of publication' whereas Cecil Day-Lewis was particularly interested in the series as typifying a new type of publication in which 'the drawings and diagrams were the principal part ... and the text in fact simply "illustrated" these drawings and diagrams'.[18] The Chairman added a further point: 'With the appearance of producers like Adprint a new phenomenon of a third party between publisher and author had arisen.'

The main clauses of the final agreement included safeguards for omnibus editions and for authors who wished to re-use their material elsewhere, and on 15 February 1944 'the Committee unanimously agreed that the Society had every reason to feel extremely well pleased with the result of the negotiations'.[19] Ushering in the opportunity for the Society of Authors (with the support of agents) to make a strong stand, and anticipating an era in which packaging and illustration would become even more important aspects of book publishing, the significance of this series went well beyond its origins in propaganda.

24 Books for the Forces

Joe Pearson

The importance of, and appetite for, the printed word before and during the
· Second World War cannot be overstated. In today's world, where the information
highway to the global village is only a mobile phone call away, it is almost impossible to visualise a world where paper was rationed and the radio was the major
source of national news. In such an environment, Penguin Books was to play a
major role in supplying the reading needs for a population desperate for information and entertainment.

At the outbreak of war the authorities were faced with the simply enormous
challenge of how both to inform and educate the massive numbers of civilians who
had been called up to serve in the Armed Forces:

> After the Munich agreement of September 1938 and following the entry of the
> Nazis into Prague six months later, public opinion had crystallised. For all that,
> when the uneasy peace finally gave way to war, there were many going into the
> forces who had no clear idea of the issues at stake: of what, in short, the 'war
> was all about'. An even larger number knew little of citizenship or 'of the mean-
> ing, structure and ultimate aims of a British democracy'.
>
> *Education in the Forces 1939–45*, N. Scarlyn Wilson, 1948

One of the prime movers in promoting the cause for education for the forces was
the Workers' Educational Association which, as early as May 1939, was already lob-
bying for a comprehensive educational scheme for the troops who had already been
conscripted. Penguin collectors will be familiar with one of the leading lights of the
W.E.A. – William Emrys Williams.

The promotion of education within the forces eventually became the remit of
the Central Advisory Council recommending in their memo 'Education in the Wartime Army' of September 1940 to the Army Council, that 'mental contentment
as well as physical comfort was essential to efficient soldiering and high morale'.
There was, it pointed out, a real danger that, accustomed in civil life to fend for
himself, the soldier with his life ordered and 'his daily requirements automatically
met' would find his mind deadened and his brain 'cloakroomed for the duration',
once the novelty of Army life had worn off.

The need then to promote a well informed and educated Fighting Force was
undeniable and, at the very outset of the war, the Library Association was quick to
set up a committee to work out a scheme for supplying books to the forces. At its
first meeting in October 1939 it resolved to call a conference to which the branches
of the Armed Forces, the Board of Education, the YMCA and other interested parties were invited. The Library Association was eventually to take on the role of

selecting books, assembling them into organised libraries and then distributing them to units. However the most immediate task was to provide books for the Expeditionary Force in France. As a first step, 100,000 selected books were brought and dispatched to the British Expeditionary Force to arrive in time for Christmas. These books were noted as being mostly of the 'Penguin and Pelican type' and so from the very outset Penguin Books' relationship with the forces was established.

The difficulties faced by the authorities in supplying books to the forces were considerable: not only was there the task of collecting and assembling libraries at a time when fewer titles were being published, but the physical difficulties of supplying books to the far-flung troops presented further hurdles. Also, the variety and variation of the forces that needed to be supplied with reading materials were vast: troops on active service; the Merchant Navy; Hospital Libraries; Hospital Ships; Convalescent Homes; Prisoner of War camps containing thousands of men; and then isolated Units of less than ten men, such as those serving in searchlight batteries. All needed to be catered for and the sheer scale of the task must have been enormous.

There was also the added burden of paper rationing which inevitably led to shorter print runs and fewer titles being published. The paper allocation to publishers was calculated as a percentage of their bulk use of paper at the outbreak of war. In this respect Penguin were more fortunate than their rival publishers, in that their pre-war sales, particularly of the Penguin Specials, had been phenomenal and consequently they received a very generous allocation of paper. Also Penguins, by their very nature, required far less paper to produce a book than their rivals, who used more expensive materials and Penguin were thus able to produce a greater number of books per ton. This resulted in Penguin having a virtual monopoly of paperback publishing as the longer established hardback publishers now lacked the paper allocation to compete with Penguin. These publishers did eventually collaborate and launch the Guild series of paperbacks but it was a rather unsuccessful rival to Penguin.

In the early stages of the war the situation wasn't particularly arduous and book production, although reduced, was fairly healthy. However, by the Christmas of 1941, the allocation of paper to the publishers had been reduced to 37% of pre-war consumption for books and to 20% for magazines. In such an environment Penguin now found themselves unable to meet the huge demand for books and printed materials and this drastically affected all aspects of the book trade, from retailers to customers, especially those in the forces.

The bulk of the task of supplying books for the forces was left to the voluntary organisations, in particular to the Red Cross and also to a lesser extent the YMCA. These organisations launched numerous appeals for second-hand books and were assisted in their task by other appeals such as those organised by individual towns, for example The Lord Mayor of London Appeal. Indeed the *Sunday Times* and later the 'Times Book Club' launched its own appeal under the slogan 'Give A Good Book', and W.I.s, department stores, churches, Scout groups and Post Offices all did their bit to gather in the harvest of books and magazines.

At the end of May 1940, the Postmaster-General authorised free transmission of books and periodicals left at post offices in any part of the country. Penguin collectors will be familiar with the entreaty printed inside many Penguins from that date.

FOR THE FORCES

When you have read this book, please leave it at your nearest Post Office, so that the men and women in the Services may enjoy it too.

These appeals were very successful, particularly in the early stages of the war. In the first year of the war the London headquarters of the Red Cross received some 500,000 books as gifts but this level of success was not maintained and the following year's appeal only attracted 255,000 and by 1944–5 this had further shrunk to 137,891. This early success was in part due to gifts from Londoners giving up their homes because of air-raids but the paucity of new publications, enemy damage and fierce competition for books led to a decline in the numbers of books raised by public appeal.

The contribution made to these appeals by way of recycled Penguins was enormous, particularly to the hospital library service operated by the Red Cross. The hospital library service, especially in the earlier years of the war, handled almost entirely second-hand books and paper-bound publications. Penguins were especially popular for hospital reading, being light in weight, but were found to have a short life unless cased in stronger bindings. At the London headquarters of the Hospital Library Service, three rooms were set aside for the work of rebinding, repairing, and casing. These activities were carried out by a staff of voluntary workers under the supervision of a professional bookbinder and one room was specifically set aside for 'Penguin' binding. Red Cross records for the London headquarters record that the 'Penguin' binding room was opened on 31 March 1941 and its total output was 111,208. Other binding and repair centres were also established in many London boroughs and in most counties. To arrive at even an approximate total of Penguins treated in this way is impossible, for records were not always kept. Those that were give some indication of the scale of this activity. The Westminster depot, in just under six years, collected, mended and recased 66,177 whilst one county, in twelve months, bound and repaired 14,177 volumes.

TO THE FIGHTING SERVICES
WHEREVER YOU MAY BE
WITH BEST WISHES
FROM
THE RESIDENTS OF
WORTHING RURAL DISTRICT
SUSSEX.

The official history of the Red Cross & St. John War Organisation 1939–1947 describes these activities:

By using voluntary labour, the cost of binding was very low. On the basis of an output of 230 books per five-day week, it came to just under 8d. per volume, of which 5d. represented the proportion of the professional bookbinder's wages and the remainder boards, paper book cloth, glue, paste, mull and extras. 'Penguin' binding was done entirely by voluntary labour; the cost – three volumes a penny at August, 1942 – was kept to a minimum by gifts of wallpaper, by using the backs of old books from the binding room, and by generous concessions from firms supplying book cloth – one for instance, met the purchase tax on material.

Between September 1939 and September 1945 the London headquarters of the Hospital Library Service distributed at home 948,375 books and magazines, the county depots another 1,745,445 books and a further 1,777,258 books were dispatched overseas by London. In all, for home and overseas, the hospital library service from London headquarters and the county depots, distributed more than 6,220,000 books and magazines. Although it is impossible to calculate how many, clearly hundreds of thousands of Penguins had their lives extended and found useful service. Indeed it isn't too difficult today to unearth examples of these 'rebound' Penguins in bookshops around the country where a glimpse inside will often be rewarded with enticing mementos of their journeys.

25 The American Publisher's Series Goes to War, 1942–1946

John B. Hench

The Second World War exalted the importance of books in many ways, most of all by clearly demonstrating the ambivalent power of books to foster evil as well as good. What was good and what was evil, of course, lay in the eye of the beholder. During the run-up to the war, the Nazis reactively burned or banned millions of books that they deemed a threat to their noxious ideology. *Proactively*, Goebbels and others of Hitler's henchmen published and circulated masses of books and other printed materials in conformity to the tenets of party doctrine. For its part, the US government, in anticipation of Hitler's defeat, responded by purchasing and funding the special publication of large numbers of American books to accomplish the goal of weaning the civilians in both overrun and aggressor nations from years of Goebbels's propaganda. As part of this undertaking, many of the burned-or-banned books were symbolically rubbed in the noses of the citizens of the shattered Third Reich. In concluding that, of all the media, books had the longest-term effect on people's minds, the government endorsed the cornerstone of the publishers' professional ideology, the notion that books were uniquely suited to perform vital cultural work.[1]

No less a personage than President Roosevelt pronounced books to be 'weapons in the war of ideas' against the fascist powers, and with his blessing a coalition of private and governmental organisations sent them into battle on both sides of the Atlantic. The war even emboldened American book publishers to become far more active players in the world's markets than they had previously contemplated or even desired. Books in series became the dominant vehicle for these vital wartime programmes.

My interest in the wartime work of books and other printed material stems from the collecting and scholarly research and writing that I have pursued for nearly a decade. I started to collect American books, magazines and newspapers that were published for the purpose of advancing certain important military, political and propaganda goals. By definition, magazines and newspapers are published in series. It soon became clear to me, however, that most of the books I came to own had also been issued in series. My collecting led directly into the research that has culminated in my book, *Books as Weapons: Propaganda, Publishing, and the Battle for Global Markets in the Era of World War II* (Ithaca, NY: Cornell University Press, 2010), from which this chapter draws material. In doing both the collecting and the research, I discovered additional war-related series of books. Preparing for this chapter gave me the chance to think about how the intellectual and marketing concepts behind the series I was collecting and studying, as well as the physical nature of the books in the series, were particularly appropriate to the needs and demands of wartime publishing and propaganda.

In this chapter, I briefly describe the various series and the circumstances of their creation, production and circulation. It is important to realise that all of these processes had to be carried out in a state of emergency, with stakes incredibly high, time short and resources limited. From there, I explore such questions as how and why the series model was well suited to wartime use, how the wartime series differed from the series norm, and how *these* particular series influenced the post-war direction of book publishing and book consumption not only in the United States but throughout the world.

The most famous of these special wartime series was the one called Armed Services Editions. Produced by the Council on Books in Wartime, a non-profit wartime agency of the publishing industry, with funding and worldwide distribution provided by the army and navy, 123 million copies of 1,322 eclectic titles were put, free of charge, into the hands of US forces in all theatres of the war. Of course, these books were meant to help soldiers and sailors to use to good advantage the time available within the 'hurry up and wait' military routine. Altogether, the books provided entertainment, cultural enrichment and education, particularly on how to prepare for success in civilian life after the war. The books, which were selected by the army and the navy, included world classics as well as more current fare, in all genres and appealing to all brow-levels.[2] For publishers, participating in the series not only contributed directly to the war effort by benefiting the morale of the military, it also held promise for stimulating the domestic market for books after the troops came home. If the great interest soldiers and sailors had shown in reading books during the war continued afterwards, Council member William Sloane remarked, the Armed Services Editions plan would 'justify itself 100 times over'.[3] The publishers didn't even have to dip into their own paper rations in the production of these special editions.

So that they could be printed economically on fast rotary presses used in peacetime for magazines and catalogues but under-utilised in wartime, most of the Council Books, as they were also called, appeared in an unusual, landscape format in two trim sizes, with the text arrayed in two columns per page, rather than one, which produced a shorter, more legible line. Though this format arose out of expediency, it resulted in a convenient size and shape for fitting into a soldier's tunic or pack and to be read comfortably while lying on one's back in a hospital bed, as one war correspondent observed.[4] After the war was over and greater and more varied press capacity became available, the last titles – produced for troops occupying Germany and Japan – were published in the standard portrait paperback format that had become prevalent in the USA in the 1930s. The Armed Services Editions were described, shortly after the war had ended, as 'the greatest mass publishing enterprise of all history',[5] a judgement that may remain unchallenged more than sixty years later.

Though by far the largest and most important, the ASEs (or Council books) were not the only series intended for GIs. Next in significance was the Fighting Forces Series, which was initiated by the *Infantry Journal*, an influential semi-official professional publication for infantry officers since its establishment in the early 1900s. Some of the titles were published by *Infantry Journal* alone, others through a loose but inventive and highly effective partnership between *Infantry Journal* and the American branch of Penguin Books. Most of the titles in the Fighting Forces series were on some military subject or other. They provided service personnel with information on military strategy, tactics and materiel, as well as descriptions of the enemies they faced and of the history, geography, flora and fauna of the places to which they were being sent to fight.[6] A key figure on the Penguin side of this enterprise was Kurt Enoch, who had come to the USA as a refugee from Hitler's Europe, and who neatly connects the Fighting Forces series with two legendary series, Albatross Modern Continental Library, which he had co-founded, and Tauchnitz Editions, which he had acquired [...].[7] Another specialist publisher, the Military Service Publishing Company, started a series called Superior Reprints, also in cooperation with Penguin USA. This line mainly featured not-very-challenging popular novels.[8]

Pocket Books, Inc., the pioneer American paperback publisher of modern times, also issued books for the soldier market, which were confusingly also designated as Armed Services Editions. Some were marked as for free distribution, while containing in the back matter lists of other Pocket Books titles available for 25 cents each. Besides issuing its own armed forces editions, Pocket Books actively promoted the sale of all of its titles by urging civilians to purchase and mail the books to loved ones in the service.[9]

Some of the most interesting, and least known, of the wartime American series were those that were not published for the GI Joes and GI Janes overseas or in training camps stateside. Among them are the two related series – Overseas Editions and Transatlantic Editions – that prompted me to undertake my research project and that form the core of my book. Both series were published to be put in the hands of European and Asian citizens as soon as possible after the defeat of the Axis powers.

Like the Armed Services Editions, the Overseas Editions were published in New York by a subsidiary of the Council on Books in Wartime in partnership with an arm of the government – in this case, the Office of War Information (OWI), the chief propaganda agency. Overseas Editions consisted of forty-one separate titles in seventy-two editions in English, French, Italian and German, all manufactured in the USA and shipped to overseas markets, where they were to be sold rather than given away. For various reasons, OWI produced the Transatlantic Editions through its London office – ten titles in French and ten in Dutch. These books were typeset and printed in Britain, using American paper, but they bore a New York imprint of Transatlantic Editions in Dutch or French.[10]

The Overseas and Transatlantic editions reflected separate, but manifestly complementary, goals of their two sponsors, the OWI and the private, non-profit Council on Books in Wartime, which the publishing industry had created in 1942 to focus its contributions to the war effort. For OWI, the exhaustively selected titles were meant to respond to the figurative and literal hunger of war-torn peoples for books free of the taint of Axis ideology and censorship and to liberate their minds from the intellectual blackout that the war had produced. For the publishers who made up the Council, the projects offered them a golden opportunity to gain a foothold in overseas markets, in which they had shown little interest until the wartime damage to the British and European book trades created a vacuum.

Another foreign-language series – Bücherreihe Neue Welt ('New World Bookshelf') – has an especially interesting publishing history.' Twenty-two titles in twenty-four volumes, all in German, were published for German prisoners of war held in camps in the United States. Like the Overseas and Transatlantic editions, these books were sold. The internees could afford to buy them because they earned small amounts of cash from required or voluntary labour in the camps and from the sale of handmade crafts. The project was undertaken late in the war when it was felt necessary to provide some formal re-education to the prisoners in anticipation of their repatriation to the defeated and devastated former Third Reich. Responsibility for the top-secret series lay with the army's Office of the Provost Marshal General, which had custody of the POWs. Handling the production and distribution were two silent partners – once again the *Infantry Journal* and the US branch of Penguin Books. Most of the texts were supplied by the rights holder, Gottfried Bermann-Fischer, a refugee German Jewish publisher and heir to the noted German publishing house, S. Fischer Verlag, who ultimately found refuge in New York in 1940. About three-quarters of the selections were books by contemporary German writers (mostly Jews) that had been proscribed by the Nazis. The remainder were American-authored titles and a few other books that Bermann-Fischer had already published in German translation through his Stockholm branch-in-exile.[11]

There are some other books worth mentioning, which may or may not meet the criteria for being a publisher's series. These were books published in foreign languages in New York largely for audiences of refugees from Hitler. There are, for example, at least three series of books published in French by firms in New York City. The targeted audiences for these were French émigrés in countries throughout the Americas, as well as Francophones around the world whose normal supply of books in French had been cut off by the war. The most notable of these was a series called Éditions de la Maison Française. The publishers were immigrants of Sephardic Jewish ancestry from Turkey and Greece who moved to the USA in the 1920s and set up a French-language bookstore in Manhattan. The shop existed until 2009. Anyone who visited Rockefeller Center in New York before then probably saw it, the Librairie de France, directly across from St Patrick's Cathedral. If so inclined, one can still purchase pristine copies of many of their wartime titles from the firm's website. André Maurois, himself in exile in New York, was the chief patron of this enterprise, which included a number of his books on its list.[12]

The other French series were similar in purpose and content to the EMFs. One was published under the name Éditions Didier and the other by the New York and Paris bookseller Brentano's.[13] Titles with the Maison Française and Didier imprints have numbers attached to them, as would befit a series. Their covers are also very uniform, but it is a uniformity of general house style and French convention, rather than specifically the uniformity of a series.

How can we define the characteristics of these various series? How much do they have in common with each other? How do they differ from the classic series of the nineteenth and twentieth centuries, like Ticknor & Fields Blue and Gold Series, Tauchnitz, the Railway Library, Albatross and the Modern Library?

First of all, they were all designed to meet one or more specific wartime needs, which included:

- providing recreational and educational books for the American armed forces;
- putting American books carefully selected for their propaganda value into the hands of civilians in liberated and Axis countries;
- re-educating German POWs prior to their repatriation;
- producing books for émigrés cut off from their homeland;
- giving publishers more access to paper, printing facilities and markets;
- providing visibility for American books in order to capture overseas and domestic markets after the war.

Even though the sponsors clearly hoped the wartime series would stimulate post-war demand, the series themselves were entirely ad hoc efforts, with no pretensions as to permanence as series. They were also highly improvised. Most were established *as* series only after other methods of satisfying the stated needs proved inadequate. For example, previous efforts to take random public donations of used books for the troops turned up too many useless and hard-to-ship titles, so plan B was the highly successful, made-to-order Armed Services Editions. Similarly, the Overseas and Transatlantic series came about because the supply of publishers' in-stock titles in English, let alone in the required foreign languages, was inadequate to meet the anticipated post-liberation demand abroad. In the case of the books for German POWs, domestic supply was likewise wanting, so a special series was commissioned.

The most significant of these series were produced with close ties to one US government agency or another, whether the army and navy, the OWI or the Office of the Provost Marshal General, but all were actually 'published' by a non-governmental entity, in the case of books aimed at foreign nationals, to mask the true origins of the books.

All the books were published in one or two standard formats. Nearly all were paperbacks, though one of the Éditions Didier titles I own is in a publisher's cloth binding. Most of the series numbered the titles in one or more sequences. The uniformity of the formats is not only a principal characteristic of publishers' series in general, but for wartime purposes it also greatly simplified the task not only of manufacturing the books but all the packing and shipping of them overseas, whether to GIs or liberated civilians, all the more so because the books were in paper rather than hard covers.

Aspects relating to the design and other paratextual features were critical elements of their character and are well worth consideration.[14] The element of uniformity of design and format, first of all, helped to create, or draw on, familiarity.

For example, the producers of the Overseas and Transatlantic editions consciously rejected the landscape format that worked so well for the Armed Services Editions in favour of a portrait paperback purposely designed to resemble the typical paperbacks of France and elsewhere in Europe. These were squatter than the typical British or American paperback, generally with tan covers printed in black and red, with few graphic touches. The books published by the three French publishers in New York were virtually identical in design to the Gallimard, Grasset and other Paris publishers' titles that the Librarie de France and Brentano's had been importing and selling in their stores for years. The publishers of these wartime series also took advantage of the characteristic of series that historians Jay Satterfield and John Spiers, among others, have noted: that is, that such books were designed, branded, marketed and sold as a coherent whole, rather than as an assortment of individual titles.[15]

Moreover, many of the paratextual features included in the books gave clear signals as to what the readers were meant to gain from reading them and, more subtly, what the sponsors wished to accomplish. The books aimed at foreign readers contained blurbs on the back cover that noted the propaganda goals (without calling them such) that the books were chosen in order to accomplish. For example, the blurb for David Lilienthal's *TVA: Democracy on the March* pointedly demonstrated that a democracy could successfully engage in social planning no less than a fascist or communist state, while Bernard Jaffe's *Men of Science in America* countered Nazi propaganda that the USA lagged in major accomplishments in the basic sciences. Bücherreihe Neue Welt titles also carried blurbs that performed propaganda work. On the back cover of John Scott's *Jenseits des Ural: Ein Arbeiter in Stahlzentrum Russlands*, for example, it was made clear that the POW readers were supposed to gain a view of America's ally the Soviet Union different from the one they had been supplied by their leaders.[16] The back-cover blurbs of ASEs were similar to what would have appeared on the original editions, including complimentary 'puffs' from noted critics and journalists. This plus the fact that the covers of the ASEs featured images of the dust jackets of the publishers' own editions was a clear sign that the firms wanted to promote their products to the GIs, who would, some day soon, be returning home and to civilian life.

The 'series-ness' of these publications was important, even crucial, to accomplishing their assigned wartime work: that is, getting them produced efficiently, on budget and as much on schedule as political, economic and technical conditions allowed them to be. Publication and translation rights for the ASEs, OEs and TEs, about which I know the most, were cleared en masse. The books were ganged-up for printing and binding. Because they were parts of a series, and the whole was greater than the sum of its parts, individual titles could be dropped during the production cycle for any number of reasons and other titles meeting the same propaganda criteria easily substituted for them. The series format produced some cost savings. For example, all the Overseas Editions were printed by the same firm, thus gaining a volume discount for the government. Volume-buying was not possible for the typesetting of the books, however, because virtually all composing houses were offered far more work than they could possibly handle, so composition had to be parcelled out to many firms. Moreover, buying good *foreign*-language typesetting commanded few if any discounts.[17] Insofar as rights holders and vendors could persuade themselves that, by participating in these programmes, they were providing patriotic service to the war effort, the governmental connections also helped, at least occasionally, to keep costs down and production on the fast track.

Finally, these series, for the most part, operated outside the normal market forces of book publishing, including other publishers' series, like Tauchnitz and the Modern Library. The choice of books to include tended to reflect the strategic goals of the series' creators more than the presumed wishes of the intended audiences, especially in the case of the series aimed at German POWs and civilians abroad. The greatest number of these books (namely, the ASEs) were given away. Others, to be sure, were sold – to civilians abroad and German prisoners of war, for example – but the products were created by US governmental entities, far removed from their customers. To varying degrees, the books were intended for 'captive' audiences. This was quite literally so for the German POWs, and essentially so for the GIs, who were captive to the full power of military discipline. Although the liberated civilians abroad by then possessed the free will to purchase the Overseas and Transatlantic offerings, or not, their market choices were highly circumscribed since there was little if anything of domestic production available to sate their widely proclaimed hunger for non-Nazi reading material.

Wars shake up the status quo, often with lasting consequences. This was certainly the case with many of the wartime American publishers' series. Historians credit the Armed Services Editions both with helping to develop a new generation of book readers and buyers and with fuelling the post-war paperback boom. Certainly the first Armed Services Edition that many of the service men and women read may have been the first book they managed to read all the way through since they were in school, if ever. Many of the troops, of course, came from small towns in rural America, far from bookstores and decent public libraries, which remained luxuries to be enjoyed mainly by those who lived in large cities, especially in the north-east. The veterans who attended college under the celebrated GI Bill of Rights would have had a chance to further develop and refine their taste for reading. Armed with a college degree paid for by the government, a good job and secure status in the middle class, the veteran might have proudly displayed the Modern Library books he read for college classes in his suburban bookcase, joined the Book-of-the-Month Club and occasionally bought other books, both in paper and in hard covers. The ASEs unquestionably helped to boost the market for Pocket Books, Penguin Books and their imitators and competitors in post-war America.[18]

The archives of the Council on Books in Wartime, sponsor of the ASEs, contain hundreds of letters suggesting how the books were read and discussed. Most were written by the servicemen themselves, and sent to the offices of the Council, while others came from civilian observers overseas. The GIs wrote tens of thousands more letters directly to the authors whose books they most enjoyed. Most of the missives were complimentary and grateful. The letters document a host of reading styles and situations: reading books in a foxhole, in the chow line, waiting for a film to begin. Sometimes copies of the books themselves provide eloquent, if silent, testimony as to how, when and where the books were read. Many were literally consumed to pieces. Some GIs preparing for D-Day held on to their ASEs even when they threw other personal items of value away to lighten their load before embarkation. Grimly, one copy displayed a bloody thumb print on page 35 and thereafter, until a place two-thirds of the way through, when it ceased to appear. One marine in the Pacific wrote movingly about finding, sticking out of the back pocket of a dead young comrade, a copy of the ASE edition of Cornelia Otis Skinner and Emily Kimbrough's *Our Hearts Were Young and Gay*.[19] Many of the ASEs in my collection bear stains whose origins I choose not to contemplate.

The letters and other accounts also provide ample documentation about how the books fostered critical communities. One platoon leader gathered up all the ASEs held by his troops and refused to give one back to any man unless he agreed to read it aloud to his comrades. A soldier wrote to the Council, from a ship en route to some battle zone, for advice. Conrad Aiken's *Silent Snow, Secret Snow*, he wrote, 'caused quite a bit of discussion and argument among us. We are not agreed upon what Mr. Aiken has in mind.' Numerous other letters testify to consensus among 'buddies' as to meanings or at least to how a book was enjoyed. A journalist noted that 'the non-coms and privates at the back of the general's tent were all reading and discussing constantly'. The books even fostered, in at least one instance, a reading community among European civilians, which produced propaganda benefits. The army's Psychological Warfare Division dropped a few of the books by parachute on an island off the coast of Yugoslavia. Those who found them, according to a senior officer in the ASE programme, 'took them to someone who could read English where groups would gather round while they were translated aloud on the spot. The warm feeling, toward American soldiers on the part of those people is in part credited to this use of books.'[20]

For many reasons, mostly having to do with distance, language barriers and the rapid post-war dissolution of the civilian and military agencies responsible for their creation, there are few traces of how the Overseas and Transatlantic editions and the Bücherreihe Neue Welt titles might have been read and appreciated (or not). There is only one letter, rather than hundreds, in the Council's archives from a reader of Overseas Editions. In it, an elderly Greek man expressed thanks, while indicating that the books had succeeded in their purpose. 'I understand now,' he wrote, 'that in reading American books the new Greek generation will little by little gain and obtain some of the precious characters that are the privilege of the practical American, and will learn to be serious and educated.'[21] As for the books for German POWs in their own language, among the many prisoners who took the books they bought in the camp canteen home with them was a man named Seffner, who thought highly enough of his copy of Thomas Mann's *Lotte in Weimar* that he had it bound up, put his bookplate in it and wrote an inscription characterising the volume as a memento of the years, 1943–6, he spent in Camp Princeton, Texas. The book is now in my possession.

The Overseas Editions, Transatlantic Editions and Bücherreihe Neue Welt books, on the other hand, stimulated in American publishers a new interest in gaining increased international market share and helped to create a taste and demand overseas for American books after the war. Participation in a wartime book series project even helped Gottfried Bermann-Fischer to achieve the goal he held throughout his years as a refugee. The titles he sold for the Bücherreihe Neue Welt series formed the core of the paperback series Fischer-Bücherei, which he established after returning to Germany in 1950 and regaining ownership and control of the famed S. Fischer Verlag.

The conference 'The Culture of the Publishers' Series', held at the University of London in October 2007, along with John Spiers's exhibition catalogue and its lively and provocative introduction, raised some excellent questions and provided some tentative answers about the origins, production, materiality, consumption and social, political and cultural consequences of the publication of books in series. It is clear that much more work can be done [...]. Spiers helpfully hinted at the importance of studying the effect of war on publishing in general and on the publisher's series in particular. He notes important work on the American Civil War, British publishing in the First World War and the US Armed Services Editions in the Second World War.[22] My chapter serves as another contribution along these lines, and I hope it demonstrates useful parallels as well as differences between books in series in peacetime and in time of war. Much more can be done, and some of it is already under way, especially with regard to book publishing during the Cold War.[23] Moreover, work on series emanating from publishing countries other than the UK and the USA should be encouraged.

One other passage from Spiers's introduction also struck a special chord with me. This was his call to focus, in studying series, 'on particulars, not grand abstractions; on individual publishers and series, not aggregates and averages; on distinct circumstances and the intentions of the actors'. Certainly I have tried to maintain such a micro-historical focus [...]. Spiers also noted the importance of 'the actual series and books themselves, gathered en masse and studied carefully'.[24] That this is possible is a tribute to collectors, both institutional and individual. I for one cannot conceive of having undertaken my study had I not uncovered its potential through the fruits of conscious labour to collect. I suspect that many of my fellow contributors to this work would feel the same about how imaginative yet disciplined collecting can itself be a powerful tool for research.

Part Six
Colonial and Postcolonial Print Culture

The role of the book industry in establishing and perpetuating global inequalities in knowledge production and exchange has been an important focus of recent research in print culture studies. New attention has been paid to the publishing industry as an institution that is economically, politically and culturally implicated in either maintaining or contesting colonial and neo-colonial ideologies. This research has involved analysing international publishing practices regarding the languages of publication, methods of book commissioning and acquisition, trade agreements and territorial copyright arrangements as well as more subtle systems for conferring international literary prestige. The texts in this section assess, from a range of ideological and political perspectives, the implications of these transnational publishing arrangements.

Pascale Casanova's theorisation of world literary systems in *The World Republic of Letters* (Chapter 26 [2004]) considers the long-term legacies of colonialism on the global publishing industry and the way in which international literary value systems are constructed. She defines a nation's position in the international cultural hierarchy according to its levels of cultural autonomy, and argues that cultural capital continues to be concentrated in the metropolitan literary centres of Paris, London and New York. She examines how many former colonial powers are defined as autonomous literary spaces, 'most endowed in literary resources' which also exercise linguistic dominance (2004: 111). Nations subjected to or emerging from colonisation are described as dominated spaces, characterised by dependence on other literary capitals and weak publishing networks (2004: 109).

In a case study that exemplifies these asymmetrical literary power relations, Robert Fraser (Chapter 27 [2008]) analyses the response of British publishers to the opportunities presented by the British Empire in the Caribbean, during the period 1926–1960. Focusing on the Edinburgh-based family-run firm Thomas Nelson & Sons, he examines the history of their *West Indian Readers*. Nelson published school books for the domestic and imperial market from the late nineteenth century, and in the early twentieth century began opening local branches across the British Dominions, and it was from Nelson's newly established Toronto branch that their business to the Caribbean was established. He charts the development of the *West Indian Readers*, a 'small and unpretentious' series that was widely criticised by the intellectual elite of the day, but was highly profitable (p. 199). Despite such commercially successful initiatives, the house of Nelson ultimately fell, due to a failure to adapt to 'macro-level' changes, in terms of management and policy making. Despite this, Fraser argues that the long-term impact of this series was broadly positive, influencing the 'unconscious mind' of a generation of school readers, including V. S. Naipaul, and thus helping 'yield up a literature' (p. 202).

A more critical portrayal of colonial and postcolonial publishing initiatives by British publishers is offered by Kenyan publisher Henry Chakava (Chapter 28 [1992]). He explains the reasons for British publishing dominance in the final stages of British colonial rule, reflecting on the privileged relationship that British commercial publishers enjoyed in this period. In Chakava's view, the decision to invite Longman and Oxford University Press to carry out educational publishing 'unleashed a multinational ogre that was to dominate the post independence publishing scene for many years' (p. 205). He charts how, after independence in 1960, 'a host of other British publishers' (p. 206) then established sales agencies and branches in Kenya, alongside the state publisher and a handful of local commercial publishers, and analyses the struggles of these local publishers to get established, in the face of foreign competition, a lack of state support, and economic and political uncertainty. The 'multinational stranglehold' over the educational publishing industry was only broken in 1977, with the wider economic and political crisis in East Africa, which led to the withdrawal of many foreign publishers, but also to the demise of both state and independent indigenous publishers in Kenya (p. 207).

The contentious nature of postcolonial publishing is illustrated in two competing analyses of Heinemann Educational's African Writers Series by Graham Huggan (Chapter 29) and James Currey (Chapter 30). This was the largest and most successful of the African literature lists established by British educational publishers in the period of decolonisation in Africa, as part of their highly profitable educational publishing programmes. Others included Oxford University Press's Three Crowns Series, Longman's Drumbeat Series and Macmillan's Pacesetters Series (Davis 2013, 2015). Huggan's influential *The Postcolonial Exotic: Marketing the Margins* (2001) includes a critique of the series in which he examines how cultural power was exercised by British publishers along neo-colonial lines: how Heinemann actively sought to market African literature by representing it as 'other', using the 'perceptual framework of the African exotic' (2001: 37) and homogenising African literature as a single entity, in an attempt to make it more readily accessible to the Western reader.

The extract from Currey's 'Africa Writes Back' (2008) reflects on his experiences as editor of the African Writers Series, which he defends as a vital forum for African authors to 'write back' to the European canon. Currey concedes that Heinemann Educational benefited from Britain's cultural dominance at the time, in particular by taking advantage of the pre-eminence of the English language in sub-Saharan Africa, and of the prestige attached to London as a publishing centre. Currey explains that the main market for the series was the schoolbook market in Africa, not the Western consumer market, as assumed by Huggan, and he also counters Huggan's assumption that all editorial decisions were made in London, and instead emphasises the involvement of African authors – most prominently Chinua Achebe – as editorial advisors to the series. Thus, in writing his own version of events, Currey aims to present a corrective to some of Huggan's theoretical speculations.

These historical and theoretical readings draw attention to the multiple ways in which the publishing industry has been, and continues to be, structured along colonial or neo-colonial lines. This is evident in Fraser, Huggan and Currey's case studies of individual publishing companies operating in colonial and postcolonial contexts, in Chakava's survey of publishing in Kenya during the period of decolonisation, and in Casanova's discussion of the balance of power and prestige in the current global media environment. Each of these studies sheds light on the intricate and complex ways in which colonial knowledge systems were created and have been maintained, long after the demise of colonial rule itself.

SUGGESTED FURTHER READING

Anderson, B., 1991. *Imagined Communities: Reflections on the Origins and Spread of Nationalism*. London: Verso.

Carter, D., and A. Galligan (eds), 2007. *Making Books: Contemporary Australian Publishing*. St Lucia: University of Queensland Press.

Chatterjee, R., 2006. *Empires of the Mind: A History of Oxford University Press in India under the Raj*. Oxford: Oxford University Press.

Davis, C. and D. Johnson (eds), 2015. *The Book in Africa: Critical Debates*. Basingstoke: Palgrave Macmillan.

Ngũgi wa Thiong'o., 1986. *Decolonising the Mind: The Politics of Language in African Literatures*. Oxford: James Currey, EAEP, Heinemann.

26 World Literary Space

Pascale Casanova

FORMS OF LITERARY DOMINATION

In the literary world, domination is not exerted in an unequivocal way. Because hierarchical structure is not linear, it cannot be described in terms of a simple model of a single centralized dominant power. If literary space is relatively autonomous, it is also by the same token relatively dependent on political space. This fundamental dependency assumes a variety of forms, particularly political ones, and operates in a variety of ways, most notably through language.

Here we encounter once again the ambiguity and paradox that govern the very enterprise of literature itself: since language is not a purely literary tool, but an inescapably political instrument as well, it is through language that the literary world remains subject to political power. One consequence of this is that forms of domination, which are interlocking and often superimposed upon one another, are apt to merge and become hidden. Thus literarily dominated spaces may also be dominated linguistically and politically: especially in countries that have undergone colonization, the fact that political domination is often exerted by linguistic means implies a condition of literary dependency. Indeed, when the sources of dependency are exclusively linguistic (and cultural) – as, for example, in the cases of Belgium, Austria, and Switzerland – literary domination is unavoidable. But it may also be the case that domination is exerted and measured in literary terms alone. These include the effectiveness of consecration by central authorities, the power of critical decrees, the canonizing effect of prefaces and translations by writers who themselves have been consecrated at the center (thus Gide introduced the Egyptian Taha Hussein and translated Rabindranath Tagore, while Marguerite Yourcenar introduced the work of the Japanese novelist Yukio Mishima to France),[1] the prestige of the collections in which foreign works appear, and the leading role played by great translators.

Since all these forms of domination are liable to become mixed together, and so obscure each other, one of the objects of the present work is to isolate and describe them, while also showing that the literary balance of power is often a disguised reflection of patterns of political domination. Conversely, however, it is also necessary to show that patterns of literary domination cannot be reduced to a political balance of power, as is sometimes done by academic critics who treat perceived differences in rank between national literatures as a simple function of economic domination, analyzed in terms of a binary opposition between center and periphery. This sort of spatialization tends to neutralize the violence that actually governs the literary world and to obscure the inequalities that arise from strictly literary competition between dominant and dominated. A purely political analysis does not allow us to understand the individual struggles waged by writers in dominated spaces against the center or against regional centers associated with different linguistic areas, much less the precise nature of literary reality and aesthetics.

A more sophisticated model would take into account a peculiar ambiguity of the relation of literary domination and dependence, namely, that writers in dominated spaces may be able to convert their dependence into an instrument of emancipation and legitimacy. To criticize established literary forms and genres because they have been inherited from colonial culture, for instance, misses the point that literature itself, as a value common to an entire space, is not only part of the legacy of political domination but also an instrument that, once reappropriated, permits writers from literarily deprived territories to gain recognition.[2]

Literary regions and linguistic areas

Linguistic areas are the emanation and embodiment of political domination. By exporting their languages and institutions, colonizing nations (which is to say dominant literary nations) succeeded in strengthening their political pole. The expansion of linguistic (or linguistic-cultural) areas therefore constituted a sort of extension of European national literary spaces. Afterward, as Salman Rushdie put it, the 'pink conquerors crept home, the boxwallahs and memsahibs and bwanas, leaving behind them parliaments, schools, Grand Trunk Roads and the rules of cricket.'[3] The age of colonialism was characterized in large part by a process of linguistic and cultural unification. One of the chief aspects of this 'propensity for self-exportation,' as the West Indian poet Édouard Glissant has noted, is that it typically generated 'a sort of vocation for the universal,' with the result that the great Western languages came to be regarded as 'vehicular languages' that 'often took the place of an actual metropolis.'[4]

Each linguistic territory has a center that controls and attracts the literary productions dependent on it. London today, even if it now finds itself in competition with New York and Toronto, continues to be central for Australians, New Zealanders, Irish, Canadians, Indians, and English-speaking Africans; Barcelona, the intellectual and cultural capital of Spain, remains a great literary center for Latin Americans; Paris is still central for writers from West and North Africa as well as for Francophone authors in Belgium, Switzerland, and Canada, countries where it continues to exercise influence by virtue of its literary eminence rather than any power of political control. Berlin is the leading capital for Austrian and Swiss writers and remains an important literary center today for the countries of northern Europe as well as for the countries of central Europe that emerged from the breakup of the Austro-Hungarian Empire.

Each of these linguistic-cultural areas preserves a large measure of autonomy in relation to the others: each is what might be called a 'literature-world' (to transpose Braudel's notion of an 'economy-world'): that is, a homogenous and autonomous sphere in which the legitimacy of its centralized power of consecration is unchallenged; a world having its own pantheon and prizes, its own favored genres, its own distinctive traditions and internal rivalries. The structure of each area mirrors that of worldwide literary space, with a subtle hierarchy being established among its various satellites as a function of their symbolic distance (which is aesthetic rather than geographic) from the center. In some regions there may be more than one center – London and New York, for example, within the Anglophone area. These capitals come into conflict with each other, each one seeking to impose its authority over the shared linguistic hinterland with a view to achieving, and then sustaining, a regional monopoly of literary consecration.

In the aftermath of decolonization, then, the major literary centers have been able to go on maintaining a sort of literary protectorate thanks to the dual character of their languages, which allows them to exert a literary form of political power. Even in the 'soft' neocolonial form of language and literature, the perpetuation of such domination is a powerful factor favoring consolidation of the heteronomous (or political and economic) pole of the worldwide literary field.

London is, of course, along with Paris, the other great capital of world literature, not only by virtue of its accumulated literary capital but also owing to the immensity of its former colonial empire. Its power of recognition, which extends from Ireland to India, Africa, and Australia, is unquestionably one of the greatest in the world: authors as different as Shaw, Yeats, Tagore, Narayan, and Soyinka (four of them Nobel Prize winners) have all looked to London as their literary capital. This power, and the correspondingly large share of literary credit it implies, continue to confer real literary legitimacy upon writers from Commonwealth nations, successors to the territories of the old empire. Among writers of Indian descent, for example, no matter whether they have wholly assimilated British values, as in the case of V. S. Naipaul, or whether they prefer to keep a critical distance from them, as in the case of Salman Rushdie, consecration by London has allowed them to enjoy literary existence on the international level, even if this form of ennoblement is not altogether untouched by political motives.

Of one of the heroes in *The Satanic Verses*, Saladin Chamcha, an Indian immigrant to London, Rushdie writes:

> Of the things of the mind, he had most loved the protean, inexhaustible culture of the English-speaking peoples; had said, when courting Pamela, that *Othello*, 'just that one play,' was worth the total output of any other dramatist in any other language, and though he was conscious of hyperbole, he didn't think the exaggeration very great ... Of material things, he had given his love to this city, London, preferring it to the city of his birth or to any other; had been creeping up on it, stealthily, with mounting excitement, freezing into a statue when it looked in his direction, dreaming of being the one to possess it and so, in a sense, become it, as when in the game of grandmother's footsteps the child who touches the one who's it ('on it', today's young Londoners would say) takes over the cherished identity ... [London's] long history as a refuge, a role it maintained in spite of the recalcitrant ingratitude of the refugees' children; and without any of the self-congratulatory huddled-masses rhetoric of the 'nation of immigrants' across the ocean, itself far from perfectly open-armed. Would the United States,

with its are-you-now-have-you-ever-beens, have permitted Ho Chi Minh to cook in its hotel kitchens? What would its McCarran-Walter Act have to say about a latter-day Karl Marx, standing bushy-bearded at its gates, waiting to cross its yellow lines? O Proper London! Dull would he truly be of soul who did not prefer its faded splendours, its new hesitancies, to the hot certainties of that transatlantic New Rome.[5]

London's power of attraction, it will be noted, shares two characteristics already observed in connection with Paris: a sizable share of literary capital and a reputation for political liberalism.

By virtue of its uncontested political power, London has very often been used as a weapon in the permanent struggle that opposes European capitals to each other. When France's cultural domination was at its height, at the end of the eighteenth and the beginning of the nineteenth centuries, its competitors sought to turn London's prestige against Paris. Between 1750 and 1770 in Germany, for example, when a national literature was in the process of being created, the 'preclassical' generation – that of Klopstock and especially of Lessing – proposed to put an end to the imitation (and therefore to the domination) of French authors by relying on English models. Lessing himself was responsible for the great shift in critical and popular opinion regarding the work of Shakespeare.

But London has seldom imposed itself outside the linguistic jurisdiction of the British Empire (now Commonwealth). London publishers today publish very few literary translations, and prizes are awarded only to works written in English.[6] It owes its credit to the vast extent of its linguistic area and to the globally dominant position now enjoyed by the English language; but because its power of consecration has always had a linguistic (and therefore often political) basis, its strictly literary credit is not of the same kind as that commanded by Paris.

In recent years the rivalry between London and New York has produced a very clear bipolarization of English-speaking cultural space. But if New York today is the unchallenged publishing capital of the world in financial terms, still it cannot be said to have become a center of consecration whose legitimacy is universally recognized. Here again the very question of legitimacy is one of the things at stake in the game, and the way it is answered depends on the place occupied by those who are prepared to wager on it. Many writers take advantage of this uncertain balance of power in order to play one capital off against the other.

27 School Readers in the Empire and the Creation of Postcolonial Taste

Robert Fraser

I begin with an image so familiar it hardly needs showing: John Constable's painting of 1823, '*Salisbury Cathedral*, from the Bishop's Grounds' (Figure 27.1).

To children everywhere it is familiar in the shape of a jigsaw puzzle, but for many who passed through the elementary school system in the British West Indies between 1926 and the early 1960s it possesses an additional resonance, reproduced as it then was on page 199 of Book v of Nelson's much-used *West Indian Readers*. Many would have encountered it aged 11 in Standard Five, and read with greater or lesser fluency the accompanying commentary by the editor Captain James Oliver Cutteridge, Director of Education for Trinidad and Tobago and a keen amateur artist. Cutteridge treats the picture as an exercise in perspective. He calls attention to the framing of the South Front by trees, and illustrates on the following page how the sightlines meet at a vanishing point at the base of the famous steeple. Then he issues a curt invitation: 'Write a paragraph describing, *in your own words*, what you can see in Constable's picture.'[1]

During the early 1940s in wartime Port-of-Spain this invitation was addressed to an elementary schoolboy of Indian ancestry shortly before proceeding to Queen's Royal College. Three decades later, from his cottage near Salisbury, he responded in literal terms to Cutteridge's challenge by conveying in his own words – and in exactly one paragraph – the image's original and continuing effects. The passage occurs towards the beginning of his novel of displacement *The Enigma of Arrival*, the narrator of which is newly arrived in Wiltshire:

> I saw what I saw very clearly. But I didn't know what I was looking at. I had nothing to fit it into. I was still in a kind of limbo. There were certain things I knew though. I knew the name of the town I had come to by train. It was Salisbury. It was almost the first English town I had got to know, the first I had been given some idea of, from the reproduction of the Constable painting of Salisbury Cathedral in my third-standard reader. Far away in my tropical island, before I was ten. A four-colour reproduction which I thought the most beautiful picture I had even seen.[2]

Figure 27.1   John Constable, *Salisbury Cathedral*, from Nelsons West Indian Readers,
Book © Victoria and Albert Museum, London

The passage is all the more revealing because disingenuous in certain respects. If this narrator really did meet that Constable landscape in school before his tenth birthday, then his reading age – and the author V. S. Naipaul's – was two years in advance of his contemporaries. I suspect also that his consciousness of the process by which the plate was reproduced – four-colour printing – owes something to popular compilations such as *The Children's Encyclopaedia*, where that technique was regularly and carefully explained, in one edition via successive impressions of a self-portrait painted in Arles by Van Gogh. The middle-aged Naipaul complains of having lacked a context for interpreting the Constable, though his paragraph places the experience of seeing the reproduction firmly against a backdrop of colonial desire. Perhaps the best-known general judgment on Constable's landscapes is given by Ernst Gombrich in his much-reprinted *The Story of Art*. Constable, remarks Gombrich, aimed 'to paint what he saw with his own eyes'.[3] To this definition of realism Naipaul responds by the disclaimer that, as a colonial child – or even initially as an adult – viewer, he had little idea of what he was seeing. The truth surely is that he saw what he wanted, and what he wanted was England. In a modern British setting the recondition of Constable's naturalism is impeded by intervening nostalgia. In the imperial environment it was obstructed by longing. The difference between these conditions is one of the themes of Naipaul's novel, which as well as addressing migration, conducts a master class in interpreting landscape and, through it, alternative histories: of the land, of architecture and of the conditioned, observing self.

Indubitably school readers of that period instilled an anxiety of influence in writers who once studied them. West Indian literature is peppered with acknowledgements to these modest books, and the detail of the references, specifying the volume and in some case even the page-numbers, suggests not only the avidity with which they were absorbed, but the frequency with which pupils failed to hand them in. Why did this standard school fare – and Nelson's Readers in particular – retain that sort of a hold? Thomas Nelson and Sons had been providing school readers for domestic and imperial use since the late nineteenth century, but the proliferation of branches and offices in far-flung dependencies had gradually entailed a localization of provision. Until about 1907 the pattern was for uniform Crown or Royal Readers, recognizable from their brown covers, which served the needs of pupils throughout the empire, including as it happens Naipaul's Mr Biswas. There was, however, an increasing tendency to regionalize the provision, a policy first evident in the Special Canadian Series issued in conjunction with the Toronto firm of James Campbell and Sons from 1882. For the first time this series employed indigenous oral and literary sources where it could find them and organized its contents imaginatively, as the Prefaces carefully explained, around the successive seasons of the Canadian year.[4] Popular and successful, these locally orientated books were systematically updated. From the Nelson archives in Edinburgh it is clear, for instance, just how anxious the firm became at the time of Great Depression to ensure that their readers were officially sanctioned as set books throughout the Dominion. Indeed, this proliferation of local provision became something of a specialty of Nelsons' own Toronto house where from the 1920s onwards, with growing competition from other companies, the priority was to work in close collaboration with directors of education in the various Canadian provinces, several of whom were appointed as consultants. With their assistance, individual readers were tailored to the needs of pupils in Quebec, Saskatchewan, Ontario and so on.

The model of regionalization and fraternization with government was then exported. Nelsons had long had their eyes on the Caribbean region as a locus for commercial expansion. Beginning in 1910, for example, they had been experimenting with converting West Indian bamboo into viable paper, a project that had culminated in 1917 in the purchase of a plantation and paper mill at St Joseph's in Trinidad, and an agreement with the colonial government permitting them to harvest bamboo from Crown Lands.[5] Since 1909, moreover, a preferential trading agreement had existed between Canada and the West Indies, extended in 1920 and again in 1925, as a result of which the Toronto branch gradually assumed responsibility for sales in the Caribbean. The turning point for educational publishing there – and the origin of the West Indian Readers – lies in the appointment in December 1922 of S. P. Jones as a travelling representative in the region. After a six-month tour through Bermuda, St Kitts, Antigua, Monserrat, Dominique, St Lucia, Barbados, St Vincent, Trinidad, Grenada, British Guiana and British Honduras, he reported that the rapid evolution of elementary education among the black and Asian population entailed a need for purpose-made textbooks. As his boss in Toronto, S. B. Watson, then wrote back to Edinburgh on 31 July 1923, enclosing Jones's recommendations: 'You will notice that on folio five he makes a definite suggestion for a West Indian Reader, or set of Readers. I am going more fully with him into this idea, and will write you a separate letter in a few days.'[6]

The following winter, Watson himself toured the Caribbean, and while in Port-of-Spain he met Cutteridge. It was the beginning of a long and fruitful association, not untouched by controversy. Four years earlier, Cutteridge had arrived in Trinidad to take over as Principal of Tranquillity Boys' Model School, perhaps the best elementary school on the island. He came equipped, not with a university degree, but with a First World War field commission, a fellowship of the Royal Geographical Society, a zeal for educational reform and an eye for a telling picture. By the time Watson turned up, he had been elevated to Chief Inspector of Schools and Assistant Director of Education. Taking a maple leaf out of Nelson's Canadian book, he volunteered not simply as consultant for the projected textbooks, but as author. He proved unstoppable. In 20 years he was to be responsible for several volumes of elementary school arithmetic, successive editions of these readers and – his all-time commercial success – *Nelson's Geography of the West Indies and Adjacent Lands.*[7] The maths was sometimes questioned, the geography scorned. The books sold mightily.

Captain Cutteridge's versatility, or hackwork if you like, was his strength, though in some it seemed a weakness. By temperament he was a geographer and artist, and his inclination to allow these interests to shape his writing was consonant with Nelson's own editorial policy. After all, the books were to be illustrated and, following the Canadian model, they were to reflect the natural environment and the social setting of their young readership. Cutteridge's revolutionary idea – though to some at the time it seemed a misdemeanor – was to situate literature in the Caribbean itself. In their distinctive red covers, his readers – six in number, including an introductory book – covered all sorts of subjects, from folklore and customs to fauna and flora and history, but the organizing theme was that of travel, and inter-connections between different places. It was a tendency enhanced by his pedagogical tactic of re-enforcing each subject by repeating it in successive volumes at different linguistic levels. Consciously or not, through graded exercises and extracts Cutteridge conveyed a vision of Caribbean culture as a continual inflow and outflow, movement and coalescence. He was less exercised by hierarchy than by variety, exploration, diversity, gravitation and change. The upwardly mobile, Garvey-inspired, middle-class Asian and Afro-Trinidadian did not forgive him. And nor did Mr Biswas.

In effect, these well-thumbed textbooks proved a quarry from which are hewn the plots of several of the more remarkable Caribbean novels of the second half of the twentieth century, together with something of the region's poetic sensibility, its sense of history, culture and place. From public reaction in the early years one would scarcely have expected this result. Far from receiving credit for his repositioning of literature in a late colonial setting, the editor was reviled by the parents whose children's eyes he was attempting to open. The assault was initiated in the late 1920s by Howard Bishop, a one-time teacher, a disciple of Marcus Garvey and editor of the *Trinidad Workingmen's Journal*, who drew attention to the Director of Education's lack of a degree. The same criticism was levelled by Eric Williams, a former pupil of the Captain's at Tranquillity, an Oxford history first and Prime Minister of Trinidad and Tobago. 'Cutteridge was not a university graduate,' Williams snobbishly pointed out. In 1942 the much-maligned Captain, who had done quite nicely out of his many publications, withdrew weeping to the tax haven of the Isle of Man. Six years later *The Clarion*, instrument of the Trinidad Labour Party, invited its readers to envisage the geriatric former Director of Education in an old folk's home, 'spending his last days in a wheel chair and wearing a bib'.[8] But his books continued to sell, in edition after revised edition, up to and beyond his death in August 1952, as Keith Sambrook, an employee of Nelsons from 1954 to 1962, well remembers,[9] and as the weekly printing and monthly sales figures preserved in archives rescued from Nelson's Parkside works abundantly confirm.[10] The figures are well in excess of those for Nelson's other principal stock-in-trade: reprints of out-of-copyright classics. Take, as an arbitrary but far from untypical example, the reports from the printing room for the first few months of 1955. In the week of 20 January alone, 90,000 copies of the first reader were run off, while 20,000 plates were required for the second primer, and 10,000 for the fourth. In the week of 3 February, there were orders for 35,000 sets of covers, text and plates for Reader One; on the 14 March orders for another 32,000 sets of plates, again for Reader One, and 10,000 plates for Reader Five. Compare these figures with those for staples of domestic educational consumption during the same weeks: 4000 for that all-time favourite, Alexandre Dumas's *The Black Tulip*, or 2000 for *The Bible for Boys and Girls*, and you can see just how profitable Cutteridge's money spinners continued to be throughout this period. The only equivalent figures are for readers intended for the African market, which belong to a different, if related, story. The *West Indian Readers*, moreover, continued in use until a drastic revision of the early 60s, a local imprint of which is available to this day.

Throughout this period these small and unpretentious books served as a link joining the folk memories of two continents. School textbooks were a staple of Nelson's business, having been so for a century or more, and many of the workforce back in Scotland drew satisfaction and a sense of purpose from the knowledge that their products were to travel the world. At much the same time as Naipaul sat enthralled before that reproduction of Constable's *Salisbury Cathedral*, a 17-year-old apprentice called Bill Reid was continuing his training on one of the large Wharfedale presses in Nelson's machine room at their neo-Gothic Parkside Works situated at the foot of Arthur's Seat in Edinburgh. His role was apparently pedestrian, yet because of its worldwide reach it also seemed grand:

> And it wasn't a terribly exciting job, but at least you were bookprinting, and you felt top of the world 'cause were part of a book that was being printed and going all over the world at that time. And, of course, you were now a year old in the trade and you were a real printer! And we used to have to print these, I mean there were millions of them![11]

Reid can even remember the ink from the covers coming off on his hands, and having to wash it off under a coldwater tap at night. It is a salutary thought that some of the residue may well have transferred itself to the fingers of young readers in the Caribbean to be similarly scrubbed off in the evening, perhaps in a bucket, perhaps at a communal pump.

In an age of virtual texts conveyed by screen we are, perhaps, beginning to forget the intimacy of touch and other sensations that once upon a time books as physical objects regularly transmitted from printer to reader. The infant Naipaul was very appreciative of the subtle tones of Nelsons' four-colour illustrative technique, but the reminiscences of Eric Martin, who joined the firm's camera department in 1953, allow us to view such visual experiences from the perspective of the producer:

> So what you did, you made up one negative with a colour filter. Then you made another one, blue, red, green, yellow. You made the negatives through these filters. Different negatives. And that brought up, you know, different parts o' the picture, and then there was other men, retouchers, they had to accentuate the colours and that.[12]

Few of these Scottish workers had ever visited the Caribbean or any of the many other parts of the Empire to which their artefacts were dispatched from the nearby port of Leith, yet they had a vivid feeling for the realities and commercial positioning of the firm, and for the place within changing markets occupied by its merchandise. Ever since the First World War the firm had, in spite of its apparent prosperity, been on something of a back foot. When Thomas Nelson III, grandson of the founder, had perished in the trenches in 1917, his place had been taken by his younger brother Ian, who by many accounts was far more enthused by the fruits of business success than the unglamorous grind of publishing. Long weekends were spent shooting at the family estate at Glenetive in Renfrewshire, the briefest of working weeks at Parkside, where the pleasure-loving director was regarded with sly and knowing affection by his lowlier employees. John Gunn, then a junior clerk in the counting room, paraphrases the prevailing attitude of the staff with some tact: 'He was a very gentle gentleman, and spoke to everybody, but he didn't actually have a hands-on job at all.'[13] The files in the Edinburgh University archive amplify this impression with glimpses of Ian's multifarious extramural activities. These included money-spinning though ultimately disastrous speculations in paper-manufacture from bamboo pulp in Trinidad and India, and a failed venture to sell off the loss-making estates in St Joseph's to the American-based manufactures of the synthetic fibre Celanese Acetate, so that the bamboo could be processed into artificial silk. For quite a long period the firm enjoyed an unusually close relationship with their banker Charles Grenfell of Morgan Grenfell ('Charlie' to the board). Nelsons personnel even managed for some of this time to serve on the board of their own auditors, and in this capacity to send stern little notes to themselves, a situation that cannot have contributed to their financial realism. By the 1930s, they evidently existed at the centre of a web of subsidiaries or aliases operating across three continents, sharing much the same list of directors and shareholders, shunting capital between themselves, even communicating with one another through telegrams phrased in code. They were repeatedly in difficulties with the tax authorities in different countries. At Christmas 1935 they were obliged to rush their office accounts to Bengal, where the inspectors were demanding returns on their Indian investments. The relevant files were sent out on flying boat *The City of Khartoum* from Croydon Airport. The plane sank in the Mediterranean while attempting to land at Alexandria, taking the requested accounts with it. As Nelsons were then able to report to India with some satisfaction, enclosing verification from the Post Office (which at least they did not own), the mail had not been held in a watertight compartment, and therefore must be presumed lost. The whole entangled saga can be followed through the archive across correspondence between various linked addresses, though it seems imaginatively to belong in one of the swashbuckling novels of John Buchan, who for the immediately preceding period (1912–29) had, as it happens, worked as chief literary advisor to the firm.[14]

These operatic distractions could not disguise a more radical problem: Nelsons were failing either to rethink their publishing strategy in the changing commercial climate of the interwar and post-war periods, or to reinvest in basic plant and stock. For generations they had survived quite satisfactorily on three highly profitable lines: the imperial educational market, cheap hardback reprints of the classics of English literature and latterly a small slice of the Bible trade. By the 1950s there were many competitors in the first of these fields, and the second was being hit hard by a paperback revolution to which Nelsons were slow to react. They carried on in Scotland, where to the very end their printing was routinely done, turning out well-loved standbys such as the school readers on outdated and aging equipment. They may have convinced themselves of the prudence of this policy in their capacity as accountants, but they could not kid the workers. If you want the truth, ask the shop floor. Here is Bill Reid again:

> But Nelsons were never great modernisers. They were never at the forefront of technology. When photo-composition came along, they didn't bother with that. The cameras were the old ones with the hood over the top and – they didn't have magnesium flares, but they had everything else I think. And they never altered all the years we were there in terms of modernising the plant. The Monotype keyboard side was making lines of type and monotype up. But the machines were very old and they cluttered and cluttered and cluttered and cluttered.[15]

The din of the machines could not drown out the bugles of impending doom. When Ian Nelson died in 1958, he was succeeded by his son Ronald, whose principal interest was in steam trains. Most Friday afternoons, Ronnie took the 4.30 Flying Scotsman from Waverley Station to London. Settling into a first-class compartment, he hung up his bowler hat and then enjoyed a good dinner, rounding it off with a double brandy. One week he had invited his recently recruited junior colleague Keith Sambrook to join him at his table when, polishing off his aperitif, he rose to his feet and announced that he would spend the rest of the journey on the footplate of the engine. This he did, timing the arrival of the express train on his silver stopwatch at each station en route before re-emerging at King's Cross, bowler hat once more on brow, to declare: 'Late at Darlington again!'.[16]

So, all things considered, it was little surprise to the labour force when, one morning in 1962, Ronnie went into close two-man conference with the Canadian plutocrat Lord Thomson of Fleet at the London office, and sold the family firm to the Thomson Organization behind closed doors. Soon the printing division was separated from the publishing house, and within five years, though their books continued in use around the world, Thomas Nelsons and Sons as a commercial enterprise were little more than a name. The Parkside Works were demolished, and the archive was rescued from the skip.[17] In the second volume in this set I shall be discussing the Oxford University Press (OUP), another British-based publishing firm with an equally global reach. OUP is not, of course, a family firm, but in its own quaint manner it has always had a patriarchal ambiance. Through an arcane combination of snobbery and flexibility, it has managed nonetheless to survive through thick and thin, as Nelsons did not. On the micro-level, in individual series, for example, Nelsons proved adaptable enough to reap success, especially overseas. At the larger macro-level, the level of management and policymaking, they failed to adapt at all adequately. Because of that higher failure, the house eventually fell.

Meanwhile, back in the Caribbean, the chorus of condemnation against Cutteridge's much-used readers had been unstinting. It was not for his alluring visions of Salisbury or London that the much-maligned captain received such opprobrium, nor for his recasting of the classics, his summaries of Defoe or Dean Swift, but for sidetracking local aspirations to universal excellence through the siren call of relevance. That conflict of interest is now a matter of history. To recognize its one-time existence, however, is to question one well-received theory that may be styled the 'reactive model' of postcolonial writing. According to this stereotyped view, school authorities throughout the Empire force-fed William Wordsworth's 'I wandered lonely as a Cloud' to their tender charges repeatedly 'til, sick of this foreign diet, they revolted by producing writing of their own. The example of Nelsons in the Caribbean tends to suggest on the contrary that – in this context at least, and over one protracted period – publishers and teachers sought valiantly to localize literary appreciation, in the teeth of parochial *petit bourgeois* elitism. But what the conscious mind of one generation rejected, the unconscious mind of the next permanently absorbed. Nelsons is now a fading memory for several generations in the West Indies and elsewhere. Nonetheless, the effect that they had on receptive young people has proved decisive. By attending, albeit temporarily and in part, to the changing needs of one particular local audience of schoolchildren, Nelsons bucked the trend, and crossed party lines. They planted seeds in the fertile soil of a vibrant culture, thereby helping in the long run to yield up a literature.

28 Kenyan Publishing: Independence and Dependence

Henry Chakava

Very little has been written on the Kenyan publishing industry even though it is one of the most important in Africa. The aim of this chapter is to attempt, for the first time, to discuss the origins and development, the successes and failures, the opportunities and challenges of the Kenyan book industry as comprehensively as possible, from the time of Kenya's independence to the present day.

AT INDEPENDENCE

At the time of independence, there were only three major publishers on the scene. The first, East African Literature Bureau (EALB), had been started by the East African High Commission (the common services organ of the British colonial government of Kenya, Uganda and Tanzania) in 1948 in response to demand from the emerging African readership for relevant homegrown reading materials following recommendations by the Elspeth Education Commission. Charles Richards, an experienced missionary printer-cum-publisher was appointed to run it.

In fact, Richards was largely responsible for the arrival of the other two publishers, Longman and Oxford University Press. He has argued consistently that it was his wish right from the beginning to support the growth of a vibrant local publishing industry in Kenya.[1] For example, instead of installing printing facilities at EALB, he encouraged commercial printers to print for him. On the publishing side, he invited British publishers to open branches in Kenya, offering to pass over to them for exploitation any viable titles developed at the Bureau.

THE COMING OF FOREIGN PUBLISHERS

Longman, which was already publishing for the market – but from London, was the first to respond, appointing a resident representative in 1950. Oxford University Press arrived four years later and set up an office very much along the lines followed by Longman. Neither company published locally; rather their function was to collect good manuscripts and forward them to London for vetting and publishing. Richards became a regular supplier of EALB-developed books to these companies, and they managed through this arrangement to publish some very profitable textbooks such as Oxford's *New Oxford English Course for East Africa* and Longman's *Highway Arithmetic*. Local printing did not start until 1965, two years after independence.

We shall mention three other categories of publishers who were active at this time although they are not central to our present study. These were the Government Printer, whose work from its initiation in 1899 was the printing of government notices, reports, and so on; it is still functioning today, but it never ventured into mainstream publishing. Among the others are the mission presses – spearheaded by the Church Missionary Society, which is reported to have printed the first Kenyan book in 1894, thereby setting in motion and eventually helping to shape the emergence of a local publishing industry. The prime concern of the mission presses was the translation of the Bible and the hymn book into African languages and any other books that they considered important for the spiritual nourishment of their newly converted followers. And after World War II, there were also small presses operated by Kenyan nationalists such as Henry Muoria and, later, Gakaara wa Wanjau, who produced handbills, political pamphlets, and booklets in their efforts to sensitize the African people in the early stages of the freedom movement, and for an alternative education from that offered by the missionaries.

RICHARDS' ABOUT-TURN

As can be seen, there was neither a privately owned local publishing house, nor a national one, at the time of independence. It is important to appreciate this point if one wants to understand the things that hampered and, in a way, still hamper the development of a strong indigenous publishing industry in Kenya. One person best placed to spearhead its establishment at the time of independence was none other than Charles Richards himself. He had done a good job publishing for the Church Missionary Society in the 1930s, had been instrumental in the establishment of Ndia Kuu Press (the first Kenyan commercial publisher) in the 1940s, and had managed EALB from its inception to 1963, when he resigned to become the manager of the newly locally incorporated branch of Oxford University Press. For some time, he continued to enjoy a special relationship with EALB, out of which the profitable and perennial *New Peak English Course* arose.

We must state at the outset that we do not believe in state publishing and are suspicious of the efficacy of parastatal organizations. We are, therefore, in full sympathy with Richards when he justifies his decision to invite commercial publishers and to launch them off with ready-made textbooks from EALB. But we should have thought that if Richards believed in commercial publishing, he would have crowned his exemplary service to publishing in Kenya by spearheading, at independence, the establishment of a locally owned commercial firm. Such a firm would have benefited from his policy of shedding off successful textbooks to enable the bureau to concentrate on his prescribed noble task of developing materials for the new literates. J. W. Chege has questioned the reasoning behind Richards' policy of developing texts and then handing them over to foreign publishers. He argues, and with the benefit of hindsight quite rightly so, that by doing this the bureau was preparing the ground for the entrenchment of foreign publishers, particularly Longman, Oxford University Press, Macmillan, and Nelson. He goes on,

> This meant that the Bureau bore all the publishing risks for these commercial publishers…. They did not have to spend their money on marketing research, or sales promotion…. The risks were borne by the Bureau which could only afford to do this at the expense of the East African tax-payer.[2]

However well intentioned Charles Richards may have been, he lost a major opportunity to leave a national monument behind after 30 years of credible service to Kenya, unleashing instead a multinational ogre that was to dominate the postindependence publishing scene for many years.

CREATING NEW INSTITUTIONS

The period after independence was one of change, experimentation, and innovation. Education, acknowledged as the key to national development, was one of the first areas to receive attention. The Kenya Institute of Education (KIE) was set up in 1964, amalgamated with the Curriculum Development Center and charged with the responsibility of drawing up new syllabi reflecting the changed priorities of the newly independent state. The first Commission of Enquiry into education, under the chairmanship of Professor S. H. Ominde, was appointed to undertake an exhaustive inquiry into all aspects of education in Kenya. The commission submitted part one of its report in October 1964, with wide-ranging recommendations that were to have far-reaching effects on the direction of education in Kenya. Although books are critical to the success of any education system, the report said nothing about them and how they were to be created, produced and distributed to serve the educational system the committee had so meticulously analyzed and restructured. And because no mention was made of books in this very vital report, about which more will be said later, a major opportunity to propose a national book publishing and distribution policy was lost.

However, the syllabi being developed by KIE and the materials that were produced by the subsequent subject panels underscored the need to have a publisher who would issue these materials. So the government created Jomo Kenyatta Foundation (JKF) in 1965 as a trust that would publish these materials and use whatever profits it made in the award of scholarships to needy children. It must be emphasized that although government later got sensitive about primary school books being published by foreign commercial publishers, and later unsuccessfully tried to use JKF as a primary school publisher, the problem was that JKF had not been set up as part of a broad national strategy toward localizing the Kenyan book industry.

THE COMING OF LOCAL PUBLISHERS

1965 was a watershed year for Kenyan publishing. Apart from JKF, several other new publishers came on the scene – the most important of which was, perhaps, East African Publishing House (EAPH). It was started by a group of academics from Eastern Africa who constituted the East African Institute of Social and Cultural Affairs, in association with the British publisher Andre Deutsch. The new publisher was expected to cater more satisfactorily to the academic and general educational needs of the local communities and to reflect a more positive image of the African heritage, which, it was felt, the existing foreign publishers had failed to do. The partnership with Andre Deutsch did not last and was discontinued the following year due to differences arising from publishing policies. Institute members then formed themselves into the East African Cultural Trust, which was to administer the publishing house, and Afropress, a sister printing works established later. The new firm was able to attract manuscripts especially from academics who were themselves members of the institute, with quite a few of their own titles coming out during the firm's first few years of publishing.

Another new publishing company that started business in 1965 was Equatorial Publishers, a private indigenous publisher set up by an entrepreneuring ex-salesman of Longman named Y. N. Okal, who also spread his interests to include bookshops and a printing press.

In the same year two foreign publishers, Longman and Heinemann, set up substantive branches. Longman, who by now had two very successful textbooks, the *Highway Arithmetic* and *Pivot English Course*, consolidated its gains by reconstituting itself into an overseas branch of Longman U.K., and in 1969 as a full company, Longman Kenya Ltd. As for Heinemann, it at first thought that its general list might appeal to the ex-colonial settlers who admittedly made up much of the general readership, and a new company, Heinemann-Cassell, was formed to carry the trade list. Heinemann soon afterwards found out that the African Writers Series and key textbooks such as *Ordinary Level Physics* and *New Certificate Chemistry* stood it in good stead. Three years later, the general company was dissolved and a new educational company, Heinemann Educational Books (E.A.) Ltd., was established in 1968. Macmillan came seeking to employ the same strategy as it had done in Ghana, Tanzania, and Uganda, but it did not find a willing state publisher to work with and had to wait until 1971, when it registered itself locally as (Macmillan) Books for Africa after its debacle in the three countries above had necessitated a fresh start.

Other publishers such as Nelson, Evans, Pitman, and Cambridge University Press, to name a few, were active at this time and appointed resident representatives. A host of other British publishers who neither had branches nor representatives in Kenya offered agencies to those who were already there, so that by about 1968, close to 80 British publishers had some form of presence in Kenya.

So, during the first five years of Kenya's independence, there were, apart from the Government Printer and the religious presses, four types of publishers coexisting amicably but potentially antagonistically with one another: the state or semistate publishers (for example, EAPH), private commercial publishers (Equatorial), and foreign publishers (Longman, Oxford University Press, Heinemann). At first, there were no major problems between the main groups or within each group; in fact, there seems to have been some cooperation. For example, Oxford University Press continued to publish the *New Peak English Course*, originally developed by EALB, refined by KIE, and now renamed *Progressive Peak English Course*. Longman copublished the title *Zamani: A Survey of East African History*, edited by B. A. Ogot, with EAPH. And, again, Longman was the publisher chosen to produce *Tujifunze Kusoma Kikwetu* – an ambitious language and reading scheme developed at KIE, in which the same color illustrations were to be used to produce the textbook in 15 local-language editions. The EAPH developed a mathematics course, *School Mathematics of East Africa (SMEA)* jointly with Cambridge University Press.

By 1970 it could be said that although Kenya had been independent for seven years, the publishing industry was largely in the hands of foreign publishers. Equatorial publishers were finding the going difficult and were surviving mostly on what they made from their printing press. The JKF was deriving most of its revenue from *Kenya Primary Mathematics*, a complete primary mathematics textbook developed at KIE, and a few teachers' guides. EAPH, either by choice or force of circumstances, was publishing mainly academic and general books, children's books and fiction, while the EALB continued on the path that Richards had charted for it on his departure, namely publishing books in African languages and adult literacy primers. The profitable textbook market, which at that time represented over 80 percent of the value of the total book market, was in the hands of foreign publishers. John Nottingham, then executive director of EAPH, has covered this period well in his various papers, drawing attention to this acute dependence in a sensitive area of vital national interest.[3]

The first response to this multinational stranglehold came from government. They set up the Kenya School Equipment Scheme (KSES), a body that was to buy books centrally and distribute them to Kenya's primary schools. The Ministry of Education then proceeded to draw up a list of recommended books to be bought by the KSES, and this included titles mainly developed at KIE and published by the JKF. As the foundation had not yet published all the books required for primary schools, the ministry had no alternative but to include textbooks from foreign publishers as well. But the government intended to protect the primary school market as a monopoly for JKF. In fact, so successful was KSES, that titles outside the scheme's list sold in very small quantities indeed – the losers being largely foreign publishers of primary school books, with textbooks such as JKF's *Safari English Course* gaining ground on the more acceptable traditional books.

The second response came from local entrepreneurs entering the publishing business – among them John Nottingham, who had resigned from East African Publishing House to set up Transafrica Publishers and Book Distributors in 1973. Fred Ojienda, the production man at EAPH, also broke off to set up Foundation Books in 1974. Others were David Maillu, a graphic artist and illustrator, who established Comb Books in 1972 with the main intention of publishing his own novels – to which local publishers had not reacted favorably. Other publishers coming on the scene included Njogu Gitene – Njogu Gitene Publications (children's books); Lennard Okola – Bookwise (educational); Ngotho Kariuki – Midi Teki (general); Abdilahi Nassir – Shungwaya (Kiswahili general); Mohammed Mbwana – Mowa (Kiswahili educational); and Munuhe Kareithi – Gazelle Books (educational/general).

THE FAT YEARS

The period between 1970 and 1977 was probably the most lively in Kenyan publishing, and the most competitive. The JKF monopoly described above did not work completely, as the foundation did not have all the primary schoolbooks required in the system. So with the exception of *Kenya Primary Mathematics*, a Kiswahili textbook entitled *Masomo Ya Kiswahili*, and the *Safari Course*, KSES procured the rest of the required materials from commercial publishers, the majority of which were still branches of multinational publishers. The indigenous publishers did not have the kind of funding required to develop textbooks that would have gotten onto the scheme, but they did get several single titles onto it. Although there was general prosperity, this period was characterized by doubt, mutual suspicion, and intrigue among the parties involved. Paradoxically, it is this situation that led to the formation of important professional associations in 1971 – the Kenya Publishers Association and the Kenya African Booksellers and Stationers Association, later named the Kenya Booksellers and Stationers Association, so as to accommodate all the nationalities involved in the book trade. It would appear that people joined these associations to guard their own self-interests rather than to strive for the common goal of working toward the welfare of the book industry as a whole. It comes as no surprise that five years later, indigenous publishers had pulled out of the Kenya Publishers Association, while the Kenya African Booksellers Association was finding it difficult to continue without the support of its more affluent Asian partners.

THE LEAN YEARS

The period of prosperity ended in 1977, with the closure of the border between Kenya and Tanzania. Kenyan publishers were no longer able to export to Tanzania or the markets farther south such as Zambia and Malawi. There had been little business with Uganda since Idi Amin's 1971 coup d'état. Thus, over this period Kenyans had lost the bulk of their export trade, which at its peak had averaged 25 to 30 percent of their turnover. To complicate matters, the home market stagnated largely as a result of the uncertainty surrounding Daniel arap Moi's succession to the presidency upon Kenyatta's death in 1978. A coup attempt on President Moi's new government in 1982 did not help matters.

The response to these problems was varied. Longman, by far the largest publisher, reacted by selling 40 percent of its equity to local people – more as a way of ensuring their own survival than as a genuine step toward indigenizing the company. And when this approach seemed not to be working, they followed the example set by Oxford University Press in declaring some staff redundant and cutting down on their publishing programs. The smaller foreign publishers (e.g., Collins, Pitmans, Cambridge University Press, Nelsons, and Evans), either closed down completely or pulled out and left their businesses in the hands of local commission agents.

State-supported publishers such as EAPH, Kenya Literature Bureau (KLB), the company that Kenya had set up in 1979 to replace the former EALB, and the JKF were all dormant, with almost no new titles coming out of them during this critical period.

But it was the indigenous publishers who took the greatest beating. Transafrica went bankrupt, while Comb Books, Foundation Books, Shungwaya, Mowa, Midi Teki, Bookwise, Njogu Gitene, all stopped publishing and, with no backlists to fall back on, went out of business. EAPH was eventually declared bankrupt in 1987.

29 African Literature/ Anthropological Exotic

Graham Huggan

The Heinemann African Writers Series (AWS) has undoubtedly performed a valuable service, both in fostering the reputations of many gifted African writers and in bringing an increasing number of African literary works – the Series now runs into the hundreds – to the public eye. The emergence of English-language African writing in the 1950s and 1960s, and the wide respect in which it is held today, would be unthinkable without the momentum provided by Heinemann's promotional enterprise, worldwide distributional networks and financial support. But *how*, exactly, has Heinemann chosen to promote African literature? A cursory history of the Series suggests that Heinemann, for all its well-intentioned activities, may have contributed to the continuing exoticisation of Africa through misdirected anthropological images; and that the Africa it has promoted by way of its talented literary protégés has been subjected to a self-empowering, implicitly neocolonialist 'anthropological gaze' (Lizarríbar 1998: chap. 4).

The development of the Series, established in the early 1960s under the stewardship of its veteran impresario, Alan Hill, must first be understood in the wider context of the African publishing crisis to which I previously alluded. This crisis, as I suggested, might itself be seen as a single component in the vast neocolonial engine that drives relations between Africa and other Third World regions and their First World 'benefactors' today. The publishing industry in Africa, indeed, affords a rueful object lesson in how structural conditions of underdevelopment produce reliance on the very outside sources that reinforce cultural, as well as economic, dependency (Kotei 1981). Low literacy rates; a fragile intellectual infrastructure; the prohibitive costs involved in printing, transporting and purchasing books in such a huge, divided and desperately impoverished continent; the perceived lack of a cultural atmosphere conducive to the development of local production/consumption networks (Irele 1990) – all of these are contributing factors to a history of catastrophically low levels of book production in Africa and to the continuing, largely enforced reliance on importation and outside agencies of support. Yet these are also indicators of a neocolonial knowledge industry: of the educationally reinforced dependency-mechanisms by which many African writers and, by corollary, their local readers are persuaded to believe that cultural value, as well as economic power, is located and arbitrated elsewhere.[1] Camille Lizarríbar, to whose pioneering history of the

African Writers Series I am greatly indebted here, sums up the position for many contemporary African writers as follows:

> African authors will often turn to foreign publishers because of a general mistrust in local publishing, and to be assured of a higher quality product. Therefore, both writers and books are geared primarily towards an outside audience. This vicious circle seems to be a well-established mechanism which hinders the growth of an African book industry by continuously directing its resources and products towards an external supplier and consumer.
> (Lizarríbar 1998: 58)

Unquestionably, this state of affairs lies behind the unparalleled success of the Heinemann. African Writers Series, and goes some way toward accounting for its (along with other leading Euro-American publishers') virtual monopoly over the distribution of African literature today.

Various myths of origin surround the emergence of the Series. Several of these relate to the formative role played by Chinua Achebe: one of the Series' founding editors; the author of its inaugural and, in several respects, catalytic volume (*Things Fall Apart*); and still far and away its leading generator of revenue (it has been estimated that Achebe's novels alone are responsible for a third of the Series' total sales). Another relates to the landmark decision of Van Milne, an experienced recruit from one of Heinemann's competitors, Nelson, to launch a low-priced trade-paperback series that would effectively piggyback on the existing African educational market. The most important figure, though, and self-designated founder of the Series, was Alan Hill, the then director of Heinemann's lucrative educational branch, Heinemann Educational Books (HEB). As Hill, now retired, relates in his self-congratulatory autobiography, *In Pursuit of Publishing* (1988), the overseas development of HEB was serendipitously connected with the demise of the British Empire. A three-day visit to Bombay in the mid 1950s was enough to persuade Hill that '[t]he India which British soldiers and administrators had lost was being regained by British educators and publishers' (Hill 1988: 93), especially Longman and Oxford University Press. Enter HEB and, shortly thereafter, the African Writers Series, which was also to profit from what Hill called 'the winds of [political] change' in Africa (Hill 1988: 192).

As Lizarríbar convincingly demonstrates, the self-important, blatantly neo-imperialist rhetoric of Hill's autobiography 'sustains contemporary theories which propose a form of neo-colonialism of Third World countries by the former colonial powers of the West, this time through economic and educational channels' (Lizarríbar 1998: 74)·In *Pursuit of Publishing* is also remarkable for its redeployment of atavistic 'Dark Continent' imagery in the service of pioneering First World enterprise, as Hill's numerous formulaic allusions to Conrad's *Heart of Darkness* attest. (Here, for example, is our man in Nigeria: 'Periodically we slithered off the wet track into the darkness of the bush; but thankfully we always skidded back on again. Occasionally we would cross a clearing with a circle of primeval mud huts. It seemed like a journey back into a deep past' (Hill 1988: 122).) As Lizarríbar concludes of the abundant light-and-dark images that traverse Hill's expeditions of African 'discovery', his vision of the creation of the African Writers Series can be seen as:

> a mixture of the … missionary mentality, which proposed education as the route into the light of Christianity, and [a combination of] western values and his own business savvy, which made him aware of the potential market involved. As a modern missionary, Hill would not merely bring light into the Dark Continent; … he would provide a light that would allow the Dark Continent to reveal its own mysteries through the mediation of literature and good business sense.
>
> (Lizarríbar 1998: 83–84)

While it would be exaggerating the case to claim that the Series has moulded itself to Hill's self-image, its marketing approach has often shown symptoms of a controlling imperial gaze. This gaze is evident, not just in patterns (especially early patterns) of selection and editorial intervention, but also in the blatantly exoticist packaging of AWS titles, particularly their covers. As emerges from early assessments of titles earmarked for the Series, a certain style and tone were expected, often conforming to Euro-American preconceptions of 'simplicity', 'primitivism' and 'authenticity' (Lizarríbar 1998: chap. 4). These preconceptions also hover round the edges of the early titles' covers, several of which feature emblematic images and designs and, in black and white on the back cover, a crudely amateurish photograph of the author for what appears to be ethnic identification purposes. These covers arguably betray a preoccupation with the iconic representation of an 'authentic Africa' for a largely foreign readership, a preoccupation also apparent in appreciative assessments of the works' putatively anthropological content. Hill's triumphal vision of the corrective role to be played by the Series shows this clearly:

> In place of the misconceptions of colonialist times [the African Writers Series] has given us a true picture of African traditional societies as they move into the modern world, depicting their humanity, their artistic achievements, as well as their cruelty and superstition – a mixture very familiar in the history of Western European civilization.
>
> (Hill 1988: 145)

This pseudo-anthropological view, in which the reconfirmation of exoticist stereotype masquerades as the newly minted expression of a previously misunderstood cultural reality, has been influential in the metropolitan reception of AWS titles – not least because of their insertion into a ready-made educational market. As an offshoot of HEB, the Series was initially intended to function within a residually colonial African educational system modelled on European standards (Lizarríbar 1998: 121). As James Currey, in charge of AWS from 1967 until 1984, remarks matter-of-factly: 'This was a series published by an educational publisher and used in Africa for educational purposes, at university as well as at school level' (Unwin and Currey 1993: 6). Yet as soon became clear, the educational function of the Series was by no means restricted to Africa; it could be geared to the education systems of Europe and America as well. And a valuable marketing strategy – particularly though by no means exclusively outside of Africa – was to play up the anthropological dimensions of literary texts often touted as virtually unmediated representations of African society, culture and history. Literature emerged as a valuable tool for the student of African customs, a notion reinforced by the provision of glossaries and other paratextual phenomena – introductory essays, photographs and illustrations, the paraphernalia of annotation.[2] Yet this well-intentioned work of sociohistorical explication, still intrinsic to the ethos of the Series, did little to correct stereotypical views of a romantic Africa of 'primitive', even primordial, tribal existence. Hill again on Achebe:

> The great interest of [*Things Fall Apart*] is that it genuinely succeeds in presenting tribal life from the inside. Patterns of feeling and attitudes of mind appear clothed in a distinctive African imagery ... [Achebe's] literary method is apparently simple, but a vivid imagination illuminates every page, and his style is a model of clarity.
>
> (Hill 1988: 121)

Hill's account of the development of the Series, charted through a series of glibly classified stages or period-movements, oscillates between a diachronic, 'historical' view of African social transformation and a synchronic, 'anthropological' view of a distinctive African culture. Both views, largely essentialised, indicate alternative reflectionist readings of African literature as either a window onto the 'real' Africa or a barometer of its changing culture.

Several caveats, however, should probably be entered here. Hill's philosophy, while influential, can hardly be said to enshrine AWS policy, which, as might be expected, has undergone numerous changes in the four decades of its existence. The Series during that time has expanded far beyond its original educational mandate, and the vision of Africa it presents is far more varied and complex than Hill's suspiciously disingenuous classifications imply.[3] The AWS, while certainly marketed for a foreign and, increasingly, a global audience, has always catered for a sizeable African reading public as well, as is still very much the case today. (This can be seen, for example, in Bernth Lindfors's 1990 statistics on the prevalent use of AWS texts as school/university set texts – Lindfors 1990, 1993.) What is more, African writers have chosen by and large to send their works to Heinemann, in the hope not just of financial reward and a large overseas, as well as African, audience, but also in the legitimate expectation of unbiased treatment and professionally conducted peer review. The view of African literature – to repeat – as an exotically cultivated export product risks falling victim to the same historical inaccuracies and cultural homogenisations of which Hill himself might stand accused. All of these might be considered as extenuating circumstances. For all that, the history of the Series, relaunched in 1987 under Vicky Unwin and still as active as ever, arguably reveals at least some of the characteristic preoccupations of the anthropological exotic: the desire for authenticity, projected onto the screen of a 'real' Africa; the insistence on the documentary value of literary and, especially, fictional sources; the attempt to co-opt African literature into a Euro-American morality play centring on the need to understand 'foreign' cultures; the further co-optation of this educative process for the purpose of lending moral credence to a self-serving romantic quest. Thus, while it remains true that the AWS has done much to provide the working conditions in which African literature continues to flourish, it has done so under circumstances that might be considered, at best, as inconsistent with many of its writers' overtly anti-colonial beliefs. And, at worst, it might even be claimed that the Series has helped – inadvertently no doubt – to project a certain image of an emergent continent, 'expressed' through its literature, that 'reinforces negative stereotypes which have defined the "Dark Continent" and its people to the Western world' (Lizarríbar 1998: 140).

As I have suggested, this negative view summons up the image-repertoire of an anthropological exotic which serves to celebrate the notion of cultural difference while at the same time assimilating it to familiar Western interpretive codes. These assimilationist tendencies are also apparent in what Achebe calls 'colonialist criticism': the type of Euro-American response that raids African writing for evidence of 'universal' (read, Western) patterns of human history and behaviour.[4] (Hill's view of the Series as providing a 'mixture [of humanity and cruelty] very familiar in the history of Western European civilization' might be taken here as symptomatic.) But at this point, what should we make of Achebe's own formative role in the development of the Series; or of the respects he pays Hill in his unequivocally appreciative foreword to *In Pursuit of Publishing*? Might there not be a danger here in subscribing to a *bifurcated* reception model – one in which African writers, through their dealings with Western 'agents of legitimation' (Bourdieu 1993), are inevitably compromised, suckered into successive reinventions of an Africa that the White Man has known all along? While there are several well-documented instances of African writers locking horns with Western publishers, reviewers and critics (within the context of the Series, two names that come immediately to mind are those of Ayi Kwei Armah and Kole Omotoso), it would be unwise to conclude from this that African literature and the Western literary/critical industry are necessarily at loggerheads; that Western publishers and critics inevitably misrepresent Africa, and that Western readers are automatically complicit in such misrepresentations; and that a guaranteed corrective can be provided for these patterns of abuse by the encouragement of homegrown epistemologies, the cultural-nationalist protection of resources, and local ownership of and control over the means of cultural production. Such 'nativist topologies', as Kwame Anthony Appiah calls them, often depend on a binary 'us/them' rhetoric which negates the transculturative potential inherent in a lengthy history of European encounters – however invasive – with Africa, as well as in more recent developments of capitalist globalisation – however uneven – that have made an irrevocable impact on the configuration and transformation of African national cultures; which blinds itself to the crucial understanding of modern African literature as a product of the colonial encounter, rather than as 'the simple continuation of an indigenous tradition [or] a mere intrusion from the metropole' (Appiah 1992: 69–70); and which risks merely supplanting the Western-academic 'rhetoric of alterity' with a form of 'ersatz exoticism', through which Africans vainly attempt to assert their cultural autonomy by fashioning themselves 'as the image of the Other' (Appiah 1992: 72). For Appiah, it is pointless trying to forget Europe by erasing the European traces of Africa's past: 'since it is too late for us to escape each other, we might instead seek to turn to our advantage the mutual interdependencies history has thrust upon us' (Appiah 1992: 72).

I would echo Appiah's insistence that Europe is, like it or not, a part of Africa; and that African literature is best regarded as neither celebratory self-expression nor reprehensible Western imposition, but rather as a hybrid amalgam of cross-fertilised aesthetic traditions that are the historical outcome of a series of – often violent – cultural collisions. The anthropological exotic in which African literature is implicated is, in part, an attempt to convert this violence into palatable aesthetic forms. This attempt, perhaps, comprises what I would call the 'postcoloniality' of African literature: its global market-value as a reified object of intellectual tourism, or as the reassuringly educative vehicle of a cultural difference seen and appreciated in aesthetic terms (see Introduction). But the anthropological exotic is also, like other forms of the exotic, a medium of unsettlement; it contains unwanted traces of the violence it attempts to conceal. As I have suggested in this chapter, the deployment of strategically exoticist modes of representation in African literature, often ironically mediated through an anthropological discourse of 'scientific' observation, has a destabilising effect on the readers it addresses. Destabilising in several senses: first, because it reminds these readers of their interpretive limits and of the inevitable biases behind their attempts to construct Africa as an object of cultural knowledge; second, because it redeploys the anthropological technique of participant-observation as the metaphor for a self-empowering, but also potentially self-incriminating, cultural voyeurism; and third, because it illustrates the 'epistemic violence' (Spivak 1987) that underwrites the colonial encounter – an encounter of which anthropology, as well as African literature, is the historical product (Asad 1972). It has been said, uncharitably no doubt, that the current 'literary turn' in anthropology is another variant on the motif of ethnographic salvage – the discipline's attempt, through heightened powers of critical self-reflexivity, to save itself from itself and from its own exoticising tendencies. I favour the more generous view – also espoused by Miller – that anthropology remains a useful, if inevitably flawed, tool of cultural exploration and self-critique (Miller 1990: esp. chap. 1). But on the question of whether anthropology is a necessary supplement to the critical work of textual analysis, I must confess to a certain scepticism. There is an anthropology *in* African literature that is less about the establishment of techniques for information retrieval and interpretation than about a cultural politics of reading in which the desire for 'information' itself becomes deeply suspect. Miller is quite right, I think, to warn about the dangers of cultural ignorance. But African literature does more than warn about these; it also suggests the dangers of a misappropriated cultural knowledge. These dangers become apparent when we turn to the global knowledge industry and to the – often predetermined – role that an ostensibly postcolonial literature is made to play within neocolonial knowledge networks. African writers, almost by definition, are well aware of this dilemma – a dilemma that several of them have chosen to dramatise in their works. Perhaps what is needed is less an anthropological understanding of African literature, more a sociological grasp of the specific material conditions under which such understandings are constructed; and a wider historical sense of how cultural knowledge about 'foreign' cultures is effected, through which channels that knowledge is routed, and in whose interests it is deployed.

30 Africa Writes Back: Heinemann African Writers Series – A Publisher's Memoir

James Currey

The African Writers Series was founded in 1962, almost exactly 25 years after the start of Penguin books. The paperback Series was to become to Africans, in its first quarter century, what Penguin Books had been to British readers in its first 25 years. It provided good serious reading at accessible prices for the rapidly emerging professional classes as the countries became independent. The colour orange for novels had been shamelessly copied from Penguin. By the time of its tenth anniversary in 1972, it had come to be called in Africa the 'orange series' and was stacked high in the key positions inside the entrances of the university campus bookshops, from one side of Africa to the other. The writer and critic Edward Blishen said at the time of the tenth anniversary in 1972: 'I shall tell my grandchildren that I owe most of what education I have to Penguins and that through the African Writers Series I saw a new, potentially great, world literature coming into being.'[1]

English was the lubricant of the English-speaking world. It was not only how authority was imposed but it was also used by the subject peoples to resist that imposition of power. Writers in India, the Caribbean and Africa came to take advantage of the language that they shared. But they had to have publishing opportunities. And to begin with, those opportunities were almost all in London. By 1962 quite a lot of work by Caribbean writers had been published in London. Some Indian writers were well established on London lists. But practically no creative work by Africans had appeared. Writers in Africa needed to get the idea that they too might get published. The title of my chapter is 'Africa Writes Back' because I have seen, over the last 40 years, how Africans achieved the confidence to write back in novels, plays and poetry about what was happening to them.

It was the received wisdom in British publishing in the early sixties that the only books that could be sold in Africa were school textbooks. There was no perceived 'general market'. The colonial authorities thought of books for a purpose – the education of a new elite. Books for enjoyment which enhanced understanding of other Africans' ways of love and death were not on their agenda. Alan Hill, the founder of Heinemann Educational Books, was described to me by the former head of the Longman Africa division as 'an inspired madman' because he did the things that other British publishers thought were a waste of time.

A grandson of missionaries in Cameroun, he grew up knowing where Africa was. On his first visit to Nigeria in 1959, he was very proud of the fact that William Heinemann had the previous year published a novel called *Things Fall Apart* in hardback. To his amazement nobody knew anything about it. At the elite University College in Ibadan, expatriate staff refused to believe that a recent graduate could have had a novel published by a prestigious London publishing house. Chinua Achebe told me that as a student he read Joyce Cary's *Mister Johnson* which is set in Nigeria. He said that he had thought to himself: 'If this man can get such a bad book about Nigeria published why don't I have a go?' A clear case of an African writing back.

Alan Hill, in the heady atmosphere of the independence years (Ghana in 1957, Nigeria in 1960) saw the need to make serious general books by Africans available in a paperback series like Penguins. It was an inspired choice to make Chinua Achebe the Editorial Adviser to the Series. The first four titles included Achebe's *Things Fall Apart* and its sequel *No Longer at Ease*. First printings were about 2500. It was a cautious start. Quickly Chinua Achebe's name became a magnet for new writing. The photograph of the author on the back reinforced the idea that Africans might get published.

By the twentieth anniversary in 1982 Heinemann had sold close on three million copies of *Things Fall Apart*; in the next 20 years sales trebled. There have been translations into many other languages. Neither Penguin nor Pan, the two major paperback series in Britain in 1958, bought rights. It now appears in Penguin Modern Classics. None of that would have happened if it had not been published in paperback as number 1 in the African Writers Series.

Paperbacks are mostly reprint series. But what to reprint when so few novels by Africans had been published in hardback by British or American publishers? In 1962, the very year of the start of the Series, Chinua Achebe was at a conference on African writing at Makerere University College in Uganda in East Africa, when he heard a knock at the door of his guest house in the evening. He found a student standing there who offered him the manuscripts of two novels. The name of the Kenyan student was Ngugi. *Weep Not, Child* and *The River Between* were the first books to be accepted for publication in hardback as well as in paperback in the African Writers Series. That was the moment when Heinemann Educational Books took on the role that was at that time almost exclusively performed in London by general hardback publishers: the *first time* publishing of new creative writing whether novels, plays or poetry. There was also the stiffening thread of political works by people with names such as Mandela, Mboya and Kaunda.

Ngugi got the idea of writing novels from the Caribbean. A range of writers from the West Indies were being accepted from the fifties onwards by established literary hardback publishers in London. Henry Swanzy's BBC Colonial Service programme 'Caribbean Voices' gave hope to Walcott, Naipaul and many other writers. Africans needed hope as well. Ngugi tells in *Homecoming* of the impact on him of the Barbadian George Lamming's *In the Castle of My Skin:* 'He evoked for me, an unforgettable picture of a peasant revolt in a white-dominated world. And suddenly I knew that the novel could speak to me, could, with a compelling urgency, touch cords deep down in me.'[2]

We take it for granted in Britain now that there are many outlets – publishers, journals, newspapers, radio stations – who are accepting creative writing all the time. And we take it for granted that there are literary agents to place work. And we know that, once a book is published, there is a whole reviewing, promotions and feature-writing industry. At that time, we needed to get that industry to take writing by Africans seriously.

A problem was that paperbacks were not reviewed in newspapers. Novels had to be published in hardback to be noticed. We needed to get the consideration of African writers in the reviewing columns along with the regular output from the hardback literary publishers. Reviews were necessary in order to get orders from public libraries who, at that time, were the main patrons of new writing. The father firm William Heinemann agreed, reluctantly, to publish Ngugi's novels in hardback first. Heinemann Educational Books later published many of the writers in hardback under the imprint 'Heinemann'. Only gradually did enterprising reviewers come to realise that there was a new vitality in the writing from Africa and looked to the orange paperbacks for something special.

Keith Sambrook was the director at Heinemann Educational Books who had been put by Alan Hill in charge of the rapid expansion of offices in what we were then starting to call 'the Third World', Keith Sambrook, with Chinua Achebe's active encouragement, built on the success of the initial four titles with a canny choice. There were anthologies of poetry, prose, short stories and plays. Some key titles such as Alex la Guma's *A Walk in the Night* came from the remarkable Mbari list in Ibadan. There were some translations from African languages. However, it was the translations from the French which helped to establish the early dominance of the African Writers Series. The Parisian publishers had been much more enterprising about publishing African writers. In 1956 first novels by Mongo Beti, Ferdinand Oyono and Sembene Ousmane, all appeared.

Some other publishers with educational lists in Africa were also starting paperback series of writers from Africa. Collins put about 20 African tines into their Fontana paperback list. Rex Collings, who had started his publishing life at Penguins, persuaded Oxford University Press to start the Three Crowns Series. He secured from Mbari the plays of Wole Soyinka, who was to be the first winner of the Nobel Prize for Literature. In 1965 Rex Collings went off, taking Soyinka to Methuens, who had one of the most distinguished drama lists. He made sure that I could inherit his publishing list at Oxford. However in 1967 the chance came to work with Keith Sambrook at Heinemann; by this time the first 30 titles in the African Writers Series had already gone a long way to establish a new canon of African literature.

The central problem at Heinemann Educational Books was that here was an educational company which needed the educational system to build up the sale of its paperbacks to keep the prices down. We did not know that the new examination boards in West and East Africa would be so enterprising in prescribing texts by young living Africans; the boards in Britain preferred their authors dead. The bookshops, universities and schools were delighted to find that the Africans were writing back. The British firms Oxford University Press, Longman, Macmillan, Evans and Nelson dominated the educational textbook market in Africa in the early sixties. Heinemann Educational Books came late but made such a success of the African Writers Series that it helped to get text-book contracts.

My more cautious colleagues were concerned that sex, religion and politics might keep the books out of schools. The inhibitions which concerned an educational publisher, only a few years after the Lady Chatterley obscenity trial, did not worry Chinua Achebe as Editorial Adviser. He wanted the Series to reflect all the richness and variety of an emerging Africa. He was concerned with the widest literary criteria. All these books had to be approved for publication by a formal committee of directors and editors sitting round a table beneath the chandeliers of the ballroom of a house in Mayfair which had belonged to Lord Randolph Churchill and his wife, Jenny. After the discussion had gone on for some time about whether certain subjects would cut out the book from schools, the Chairman Alan Hill would say, 'Well, James, what did the old Chinua say?' He knew, everyone round that table knew, that if I had brought the proposal to the meeting then young Chinua Achebe would already have said 'yes' (even if it was on the telephone while passing through London from the Uli airstrip in Biafra to raise funds in America). So Alan Hill would say 'Right James. You want to do it? Go ahead and do it?' With the imaginative support of Chinua Achebe for the first 100 titles in the series, Heinemann had established that there was a general as well as an educational market in Africa.

I visited Chinua and Christie Achebe at the University of Nigeria at Nsukka at the end of the civil war. The house was a shell. The walls were black. There was no power. Chinua Achebe gave me the manuscript of his short stories called *Girls at War*, which became No. 100 in the Series when published in 1972. He said that the time had come to hand over his role as Editorial Adviser to another African writer and he and I agreed that Ngugi would be absolutely appropriate. Ngugi immediately accepted but then after six weeks understandably decided that the duties would interfere with his own writing.

Keith Sambrook and I set out to widen the African input. By the tenth anniversary of the Series, Heinemann had an active editorial office in Nairobi as well as Ibadan. So we suggested that, rather than a single Editorial Adviser to the Series, there should be a triangular system of consultation between the publishing editors in Ibadan, Nairobi and London. Aig Higo, himself a poet, had worked with Chinua Achebe almost from the start and continued to keep us in touch with the active Nigerian and Ghanaian literary scenes. Chinua Achebe and Ngugi, along with a host of other writers and academics, were to continue to give reports and recommend new manuscripts. Henry Chakava, Simon Gikandi and Laban Erapu in Nairobi were from a second generation. They were to make Heinemann the publisher of first choice in East Africa, as it already was in West Africa. I would continue to draw on the exile community and the new publishers of resistance to represent South Africa, Rhodesia and the Portuguese colonies. Central to the policy was enthusiasm. Nobody had a veto. All three offices usually came to an agreement over novels. Selection of poetry tended to be a much more individual choice. Anthologies of plays tried to represent work from across the continent and from different traditions.

Heinemann had built an active international network of choice in Africa. Consultation was not without considerable effort and expense. Again and again one is reminded that telephoning was expensive and unreliable. Cables were the text messages of the time and just as likely to be ambiguous. Photocopying the wide range of hopeful manuscripts to share between three offices was still relatively expensive. Airfares were still high (In 1959 it had cost Oxford University Press almost as much as my annual salary to fly me to South Africa). I was only able to justify the heavy costs of travel by going to see the educational authorities about textbook adoptions during the working day; in the evenings I and my African colleagues could drink and eat with the writers or go to their plays. It would never have been cost-effective to go round Africa just to see the creative writers.

We could accept only a fraction of the piles of manuscripts received by the three offices. (I should guess 1 in 30 or 40). We spent a lot of money on reports. If the first reaction was hopeful I would get a second report. If both the reports were hopeful and had suggestions about rewriting I would, even if we were rejecting the manuscript, send them to the writer. We felt that it was constructive to pass on the reactions of our readers. Writing is a lonely business and if some advice comes it is better than a cold rejection slip. We invested all this effort to bring on new writers. Increasingly there were publishers in the larger African countries encouraged by the market which had grown for creative writing. In Nairobi the East African Publishing House had a rival Modern African Writers series. However, elsewhere the African Writers Series was so dominant that most of the writers offered their work to us first.

It has often been said that it was inappropriate for the African Writers Series to be published in the old imperial capital of London. Individuals, usually European or American, have accusingly said to me, 'A series of African writers should be published in Africa.' However, the writers wanted to be published in London, and the common hope was that they would be treated as 'writers' rather than 'African writers'. With Heinemann the most outstanding writers could often have it both ways with hardback and paperback publication. From a London base we were able to make the literary contacts which introduced these writers to readers not only in Britain and America but also in places as wide apart as Canada, India, the West Indies and Australia. And we sold translation rights in the major languages of Europe and Asia.

At the same time, through the medium of English, we often introduced African writers in Portuguese and French to a larger audience than they were able to reach in the original language. Mongo Beti wrote to me on 8 December 1975 and said, 'J'ai aussi parcouru avec étonnement les chiffres de vente' ['I too went through the sales figures with astonishment']. The Egyptian publishing industry was the largest in Africa. Colloquial Arabic was used in the modern novel in spite of religious opposition. The first ever publication of English translations of the novelist Naguib Mahfouz appeared in the African Writers Series as well as in Heinemann's parallel series called Arab Authors. This Egyptian novelist was to be the third winner from Africa of the Nobel Prize for Literature; work by Wole Soyinka, Nadine Gordimer and Naguib Mahfouz had appeared in the Series long before they received the Prize.

Intrinsic to our handling of African writers was the need to build bridges: to literary agents, to hardback publishers who would get reviews and library sales, to broadcasters, to US publishers, to publishers in foreign languages. We found excitement in providing an international network. We knew a great deal about the literary industry in London and New York. We took a pride in getting the outstanding writers known in the literary circles there.

At Heinemann we all – in Africa, in London and at offices round the world – took advantage of English to provide an international network. We used the advantages of being in London to stimulate an explosion of creative writing in Africa. In these days of so much Afro-pessimism one can say that African writing and African music have reached out across the world. One can really say that Africans have learned to write back.

Part Seven
Women and Print Culture

The readings in this section reflect on women's historical exclusion from print culture and on their responses to these exclusions and inequalities. They include studies of the methods employed by women during the 'second wave' of feminism in the late twentieth century to gain control of printing and publishing and to give women writers more prominence, and also of the ways in which digital technology enables women writers to circumvent gender inequalities in the contemporary publishing industry.

Virginia Woolf's *A Room of One's Own* (1967 [1929]), based on two lectures given at Cambridge in 1928, reflects on reasons for the lack of a female literary heritage. She considers the absence of women from history books and the gaps in our historical knowledge about women's lives prior to the eighteenth century, and tells the tragic story of a hypothetical sister of Shakespeare, as gifted as her brother but without education, money or independence, concluding that, 'It would have been impossible, completely and entirely, for any women to have written the plays of Shakespeare in the age of Shakespeare' (p. 227). The tract (Chapter 31) reflects on the way that women authors in the nineteenth century exhibited signs of 'inner strife' through seeking anonymity and adopting male pseudonyms, and concludes that the female author continues to be hampered by the myth of female mental inferiority, by a lack of financial independence and by a lack of physical space to write without interruption. Woolf's argument that certain material conditions, namely 'money and a room of her own', are essential for the creation of fiction has been criticised for its political evasion and 'strategic retreat' (Showalter 1977: 284) and for its capitalistic aspirations for private property (Solomon 1989: 334), but it remains a foundational text of feminist criticism and influential feminist critique of print culture.

The development of feminist publishing in the global south is surveyed by Urvashi Butalia and Ritu Menon in this extract (Chapter 32) from *Making a Difference: Feminist Publishing in the South* (1995). In the context of significant obstacles affecting the publishing industry across regions of Asia, Africa and Latin America, they chart how feminist activists engaged with printing and publishing. Several of these ventures arose from women's groups and women's studies programmes, but some were more commercial enterprises, and feminist publications ranged from more ephemeral pamphlets and magazines to fiction, self-help and academic women's studies books. This was a considerable struggle, and those companies that survived relied on either donor funding or a flexible approach towards publishing across a range of genres and markets. The authors describe their own work in establishing the publishing firm Kali, with the aim to 'reverse the flow of ... information, which has traditionally been from North to South, West to East'.

One of the most prominent and enduring of the feminist publishing imprints is Virago Press. Simone Murray (Chapter 33 [2004]) examines Virago's complex history and mission, and reflects on the tensions resulting from a publisher's competing objectives to unite politics and profit: to serve ideological objectives while also reaching a wide readership. Virago was established in 1973 in London as a publisher of non-fiction and fiction by women writers, in both original and reprinted form. Murray explores the implications of the firm's complex history of ownership, from its origins as an independent publisher, its mixed experiences of corporate partnerships, and finally its establishment as an imprint within a media conglomerate. She considers the difficulty the company faced in maintaining its identity in the mid-1990s, in the face of a lack of financial independence and the prevailing sense that gender politics was 'embarrassingly passé' (p. 237). The resulting ideological contradictions were manifested, in Murray's view, in the paratext of Virago's books, which she describes as an attempt 'to clothe generally oppositional texts in the guise of the mainstream' (2004: 58). Her key argument is that 'Feminist presses must locate for themselves a position on the continuum between an idealized independence, on one hand, and total integration into a conglomerate structure on the other' (2004: 52).

The final extract (Chapter 34) by Mohanalakshmi Rajakumar and Rumsha Shahzad (2015) questions whether, in the twenty-first century, online self-publishing offers a viable alternative for women writers, in view of the persistent and pronounced gender bias in the traditional publishing industry. Their survey of female authors reveals that many are turning to self-publishing as an alternative to mainstream publishing, and that although this presents certain challenges and uncertain financial rewards, one of the main advantages of the digital environment is its possibility for author collectives and communities.

These readings analyse the success of feminist interventions in tackling gender discrimination and in providing new forms of political and social expression for women, from the early twentieth century to the present day. They also reveal the ways in which both printed and online publishing have contributed to the formation of women's writing communities, and to new, gendered senses of affiliation and belonging.

SUGGESTED FURTHER READING

Cadman, E., C. Gail, and P. Agnes., 1981. *Rolling Our Own: Women as Printers, Publishers and Distributors*. London: Minority Press Group.
Foster, L., 2016. 'Spreading the word: Feminist print cultures and the women's liberation movement', *Women's History Review*, 25, 812–831.
Groeneveld, E., 2016. *Making Feminist Media: Third-Wave Magazines on the Cusp of the Digital Age*. Waterloo, Ontario: Wilfrid Laurier University Press.
Howe, F., 1995. 'Feminist publishing,' in P.G. Altbach and E.S. Hoshino (eds), *International Book Publishing: An Encyclopedia*. New York and London: Garland, 130–137.
Simons, J. and K. Fullbrook (eds), 1998. *Writing: A Woman's Business: Women, Writing and the Marketplace*. Manchester: Manchester University Press.

31 A Room of One's Own

Virginia Woolf

It was disappointing not to have brought back in the evening some important statement, some authentic fact. Women are poorer than men because – this or that. Perhaps now it would be better to give up seeking for the truth, and receiving on one's head an avalanche of opinion hot as lava, discoloured as dish-water. It would be better to draw the curtains; to shut out distractions; to light the lamp; to narrow the enquiry and to ask the historian, who records not opinions but facts, to describe under what conditions women lived, not throughout the ages, but in England, say in the time of Elizabeth.

For it is a perennial puzzle why no woman wrote a word of that extraordinary literature when every other man, it seemed, was capable of song or sonnet. What were the conditions in which women lived, I asked myself; for fiction, imaginative work that is, is not dropped like a pebble upon the ground, as science may be; fiction is like a spider's web, attached ever so lightly perhaps, but still attached to life at all four corners. Often the attachment is scarcely perceptible; Shakespeare's plays, for instance, seem to hang there complete by themselves. But when the web is pulled askew, hooked up at the edge, torn in the middle, one remembers that these webs are not spun in mid-air by incorporeal creatures, but are the work of suffering human beings, and are attached to grossly material things, like health and money and the houses we live in.

I went, therefore, to the shelf where the histories stand and took down one of the latest, Professor Trevelyan's *History of England*. Once more I looked up Women, found 'position of' and turned to the pages indicated. 'Wife-beating', I read, 'was a recognised right of man, and was practised without shame by high as well as low…. Similarly,' the historian goes on, 'the daughter who refused to marry the gentleman of her parents' choice was liable to be locked up, beaten and flung about the room, without any shock being inflicted on public opinion. Marriage was not an affair of personal affection, but of family avarice, particularly in the "chivalrous" upper classes…. Betrothal often took place while one or both of the parties was in the cradle, and marriage when they were scarcely out of the nurses' charge.' That was about 1470, soon after Chaucer's time. The next reference to the position of women is some two hundred years later, in the time of the Stuarts. 'It was still the exception for women of the upper and middle class to choose their own husbands, and when the husband had been assigned, he was lord and master, so far at least as law and custom could make him. Yet even so,' Professor Trevelyan concludes, 'neither Shakespeare's women nor those of authentic seventeenth-century memoirs, like the Verneys and the Hutchinsons, seem wanting in personality and character.' Certainly, if we consider it, Cleopatra must have had a way with her; Lady Macbeth, one would suppose, had a will of her own; Rosalind, one might conclude, was an attractive girl. Professor Trevelyan is speaking no more than the truth when he remarks that Shakespeare's women do not seem wanting in personality and character. Not being a historian, one might go even further and say that women have burnt like beacons in all the works of all the poets from the beginning of time – Clytemnestra, Antigone, Cleopatra, Lady Macbeth, Phèdre, Cressida, Rosalind, Desdemona, the Duchess of Malfi, among the dramatists; then among the prose writers: Millamant, Clarissa, Becky Sharp, Anna Karenine, Emma Bovary, Madame de Guermantes – the names flock to mind, nor do they recall women 'lacking in personality and character.' Indeed, if woman had no existence save in the fiction written by men, one would imagine her a person of the utmost importance; very various; heroic and mean; splendid and sordid; infinitely beautiful and hideous in the extreme; as great as a man, some think even greater.[1] But this is woman in fiction. In fact, as Professor Trevelyan points out, she was locked up, beaten and flung about the room.

A very queer, composite being thus emerges. Imaginatively she is of the highest importance; practically she is completely insignificant. She pervades poetry from cover to cover; she is all but absent from history. She dominates the lives of kings and conquerors in fiction; in fact she was the slave of any boy whose parents forced a ring upon her finger. Some of the most inspired words, some of the most profound thoughts in literature fall from her lips; in real life she could hardly read, could scarcely spell, and was the property of her husband.

It was certainly an odd monster that one made up by reading the historians first and the poets afterwards – a worm winged like an eagle; the spirit of life and beauty in a kitchen chopping up suet. But these monsters, however amusing to the imagination, have no existence in fact. What one must do to bring her to life was to think poetically and prosaically at one and the same moment, thus keeping in touch with fact – that she is Mrs. Martin, aged thirty-six, dressed in blue, wearing a black hat and brown shoes; but not losing sight of fiction either – that she is a vessel in which all sorts of spirits and forces are coursing and flashing perpetually. The moment, however, that one tries this method with the Elizabethan woman, one branch of illumination fails; one is held up by the scarcity of facts. One knows nothing detailed, nothing perfectly true and substantial about her. History scarcely mentions her. And I turned to Professor Trevelyan again to see what history meant to him. I found by looking at his chapter headings that it meant –

'The Manor Court and the Methods of Open-field Agriculture ... The Cistercians and Sheep-farming ... The Crusades ... The University ... The House of Commons ... The Hundred Years' War ... The Wars of the Roses ... The Renaissance Scholars ... The Dissolution of the Monasteries ... Agrarian and Religious Strife ... The Origin of English Sea-power ... The Armada ...' and so on. Occasionally an individual woman is mentioned, an Elizabeth, or a Mary; a queen or a great lady. But by no possible means could middle-class women with nothing but brains and character at their command have taken part in any one of the great movements which, brought together, constitute the historian's view of the past. Nor shall we find her in any collection of anecdotes. Aubrey hardly mentions her. She never writes her own life and scarcely keeps a diary; there are only a handful of her letters in existence. She left no plays or poems by which we can judge her. What one wants, I thought – and why does not some brilliant student at Newnham or Girton supply it? – is a mass of information; at what age did she marry; how many children had she as a rule; what was her house like; had she a room to herself; did she do the cooking; would she be likely to have a servant? All these facts lie somewhere, presumably, in parish registers and account books; the life of the average Elizabethan woman must be scattered about somewhere, could one collect it and make a book of it. It would be ambitious beyond my daring, I thought, looking about the shelves for books that were not there, to suggest to the students of those famous colleges that they should rewrite history, though I own that it often seems a little queer as it is, unreal, lop-sided; but why should they not add a supplement to history? calling it, of course, by some inconspicuous name so that women might figure there without impropriety? For one often catches a glimpse of them in the lives of the great, whisking away into the background, concealing, I sometimes think, a wink, a laugh, perhaps a tear. And, after all, we have lives enough of Jane Austen; it scarcely seems necessary to consider again the influence of the tragedies of Joanna Baillie upon the poetry of Edgar Allan Poe; as for myself, I should not mind if the homes and haunts of Mary Russell Mitford were closed to the public for a century at least. But what I find deplorable, I continued, looking about the bookshelves again, is that nothing is known about women before the eighteenth century. I have no model in my mind to turn about this way and that. Here am I asking why women did not write poetry in the Elizabethan age, and I am not sure how they were educated; whether they were taught to write; whether they had sitting-rooms to themselves; how many women had children before they were twenty-one; what, in short, they did from eight in the morning till eight at night. They had no money evidently; according to Professor Trevelyan they were married whether they liked it or not before they were out of the nursery, at fifteen or sixteen very likely. It would have been extremely odd, even upon this showing, had one of them suddenly written the plays of Shakespeare, I concluded, and I thought of that old gentleman, who is dead now, but was a bishop, I think, who declared that it was impossible for any woman, past, present, or to come, to have the genius of Shakespeare. He wrote to the papers about it. He also told a lady who applied to him for information that cats do not as a matter of fact go to heaven, though they have, he added, souls of a sort. How much thinking those old gentlemen used to save one! How the borders of ignorance shrank back at their approach! Cats do not go to heaven. Women cannot write the plays of Shakespeare.

Be that as it may, I could not help thinking, as I looked at the works of Shakespeare on the shelf, that the bishop was right at least in this; it would have been impossible, completely and entirely, for any woman to have written the plays of Shakespeare in the age of Shakespeare. Let me imagine, since facts are so hard to come by, what would have happened had Shakespeare had a wonderfully gifted sister, called Judith, let us say. Shakespeare himself went, very probably, – his mother was an heiress – to the grammar school, where he may have learnt Latin – Ovid, Virgil and Horace – and the elements of grammar and logic. He was, it is well known, a wild boy who poached rabbits, perhaps shot a deer, and had, rather sooner than he should have done, to marry a woman in the neighbourhood, who bore him a child rather quicker than was right. That escapade sent him to seek his fortune in London. He had, it seemed, a taste for the theatre; he began by holding horses at the stage door. Very soon he got work in the theatre, became a successful actor, and lived at the hub of the universe, meeting everybody, knowing everybody, practising his art on the boards, exercising his wits in the streets, and even getting access to the palace of the queen. Meanwhile his extraordinarily gifted sister, let us suppose, remained at home. She was as adventurous, as imaginative, as agog to see the world as he was. But she was not sent to school. She had no chance of learning grammar and logic, let alone of reading Horace and Virgil. She picked up a book now and then, one of her brother's perhaps, and read a few pages. But then her parents came in and told her to mend the stockings or mind the stew and not moon about with books and papers. They would have spoken sharply but kindly, for they were substantial people who knew the conditions of life for a woman and loved their daughter – indeed, more likely than not she was the apple of her father's eye. Perhaps she scribbled some pages up in an apple loft on the sly, but was careful to hide them or set fire to them. Soon, however, before she was out of her teens, she was to be betrothed to the son of a neighbouring wool-stapler. She cried out that marriage was hateful to her, and for that she was severely beaten by her father. Then he ceased to scold her. He begged her instead not to hurt him, not to shame him in this matter of her marriage. He would give her a chain of beads or a fine petticoat, he said; and there were tears in his eyes. How could she disobey him? How could she break his heart? The force of her own gift alone drove her to it. She made up a small parcel of her belongings, let herself down by a rope one summer's night and took the road to London. She was not seventeen. The birds that sang in the hedge were not more musical than she was. She had the quickest fancy, a gift like her brother's, for the tune of words. Like him, she had a taste for the theatre. She stood at the stage door; she wanted to act, she said. Men laughed in her face. The manager – a fat, loose-lipped man – guffawed. He bellowed something about poodles dancing and women acting – no woman, he said, could possibly be an actress. He hinted – you can imagine what. She could get no training in her craft. Could she even seek her dinner in a tavern or roam the streets at midnight? Yet her genius was for fiction and lusted to feed abundantly upon the lives of men and women and the study of their ways. At last – for she was very young, oddly like Shakespeare the poet in her face, with the same grey eyes and rounded brows – at last Nick Greene the actor-manager took pity on her; she found herself with child by that gentleman and so – who shall measure the heat and violence of the poet's heart when caught and tangled in a woman's body? – killed herself one winter's night and lies buried at some cross-roads where the omnibuses now stop outside the Elephant and Castle.

That, more or less, is how the story would run, I think, if a woman in Shakespeare's day had had Shakespeare's genius. But for my part, I agree with the deceased bishop, if such he was – it is unthinkable that any woman in Shakespeare's day should have had Shakespeare's genius. For genius like Shakespeare's is not born among labouring, uneducated, servile people. It was not born in England among the Saxons and the Britons. It is not born to-day among the working classes. How, then, could it have been born among women whose work began, according to Professor Trevelyan, almost before they were out of the nursery, who were forced to it by their parents and held to it by all the power of law and custom? Yet genius of a sort must have existed among women as it must have existed among the working classes. Now and again an Emily Brontë or a Robert Burns blazes out and proves its presence. But certainly it never got itself on to paper. When, however, one reads of a witch being ducked, of a woman possessed by devils, of a wise woman selling herbs, or even of a very remarkable man who had a mother, then I think we are on the track of a lost novelist, a suppressed poet, of some mute and inglorious Jane Austen, some Emily Brontë who dashed her brains out on the moor or mopped and mowed about the highways crazed with the torture that her gift had put her to. Indeed, I would venture to guess that Anon, who wrote so many poems without signing them, was often a woman. It was a woman Edward Fitzgerald, I think, suggested who made the ballads and the folk-songs, crooning them to her children, beguiling her spinning with them, or the length of the winter's night.

This may be true or it may be false – who can say? – but what is true in it, so it seemed to me, reviewing the story of Shakespeare's sister as I had made it, is that any woman born with a great gift in the sixteenth century would certainly have gone crazed, shot herself, or ended her days in some lonely cottage outside the village, half witch, half wizard, feared and mocked at. For it needs little skill in psychology to be sure that a highly gifted girl who had tried to use her gift for poetry would have been so thwarted and hindered by other people, so tortured and pulled asunder by her own contrary instincts, that she must have lost her health and sanity to a certainty. No girl could have walked to London and stood at a stage door and forced her way into the presence of actor-managers without doing herself a violence and suffering an anguish which may have been irrational – for chastity may be a fetish invented by certain societies for unknown reasons – but were none the less inevitable. Chastity had then, it has even now, a religious importance in a woman's life, and has so wrapped itself round with nerves and instincts that to cut it free and bring it to the light of day demands courage of the rarest. To have lived a free life in London in the sixteenth century would have meant for a woman who was poet and playwright a nervous stress and dilemma which might well have killed her. Had she survived, whatever she had written would have been twisted and deformed, issuing from a strained and morbid imagination. And undoubtedly, I thought, looking at the shelf where there are no plays by women, her work would have gone unsigned. That refuge she would have sought certainly. It was the relic of the sense of chastity that dictated anonymity to women even so late as the nineteenth century. Currer Bell, George Eliot, George Sand, all the victims of inner strife as their writings prove, sought ineffectively to veil themselves by using the name of a man. Thus they did homage to the convention, which if not implanted by the other sex was liberally encouraged by them (the chief glory of a woman is not to be talked of, said Pericles, himself a much-talked-of man) that publicity in women is detestable. Anonymity runs in their blood. The desire to be veiled still possesses them.

32 Feminist Publishing in the South

Urvashi Butalia and Ritu Menon

Feminist publishing in the Third World has followed a somewhat different trajectory from its counterpart in the West. Many countries in this part of the world have come to publishing relatively recently, and to indigenous publishing even more recently. Partly this has to do with colonization and empire: in erstwhile colonial countries part of the project of colonialism was to destroy or displace indigenous systems of knowledge, and to put new ones in their place. One of the consequences of this was the marginalization of oral cultures and the gradual turning towards print. As a first step here languages which did not have an orthography had to be 'given' one, again something that was often undertaken by the colonizers. Once introduced, however, publishing and books became major instruments in the educational process, a development that was not entirely without problems. The first of these was to develop indigenous authors, something which cannot be done overnight, and something which is doubly difficult to do without adequate resources. For some considerable time, books had to continue to be imported. Not only was this expensive, but it also continued the process of the colonization of knowledge begun by the colonizers.

It is not our intention to simplistically put the blame for the late development of publishing in southern countries on colonialism. But it is important, when looking at publishing in the South, to take into account the very real impact that colonialism had on it. In the early and mid-1970s, a number of universities all over the Third World still had a large number of expatriate staff: local people came into the academy in large numbers somewhat later. And often, it was their entry, especially that of women, which brought women's studies courses into being.

For reasons of history, economics, and politics, many Third World countries have also been lacking in the material resources necessary to set up publishing units. Few produce enough paper to meet the needs of the publishing industry. While the actual raw materials may exist, the infrastructure of production, factories, and machinery are lacking. Nor are such countries able to purchase this equipment from outside – more often than not, the exchange rates are unfavorable. Sometimes restrictive import policies do not allow easy import of paper.

In several Third World countries while books are still among the most widely used of media, high rates of illiteracy make it difficult for publishing to survive. Shortages of money, and what are universally seen as more urgent needs such as food, water, shelter, are also things to contend with. If people do not have a roof over their heads, how can you convince them to spend scarce resources on buying books? Several parts of the Third World have also – for many years and for a variety of reasons, many of which are not of their own making – been in the grip of politically volatile and repressive situations. The fundamentalist backlash sweeping through much of the Muslim world has made it difficult for independent publishers to survive. For women's voices to be heard in such an environment is well nigh impossible. In countries such as Algeria the first people to have been the targets of attack have been intellectuals and writers – the wide swathe of killings and executions has not spared women. In Bangladesh, the now well-known writer Talsima Nasreen has had to flee the country for having spoken out. Nor has the backlash been limited to the Muslim world. In India it is becoming increasingly difficult to counter the fundamentalism of the majority community. In Mauritius writer Lindsey Collen has had to face the wrath of the Hindu community for her novel *The Rape of Sita*, which was published in 1993 and banned within three days of its publication.

For publishing to survive anywhere in the world there must be writers, and readers. Because of their histories of colonization many Third World countries have been at the receiving end of knowledge and information about themselves from the West or the North. It is not uncommon to find, in say Africa or Asia, numbers of Western scholars who have access to both funds and opportunities for publication and who come and do research for short or long periods and then produce the definitive book on a specific subject. With women's books this follows a somewhat different pattern: because of the solidarity built up by women's movements internationally, groups in the Third World are often more open to scholars from other countries than might be the case normally. In the process they lose control on their own histories, only to have them reproduced by 'outsiders'. Published expensively in the North, such books often have to be purchased by Third World groups and individuals simply because local material is so scarce. Additionally, because they are produced well, and because they are imported, they often carry a legitimacy and importance that many 'foreign' articles do in Third World countries. Would-be feminist publishers have had to contend with this phenomenon, and yet, conversely, it is precisely this that has, in some instances, provided the impetus to set up local publishing houses in an attempt to 'redress the balance'.

WOMEN'S BOOKS AND WOMEN'S MOVEMENTS

In the Third World one of the strengths of feminist publishing has been the close links it has with the women's movement. Indeed, had it not been for the kinds of questions thrown up by women's movements, and the environment of interest and empathy provided by them, feminist publishers would have found it hard to survive. Not only publishing, but also the introduction of women's studies and courses on gender in the academy have been occasioned by the gains of women's movements across countries. And women's studies has in turn led to the need for materials for teaching and training, which have provided much of the base for publishing.

While women's studies and women's publishing are closely linked, the impetus for setting up women's publishing houses has also come from other sources. Thailand, for example, does not have a long history of women's studies courses, and its key feminist/women's publishing house, Genderpress, publishes mainly 'popular' works such as novels by women writers and translations of well known classics into Thai. Similarly, though the Women's Action Forum and other activists in Pakistan did provide one of the impetuses for the setting up of women's publishing, both Simorgh and ASR (Applied Socio-Economic Research) initially began publishing as women's groups, bringing out pamphlets and the occasional book as part of their work. ASR later developed a full fledged publishing program as one arm of its work and now regularly attends book fairs and book related events.

In the Third World, as indeed in many countries in the First World, a great deal of women's publishing takes place outside of publishing houses. Research institutes and women's groups bring out numbers of books and pamphlets which feed into the overall creation of knowledge and information on women. In Zimbabwe, for example, the Zimbabwe Women Writers Group is not a publishing enterprise. Their main work is to get writers together, and to hold discussions and workshops on women's writing. As part of this, however, they have published a few books by the women who are members of the group. Similarly in Malaysia a small group of activists and academics called Sisters in Islam, has begun a process of questioning Islam from within. Can the religion be as inegalitarian as the clergy would have it seem? Using meticulous and detailed research, Sisters in Islam initially brought out two pamphlets. These have now been followed by a book, and their future plans include other, similar publications. In Manila, Isis International, (a group originally founded by two women, Jane Cottingham and Marilee Karl, and based then in Rome), have a range of activities which include the publication of books and pamphlets which are distributed all over the world. Much of this kind of 'outside' publishing is funded with grants from donor agencies, and it is often short lived. But it is nonetheless important to take it into account.

Where books are difficult to publish, groups in the South have often started with the occasional pamphlet or booklet and, in many cases, journals and magazines. This is particularly true in Latin America where some feminist magazines have acted as precursors to publishing houses. Magazines are, of course, not easy to publish or sustain. Most of these, however, are not commercial magazines, but those associated with women's groups and usually funded on a non-commercial basis. The kind of knowledge base created by such occasional publishing has often proved useful for groups that may later go in for books: it provides ready-made and only partially circulated material which can be put together into book form at some point. Several publishers in Third World countries have gained from such efforts.

The different political and economic situations in countries in this part of the world, as opposed to the North, have combined to produce both strengths and weaknesses in Third World feminist publishing. In relatively poorer countries labor comes cheap; new technologies are expensive and often late entrants. This may, on the one hand, mean that in terms of quality, books produced in the South may not always be able to compete with those in the North. On the other, publishers are often able to experiment with innovative things that may well be expensive, or virtually impossible to do, in the north. Some years ago, the Indian feminist publishing house, Kali for Women, brought out a book on women's bodies and women's health, written by rural women from the north Indian state of Rajasthan. The book has an interesting history: it was initially 'written' as a result of a series of workshops on health that were conducted in different districts in Rajasthan among rural women. At the end of the workshops, some 100 women got together to 'produce' (make by hand) two or three copies of the book entitled *Shareer ki Jaankari* (Know Your Body), which held information and knowledge that they felt was needed by them, and therefore probably by other women (especially rural women) as well. In the initial stages the book carried illustrations of naked women with different parts of their bodies marked, but this was not well received in the villages where these initial two or three books were tested. People said the illustrations were not true to reality: if you did not see a naked woman in a village (i.e. if the women were well covered), how could a book about village women represent them differently? The women then returned to the drawing board so to speak, and produced a different version of the book, one that had both women and men traditionally dressed, and therefore modest, with small flaps pasted on in strategic places which could be lifted up and people could see the processes of menstruation, etc.

The important thing about such a book was that it had to be priced very low in order that it could become accessible to its target readership – village women. For most mainstream publishers this would not have been a viable proposition. The feminist publishing house Kali, however, took on the task of producing this book. The most complicated – and potentially expensive – part of the book was the binding. But since most binding in India is done by hand, it was eventually possible to get the book bound, flaps and all, quite cheaply (and interestingly, by a group of women binders who had been trained in binding as an income generating activity). Elsewhere, it would probably have been quite difficult to keep the price of such a book so low, and indeed to get the complicated work of binding and pasting done so painlessly. Nor would most mainstream publishers have been interested in such a labor intensive, small-economic-return activity. But for feminist publishers, the returns are often considered not only in economic terms.

While this kind of thing may be more easily possible in countries in the southern hemisphere, there are other, major constraints on publishing. These include shortages of resources and raw materials, paper, adequate machinery – problems which are compounded by the lack of efficient postal systems, expensive postal and freight rates, the absence of a good library or retail system, as well as the many other problems such as illiteracy, lack of buying power etc., that we have discussed earlier. These are things that impact on publishing as a whole: but something like feminist publishing is further affected for a number of reasons.

MARKETS AND BUYERS

In many Southern countries the received wisdom is that the main buyers of books are libraries. Sometimes this figure, as in India, is said to be as high as 80 per cent. This almost automatically places feminist publishing at a disadvantage. Not only are library purchase systems slow and bureaucratic, but many librarians are also fairly conservative in their tastes and choices. Women's writing is seen as peripheral and non-serious by many. The range and type of subjects covered do not easily fall under accepted categories. Women's studies is a somewhat mixed discipline which includes work by both academics and activists. If a library does not have funds allocated for this, it may be extremely difficult to open up the system to the purchase of feminist titles. The word feminist is itself suspect in many southern countries because of the baggage of westernization and alienation it carries. All of this makes for a difficult situation for book purchase.

Additionally, in their writing and publishing women-have opened up a range of new areas and subjects. Again, many of these are not always accepted as being 'serious' enough for library purchase (this relates, in particular, to material about sexuality, lesbianism, the experiences of minority groups and so on). Many librarians are also constrained by having to purchase from recognized outlets and at fixed discounts. This more or less rules out much of the non-formal type of material that women's groups generate and which would benefit greatly from the wider exposure libraries could provide.

Typically, however, women publishers have proved equal to the challenge. Not to be outdone, they have turned around this apparent disadvantage and have worked hard to create and develop markets among individuals, groups of feminists, international donor agencies, policy planners and others. Publishing from a niche has certain advantages, particularly when the issues that occupy the inhabitants of that niche are simultaneously being articulated by a widespread political movement – which feminism across the world is. Thus, feminist materials find a ready market among non-governmental organizations (NGOs), policy planners, some donor agencies, as well as generally. Publishers put some effort into reaching these markets and keeping them informed about new titles and projects.

There are other things that differentiate feminist publishing in the South from its counterpart in the North. Because of their roots in activism, publishers and groups in the South have often chosen not to specialize in the way that northern publishers have. The bulk of publishing in many countries is educational – as that is the priority. While academic books do exist, in greater or lesser degree depending on the country, there is not that much of what is known as trade publishing. Thus, whether it is in Indonesia, or Malaysia, or Nigeria or Chile, one may be almost sure that educational and academic books will have priority. Here, because there are very few courses which are open to the kinds of books feminist publishers are publishing, it becomes difficult to find a point of entry. Then again, in many places feminist publishing in the West seems to be divided into the kind of books that feminist presses do more of – fiction, self help, memoirs, autobiography, etc., – and the more 'academic' books produced by university presses who run strong women's lists. This is not a situation that is commonly found in countries of the South: publishers and women's groups produce a range of things which can include practically any and every sort of book, from the textbook to the children's book to the handbook or activist book, to fiction and academic works. Below we look in detail at some of the kinds of books and materials feminist presses in the Third World are producing, and we trace, in as much as it is possible, a kind of history of feminist publishing in different parts of the Third World.

33 'Books with Bite': Virago Press and the Politics of Feminist Conversion

Simone Murray

> By no stretch of usage can *Virago* be made not to signify a shrew, a scold, an ill-tempered woman, unless we go back to the etymology – a man-like maiden (cognate with *virile*) – and the antique meaning – amazon, female warrior – that is close to it. It is an unlovely and aggressive name, even for a militant feminist organisation, and it presides awkwardly over the reissue of a great *roman fleuve* which is too important to be associated with chauvinist sows.

> Anthony Burgess in a review of Dorothy Richardson's *Pilgrimage*, reissued by Virago in 1989 (quoted in Scanlon and Swindells 1994: 42)

> Twenty years since Marilyn French's *The Women's Room*, one of the most influential novels of that time, women's lives have changed. There is a new spirit in women's writing which Virago salutes with its new 'V' imprint. The launch titles are as diverse as women themselves; but the young authors share a liberating sense of irreverence and risk-taking. The 'V' aim is to avoid political correctness at all costs: these are books by women which speak to men as much as women.

> 'Wayward Girls & Wicked Women', Virago relaunch promotion (*Guardian* 1997)

There is some considerable distance between being lambasted by a characteristically curmudgeonly Anthony Burgess for militant political chauvinism, and squeamish recoil from ideological commitment under the guise of avoiding 'political correctness'. That both of these quotations refer to the public face of Britain's Virago Press during the course of a single decade highlights the extent to which the women's publishing house has reinvented itself for a new generation of readers. Such a marked volte-face must derive either from a suspiciously late twentieth-century obsession with self-reinvention and novelty for its own sake or, more fundamentally, from a crisis of house identity suffered by Virago and its directors. Such a seizure of self-doubt can be pinpointed with unusual accuracy: the linchpin between the two faces of Virago outlined above is the sale of the press in November 1995 to Little, Brown & Co. UK, a subsidiary of the US-based multinational Time Warner.[1] The sale, and the flurry of negative publicity that surrounded it, represented a critical phase not only for Virago, but for feminist publishing as a whole, as falling profits and uninspiring frontlists forced reconsideration of feminist publishing's agenda – a thorough-going industry soul-searching of the kind that Virago had not undertaken publicly in the course of its 23-year history. For this reason, the 1995 sale of Virago serves as a critical vantage point from which to survey the press's history and against which the company's post-1996 relaunch can be measured. Beneath the breathless rush of the new Virago's promotional copy, it is possible to discern a frantic search for the winning formula by which Virago formerly united its profits with its politics – and the belief that this elusive link is capable of being reconstituted in the consumer-dominated, politically skittish 1990s and beyond.

The sale of Virago Press to publisher Philippa Harrison's Little, Brown UK group for a rumoured £1.3 million on 2 November 1995 bears closer analysis because of the wider debates around feminist publishing which the incident sparked in the international media (Rawsthorn 1995: 7; *Bookseller* 1995b: 8). Essentially three strands are discernible in the journalistic coverage of the sale: the personality-dominated 'feuding feminists' angle (*Evening Standard* 1995: 8; Shakespeare 1995: 12; Porter 1995: 1, 25; Rawsthorn 1995: 7); the accusation of mismanagement and poor business practice (Pitman 1995; Alberge 1995: 3); and – most common among left-identified newspapers – the lament for a passing golden age of feminist and publishing history represented by Virago (Dalley 1995: 21; Baxter 1995: 9). The first of these approaches, that focusing on the personal animosity between Virago's founder, Carmen Callil, the firm's original director and former chairman [sic], and Ursula Owen, initially Virago's editorial director and later its joint managing director, follows the convenient journalistic practice of reducing complex issues to personal antagonisms. Epitomising this hostile coverage is Henry Porter's exposé of 'feminist publishers – their angry struggle' in his feature article for the *Daily Telegraph*, entitled 'The Feminist Fallout that Split Virago' (1995). Strategically juxtaposing photographs of Callil and Owen, Porter paints a scenario of maenadic fury, the obvious subtext of which urges that sisterhood is at best merely spectral – suitable for a rallying cry but a risible failure when put to the test.[2] In pursuing the feminist catfight line, the article ploughs an increasingly overworked media furrow. The early 1990s war-by-fax waged between tireless self-promoters Camille Paglia and Julie Burchill was belaboured in the mainstream press in precisely the same manner, as were the ideological differences between Australian author Helen Garner and younger feminists in the newspaper flurry over Garner's book about sexual harassment within universities, *The First Stone* (1995). According to such journalistic practice, the mergers and buy-outs of largely male-run multinational publishing companies are read as auguries of market trends; those of feminist publishing companies betoken nothing more significant than the hysteria of the wandering womb. As an unidentified 'ex-Virago' confided to Jan Dalley in her *Independent on Sunday* article: 'When men have boardroom battles, it's heroic and Titanic and serious. When women do the same, it's a catfight' (1995: 21) [...].

Of the many articles published about Virago in late 1995, those of most significance for the purposes of this discussion are the pieces appearing in the UK's centre-left broadsheets – the *Observer* and the *Independent on Sunday* in particular – for they invoke the issue of Virago's loss of independence to survey the general state of feminist publishing, and to reignite then latent debates about the political viability of such enterprises. During the high point of Virago's commercial success in the late 1970s and early 1980s, the substantial backlist sales generated by its fiction reprint series, the Virago Modern Classics, and its unmatched reader loyalty tended to obviate the need for any such debate. Virago was phenomenally successful, and commercial success was seen to constitute the litmus test of its publishing philosophy. The subsequent nadir of the company's fortunes in late 1995 is attributable to a variety of causes: a profit of barely £100,000 on sales of over £3,000,000 (a margin of under 5 per cent); the resignation of senior directors Carmen Callil, Harriet Spicer and Lennie Goodings within a period of eight months (*Evening Standard* 1995: 8; *Bookseller* 1995d: 6; Buckingham 1995: 4); low staff morale; staleness induced by slow middle-level employee turnover; and ferocious competition from the feminist lists of mainstream houses for high-profile female authors and titles (Ezard 1995: 3).

Yet, more pervasively, Virago's loss of direction is attributable to a crisis of confidence in the political and cultural role of a feminist publishing house, a deep-seated suspicion of its own irrelevance in an age that has broadly appropriated feminist positions as mainstream thinking, but which simultaneously eschews explicit gender politics as embarrassingly passé. Such defeat points, paradoxically, to the old-style Virago's victory: so successful was its publishing philosophy that its radical avant-gardism of the early 1970s appeared to the jaded mid-1990s as banally self-evident. Hence Virago's 1995 directors might have been forgiven for wondering whether they should preside over the company's demise or respond with a Mark Twain-like salvo to the effect that reports of its death had been greatly exaggerated.

Should Virago's sale to the world's largest media conglomerate be taken as evidence that feminism's battle for representation from the margins of political and cultural power has been won, and that its place in the cultural mainstream has been established? Alternatively, is the subsumption of Virago within the capacious corporate structure of Time Warner the final victory of market forces and economic rationalism over political commitment – the selling out of a feminist dream? It is in keeping with the complex ambiguities of feminist publishing that the fact of Virago's sale should be susceptible to both readings, but both represent an oversimplification of the issue. For Virago's 1995 crisis is attributable chiefly to a loss of confidence in what had, until that point, proved a delicate balancing act between the seemingly irreconcilable forces of politics and profit. By refusing to acknowledge that commercial success need necessarily vitiate political integrity, Virago attained a profile among the general reading public higher than that of any feminist press worldwide. The savvy and legerdemain by which such a delicate balance was achieved bears closer scrutiny, not only for the light that it casts on the fate of Virago Press in particular, but because it represents an optimal – though precarious – point on the continuum strung between feminist oppositionality and market centrality.

The characteristic that distinguishes Virago from many other feminist presses which sprang up under the invigorating influence of women's activism from the late 1960s is the duality of its self-conception: it perceived itself simultaneously both as a commercial publishing house *and* as an intrinsic part of the British women's liberation movement. With the mutation of international leftist politics towards the centre over the course of the 1980s and 1990s, it is difficult now to recapture the anomalousness of such a position in the socio-political climate of the early 1970s. With feminism regarding the progressive left as its natural political home, such a flagrant embrace of capitalist principles on the part of Virago engendered some suspicion, and attracted substantial criticism from the socialist wings of the women's movement (Owen 1998b). Yet, the insistence that politics and profitability be brought into a working relationship is, in retrospect, a radical proposition.[3] Virago's *raison d'être* was to publish books informed by the feminist politics of the time and to make them profitable – in foundation member Harriet Spicer's terms 'to make profitable what you wanted to do' (Spicer 1996).

The attempted unification of capitalist and feminist agendas placed Virago in a borderland position, between the feminist sisterhood (with its preference for experimental, collectively run co-operatives such as the British periodical *Spare Rib*) and the traditional power centres of mainstream London publishing (which regarded politically identified publishing – let alone *feminist* publishing – as a commercial non-starter and as a somewhat distasteful predilection). Nevertheless, Virago's protean house identity proved the key to its success. Because the press maintained a double outsider status in relation to both groups, it was able to weather the enormous changes in industry organisation and feminist thought that occurred during the 1970s and 1980s. Significantly, it was in the early 1990s – as feminism embraced the cultural possibilities of ambivalence and irony – that Virago appeared to harden in its political stance and to suffer recurrent financial losses. In the apt colloquialism of former Virago employee Sarah Baxter, 'Virago lost the plot' (1995: 9). The vagaries of fashion in feminist thought, not to mention the unpredictability of complex consumer economies, reward feminist presses that state their politics up front, but which are canny enough to factor in a buffer zone of ambivalence and allowances for revision. Provisional certainties, not lapidary pronouncements, have the best chance of securing market rewards.

The borderlands between divergent political systems and ideologies can, however, prove fraught and uncomfortable ground: original Virago member Ursula Owen speaks wryly of 'get[ting] flak from the left and right, but I'm fairly resigned to that' (Macaskill 1990: 434). Alexandra Pringle, who joined as Virago's fourth member in 1978, casts the press's dual outsider status in a more playful light: 'Does it make you feel that you're under siege? Well, yes. But it's quite fun that, you feel you're out there battling...up there on the barricades' (1996). This concept of strategic self-positioning in order to partake in both feminist activism and commercial publishing – but combined with a refusal to be defined or contained by either – is key to Virago's achievement and its current remarketing. Within this general framework of Virago as a political and publishing fringe-dweller – though a powerful one by reason of its fringe-dwelling status – this discussion analyses the company from its origins in 1972, including its post-sale relaunch in mid-1996 and taking into account subsequent seasons' developments. The first section presents a general overview of the company's history and its changing institutional niches, rebutting the misconception present in much writing about Virago's 1995 sale that Virago had, until that point, been a fully independent company (Ezard 1995: 3; Henry 1995: 13; *Bookseller* 1995b: 8). Secondly, the discussion explores the facet of Virago's identity that is broadly feminist, focusing on Virago's complex relationship with the women's movement and with the academic wing of feminist politics – university-based women's studies programmes. The discussion then proceeds to site Virago within the context of the publishing industry, focusing on three key issues: the significance of independence for feminist presses; Virago's marketing of feminism for a mainstream readership; and Virago's role in the creation and appropriation of a market for feminist books. Lastly, Virago's current state of play is analysed, as is its most recent attempts to remarket itself as a trade publisher with special appeal to a younger, more politically jaundiced, readership. The structure of this chapter, analysing Virago firstly against the background of feminist politics and, in the second instance, against publishing industry dynamics, is the result of convenience rather than of any absolute theoretical distinction between the two spheres. Publishing and politics are, in the case of Virago, indisputably interlinked; the disentangling of Virago's relationship with first one and then the other area serves merely as an analytical device to cast light upon the unique position that Virago occupied at the cusp of the profit-driven publishing industry and the politically driven women's movement.

A KITCHEN TABLE IN CHELSEA: SELF-MYTHOLOGISATION AND THE ORIGINS OF VIRAGO

The origins and publishing history of Virago Press have been so often recapitulated in the firm's promotional material that the division between past and present has all but dissolved – history is recycled as publicity in a manner that occasionally owes more to directorial agendas than to historical veracity. The self-mythologising strain in Virago is comparable in publishing history only with Allen Lane's famous championing of the early Penguin paperbacks: because both ventures were innovatory for their time, the fact of their existence – aside from any individual title they produced – has become in itself a badge of their founders' achievement. The origins of Virago lie in the oft-repeated detail that the press began at founder Carmen Callil's kitchen table in her home in Chelsea, and that it was fuelled by red wine and late nights spent arguing over the politics of the emerging women's liberation movement, all undertaken against a backdrop of economic buoyancy and political possibility (Lowry 1977: 9; Macaskill 1990: 432; Durrant 1993: 93; Gerrard 1993: 61). The company's initial self-description – 'the first mass-market publishers for 52% of the population – women. An exciting new imprint for both sexes in a changing world' (Virago publicity pamphlet 1996: 1) – encapsulates both the optimism and the determinedly non-sectarian vision of the press for which its founders strove. The house's success over the following two decades and its immense brand-name recognition fostered celebrations not so much of the firm's individual achievements, but of the press's very existence: in 1993 *A Virago Keepsake to Celebrate Twenty Years of Publishing* neatly conflated in its title the individual press with the concept of feminist publishing. The self-celebratory tone of the book, distributed free to bookshops by Virago, earned the press censure from some sections of the women's movement who critiqued the discrepancy between Virago's profits in the 1980s and feminism's political retreat:

> In the Virago *Keepsake* a further shift has taken place; a move from the individual author to the Virago author, a celebration not of the women's movement, or of women's writing, but the survival of the press itself – a recognition of what it stands for, not so much in terms of political achievement, but brand loyalty and quality writing.
>
> (Scanlon and Swindells 1994: 42)

The choice of year in which, to celebrate Virago's twentieth anniversary was itself contentious. The exact date of the press's foundation – either 1972, when Callil registered the company, or 1973, when Virago's first title appeared and when Ursula Owen was granted shares in the company – tends to vary in Virago's publicity according to the political make-up of the board at the time of writing.[4] For a publishing house that conceptualises its very existence as a political achievement there is much feminist cachet to be had in presenting oneself as its sole founder.

The myth of Virago's genesis (an apt term, given the firm's wryly anti-Edenic bitten apple logo) often glosses over the exact financial conditions under which Virago's initial nine titles were produced. Between 1973 and 1976 Virago was an 'independently owned editorial imprint' of Quartet Books, publishing under its own name but with copyright and production of its titles controlled by Quartet (Virago publicity pamphlet 1996: 1; Spicer 1996; Owen 1998b). Unsurprisingly, given that this same corporate niche was later to prove so uncongenial to feminist publishers The Women's Press,[5] Virago's former directors speak meaningfully of learning during those years about the importance of the power to publish. They evince a hard-won awareness that 'any requirement to refer to others on editorial decisions, however benevolent those others might be, is a constraint' (Owen, U. 1988: 89). Budgeting and editorial conflicts with Quartet led to a 1976 management buyout, funded by a £35,000 bank loan and personal pledges from Virago's directors. The period of independence that followed was one of steady expansion for the firm, with sales of the non-fiction Virago Reprint Library of early twentieth-century socialist and Fabian books such as Margaret Llewelyn Davies' *Life as We Have Known It* (1977 [1931]) and Maud Pember Reeves' *Round About a Pound a Week* (1979 [1913]) being compounded by the marketing triumph of the Virago Modern Classics. This later series, a fiction reprint list of 'lost' women writers whose out-of-print, copyright-free works were attractively repackaged for a new generation of feminist readers, achieved such success that its titles came to define the public image of the firm. Coinciding profitably with the rise of women's writing courses in academia, which were in turn fired by landmark texts such as Elaine Showalter's *A Literature of Their Own: British Women Novelists from Brontë to Lessing* (1978 [1977]), the Virago Modern Classics series blossomed, underpinning the firm's expansion into publishing fiction by living writers. The flagship series incontestably achieved its original aim of showing 'the imaginative range

of women's writing and ... celebrat[ing] the scale of female achievement in fiction'
(Owen, U. 1988: 93). The removal of the pejorative sting from the phrase 'woman
writer' has proven to be the series' most influential legacy. Nevertheless, as Virago
Modern Classics editor Ruth Petrie observed in 1993, at the time of its launch in
1978 (with the republication of Antonia White's *Frost in May* [1933]) it was non-
fiction rather than fiction that the women's movement felt harboured the greater
revolutionary potential:

> In those days [the mid-1970s] we all thought our politics were based in non-
> fiction writing, in issue-related titles. Fiction was what you gave yourself as a
> source of pleasure and distraction. It wasn't going to offer a commentary on life
> in quite the same way.
>
> (quoted in Norden 1993: 15)

Virago experimented with a second period of corporate partnership with its sale
in February 1982 to the Chatto, Bodley Head and Cape Group (CBC), which was
to provide Virago with the high-outlay distribution and production services it
required, but which would guarantee the press's editorial autonomy, thus differentiating the carefully negotiated arrangement from the invasive paternalism of the
earlier Quartet alliance. Although Callil later justified the manoeuvre to a Women
in Publishing forum as having 'written into it safeguards orchestrated by ourselves'
(Callil 1986: 851), Virago by 1986 had began to demur from an arrangement in
which it was required to shoulder losses from other houses in the umbrella group,
and under which it lacked access to 'information about what bits of [the] business
were generating profit' (Jones, N. 1992: 21–22; McPhee 2001: 208). With the
(then) US-owned giant Random House poised to take over the CVBC Group, Virago
instigated a successful management buyout in November 1987, netting substantial
profits for the firm's directors but necessitating the closure of the flagship Virago
Bookshop in London's Covent Garden as a condition of their financiers' backing.[6]
Again, Virago's perceived prioritising of company profits over sisterly allegiance was
criticised in the British feminist press, with *Everywoman* magazine tartly reporting
that 'staff made redundant at the bookshop' would, according to Virago, 'unfortunately not' be employed elsewhere, in the company (Everywoman 1987: 11).

During the early to mid-1990s the series of recessions within the book publishing sector generally accentuated a loss of direction and quavering confidence
within the firm. Repeatedly throughout the period Virago announced cutbacks in
the frontlist, changes in editorial focus and retrenchment of staff – all undertaken
without securing the desired result of long-term growth. Hence Virago's twentieth
birthday celebrations and managing director Harriet Spicer's 1993 international
promotional tour carry beneath their ebullience overtones of discernible unease;
the *Virago Keepsake*'s strident best wishes for 'more than another twenty years of
successful publishing' (1993: viii) betrays the suspicion that, though ideal; this
outcome was not necessarily certain. Virago was attempting to ensure future sales
by invoking the magic of a brand name that had in the past proven so bankable an
asset; a standard promotional tactic, it was nevertheless a vulnerable one for a firm
entering its third decade.

The period from 1993 to the company's sale in late 1995 was dominated by boardroom disputes, further staff and list cutbacks, and directorial resignations: a briefly returned Carmen Callil resigned as chairman in February 1995; managing director Harriet Spicer followed in July 1995; and publishing director Lennie Goodings compounded the trend by announcing her intention to quit in September 1995. This last departure was recorded in the *Bookseller* on 13 October, with a fellow Virago director attributing Goodings' departure to 'editorial differences, including the decision to publish books written by men' (*Bookseller* 1995d: 6). With the sale of the company imminent, Goodings' recorded preference for independence may have also prompted her resignation, for two years earlier she had remarked that 'being independent has meant survival for us. We control our own costs and savings, we decide ourselves where we will compromise and where we won't. We choose the books we want to publish' (1993: 27). That new owner Philippa Harrison persuaded Goodings in November 1995 'to change her mind about leaving the company' and to take up the position of publisher for the now fully owned Little, Brown subsidiary would appear fundamentally to contradict Goodings's earlier avowals of press independence (*Bookseller* 1995b: 8). Moreover, the commitment to women-only publishing attributed to Goodings was contradicted by the first list overseen by her as publisher to the Virago imprint, containing as it did *Sons & Mothers* (1996), an anthology co-edited by Matthew and Victoria Glendinning. Viewed in one light, these changes reflect the dynamic, strategic adaptability that has characterised Virago's history; viewed in another, they underline former director Alexandra Pringle's observation that 'Virago as we have known it is now completely over' (1996).

34 She Needs a Website of Her Own: The 'Indie' Woman Writer and Contemporary Publishing

Mohanalakshmi Rajakumar and Rumsha Shahzad

Despite the social and political gains women have made in the developed world over the last century, contemporary female writers are still being told by their publishers that 'more people will read authors who are men than are women'.[1] Anecdotal evidence suggests such thinking continues to pervade the publishing industry.[2] Joanna Rowling, whose Harry Potter series placed her on *Forbes's* billionaire list, was famously advised by her publisher to use her initials J.K. in order to ensure her appeal to young male readers. Feminist poet and columnist Katha Pollit argued that 'the kind of rapturous high-cultural reception given to writers who are white and male and living in Brooklyn'[3] is rarely accorded to women writers, because it is assumed they only address 'stereotypically feminine topics' such as the family, whereas male authors who write about the family are considered to be writing about 'the human condition'. Evidence from the organization for Women in the Literary Arts (VIDA) suggests women's writing is also less likely to be reviewed by significant literary outlets. Since 2009 the 'VIDA Count' has tracked the number of male and female authors reviewed in significant literary journals in America and Britain. Although the count does not include data on submission by gender, the gender disparities in reviews and reviewers are still striking. In prestigious publications such as the *New York Review of Books*, the *Times Literary Supplement*, the *London Review of Books*, and the *New Yorker*, more than 70% of the books reviewed in 2013 were authored by men. The gender imbalance extended to critics, with many outlets featuring four times more male reviewers than female reviewers. The 2013 VIDA Count showed some signs of progress, noting that a few periodicals such as the *New York Times Book Review* had increased the proportion of female authors reviewed from 33% to 41%. Given the extensive media interest in the VIDA Count and the encouragement of visitors to the website to contact editors to express their disappointment about gender ratios, this may suggest the way the Internet is enabling efforts to focus attention and action on gender inequalities in the publishing industry.

While evidence of gender bias in traditional publishing remains anecdotal, taken together the stories present a disturbing-picture. The *New Republic's* examination

243

of the 2010 fiction catalogs of ten major publishing houses found that many more men than women are being published across the sector.[4] Women are also published much less often in literary magazines, a vital means by which creative writers can win not only readers but agents and grants that will enable future publications.[5] One study suggests that women are much less likely to submit their work to creative journals, attributing the startling gender divide in submission rates to the persistence of stereotypes that equate femininity with passivity.[6] The barriers to publication are especially high for women of color. Traditional publishing houses have tended to consider themselves diversified if they could include a token Asian or other non-white writer. As Ama Ata Aidoo observed, 'it has to do with the limited publishing opportunities and also the straightjacket to be a "third world woman." Maybe with us the pressures are heavier because ... Someone can declare that your manuscript doesn't read like a manuscript from a third world person.'[7] The challenges for women of color continue, leading many of them to consider self-publishing. British Sudanese writer Leila Aboulela noted that 'Early in my career when I was struggling to get published, I did consider it. If I ever in the future fail to find a publisher, then I would certainly consider self-publishing.'[8]

The development of recent alternatives to legacy publishing offer women writers new options for putting their books in front of a potentially global audience. But as the comments by Aboulela indicate, independent publishing has its own problems, not least the stigma associated with authors who self-publish. To what extent then have the new publication choices helped women authors? This essay examines the experience of the female 'indie' author – a term characterizing women who self-publish online – to offer some preliminary evidence of how the digital era is impacting the literary careers of women.

INDEPENDENT PUBLISHING

Originally used to refer to small presses or academic presses that were considered independent of the commercial mainstream, the term 'independent publishing' now encompasses a range of publishing options for individual authors using a variety of digital platforms. The popularity of e-books and e-readers have given rise to new methods of retailing books from Print on Demand to new platforms for publication, such as Amazon's Kindle Direct Publishing, a program through which Amazon allows writers to upload their books and offer them for free over limited periods of time in exchange for exclusivity with Amazon.

While a number of traditional publishers such as Simon & Schuster offer pay-to-publish services under separate imprints,[9] differences in author compensation and control continue to distinguish independent and traditional publishing. In independent publishing, the author is the one making 'the publication decisions', paying the bills, and hoping for profit in lieu of royalties.[10] According to Steinitz and Baverstock, 'the most common reason cited by authors for the choice to publish independently was the desire for control. Respondents wanted to have the final say on the timeframe and on every aspect of the book's writing, editing, design, production, distribution, and marketing.'[11] Independent publishing and traditional publishing may also be distinguished in terms of status. To be sure, some reports suggest the longstanding stigma associated with self-financing publications may be disappearing:

> They used to call it the 'vanity press,' and the phrase itself spoke volumes. Self-published authors were considered not good enough to get a real publishing contract. They had to pay to see their book in print. But with the advent of e-books, self-publishing has exploded, and a handful of writers have had huge best sellers.[12]

However, doubt as to the merit of self-published authors still remains, aggravated by fears about a 'flooding of markets' due to the convenience and speed of self-publishing. Carolan and Evain allude to the common perception that 'the seas of books that are being produced every year' are altering the 'publishing paradigm' in a less than positive fashion.[13] The professional publisher's seal of approval is generally considered a 'gauge of quality',[14] ensuring that readers get the right value for what they're paying. But since self-published books, especially those available for download over the Internet, are priced extremely low, the risk to readers in taking a chance on a book has significantly diminished.

Independent publishing is being hailed as leading to a diversification of the industry, one that may be particularly beneficial for women.[15] Certainly women appear to be gravitating towards nontraditional publishing in significant numbers. A recent survey of self-published authors in the UK found that women in their 40s and 50s accounted for '22% and 19% of the sample, respectively, compared to their shares of 9% and 8% of the national adult population'.[16] Does the Internet offer women the opportunity to 'theorize their own authorship', setting their own priorities in the types of books they write, rather than bending to market-driven decisions, usually made by publishing executives chasing bestselling trends?[17]

To explore women's experiences with independent publishing further, we conducted an online survey of women who identify as 'indie' authors. The initial ten-question survey was advertised from November 2014 through February 2015 to independently published female authors, through online Facebook or LinkedIn groups tagged with the words 'indie', 'independent', or 'self-published'. The title of the survey invited women who identified as indie or self-published authors to respond about their publishing experiences. The 106 respondents participated anonymously. The majority of the respondents were 59 years old or older and 97% were self-published; most of the women indicated they came from Europe (31%) or America (53%). Only five women in our sample identified as nonwhite (Latino and African American). Almost half the writers indicated they wrote memoirs (48.39%), with literary fiction (45%) and romance (29%) as the second and third most popular genres. The majority of our sample (62%) had been writing for ten years or more, with several claiming more than 20 years of experience.

Given how few of the respondents identified as women of color we were unable to explore the experiences of nonwhite indie writers in any detail. We note, however, the comments of one African-American respondent that suggest the value of exploring independent publishing by women of color further, as an option chosen in response to perceived racial bias in the industry. Natasha (not her real name) indicates feelings of under-representation in the industry overall:

> African-Americans are only 1% of the decision makers in traditional publishing. ... As an African-American female, I feel excluded more for my color than my gender. Don't believe me? Go to the stores and look at the titles. Notice who are the authors.[18]

BANDING TOGETHER

A striking feature of authorship in the digital era is the ease and speed with which authors are able to mobilize and form collectives to share information about publishing, to mentor each other, and/or to share the costs and risks of independent publishing. Some groups such as *Best Selling Reads* are aimed at established writers; members must have a bestselling title to participate and pool a shared budget to host a blog as well as prizes. Through their combined social media platforms on Twitter, Facebook, and individual blogs, the group amplifies their reach across a diverse section of genres and readers. Other collectives like the Alliance of Independent Authors, and Independent Authors International are more inclusive, gathering together groups of writers to share tips, strategies, and work. Within these collectives, largely created, managed, and participated through Facebook groups, there is a niche for female-focused writers' groups. These include *SheWrites*, which boasts 20,000 active members, and *Women on Writing* (Wow), a free e-zine for female writers, which has 6800 'likes' on their Facebook page.

Countering conventional perceptions of writing as a solitary activity, female indie writers represent themselves as a community, often alerting each other to dangers. They are quick to point out predatory publishing schemes by disreputable publishers or even overpriced strategies like that of Simon & Schuster's Archway. Author Nadia Lee's blog post about the launch of Archway is tagged as 'Public Service Announcement', 'scam', 'vanity publishing', and 'writerbeware'.[19] Lee speaks straight to her audience of aspiring writers. 'It is a vanity publishing venture, *designed specifically to make profit by taking money from authors, not* selling books to readers' (emphasis in the original).[20] She provides a chart comparing the three types of categories in publishing, Traditional Publisher, Vanity Publisher, and Self Publisher, but in case anyone has missed her overall conclusion, she directly advises 'Do *not* sign up for it' (emphasis in the original).[21] Lee's post is typical of the industry advice blogs that indie authors provide to fellow writers.

The sense of community and camaraderie is bolstered by online author organizations. Examples include *World Literary Café* or *Best Selling Reads*, through which authors share promotional and publication information. But such sites are also examples of the rise of a service industry to support indie writers.

Many respondents to the Women and Writing survey indicated that the role of author-as-marketer was the most challenging for them. Mary (not her real name) perceives the categories as somewhat mutually exclusive, noting that: 'Writers are not necessarily good marketers.' Writing a book, releasing it online, and setting up social media channels is not the simple path to sales, as Melissa (not her real name) indicated. 'Being an indie author is very difficult [it's hard] to find the audience and bring them back. Social media is oftentimes difficult for introverts.[22], While there are plenty of opportunities for independent writers, the persistent challenge of the book industry – how to get your title to stand out – remains.

In response, new roles are emerging in the publishing industry. Brooke Warner, a former executive editor of Seal Press, typifies the female expert who has flourished in the contemporary hybrid publishing landscape. Warner's experiences at Seal Press give her the credentials that make her the type of person others would want to hire as freelance writing consultant or coach. Her collaboration with Kamy Wicoff, founder of the online community for female authors, *SheWrites.com*, has led to the founding of *She Writes Press*. Aspiring writers can hire Warner to advise on how to develop their manuscript or sell their book project; they can also submit it for her consideration for publication by *She Writes Press* (SWP), which describes itself as an 'independent publishing company'.[23] SWP also promises transparency in what clients' money is purchasing, a highly touted value of the independent publishing community. Writer and founder of *Novel Publicity*, Emlyn Chand, is another example of the new service industry supporting indie writers. Chand began as an author and her discovery of independent publishing echoes that of others who were persuaded by the many options it offered:

> I started my literary journey with an agent for one novel while working toward self-publishing another. I loved self-publishing so much, I ended my contract with my agent and went full speed ahead into the indie publishing world. I've had flirtations with some small pub houses as well, but my heart really does belong to self-publishing.[24]

Chand's company offers services to writers across multiple genres. She customizes blog tours for independent authors to gain reviews and exposure to a wider audience and the company offers a wide range of other support, including design, editing, and marketing.

For the indie writers we examined, the self-publishing industry is author directed; it offers women the opportunity to set their own sales goals, and in many instances create second careers for themselves as writers. Access to low-cost publishing platforms like Amazon's KDP, as well as hybrid publishing models, appear to be lowering some of the start-up costs associated with self-publishing, which may permit a wider range of voices to be heard through publication. Despite the entrepreneurial language in which indie publishing is framed by indie writers we studied, the importance of community to indie writers and the thriving author collectives may explain why self-publishing is still spoken about by participants such as Chand as a personal passion, something that is 'loved'. It remains to be seen what the new practices associated with being an 'indie' author can do to challenge the gender inequities of the traditional publishing landscape.

Part Eight
Literary Prize Culture

Literary prizes play an increasingly important role in the approbation and commodification of books and in the public performance of authorship. The most prominent literary awards – for example, the Nobel Prize in Literature, the Prix Goncourt, the Pulitzer Prize and the Man Booker Prize – are now major celebrity events, but there has also been a proliferation of book awards throughout the world, sub-categorised by language, by geographical region, by form (including for novels, drama, short stories and poetry) and by genre (including historical fiction, science fiction, horror fiction, crime fiction, comedy, satire, romance and biography). There are also awards for specific categories, for example women's writing, children's literature, literary translations, first books and unpublished works. Literary prizes attract wide-scale criticism regarding the political, regional and linguistic bias of specific awards, and more generally for their role in the commercialisation of literature and use as marketing ploys by corporate capitalism. Individual prizes have also been subject to controversy, regarding the judging criteria, the constitution of the judging panels, the judges' decisions and the recipient's response.

The impact of the burgeoning literary prize culture on authorship in Britain in the late twentieth century is assessed by Richard Todd (1996). Explaining the main transitions of authorship as a profession, he focuses on the financial impact of literary prizes on an author's career, and the potential of literary awards to provide authors with an instant global profile. He compares the economic significance of British literary prizes with the French Prix Goncourt and the Italian Premo Strega, or the Nobel Prize, and observes that, for the first time since the early twentieth century, literary prizes now offer the transformative potential to writers to actually make a living from writing fiction.

In the second excerpt, Tom Maschler (2003) offers a first-hand account of the origins of the Booker Prize, explaining his own role in its inception. From the outset, his goal was to create a promotional as well as a competitive climate for literature, and to model the Booker on the Prix Goncourt, hoping to emulate its success in stimulating sales of prize-winning books each year. Maschler tells the story of how he managed to persuade Booker – the sponsors – to fund the prize and how he managed to achieve his goal of creating a widely publicised and eventually televised literary event.

The role of the literary prizes in the process of recognising and conferring value on literature is explored by Claire Squires in *Marketing Literature: The Making of Contemporary Writing in Britain* (2007). In this extract, she discusses in particular the role of prizes in contributing to genre classification and definition, as a site of the 'interaction between genre and the marketplace' (p. 256). She maintains that a study of various literary prize entry requirements reveals a hierarchy of literary value, with prizes for specific genres and categories of literature (for example, the best crime writing or the best Scottish novel) occupying a lower place in the hierarchy than those, like the Booker Prize, which award prizes to 'the best novel'. She also considers what literary awards like the Whitbread Awards (now named the Costa Book Awards) reveal about late twentieth-century and early twenty-first-century reading practices, arguing that 'the structure of the awards is such that the very notion of genre boundaries is contested, both supporting and undermining genre divisions in the promotion of books and reading' (pp. 258–259). For Squires, literary prizes contribute to the processes of literary categorisation and canonisation, which are integral aspects both of literary marketing and also of the process of creating cultural meaning.

James English (2005) decodes the unspoken rules and practices underlying literary prizes, with reference to Bourdieu's field theory. In this extract from *The Economy of Prestige Prizes, Awards, and the Circulation of Cultural Values*, English identifies a new form of capital in circulation in the major literary prizes: the currency of scandal. Examining various forms that this currency takes, and the way in which it operates in all the major prizes, he draws attention to typical examples of scandals: when 'great artists' are overlooked in favour of lesser-known authors; when prizes are awarded to controversial authors; and when judges are deemed inept, unqualified or corrupt. He maintains that their function is not simply to promote the authors and the prize but also to keep afloat the concept of the author as a 'special category of person, and hence in Art as a special domain of existence' (p. 265).

These four readings chart the historical development of literary prize culture, and account for the exponential growth of book awards over the course of a century. Interpreting the rules and strategies in operation in literary prize culture, they make important contributions to ongoing debates about the dual role played by prizes as cultural and commercial agents in the literary field, and about the significance of literary prizes in contributing to authors' and publishers' profitability and global prestige.

SUGGESTED FURTHER READING

Huggan, G., 1997. 'Prizing otherness: A short history of "The Booker"'. *Studies in the Novel,* 29 (3), 412–432.

Moran, J., 2000. *Star Authors: Literary Celebrity in America.* London: Pluto Press.

Squires, C., 2004. 'A common ground? Book prize culture in Europe' in *Javnost The Public* 11 (4), 37–47.

35 Literary Prizes and the Media

Richard Todd

At about the beginning of the 1980s, Britain's literary culture in respect of the novel began to undergo a series of rapid and fascinating changes. Prior to this time – in other words during the immediate post-war period until well into the 1970s – Britain's serious literary novelists were likely to achieve notice through either (a) the production of one title that captured the public imagination, or (b) a steady output that contrived to reach a faithful, and usually increasing, readership. Among the best-known examples of the former are the successes of William Golding and John Fowles. Golding's *Lord of the Flies* first appeared in 1954; by the 1960s it had become a 'set text' both in Britain and overseas. By the 1980s Fowles's *The French Lieutenant's Woman* (1969) had taken its place in academe as Britain's best-known postmodernist novel. Both books were subsequently filmed, Fowles's novel more recently and famously as we have seen, than Golding's (although it was Peter Brook who wrote the screenplay for *Lord of the Flies*). Well-known examples of the latter category of steady output include the achievements of Graham Greene from the 1940s onwards, and Doris Lessing, Iris Murdoch and Muriel Spark from the 1950s onwards.

There were prizes to be won by the serious literary novelist, to be sure, but their significance was not noticed by the majority of the reading public, nor were they promoted as being of interest to consumers of contemporary fiction, whether borrowers or buyers. These awards still exist. They include the James Tait Black Memorial Prizes (these were established in 1918 and are awarded annually, one for fiction and one for biography), the Geoffrey Faber Memorial Prize (then a relative newcomer that was established in 1965 and awarded in alternate years for verse and prose fiction), the Hawthornden Prize (established in 1919 and awarded for 'the best work of imaginative literature published during the preceding year by a British author'), and – most significantly – the Somerset Maugham Awards (first made in 1947 and intended to encourage writers under 35 to travel). None is specifically for the novel.

The prestige that went with winning any of these prizes in the 1960s was confined to the literary world. The sums of prize-money were certainly appreciated by the winners, but they were not substantial by today's standards (it would have been impossible to turn to writing full-time on the proceeds unless one were already of independent means), and the awards themselves had no really discernible effect on an author's sales.

The British literary establishment (as was often lamented) had no equivalent of France's Prix Goncourt, established in 1903, whose (symbolic) financial value is a nugatory 50 francs or Italy's Premio Strega, whose monetary value is 1m lire (about £400). However, to win the Goncourt or the Strega was and is to be assured of massive sales. The total readership for a winning novel is of a size rarely if ever achieved in Britain. For example, Jean Rouaud's first novel, *Les Champs d'honneur*, was a highly regarded recent winner. Published on 1 September 1990, it had sold several thousand copies; after the prize was awarded in November it went on to sell a further 1m copies on the basis of the prestige of the prize and favourable reviews.

For British writers, as for their colleagues worldwide, there always remained the phantom of Nobel Prize recognition. Whatever else might be said about it, the Nobel Prize remains the most financially lucrative award in the entire world. Its 1994 value has been placed variously at between £650,000 and £900,000. Although Nobel laureates from Britain and Ireland in the first half of the twentieth century included Rudyard Kipling in 1907, W. B. Yeats in 1923, John Galsworthy in 1932 and T. S. Eliot in 1948, the only Britons to have won the Nobel Prize for Literature in the second half of the century, as the 1970s came to an end, were the philosopher Bertrand Russell in 1950 and the historiographer Winston Churchill in 1953. Of the entire list, only Kipling and Galsworthy could be counted as novelists. Their number was swelled by the Irish-born French-speaking exile Samuel Beckett in 1969. In 1983 William Golding became to date the only post-war British novelist to be awarded the Nobel Prize. His achievement, however, was marred by an apparent breaking of ranks from within the Swedish Academy, with a sour press as the result. There has been a very recent spate of English-language (though not British) Nobel laureates: Nadine Gordimer in 1991, Derek Walcott in 1992, Toni Morrison in 1993 and Seamus Heaney in 1995.

By the 1990s Britain's prize culture had changed dramatically. Any of the writers mentioned or discussed in this book is in theory eligible for between forty and fifty literary awards, only a minority of which are not made annually. Of these awards, at least half-a-dozen now available to novelists published in Britain exceed (sometimes considerably) £10,000. Winning one of these more significant prizes not only brings the novelists a cash windfall: it can exercise spectacular effects on sales figures. On several occasions, as we have seen with A. S. Byatt's *Possession* and will see in subsequent instances, a big win has catapulted hitherto less well-known or even unknown writers to fame, enabling them to devote their careers to writing full-time. This, coupled with shrewd business sense on the part of a publisher and/ or an agent, can empower writers to achieve a global profile that would otherwise have been out of their reach.

One could make out a case in terms of success of this kind for at least ten or fifteen, and probably more, writers of serious literary fiction working today and published in the first instance in London since 1980. It is probably true to say that not since before 1914 have so many serious literary novelists been able to make a living from writing fiction in Britain. Of Arnold Bennett, for example, Frank Kermode observed well over ten years ago:

> It may not seem credible, but I calculate that [his] income in 1913, expressed in terms of our money in 1982, amounted to something over £800,000.[1]

The presence in the modernist literary canon of writers such as James Joyce and Virginia Woolf (both 1882–1941) may blind many of their academic readers to the fact that each sold relatively poorly in their lifetimes.[2] In the 1920s Woolf, for example, could not have begun to envisage the kind of sales she achieved posthumously more than half a century later (prior to coming – briefly – out of copyright, Woolf was published by Penguin in arrangement with The Hogarth Press). An indication of Woolf's current sales is given by the effect of the 1992 filming of *Orlando* (1928). In March 1993 Virago issued an offset of the 1990 Vintage edition of the novel, having bought the rights to a film tie-in cover from Penguin; in 1993 alone Virago's sales of *Orlando* (that is, sales excluding the Vintage and Penguin editions of the novel) totalled 15,000 and by September 1994 had exceeded 17,000 – this in addition to continuing steady Penguin and Vintage paperback sales.[3] These figures exceed the original world sales of *Orlando* in the four-and-a-half years between November 1928 (the date of its appearance) and February 1933.[4]

Today's serious literary novelists in Britain, however, unlike those of sixty to seventy years ago, are alive to commercial possibilities that for most of the twentieth century have been available only to writers deliberately aiming at the best-selling, genre-fiction end of the market such as crime or science fiction. The media consequences for this new constituency have been varied and lucrative. A TV serialization or the sale of film rights have been frequent occurrences; once again, in shrewd hands these can generate vast amounts of extra income, fame and far wider prestige than was the case a generation ago. I am not arguing that external events have only recently begun to assist sales; I am drawing attention to the fact that such sales are no longer exclusively the preserve of the genre-fiction writer. Agatha Christie's carefully scripted and notorious 'disappearance' in 1926 boosted her sales considerably, beginning with *The Murder of Roger Ackroyd*, which had appeared earlier that year. A fictional instance, quite possibly inspired by the Christie case, occurs soon afterwards in the work of Dorothy L. Sayers. Sayers' *alter ego*, the detective writer Harriet Vane, having been acquitted of murdering her fiancé thanks to the persistent genius of the sleuthing aristocrat Lord Peter Wimsey, finds herself 'a very much richer woman than she had ever dreamed of becoming' as a result of increased sales of all her titles and – interestingly – transatlantic coverage arising from intense press curiosity about the case.[5]

The element of good fortune that can attend the early stages of a career should not be underestimated, although in mentioning it one is in no way trying to belittle individual achievement. The celebrated 'two-horse races' between William Golding's *Rites of Passage* and Anthony Burgess's *Earthly Powers* in 1980, and D. M. Thomas's *The White Hotel* and Salman Rushdie's *Midnight's Children* in 1981 impressed the Booker Prize on the public imagination. The serious literary novelists of the 1980s and 1990s tend to have a much higher media profile than their peers of a generation ago.

36 How It All Began

Tom Maschler

At the age of eighteen, during the autumn of 1951, I spent three months in Paris. I well remember sharing in the excitement which surrounded the literary prizes throughout that season. The Prix Goncourt above all, but also the smaller ones. Virtually every evening the subject would come up. Before the prizes were announced, the merits or demerits of the winner were analysed. Within a brief period of the announcement, half the people I met seemed to have read the Goncourt winner. Such intellectual fervour left a lasting impression on me.

A few years later, I found myself working in British publishing and I learned that there were a number of literary prizes in England also. In terms of extra sales generated by a book winning one of these prizes, the most significant prior to The Booker Prize was probably the Somerset Maugham Award. The winner might sell an additional 500 to 1,000 copies. Not much in comparison with the Goncourt winner, who might expect to sell an additional 500,000 copies! No wonder that in England, literary prizes were considered irrelevant.

When the opportunity arose, I used to speak of my French experience and when I was invited by the Society of Young Publishers to give a talk I took the opportunity to campaign for an English prize. My goal was not simply to found a prize for the benefit of a winner, nor for the sake of the bookshops, but to stimulate interest in serious British fiction as a whole. I aspired to create a competitive (and a promotional) climate by announcing a shortlist each year. The aim was to catch the imagination of the press followed by that of the public. My talk seemed to find favour. Several people commented that, desirable as the scheme was, nothing would happen unless I made it my business to find a sponsor. Once the money was there the prize would be relatively easy to set up.

At first I found the idea of raising a substantial sum of money rather daunting. But then it occurred to me that my company, Jonathan Cape, had a relationship with a possible candidate, Booker Brothers. Booker had set up a subsidiary to purchase the copyright in the work of certain enormously successful authors such as Agatha Christie and Ian Fleming. Given the fact that we published Fleming, I was aware of the degree of financial success Booker had enjoyed from this venture. So I thought they might be persuaded to plough a small percentage back into a literary prize. Thus it was that my colleague, Graham C. Greene, and I went off to see Charles Tyrell and John Murphy at Booker. We put our case and we were frank about the fact that the prize would take several years to make a mark. We pointed out that once it did so (as we were convinced it *would*), Booker might well find their sponsorship something they could be proud of. It might even have a commercial value. Messrs Tyrell and Murphy said that they were personally in favour but that they would have to discuss the proposition with their colleagues. A formal agreement came through rather quickly and then serious planning meetings began.

'It's the most important thing I've done in my career.'

Tom Maschler, founder of The Booker Prize

Of course it was several years before the prize became so important that the event as a whole was televised. However, it made a mark right from the start. I shall never forget our pride and joy when the very first novel to win The Booker, P.H. Newby's *Something to Answer For*, appeared on the *Evening Standard* bestseller list. It was the first time that a British novel had found its way onto a bestseller list purely as a result of winning a prize. From the time that the prize was televised regularly, the impact was such that not only the winner but also the shortlist appeared on the bestseller list.

It is not for me to assess the achievements of the prize but I do believe that it has richly fulfilled our hopes and ambitions. However, I have two particular concerns. One is that on a number of occasions the winner seems to have fallen far short of attaining our goal; it was inordinately difficult to recognise the winner as 'the best book'. Clearly this is a highly subjective question. Nonetheless, some of the novels have been such very strange choices that it is really difficult to make sense of them. My other reservation is related to the question of secrecy. Keeping the winner a secret until the dinner is an important element in suspense and in the resulting media interest. If the outcome were known to the shortlisted authors, they would have the choice of attending the dinner or not attending at all. As things stand, the secrecy leads to considerable tension. Though they have attempted to put a brave face on it, I have frequently seen authors put through anguish. Such anguish that I cannot help thinking that it might be better for the secrecy to be abandoned.

37 Genre in the Marketplace

Claire Squires

LITERARY PRIZES

Literary prizes are one of the wider agencies involved in book marketing, and are not, on the whole, initiated, let alone controlled, by publishers. Nonetheless, prizes still play a crucial role in the interaction between genre and the marketplace, and are one of the forces that come to influence notions of cultural value and literariness. Ostensibly, what every book award might claim to do is to recognise and reward value. A corollary part of this mission is, then, the promotion of the winner or winners: literary prizes can bring relatively unknown writers to public recognition, enhance the reputation of already established authors, turn the attention of the media to books, and so support the consumption of literature generally. As such, the role of literary prizes is already more complex than as an index of literary achievement, and they have a broad range of motivations and implications.[1] Moreover, awarding a prize to a book acts not only to indicate value, but also to confer it. Value is thus doubly constructed in the realm of literary prizes. Yet even before the role of literary prizes in constituting notions of value is assessed, and the contingent nature of value examined, the organisational structures of prizes suggest how they contribute to genre definition and literary categorisation. The entry requirements for each prize provide the key to this. The Booker Prize, for example, 'aims to reward the best novel of the year written by a British or Commonwealth author'.[2] The novel must also be originally written in English and published by a UK-based publishing house. The definition that the prize gives is to do with national and regional identity, and also the market through which the novel has been published. This definition has contributed to analyses of the Booker Prize as promoting post-colonial writing from within the context of UK cultural imperialism.[3] What is of greater direct impact on the definition of genre, though, is the first part of the description: 'the best novel'. This may seem at first glance to be an absolute definition (within the already circumscribed entry requirements), but by placing it alongside the entry requirements of other prizes its function with regard to genre becomes apparent. A brief survey of the 'Prizes and Awards' section of the *Writers' and Artists' Yearbook* yields, among others, a list including the Boardman Tasker Prize (for the best book 'concerned with the mountain environment'), the Arthur C. Clarke Award (for 'best science fiction novel'), the Betty Trask Award (for the best first novels 'of a romantic or traditional nature'), the Crime Writers' Association 'Daggers' (for best crime writing), the Encore Award (for 'best second novel'), the Lichfield Prize (for the best novel 'based recognisably on the geographical area of Lichfield District, Staffordshire'), the Saltire Scottish Book of the Year (for the best book by 'any author of Scottish descent or living in Scotland, or for a book by anyone which deals with the work or life of a Scot or with a Scottish problem, event or situation').[4] Some, such as the Arthur C. Clarke and the Crime Writers' Association awards use traditional genre definitions, while others choose quite different categorisations. What these entry requirements do, be they stated in terms of the book's subject matter, genre, or author biography, is to indicate a series of *relative* 'bests'. It is in this comparative light that Booker's definition of 'the best novel' acquires generic implications. For the Booker is awarded to the best non-genre novel or, in other words, the best 'literary' novel. By not naming the category, though, what the Booker does is to confirm the 'literary' novel at the top of genre hierarchies. The phrase 'best novel' equates with 'best literary novel', and so it is implied that the winner of the Booker is better than the winner of the Arthur C. Clarke.

Based on the categories of their entry requirements, literary prizes construct notions of value through their choice of winners. Richard Todd's *Consuming Fictions* is premised on the idea that the Booker Prize and its winners have been crucial in broadening the appeal of 'serious literary fiction' from UK publishers, both in home and overseas (particularly the US) markets.[5] Todd's thesis is that the increasing commodification of literary fiction through the course of the 1980s and 1990s, a development led by the Booker Prize, has had the effect of turning writers to particular themes and treatments of themes:

> the novelists I discuss have worked in an increasingly intensified atmosphere, one in which both the promotion and the reception of serious literary fiction have become steadily more consumer-oriented. How many of even the most interesting postcolonial writers of recent years, for example, are – however subconsciously, with whatever desire to say something new – now responding both aesthetically and commercially to the 1980s as 'the Rushdie decade'? Or – likewise – how many slush-pile literary detective novels with a double historical time-scheme has A. S. Byatt's *Possession* spawned?
>
> Such self-conscious commercial categorization offers a real challenge to today's novelists, agents, publishers and readers.[6]

Todd's claim is an interesting one, though difficult to sustain in terms of textual analysis. The real benefit of his thinking, though, is to suggest how agencies such as literary prizes alter perceptions of success, and thus construct notions of genre and value.

The Whitbread Book Awards are particularly apposite to the question of the interaction of literary prizes and genre because of their idiosyncratic organisation. Unlike the Booker, whose parameters are only occasionally interrogated, and much more often on the grounds of its nationality requirements and its post-colonial eligibility structures, the Whitbread's structure of categories casts its observers into immediate ontological doubt. Since 1985, the Whitbread has operated with five separate category awards, each with its own judging panel, shortlist and section winner. In 1999, for example, the section winners were Rose Tremain's *Music and Silence* (1999) for the Novel Award, David Cairns's *Berlioz Volume Two: Servitude and Greatness 1832–1869* (1999) for the Biography Award, Seamus Heaney's *Beowulf* (1999) for the Poetry Award, and J. K. Rowling's *Harry Potter and the Prisoner of Azkaban* (1999) for the Children's Book of the Year.[7] The final judging stage then pits category against category: biography against poetry, first novel against later novels, a task which must yearly fill the judges with a momentary horror as they scrabble for a critical vocabulary to make sense of such disparate artistic forms. The very idea of having a separate category for the novel and the first novel starts to unravel if the first novel section winner goes on to win the main award, as Kate Atkinson's *Behind the Scenes at the Museum* (1995) did.[8] How are the judges to compare an elegantly slim volume of poetry and a encyclopaedically mammoth life? What, moreover, is a panel to make of a book of poetry that is also heavily autobiographical, such as Ted Hughes's *Birthday Letters* (overall award winner of 1998)?[9] These questions of category – questions which demand the comparison of different genres – are not insurmountable, as the Whitbread judges prove each year. Rather, what the questions do is to foreground the construction of value through genre, enshrining a notion of hybridity in its cross-genre judging system. Bud McLintock of Karen Earl Ltd., the Director of the Awards, believes this echoes contemporary reading practices: 'Readers don't tend to make the distinctions that critics make in their reading habits, and the Whitbread Book Awards reflect this.'[10] The model of a cross-genre reader, choosing his or her reading matter from a variety of types and sources, is in accord with Connor's analysis of post-war reading in *The English Novel in History 1950–1995*, in which he writes that:

> If there ever was a moment in which it could be assumed that readers were identical with the readerships to which they belonged [...it] has given way to a condition in which readers [...] typically have multiple affiliations and participate in multiple readerships and forms of reading. [...]

> Positing the existence of interpretive groups, or communities of taste, may be useful mostly in order to help to register the effect of the multiple allegiances which precisely work to dissolve the clarity of such groups.[11]

Connor's reference, by way of 'interpretive groups, or communities of taste', to Stanley Fish's theories, suggests the complexity of post-war reading patterns, something which Delany also asserts in noting the shift from product differentiation to market segmentation. This is precisely the challenge to both the industry and its analysts: to 'register the effect of the multiple allegiances' both in terms of patterns of consumption and the impact on the material product.

The addition of the Children's Book of the Year to the overall Whitbread Awards [...] highlights the dialogue the literary prizes have with genre, the marketplace and its consumers. For while Whitbread's exercise in genre comparison might be thought an experiment that threatens to loose the riotous border-crossing of relativism upon demarcated aesthetic boundaries, it should also be seen as a self-conscious example of the general function of literary prizes with respect to genre. The structure of the Awards is such that the very notion of genre boundaries is contested, both supporting and undermining genre divisions in the promotion of literature and reading.

Literary prizes, then, use literary categorisation, both by confirming and contesting existing categories and creating and influencing new ones. They are integrally involved with the processes of canonisation, both by choosing works to reward and promote, but also by defining the ways in which they are chosen. Genre, as well as being created and reflected by the book itself, by branding, by imprints and by retail practice, is crucially influenced by the interventions of wider agencies, such as literary prizes. In addition to being an integrated and integral part of the publishing industry's business practice, marketing therefore operates via a range of publishing activities and publishing intermediaries in order to represent books and authors in the literary marketplace. In so doing, it actively influences reception, negotiates with genre and constructs and reshapes notions of literary value and taste. Through branding, through packaging, through imprints, through bookshop shelving strategies, and through literary prizes, the marketing of literature works actively to create cultural meanings.

38 Scandalous Currency

James F. English

As we've already noted, the discourse surrounding cultural prizes has long been predominantly negative in tone.[1] Historically, it is difficult to find anyone of any stature in the world of arts and letters who speaks with unalloyed respect for prizes, and still more difficult to find books or articles (other than those under-written by the prize sponsors themselves) that do not strike the familiar chords of amused indifference, jocular condescension, or outright disgust. It seems moreover to be the case that the most prestigious awards draw the most intensely critical sniping. It is not the little start-up prizes, or the eccentric, whimsical prizes, or the prizes in low-prestige genres like romance or pornography, which 'everyone hates' (though these are often the object of dismissive, just-what-we-need-another-prize remarks), but rather the very prizes which we should have thought everyone wanted to win: in America the Pulitzers or Academy Awards, in Britain the Booker or the BAFTAs, nearly everywhere the Nobel. And not only are the high-prestige, high-culture prizes the ones most frequently and bitterly derided, but the most derisive commentators tend to be the highest-prestige authors and artists and critics – the very people who constitute the pool of potential judges and prize-winners, and from whom we might therefore have expected a certain degree of diplomacy, if not an actual endorsement.

What sort of event or system of exchange is this, which seems to secure cultural esteem by maximizing the flow of disesteeming discourse through and around it? How and why do cultural prizes discourage, except in blandly official statements, unequivocal expressions of affirmation and assent? And if we are not really expected to believe in the prize, to take it altogether seriously, then in what sense is it an effectual practice of 'collective make-belief' or 'social alchemy'? What collective cultural function can the prize possibly serve when so many consequential participants have announced in advance their disdain for its procedures and outcomes?

These are important questions because, to begin with, they get to the heart of the *game* element in prizes, the unspoken rules and unconscious strategies that structure everything from acceptance speeches to op-ed commentaries, and that cue observers to praise an adept or expert 'player' like Dustin Hoffman at the 1985 OBIEs ('This is a very tough fucking *house*. How can you *beat* this house?') or Bill Murray at the 1999 New York Film Critics Circle Awards (removing his coat and rolling up his sleeves: 'We might as well get comfortable. I'm going to be up here for a while') while deprecating a maladroit one like Sally Field at the 1980 Academy Awards ('You *like* me! You really *like* me!').[2] But they are also important questions because they point to a central difficulty in the critical analysis of prizes – namely, the fact that critique, at least in its usual forms, is itself a fundamental and even in many circumstances an obligatory part of the game, a recognizable mode of complicitous participation. One cannot get very far toward understanding what prizes are and how they work, let alone toward challenging the material and symbolic bases of their efficacy, simply by joining with the long-dominant tendency to abuse them, labeling them a farce and a circus and an embarrassment, or permitting oneself to tolerate their existence with barely concealed distaste. Rather, we must subject this tendency itself to critical examination, tracing its recent history and assessing the kind of cultural work it performs in our era.

Because it is a tendency that becomes stronger rather than weaker as the prize in question becomes more valuable and the field of its application more elevated or culturally legitimate, I will focus in this part of the book on the higher, 'art' end of the art-entertainment spectrum, where the forms of critical sniping at the prize and, to borrow another term from Bourdieu, the 'strategies of condescension' at work within the prize presentation itself, are somewhat more elaborate. Of course there is no shortage of attacks on 'entertainment' prizes: sometimes it seems as if the whole point of the Grammys and the Tonys and the Emmys is to give newspaper columnists an opportunity to hurl abuse at them. Remarking that the Oscars are 'a joke' and the Grammys 'an even bigger joke,' a writer for the *San Francisco Chronicle* adds that, 'as for the Emmys, the idea that they actually give awards for series television is probably the biggest joke yet.'[3] But prizes for painting, literature, opera, sculpture, dance, and so forth – the fields belonging to the 'sphere of legitimacy,' the sphere over which academic authorities exercise their legitimate domination and enforce their methodical hierarchies and universal claims – are different from prizes for sitcoms and docudramas.[4] If prizes for these legitimized arts can still be derided as a kind of joke, it is a somewhat different joke from that of the Emmys. It is not a matter of the supposed aesthetic worthlessness of the entire field being honored, the illegitimacy of its claims to value (though, as we will see, there are moments when that broadly satiric view of, say, contemporary literature or contemporary art is put strategically into circulation). It is, rather, a question of the awkward or embarrassing or somehow compromised relationship between that field and the kind of honor the prize represents. If prizes for daytime talk shows are an idiocy, prizes for poetry or painting are a *scandal*. And there is perhaps no device more perfectly suited than scandal to making things happen on the field of culture; it is the 'instrument *par excellence* of symbolic action.'[5]

Though there seems never to be a shortage of prize scandals, the scandals invariably sort out into just a handful of basic and well-established types, all of which ultimately derive from the scandalous fact of the prizes' very existence, their claim to a legitimate and even premier place on the fields of culture. While any of the participants in a cultural prize – from sponsors or administrators to winners and losers to friends in attendance at the ceremony – can be fodder for the journalistic apparatus that produces awards scandals, the most common and generic scandals concern the judges, specifically the judges' dubious aesthetic dispositions, as betrayed by their meager credentials, their risible lack of habitus, or their glaring errors of judgment. The Nobel Prize in Literature set off a judging scandal in its very first year, when the Swedish Academy failed to name Leo Tolstoy its laureate, presenting the prize instead to the minor French poet Sully Prudhomme.[6] And then, amid the consequent storm of protest, the academy was loath to appear contrite (or vulnerable to the pressure of public opinion) and so persisted in neglecting the Russian until his death in 1910.[7] The scandal of appalling omissions from the roster of Nobel laureates (Tolstoy, Hardy, Ibsen, Kafka, Proust, Valéry, Rilke, Joyce, and others), so often invoked against the prize by present-day observers, was thus already firmly lodged in the field of discussion by 1902.

In this case, the scandal was the judges' blindness to great art, their inability to mark a distinction between truly extraordinary and relatively undistinguished work. The academy's scandalized critics, including forty-two Swedish writers, critics, and artists who signed a statement of protest, stressed above all the 'genius' of the artist who had been passed over. Just as often, however, these scandals are concerted around the choice of an egregiously 'bad' artist, one who affronts the dominant taste with work that appears pornographic, morally corrupt, politically unpalatable, or simply 'worthless' according to prevailing standards of evaluation. In such cases, the ostensible deficiency of the judges' taste is a matter not of their undervaluation of true art, but of their overestimation of 'garbage' or 'gibberish.' Allen Tate and his fellow New Critics, who in 1949 awarded the inaugural Bollingen Prize to Ezra Pound, came in for just this sort of abuse; the *Pisan Cantos* were derided as fraudulent nonsense, while Pound himself, an indicted and incarcerated fascist war criminal, was seen as beyond the pale of consideration for national honors and awards. Since this was a prize administered under the auspices of the Library of Congress, it enjoyed the implicit endorsement of the federal government, an unusual feature in U.S. literary awards (though more common elsewhere), and one that led outraged congressmen to join the chorus of book reviewers and literary journalists in their harangues against Tate, T. S. Eliot, and the other Bollingen judges. Indeed, the outcry was so fierce that Congress withdrew from the library its license to make awards of this kind – reinstating that power only in 1989, with the founding of the biennial Rebekah Johnson Bobbitt National Prize for Poetry.[8]

Whether critics of a prize focus positive attention on the loser or negative attention on the winner – and whether they take a populist or a high-culturalist perspective, attacking the jury for its elitism or for its commercialism, for the inaccessibility or rather for the aesthetic unambitiousness of its selection – their cries of 'scandal' are directed not at some minor imperfection in the prize's structure or bylaws (though they sometimes seem to be) but at its very roots. With the Nobel, the Bollingen, and countless other prizes, judging scandals arise practically from the moment of the inaugural award presentation precisely because such scandals go to the very heart of the prize's initially fragile claim to legitimacy. Every new prize is always already scandalous. The question is simply whether it will attract enough attention for this latent scandalousness to become manifest in the public sphere.

Most of the other types of judging scandal in which prizes become enmeshed are simply variations on this original outcry against the jury's imposition of wrong aesthetic preferences. There are, for example, corruption scandals, in which judges presumably capable of making correct artistic distinctions are accused of selling, trading, or otherwise rigging their votes for the sake of personal gain. As mentioned earlier, this type of scandal has hounded prizes since their invention by the Greeks, and no prize can be immune to it. The furor over Pia Zadora's 1981 Golden Globe Award for Best Actress was only the most notorious instance of the perennial corruption scandals that surround those awards and the voting members of the Hollywood Foreign Press Association – a group that is widely regarded as both undercredentialed and overeager to cast votes in the direction from which the most lavish trips and presents are flowing. (Among other enticements, Zadora's husband flew the entire association membership to Las Vegas.)

Often, judging scandals concern alleged corruption not by money but by some undeclared conflict of interest. In the small, quarreling-family milieu of British book prizes, for example, such conflicts have been attributed to a judge's desire to please a spouse or lover who happens to be on the slate of nominees. These scandals of excessively *intimate* social capital began at the Booker Prize in 1974, when Kingsley Amis' wife, Elizabeth Jane Howard, was on the panel of judges that shortlisted Amis' *Ending Up*. In 1994, the chair of the Booker judges, John Bayley, withdrew a novel by his wife, Iris Murdoch, from consideration; but a fellow juror, James Wood, was denounced for not following suit with respect to a novel by *his* wife, Claire Massud, which he supported for the shortlist. As Mark Lawson (himself a former Booker judge) put it in the *Independent*, other judges may have blundered from time to time, but 'we all got through our duties without running the risk of the £20,000 winner's cheque being sent to our own address.'[9] A year later, Sheridan Morley, one of the judges for the AT&T Non-Fiction Prize, was chastised for arranging to have his fiancée, Ruth Leon, fill another spot on the panel, and then withholding from his fellow judges the fact of their engagement. Told after the fractious ceremony that Morley and Leon were a couple and would soon be married, the chair of judges, Lord Clark, reportedly said, 'They deserve each other.'[10] Somewhat less entertaining variants of these conflict-of-interest scandals may involve a judge who is perceived to be returning a favor to an editor, publisher, or producer (the sort of scandal that has been virtually normalized in the major French book awards) or reciprocating an artist who has recently supported the judge when their roles were reversed (as has sometimes occurred in American poetry prizes). All such scandals are pitched against the 'politics' of prizes, their inescapable entwinement with the movements not just of money but of social capital. As we have seen, social capital is often an even more important factor than symbolic capital (and far more important than money) in persuading a prestigious artist or critic to serve as a judge; it is an indispensable currency for any new cultural prize. By the common or journalistic definition, therefore, prizes are unavoidably 'political' from the moment of their inception, and hence always open to scandals of this kind.

Here again, scandals can take either positive or negative form: critics may accuse judges of having too cozy a relationship to the (unworthy) winner or harboring unfair, merely 'personal' animosity toward a (more worthy) contender, or even nursing such fierce antagonism toward a fellow judge, administrator, agent, or other player as to preclude support for that person's candidate. The latter form of scandal, concerned with grudges and hostilities and quarreling in the back rooms of the prize, is the staple of countless journalistic exposés and tell-all cultural memoirs. 'Prizefighting,' as it is called in many headlines, is the very stuff of awards lore. Yet although such insider accounts are routine, they themselves are often treated as another form of scandal – the scandalous lapse of etiquette that leads a judge or other insider to air the prize's dirty laundry in public. When someone whispers a scandalous bit of backroom gossip to the press, the scandal of the 'leak' is often given more play than its ostensible substance.

This capacity on the part of commentators to cast the very fact of a scandal as itself a scandal – and thereby to layer scandal upon scandal, implicating all sides of a dispute – is an increasingly significant feature of the awards scene. It is apparent in such instances as the 1994 Booker Prize, when the scandal of the prize being awarded to an 'unreadable,' 'interminable,' and 'obscene' 500-page novel of densely rendered Glaswegian dialect in which the word 'fuck' reportedly appears more than 4,000 times (James Kelman's *How Late It Was, How Late*) was bound up with the scandal of the especially fierce bickering and maneuvering of the judges, who appear to have landed on Kelman's (altogether remarkable and important) novel not because it was anyone's first choice but because it was used by several judges in their efforts to block the first choices of others. This scandal was, in turn, bound up with the outrageous behavior of one judge, the rabbi Julia Neuberger, who proceeded immediately after the award ceremony to denounce the winning novel ('crap'), its author ('just a drunken Scotsman'), and her fellow judges in a public statement condemning the bad faith and excessively political nature of the decision-making process, a process that she described as 'completely mad.'[11]

Breaches of etiquette such as this are scandalous not only because they violate the acknowledged rules of the game (judges agree to keep their deliberations confidential), but because they violate a broader and less explicit code of what might be termed cultural sportsmanship. Neuberger was behaving as a sore loser; her book didn't win, so she sulked and complained and did everything possible to tarnish the victory of Kelman. A great deal of the anecdotal lore through which the history of prizes has been conveyed is organized around these transgressions of a presumed collective sense of cultural sportsmanship – not only as regards judges but, especially, in connection with winners and losing contenders. The commentary on prizes assumes a certain investment, on the part of readers, in the question of whether an artist is a good sport; and structuring that question in all its various forms is a broader assumption: that we all recognize a game-like element in cultural practice and have a shared sense of the rules of the game. Or, to put this differently, one function of prize scandals is to clarify and disseminate, as well as at times to assist in modifying, the contemporary rules governing the behaviors and dispositions of 'artists' or other authorities in matters of art – rules which are understood to be different from those that obtain for ordinary people in ordinary walks of life, meaning those outside the art-game. The astonishing degree of journalistic interest in how the participants in an award ceremony behave, how the losers take the news, how the winners express their gratitude, how the old grudges and rivalries manifest themselves, is more than idle curiosity about celebrities. At stake in the minute and always ready-to-be-scandalized attendance to matters of prize etiquette is the very belief in the Artist as a special category of person, and hence in Art as a special domain of existence. And, as we will see, the scandalous currency that prizes put into circulation functions not to deflate this belief but, on the contrary, to keep it aloft, assuring its persistence in the face of heavily contrary historical pressures.

Part Nine
Globalisation and the Book

A series of rapid takeovers, mergers and acquisitions in the publishing industry from the late twentieth century led to the development of a handful of media conglomerates operating internationally and resulted in a book publishing industry closely intertwined with affiliated media such as film, TV, radio, newspapers, periodicals and computer gaming. The development of digital communications systems and the adoption of the English language as the world's main commercial language are further factors contributing to the conglomeration and globalisation of publishing businesses. These major structural changes in the publishing industry have, of course, stimulated much controversy and debate.

The changes wrought to the media and publishing industries through the recent rounds of consolidation and neo-liberal deregulation are the subject of André Schiffrin's *Words and Money* (2010). Former editor-in-chief of Pantheon Books in New York, he was dismissed in 1990 following a takeover by Random House, and became a particularly vocal critic of publishing conglomerates. He reflects in this chapter on the incorporation of publishing within 'modern capitalist society, which allowed for no exceptions and which was ravenous in its demands' (p. 273), and argues that this has led to pressure on each book title to generate much greater profits along with the awarding of extortionate salaries to directors of publishing companies. The result, he maintains, is a profit-driven corporate book industry in which publishers have become 'investors, bankers of a kind', in contrast with a bygone age, when: 'Publishing was seen as a profession, not just as a business' (p. 271). He pessimistically states that this is leading to the homogenisation and standardisation of publishing output, due to the imperative for titles to sell in huge numbers across diverse markets. Meanwhile, authors struggle to find a publisher and to make a living from writing, and independent publishers face increasing difficulties in staying afloat and competing with corporate publishers, with their advantages of economies of scale.

The current concentration of the international publishing industry in the hands of a small number of companies based in the West is a further subject of concern. Anthony Smith's *Books to Bytes: Knowledge and Information in the Postmodern Era* (1993: 18) describes the ambivalence of the internet, on the one hand as a medium for individualism and democracy, but on the other hand as a vehicle for cultural imperialism. He writes of 'a growing phenomenon of global cultural domination, produced not by powerful armies, but by powerful international companies' (1993: 18). Walter Bgoya's 2001 article in this section provides a still-resonant critique of globalisation and particularly the worldwide ascendency of the English language. He describes globalisation as closely affiliated to colonialism: a 'continuation of the same strategy of world domination', and describes how 'powerful forces that recognise no boundaries or sanctity of any values – material and spiritual – if they happen to be in the way of profit are driving it' (p. 279). Bgoya traces how European languages are widely, and willingly, adopted across Africa as the national languages and languages of instruction because 'foreign languages are synonymous with knowledge and privilege' (p. 280), with the result that many African languages are threatened with annihilation, because of the aggressive marketing of European and American media and publications. Bgoya proposes not an entrenched resistance to the use of English and other European languages, but instead that Africans should embrace multilingualism, while emphasising first and foremost the 'principal language of one's being and one's culture' (p. 283).

Angus Phillips's discussion of 'The Global Book' from *Turning the Page* (2014) also focuses on the problem of linguistic homogenisation as a result of globalisation and digital transformations. His investigation centres on the 'translation gap' (p. 285) existing between translations from and to English. On the one hand, his evidence suggests that digital developments open up possibilities for greater diversification, for example through machine translation and the possibilities of global distribution of e-books across linguistic borders, but his main argument confirms that of Bgoya's, that 'the dominance of English, especially in commercial fiction' is leading to a lack of linguistic diversity in international book markets (p. 285).

Suman Gupta's *Globalization and Literature* (2009) ponders the implications of globalisation in the literary publishing industry. His case study of the English-language publishing industry in India complicates the conventional view that multinational publishing leads directly to homogenisation and a lack of linguistic and creative diversity. Instead he argues that in India there is evidence of an increase of literary publishing in Indian languages by international publishing conglomerates and independent publishing firms, and to a greater localisation of book circulation. Gupta draws conclusions about the effects of the global literary marketplace on literary institutions: how media corporations manufacture reader communities and celebrity authors, and how they attempt to commodify and monetise intellectual and artistic creativity through copyright legislation.

Sarah Brouillette's *Postcolonial Writers in the Global Literary Marketplace* (2007) addresses the relationship between the postcolonial author and the globalised marketplace in which the writer's work is published, promoted, disseminated and received. She presents a perceptive analysis of the literary publishing industry, in which 'conglomerates control the rules of the game, having access to those aspects of publishing and marketing that require significant capital' (p. 305), and the effect of this on the market-dependent author. Although this has led to a distinct blockbuster phenomenon, niche fragmentation and market expansion have in her view resulted in greater diversification of literary publishing, which has led to the proliferation of specific genres, including that of postcolonial literature. She notes that although this 'global market expansion' has occurred within transnational publishing, the centre of production has been restricted to a few cities in Europe and America – in particular New York, and to a lesser extent, London (p. 306). The corporatised publishing industry seeks to make 'claims to inclusivity and universality that justify its particular form of dominance' (p. 308). by attempting to address the lack of diversity in its workforce and its publishing output. One response is to seek to incorporate postcolonial writing for global distribution. Brouillette notes that this literature has certain characteristics, namely a tendency towards 'sophisticated', generally anti-realist and politically liberal novels, written in European languages and particularly in English; she notes that the genre has been widely disparaged by critics as 'a feature of capitalist accumulation in the culture industries' (p. 310).

These debates about conglomeration and globalisation represented in this section indicate some of the dichotomies and contractions in the current international publishing environment. On the one hand, structural changes in the publishing industry have led to greater linguistic homogenisation and to significant disparities in international knowledge production and access, but on the other hand, global publishing corporations recognise the necessity for greater literary and cultural diversification, while digital and online technology offer unprecedented democratisation for writers and readers.

SUGGESTED FURTHER READING

Doueihi, M., 2008. *Digital Cultures*. Cambridge, MA: Harvard University Press.
Epstein, J., 1997. *Book Business: Publishing Past, Present and Future*. New York: Norton.
Hesmondhalgh, D., 2007. *The Cultural Industries*. London: Sage.

39 The Future of Publishing

André Schiffrin

One of the reasons the development of publishing throughout the world is so interesting is that it is truly a microcosm of the different societies in which it exists and a mirror of the way in which modern capitalism has evolved. Technically, there is no inherent reason for publishing to be very different from what it was in the nineteenth century. Until quite recently, it still followed the traditional artisanal model rather than the modern corporate one, and in fact was not so different from the enterprises Balzac describes in *Lost Illusions*. More important, publishing was seen as a profession, not just as a business. People who were really interested in making money did not choose it as a career. Though of course publishers needed to make enough to keep their companies going, none expected the business to be wildly profitable. As I pointed out in *The Business of Books*, the average profit of publishing houses throughout Western Europe and the United States, during much of the nineteenth and most of the twentieth century, was in the range of 3 to 4 percent per annum, roughly the amount of interest paid by a savings bank. Until the firms began to be bought up by large media conglomerates, only a few decades ago, that percentage was considered perfectly adequate. It was only when the new owners began to compare the profits of their publishing houses with those of their radio networks, television stations, newspapers, and magazines that they began to worry. How could they justify 'subsidizing' their book publishers at the expense of their other holdings? This is the way they often explained their position. Surely the publishers could manage to earn at the very least 10 percent a year, if not 15 percent, bringing themselves into line with what the others were making.

As I have argued, this entailed not only a major change in what was being published but in the attitudes of those running the publishing houses. Coming up with these new figures became the primary goal, to be accomplished within a fiscal year – or even better, on a quarterly basis. Growth was another 'target,' as it is euphemistically called, and the largest conglomerate, Bertelsmann, publicly called for 10 percent annual growth as well as 15 percent profit, a policy that forced publishers to continually seek out new companies to buy, since there was no way that such growth could be produced by the books already being published.

Gradually, publishers became investors, bankers of a kind, desperate to find both the best sellers and the new firms, or acquisitions, that would satisfy their new owners or the banks that had lent them the money they needed. Accordingly, the heads of the houses felt that their pay should be closer to the salaries of bankers than to those of the editors they once had been. Not, of course, the billions paid to the gamblers and traders of the last decades. But at least something in the seven-figure range. When I first started in publishing in the 1960s, the highest salary in Britain was a notorious 10,000 pounds a year, which of course was worth much more then than it is now, but still infinitely less than today's wages. But most publishing salaries were similar to those paid in universities. A senior editor might make as much as a professor, a beginner the equivalent of a lecturer. By the time I left Pantheon, then a part of Random House, in 1990, its president was making well over a million dollars a year. Others were making even more, the highest at the time being $2.2 million, for the head of McGraw-Hill.

Within the houses, editors are now judged by the amount of money their books made. Careful tallies are kept, and the young editors I interviewed in recent years knew to the last decimal point what their annual profit was. I remember once interviewing a young editor who wanted to leave Oxford University Press. What were our signing quotas, she asked me. I wasn't familiar with the term, so she explained it meant that she had to sign up books that would sell at least a million dollars' worth of income for the firm, and that at a famous university press!

While visiting China earlier this year I was astonished to see the degree to which they had developed a similar system. I had not been to China for more than twenty years and was curious to see how publishing had evolved there. Certainly the bookstores showed a great variety of books being published, particularly books explaining the workings of a capitalist economy. In Shanghai and Beijing, the major bookstores had whole walls filled with texts on business management. I went to visit an old colleague, who had been an intern at Pantheon Books in the late 1980s, just before my and my colleague's departure. He now headed one of the major Beijing publishing houses, doing over $100 million of business every year. I asked him and his colleagues how they were remunerated. Their basic salaries were generous by Chinese standards and, while not as high as in the West, were certainly better than those of their academic counterparts. But the basic salaries were supplemented by a percentage of the sales of any book that might become a best seller, and these bonuses could easily double an editor's income. When I asked how their books were chosen, my old colleague laughed embarrassedly and said, 'That's easy. It's whatever will sell best.' The system was geared to ensure these results, and everyone was 'incentivized' to ensure maximum profitability. The lessons of the business management texts had been well learned, and once again, publishing showed itself a microcosm of the greater society, marching with the rest of China toward a new and very thorough form of capitalism.

What is striking is that changes of this nature have been taking place not only throughout the world but also in what used to be known as the liberal professions, careers that used to be primarily free of the pressure to make money. A few years ago, I gave a talk to a reunion of my Yale University classmates, all graduated in 1957. When I described to them the change that had taken place in publishing, many came up to me to complain that the same had happened in their fields. Lawyers were rewarded according to the amount of money that their clients brought, and 'rain-making,' finding lucrative clients, was the most important activity. Architects told me they were no longer expected to build the most beautiful buildings they could design but simply to maximize the amount of rentable space in the containers they were expected to fashion. Even doctors explained that they could no longer practice medicine as they wished but were expected to deliver whatever care was most profitable to the hospitals in which they worked, skimping on those patients with the least insurance, using the most expensive machinery on those who could best reimburse the ever rising costs of medical care (including spiraling administrative costs, since multimillion-dollar salaries are common among the heads of hospitals).

None of these changes were due to the internal demands of these professions. Indeed, they are contrary to the needs of the practitioners and their clients. But they were part of the inevitable monetization of modern capitalist society, which allowed for no exceptions and was ravenous in its demands. What we have seen in the last couple of years has been the temporary collapse of some of the most extreme parts of this exercise. The banks and investment houses were unable to control their greed and increasingly gambled with the money that had been entrusted to them, while expecting to be rewarded with vast amounts as a result. Even though their system collapsed, many of its proponents have continued to defend it and have returned to their former practices and their obscene remuneration.

The system has proved remarkably able to defy the consequences of its failures. In the United States and Europe, bankers and speculators have stubbornly defended their outrageous salaries and bonuses. In the City of London, bankers were arguing that England would lose its role as a financial center if financial salaries were curtailed, and bankers in other countries made similar arguments. Aided by the same governmental officials who urged the deregulation of the markets in all of these countries, the financial sector has been able to stave off many of the reforms that at first had seemed an inevitable consequence of the crisis and the public anger that accompanied it. In the United States, President Obama surrounded himself with the very officials who had been in large part responsible for the crisis. We have yet to see what, if any, reforms can be imposed by the left-of-center governments of Britain and the United States, and 'any' becomes less likely with every passing day.

The question that those interested in books and the media must ask is whether this new form of capitalism will prove to be interested in an area that has, at best, limited profit potential. As was stated in the introduction to this book, the best a publishing house is able to produce in the way of annual returns is well below what the banks and speculators hope for from a business and have come to expect. By applying the methods of leveraged buyouts to publishing, it has been possible for a handful of businessmen to make millions, but at the cost of abandoning the interests of their firms and of their colleagues. The economic crisis does not appear to have changed the way these investors think. The 25 percent per year that groups like Wendel expected to make from their publishing venture was not based on the housing boom or even on the gambling of traders. It was what seemed to them a reasonable return on their investment. As we have seen, this can be greatly exceeded by buying and selling publishing houses, but not by simply producing and selling books, even the most commercially successful.

It is too early to predict exactly what will happen to the large publishing groups. But we have already seen the pattern to expect, even before the economic crisis that greatly accelerated it. The pressure is to produce fewer books, concentrating on those with the highest sales potential, eliminating vast areas that used to be the hallmark of many of these houses. In the past I have joked that publishers progressed from infanticide, neglecting the new books that show no sales promise, to abortion, canceling existing contracts of books no longer thought to be financially worthwhile. The goal now is contraception, preventing such titles from ever entering the process at all.

In *The Business of Books*, I analyzed the contents of five decades worth of catalogues from the largest houses. Some, like the output of HarperCollins, taken over by Rupert Murdoch in 1987, had changed so much as to be unrecognizable. Their lists from the fifties and sixties resemble what is now published by only the best of the American university presses. The current contents justify the firm's boast of being part of the 'entertainment industry,' tying in as many books as possible to the content of films and television. Even so, those managers who directed the transformation of Random House and HarperCollins have been let go, not having brought in profits enough to please their owners, whether Bertelsmann or Murdoch.

As a result of this concentration, fewer and fewer authors are able to find a publisher at all. Most of those who do find that they will not earn much from their books. Many calculate that they barely earn the minimum wage, considering the time it takes to write a book. In France, according to the union leader Martine Prosper, only 900 authors can claim an income of more than 16,500 euros a year from all of their titles.[1]

The pressure now is not so much to increase as to preserve profit. As always, part of the solution is to fire as many people as possible, and hundreds have lost their jobs in the large American firms during the current recession. They are unlikely to be hired back. Florence Noiville, one of *Le Monde's* literary editors, has just published a fascinating book called *J'ai fait HEC et je m'en excuse* (*I Went to Business School and I'm Sorry*)[2] in which she shows how the major thrust of the curriculum at France's leading business school is not to show how business or the economy works, but to teach its students how to maximize profit, partly by firing as many people as possible. These graduates have found willing employers in most conglomerates, and one can see their training at work. Likewise, in America as in Europe, there is a growing trend toward centralization, with the conglomerates amalgamating what used to be independent firms into larger entities and thereby eliminating even more jobs. We now see in the literary pages of the *New York Times* the curious ads of what is called the Knopf Group, in which books that once were published by houses as diverse as Doubleday or Pantheon – which used to be at opposite ends of the publishing spectrum – are now listed without mention of the putative publisher, 'publisher' having clearly become an unimportant and even meaningless label. The remaining staffs have been merged under one centralized management. Reports from France suggest that the same process may have been started by Planeta as it begins to examine the overpriced Editis group it now controls.

None of this is to suggest that the large conglomerates will fade away, as some have suggested. They will doubtless continue, publishing best sellers and benefiting from the sales of their backlists, built in better times. Their new output will continue shrinking, as they limit production to provide the required profit. This will be a difficult time for the many good people still working for these houses, trying to protect what they have been able to do in the past and fighting to the best of their ability the unending pressures from their owners. But even they will admit that more and more of the books that they used to publish, and would still like to publish, are coming from the small independent houses that have begun to spread in recent years, both in Europe and in the United States. (In Italy, literally hundreds of new houses have been started in the past decade.) The flourishing of these small independent houses is an encouraging sign, particularly since young people have started many of them. But they face enormous difficulties, both in distribution and in covering their costs. It is calculated that the major distributors demand a minimal sale of 300,000 euros a year to take on a publisher. This excludes most of the smaller firms, which have to work out their own system of distribution and sales fulfillment. While the smaller houses account for a third of the 38,000 titles published annually in France, their total sales come to less than 1 percent of the annual volume.[3] In the US, the small publishers account for a similar tiny percentage, though the number of intellectually important books is far greater. Until recently, the hundred or so American university presses also accounted for less than 2 percent of total sales.

40 The Effect of Globalisation in Africa and the Choice of Language in Publishing

Walter Bgoya

According to the Rural Advancement Foundation International,

> Linguists who monitor the status of surviving languages predict that approximately half of the 6,000 languages spoken in the world today will die during the 21st century. As each language vanishes, tens of thousands of years of cultural heritage and traditional knowledge are lost
>
> (Wheeler quoted in Hope 1997: 2)

Many of those languages will be in tropical Africa. This loss of linguistic heritage will not be a result of uprooting people from their society, as happened, for example, during the period of slave trade. It will, nevertheless, be a result of pressures exerted on people and their languages, which they will not be in a position to resist successfully. It must not be assumed either that the threatened languages are only those that are spoken by a few thousand people in isolated places in forests and tropical grasslands. All languages which, for one reason or another, are denied the potential for their fullest development are threatened. One of the threats comes from the phenomenon of rural to urban migration. Many young unemployed people perennially leave rural communities in search of employment in urban areas where either a foreign language or one indigenous language dominates the other languages and becomes ipso facto a 'national language'. Over time, the 'smaller languages' will lose out. Moulding diverse language communities into nations, with inter-ethnic marriages in which third languages replace mother tongues, will result in new generations of people who do not have a 'mother tongue.'

There is a crudely utilitarian view which proposes that, as language is primarily a vehicle of communication, it does not matter which one eventually succeeds in imposing itself on a given society, and by extension, on the world. According to this view there would be nothing lost if in Africa, for example, the colonial languages replaced indigenous languages. English, which is by far the preferred foreign language, could even replace French, Portuguese and Spanish. In Mozambique, which has recently joined the Commonwealth, it is very likely that English will replace Portuguese in the next 15 to 20 years. The demand for English is very high, its popularity and influence being facilitated by the revolution in information and communication technology. Communication between international business partners (those in the south being mostly agents rather than real partners), between research centres and a myriad networks of NGOs and cultural industries has given English the upper hand. Globalisation of English is, indeed, a phenomenon of far-reaching implications and threatens to annihilate many indigenous languages.

THE MYTH OF BENEFITS OF GLOBALISATION

There is a prevalent myth about benefits of globalisation of trade and industry and the revolution in information technologies, in respect of the lives of people in poor countries. The first myth is about the benefits that supposedly result from the ability to move vast sums of money from one place to another in practically no time. Another is about the ability to transmit images of events taking place in one country to viewers in any country in the world instantaneously. However, most of the supposed benefits of these developments are false and misleading. An example of the consequences of moving vast sums of money to enclaves in third world countries (and in what were not so long ago called 'second world' countries) is the economic and social crisis that the so-called Asian 'tiger' economies have been experiencing. Until recently hailed as examples of dynamic development to be emulated by other developing countries, the tiger economies a couple of years ago were going through unprecedented crises which escalated into violence and suffering and threatened the very survival of those nations. The tiger economies depended heavily on foreign finance capital which went into unproductive speculative investment – stock markets, high rise buildings and other real estate ventures, financing of imports of consumer goods – and not into production and stimulation of further domestic savings and employment.

The impact of the crisis has not been limited only to those countries; many others feel the effects of this crisis and the instability therefrom. The lesson to be learned from it is that there is no miracle to be expected out of unbridled market mechanisms anymore than there is one to be realised in state controlled and heavily bureaucratised economies. Only in a system based on the fullest participation of the people in politics and the economy and committed to fair distribution of income through taxation, can the center of development shift from the speculators to the people.

GLOBALISATION FOR WHOSE BENEFIT?

The motive force behind the information and media revolution is the desire and determination by the masters of the global economy and cultural industries to control and manipulate political and economic decision makers everywhere to do their bidding. Using the immense financial resources at their disposal they install and remove politicians so that, both at home and abroad, governments do what they want. This alliance of business and government is the pillar of the strategy to strengthen the political and economic power centres in Western capitals for global exploitation.

The significance given to events in the global media is dependent on how the events affect the interests of these power centres. Reporting on third world issues and crises is biased in favour of the side that serves interests of the 'investors'. Events are superficially treated, distorted or ignored. Media networks are interested in the next disaster or conflict in the third world, today's headlines erasing those of yesterday even before their causes and outcomes are clear. At every turn, the basic objective of the owners of the media is to undermine any form of resistance to the wholesale exploitation of resources and labour world wide.

English is the language of this globalisation and English serves fundamentally the interests of those for whom it is both an export commodity and a language of conquest and domination. That events taking place in one area can be projected on screens all over the world instantaneously is not important for those who do not and cannot relate to those events in any meaningful way. This is the more so when events being screened are about violence resulting from political and ethnic conflicts which have their roots in colonialist/imperialist legacies – whether the scene of conflict is Middle East, Rwanda, Burundi, the Congo or South East Asia. Constant barrages of news and reports are not synonymous with accurate and balanced reporting. On the contrary it would appear that the more the bombardment the less the veracity of the messages.

Is there an intrinsic evil in the spread of the English language? No. On the contrary, any language that mediates between other languages and literatures is without doubt an important acquisition and English fulfils that role very well. By the same argument new information technologies that have revolutionised the printing and publishing industry are to be welcomed.

The issues of contention in the globalisation debate and specifically on the effect of English and other European languages on education and culture in African countries can be summed up in a series of questions. The following are a few of those questions. Are there objective imperatives for English, French, Portuguese or Spanish to be the languages of education and culture? What are implications of this form of dependence on the non-European countries? Are chances of economic and social development improved by adopting those foreign languages, as it is argued? Are all African languages sufficiently capable of serving as mediums of instruction at all levels of education? How many languages can individual countries in Africa afford to use when there may be anywhere from two to several hundred languages in a particular country? This short article does not attempt to answer those questions. There are other contributors to this special issue of IRE, however, who are specialists in this field and who comment on some if not all of them. However, the reality that has emerged in the countries where measures were taken to force the English language to become the language of instruction and/or the official language, is evidence enough of the falseness of the assumptions that led to those decisions being taken.

In the Philippines, Hong Kong, Tanzania and in other so-called English speaking countries the policy has failed. It is equally true in the so-called French speaking countries. The more the emphasis has been on entrenching the foreign language in the classroom to the exclusion of mother tongues, the more the mother tongue has claimed its social roles outside, and in the end the foreign language has been ineffective.

Regarding the question of primary imperatives for adopting a foreign language as a national one, it is clear that there is none. On the contrary, there are numerous reasons to support the argument that such linguistic imposition does more harm than good. When a language is artificially imposed, students are rarely able to master it sufficiently to work comfortably in it. Not only do they fail to acquire proficiency in the foreign language; they also lose proficiency in their own languages, becoming twice disadvantaged.

Dependence on a foreign language, like other forms of dependence, is a liability that a nation can ill afford. Ali Mazrui raises the question:

> Can any country approximate first-rank economic development if it relies overwhelmingly on foreign languages for its discourse on development and transformation. Will Africa ever effectively 'take off' when it is so tightly held hostage to the languages of the former imperial masters?
>
> (Mazrui 1996: 3)

With the experience of colonialism and cultural imperialism it is clear that globalisation is the continuation of the same strategy of world domination. To systematically relegate indigenous languages to performing simple social functions is a step towards killing those languages. Constant bombardment of societies in the South with European languages, and the aggressively marketed notion of the superiority of things and ways western, can only lead to pressures on the societies in the south to accept to abandon their cultures and to adopt the American way. Underlying all this is the gospel of the market and money and consumption as the ultimate values. 'No relationship is now more important than the one between a human being and his/her cash,' writes John Pilger in his excellent and eye opening book, *Hidden Agendas*.

> You must be a consumer/customer. Railway passengers and hospital patients are consumer/customers. People who drink water are consumer/customers. Time, music, cultural heritage and the forests are there to be consumed. Moreover, consumers have rights which non consumers do not share.
>
> (Pilger 1998: 68)

Globalisation on whose terms? This is a pertinent question but like its predecessors, imperialism and colonialism, globalisation is not asking its victims whether they will have it or not. Powerful forces that recognise no boundaries or sanctity of any values – material and spiritual – if they happen to be in the way of profit are driving it. Other languages and their cultural wealth are dispensable in the market place. But just as people struggled against colonialism and are still struggling to be able to provide their basic needs, including their cultural heritages, it is necessary to take up the challenge and to close ranks with others in the same position to defend their interests.

What are the choices for the satisfactory resolution of the problem for African and other affected countries? The problem is complicated for those countries in which various linguistic identities refuse to accept a single national language. However, it is also often exaggerated because in countries where there are several or a multitude of languages, one of them usually serves as the lingua franca and over time it assumes a unifying role. In the very large countries – Nigeria, for example – with huge populations, what are called 'tribal languages' are in reality spoken by millions of people. Yoruba, Hausa, Igbo, Fulani and other languages are spoken by more people than the populations of some European countries. But Europeans would never for a moment think of adopting a foreign language and declaring it national or official.

Language problems often also reflect problems caused by bad and divisive politics with opportunist politicians using cultural pretexts to secure political and economic power. Democratic politics and equity in sharing national resources would create conditions for resolution of this problem peacefully in a beneficial manner to all. The starting point in Africa is to open up the issue to debate. At the present, however, the majority of the people who have the least reason to want a foreign language as medium of instruction in schools would actually demand it because they have been led to think that foreign languages are synonymous with knowledge and privilege. It is incumbent, therefore, upon an enlightened leadership to take up the issue and to decide in favour of African languages.

PUBLISHING IN AFRICA – CHOICE OF LANGUAGE

Languages grow and flourish with and through the development of literary culture; and literary culture cannot develop without books. The publishing industry is, therefore the backbone of language development. The choice of a publishing language defines who is the object of publishing. The decision on the language of instruction in schools should obviously precede that on the language of publishing, although in certain circumstances the reverse could also be true. In either case, if language as a cultural and development imperative is not integrated in national policy, it is improbable that publishing will develop in the national language/s or in any language for that matter.

Unfortunately in all African countries, the battle seems to have been lost before it has even begun. Although literacy rates are low and European language speakers are few, it is still the foreign languages that are given the honour of 'national' or 'official' language status. Rather than developing their own languages, most of them argue for the use of English as the easier and more economical of the options available to them.

One can appreciate the complexity of the issue in countries where there are many languages, and none has imposed itself as the lingua franca. But for a country like Tanzania, where Swahili is spoken by all the population and is the language of instruction in primary schools, there can be no reason to justify continued dependence on English. For over 30 years a false debate has gone on about whether to use Kiswahili for secondary and post secondary education. Because English was not and could not be taught well enough in primary schools (there is no reason to think that it ever will be) to enable pupils to learn via that medium in secondary schools, the country has ended up with neither English nor education.

The problem starts with the false notions that:

(i) African languages are not developed sufficiently to be media of instruction, in some countries even at the primary level; and that

(ii) African languages are not capable of handling scientific terms and scientific concepts.

The proponents of these ideas fail to see that vocabulary for science and scientific work can only develop through science related work. In other words, vocabulary does not precede invention or discovery. The vast vocabulary in Kiswahili describing foreign things and ideas is proof of that. If a society and its people are not prepared to invest in developing its language, it has only itself to blame if the language remains inadequate. There is no language that is incapable of developing to meet the needs of its people, if the people decide to make that language meet those needs.

The languages of sub-Saharan African publishing are English, French, Afrikaans, Portuguese and Spanish. It is not surprising, because those are the languages of education in the ex-colonies. The situation in South Africa, where the publishing industry is the most developed in sub-Sahara Africa, exposes the problem clearly. According to the South African National Bibliography for 1994, out of a total of 4,149 titles published, only 436 or 10.50% were in African languages. For 1995, the total number of titles published was 4,963 and 713 or 14.36% were in African languages.

This picture does not even reflect the real situation because the 1145 titles published in African languages in the two years cover many languages. The language with the least number of titles, isiNdebele, had six and three titles in the two years consecutively and only one non-fiction title in 1995. For English the titles were 2,509 in 1994 and 2,716 in 1995. For the Afrikaners, who number less that 10% of the population of South Africa, the numbers of titles published in Afrikaans (1,379 and 1,676 in 1994 and 1995 respectively) are an unmistakable indicator of their privilege on one hand and the marginalisation of the black people on the other. The situation in most African countries is not different from this and in a number of countries it is much worse.

THE ECONOMICS OF PUBLISHING IN INDIGENOUS LANGUAGES IN AFRICA

Publishing in Africa generally and in indigenous languages in particular has, until very recently, been based on print runs that could not be cost effective. With short print runs the unit costs run so high that the prices are unaffordable. With long print runs the unit cost and prices are relatively low, but there are too few outlets for selling books and too few customers to get long print runs sold. Absence of bookshops and other outlets, as well as weak purchasing power, especially in rural areas, reflect the general poverty of African societies.

Even where, as in Tanzania, primary education is offered in Kiswahili, and there is a fairly high rate of literacy, publishing in Kiswahili is for the most part limited to textbook publishing. This should point in the right direction, but as long as higher education, and therefore culture at a higher level of creativity and enjoyment, is not in Kiswahili, the problem will remain. The erroneous notion that African culture is only its folklore, including its oral tradition, music, dance, rites of passages and their rituals, frozen in a kind of static and idealised time and space, is not helpful. Little room is given to creativity that demands higher levels of education, higher levels of interpretation of contemporary realities, using but not limited to traditional props and traditional genres. This is particularly important because global culture – read American popular culture – often finds a vacuum where there are limited opportunities for engaging cultural activities, especially for young people.

There are resource limitations to offering entertainment, sports and other cultural activities that would engage the youth in constructive and healthy ways. Publishers offer only basic educational books, and little by way of interesting and relevant fiction, poetry, and drama. Other forms of entertainment, such as radio and television, do not offer exciting programmes that would be the alternative to American imports. But above all, if the leaders are themselves the apostles of consumerism and slavish followers of Western fashion and junk culture it is unlikely that they will set aside resources for a counter culture. One only has to attend so-called modern weddings, baptisms, confirmations and similar events in African cities – and alas now in villages too – to see the extent to which indigenous culture has lost out to versions of Euro-American practices.

NEW TECHNOLOGIES IN AID OF AFRICAN PUBLISHING

As a result of development of the technology of digital printing, it is becoming relatively easier to publish in small quantities at reasonable cost (and prices are going down all the time) than would have been possible two to three years ago. For those minority languages where large print runs would be uneconomical, it is already possible to print as few as 200 to 500 books at reasonable cost, and in the next year or two it will probably be possible to print even fewer. Development and publishing of dictionaries, grammar books and other important material that would have not survived without the technology of digital printing and electronic publishing (CD-ROM) will ensure that languages have a chance to survive this period.

CONCLUSION

Globalisation is here and is not going away and there are really two responses to it: to accept its inherent anti-people logic and to succumb to its power; or to understand it, and to decide consciously to strengthen the local base and its own capacities for internal generation. As far as language is concerned, the struggle must not be reduced to English versus indigenous languages; rather it should be elevated to indigenous language plus English – or any other foreign language for that matter. It is clear now that it is necessary to be fluent in at least three or four languages to function well in the modern world environment. This is not difficult for Africans who already operate with three or four languages all the time (except the youth who speak only one or two at best). It would not make a big difference to add one or two others to the three or four. The important thing to keep in constant focus is to ensure that the correct emphasis is put on the principal language of one's being and one's culture. There should be no compromise on that.

41 The Global Book

Angus Phillips

Publishers are repositioning themselves to take advantage of the globalization of book markets. They are reviewing their internal structures and are keen to obtain the world rights to potential bestsellers. The success of authors such as Stephanie Meyer and Stieg Larsson has shown how books can sell in large numbers across a variety of markets, and franchises can develop in other media. Will the growth of ebooks drive the penetration of bestsellers across different markets? What will happen in smaller markets, faced with competition from the global players?

For books two key trends are driving globalization: digitization and the growth of reading in English around the world. A bestselling author has the opportunity to see revenues from rights deals in other languages, and from export editions in the original language. With the global reach of ebooks, the original language edition can be accessed directly by a consumer. If the printing press enabled scalability, so that one book can reach many different readers, then the ebook is even more scalable in that demand can be satisfied straight away almost anywhere in the world.

HOMOGENIZATION AND TRANSLATION

What evidence is there already of a homogenization of tastes around the reading of books? Studies of bestseller lists in Europe by Miha Kovač and Rüdiger Wischenbart have showed a reasonable level of diversity.[1] Overall the majority of bestsellers were either written in local languages or translated from the larger languages of English, French, German, and Spanish (a notable exception was Swedish). In their research they developed an impact factor for authors, showing that for western Europe, in the period 2008–9, 19 out of the 40 authors with the highest impact factor were writing in English, and 21 in other languages. An examination of book markets in eastern Europe revealed that of the 40 authors with the highest impact factors, 13 were writing in English, 10 in other languages, and a further 17 were domestic authors. A startling finding was that no work originally written in an eastern European language could be spotted on the western European bestseller lists; in addition no domestic bestseller in an eastern European country had transferred to other markets in that region. This does suggest a one-way street in favour of the larger languages. This is confirmed by a 2006 study of 15,000 translations appearing in the Serbian language, which discovered that 74 per cent were from English, 8 per cent from French, and 6 per cent from German, leaving only small percentages to Polish, Slovenian, and Bulgarian.[2] In the Netherlands, three out of four translations are from English; and only 10 per cent of all translations are from languages other than English, French, and German.[3]

Digging deeper into the statistics does start to tease out more diversity. For example, although the percentage of translations from other languages has remained stable in the Netherlands, the range of languages has become broader compared to the 1980s.[4] If we turn to France, whilst there is a low level of diversity in the area of bestsellers, the picture changes with the examination of literary fiction. For example, amongst one series of bestsellers (crime, thrillers, and science fiction), three-quarters of the books were translated from English, and one-quarter were titles written in French. By contrast for series of literary fiction, of the titles analysed in one study, only between one-quarter and one-third were translated from English, with works translated from up to 36 languages.[5] Gisèle Sapiro writes that 'With regards to linguistic and geographic origins of translations, the opposition between homogenization and diversity thus coincides with the opposition between commercial and upmarket.'[6]

In the Brazilian market there is a contrasting picture between non-fiction and fiction. In non-fiction, local authors dominate and in recent years there have been a number of successful narrative tides, for example about the history of Brazil. Examination of sales data over a two-year period (2011–12) shows how for the top 20 selling non-fiction tides, 16 were by domestic authors, and their books sold 81 per cent of the total number of copies. In the area of fiction, however, the bestseller lists were dominated by commercial fiction translated from English. Out of the top 20 titles, 18 were translations and just two by Brazilian writers, Fábio de Melo and Jô Soares; and of those 18, just one title (by Umberto Eco), was not translated from English. Of the total copies sold of the top 20 titles, 88 per cent were of the translated titles from English.[7]

Clear across a number of markets is the dominance of English, especially in commercial fiction, and the benefits for writers who can write for an international market. The 'translation gap' has been well documented and figures on translations from UNESCO's Index Translationum show the imbalance of translations from and to English. Table 41.1 shows the top ten languages from which translations have been made; the database was started in 1979. Table 41.2 shows the target

Table 41.1   Top ten languages from which translations have been made since 1979

	Original language	Number of translations
1	English	1,226,389
2	French	217,841
3	German	201,193
4	Russian	101,771
5	Italian	66,697
6	Spanish	52,872
7	Swedish	39,149
8	Japanese	27,014
9	Danish	20,892
10	Latin	19,321

Table 41.2   Target languages for translations since 1979

	Target language	Number of translations
1	German	290,918
2	French	239,655
3	Spanish	228,272
4	English	153,433
5	Japanese	130,625
6	Dutch	111,242
7	Russian	83,278
8	Polish	76,616
9	Portuguese	74,705
10	Swedish	71,107

Source: Index Translationum, September 2012. The database can be interrogated for the most up-to-date figures: http://portal.unesco.org/culture/en/ev.php-URL_ID=7810&URL_DO=DO_TOPIC&URL_SECTION=201.html

languages for translations over the same period. Around eight times more titles were translated from English compared to the other way round. By comparison the totals were far more equal for French, German, and Russian. The most translated author, by a considerable distance, is the English author Agatha Christie.

Johan Heilbron argues for a core–periphery view in order to model the languages originating translations, in which English occupies a hyper-central position, with over 50 per cent of translations. Next there are two languages, French and German, with a central position, followed by around seven or eight languages (for example Spanish, Italian, and Russian) with a semi-central position. After this there are all the other languages, with only about 1 per cent of book translations. 'These languages can be considered to be "peripheral" in the international translation economy, in spite of the fact that some of these languages have a very large number of speakers – Chinese, Japanese, Arabic.'[8] The logical consequence of such a model is that rates of translation *into* a language will be lower in countries with languages towards the centre, and higher in countries with languages towards the periphery. Further, some authors now write in English rather than their native language, and are then translated into their domestic market. One example is the Slovenian philosopher Slavoj Žižek, who writes in English and is then translated into Slovene.

The website Three Percent, which advances the cause of international literature, takes its name from the 3 per cent of all books published in the USA which are translated works.[9] Chad Post writes about our reasons for wanting to read international literature, and perhaps makes some of us feel uncomfortable. He believes that books should stand on their own merits, regardless of their origins:

One of the reasons that a lot of people give for why they do (or why they should) read international fiction is to 'get a sense of what life is like in other cultures."

Which is sweet and admirable and maybe a bit LolliLove [a mockumentary in which a rich couple try to make a difference by giving the homeless lollipops], but makes a degree of sense. Or does it? Why do we assume that a Japanese writer is going to 'explain' something about Japanese culture?[10]

But if we are going to move away from a Eurocentric view of what is world literature, it is important that we broaden our horizons, whatever the motivation. As people have travelled more, they are more receptive to new cultures and experiences, and there is no reason why they cannot expand their reading to other literatures.

Lawrence Venuti has been highly critical of the trade imbalance in translations, which he believes has serious cultural ramifications. Not only does the imbalance support the expansion of American and British culture, it also promotes a monolingual culture in those countries. In addition readers have become accustomed to fluent translations, which are eminently readable and consumable, to the neglect of texts which might be seen as more difficult. He argues for a higher value to be placed on the work of the translator, to offset their 'invisibility': 'Under the regime of fluent translation, the translator works to make his or her work "invisible," producing the illusory effect of transparency that simultaneously masks its status as an illusion: the translated text seems "natural," that is, not translated.'[11] He maintains that the translator has only a shadowy existence in British and American cultures, and cites how in 1981 John Updike reviewed in the *New Yorker* works by Italo Calvino and Günter Grass with only the barest mention of the translators.

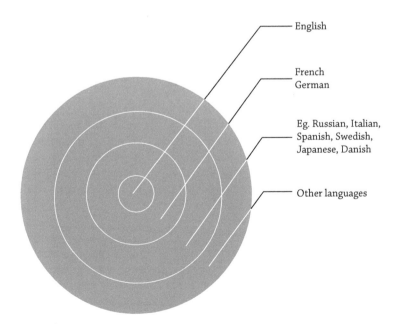

Figure 41.1 Core–periphery model

The situation has improved to some extent, and translators such as Anthea Bell are more visible, celebrated and promoted as a selling-point for their translations. But if publishers have found that the best way to push world literature is to present it as mainstream, then highlighting the work as a translation per se could be counterproductive. That Scandinavian crime fiction (and now drama, with the success of *The Killing* a prime example) can be successful on its own merits is a vindication of this strategy. Christopher MacLehose, the publisher who brought Stieg Larsson to the English-speaking world, says that 'A publisher should go where the books are, wherever that may be. The fact that Larsson is in translation has been completely overshadowed in readers' minds by the fact that it is something they want to read. Surely that's as it should be.'[12] Jo Lusby, head of Penguin's office in China, agrees with this approach, talking of their books purchased for translation into English: 'We have approached the books purely from a publishing standpoint, and to look for books that we believe will work.' She bought the English language rights for the Chinese bestseller by Jiang Rong, *Wolf Totem* (2008), and the book went on to win the first Man Asian Literary Prize and sell hundreds of thousands of copies. She suggests that in order for books to succeed, they first need to work at a local level: 'We all know that books are local, and the success of a book will begin with your next-door neighbour reading a copy, or the postman reading a copy ... Books will always start locally and radiate outwards, always, even with the best marketing campaign.'[13]

Venuti maintains that we should be reading some texts which are difficult, yet research for the Global Translation Initiative into the area of literary translations suggests that their perceived difficulty remains a major obstacle to their success.[14] They suffer from the perception that they are more difficult reads, and therefore hold less potential for popularity. When questioned about likely bias against translations, each part of the book chain looked to other areas. Translators see a bias against translations on the part of publishers, publishers point to a bias in the media, and the media perceives a bias on the part of readers. Yet booksellers, who have the most direct contact with readers, believe that any reader bias against literary translation is minimal.

English has a further role in the world of translations as an intermediary or bridge language between minority languages, alongside the traditional bridge languages of French and German. A detective story can be translated, for example, from Swedish to Hungarian, using the English translation as the mediating text. This reflects a shortage of translators able to work directly between the two languages, and the likelihood that there will be someone available to translate to and from the English. Miha Kovač comments on the situation in Slovenia:

> Translating from English is quite easy. Finding a good translator from Spanish is manageable, and finding a translator from Croatian or from Serbian is also manageable, but for example we had huge problems with Orhan Pamuk. There is only one person who can translate from Turkish to Slovene. So we translate many books from English which are not primarily written in English.[15]

An edition of a book in English also facilitates its transition into a range of other languages in other ways, as Barbara J. Zitwer suggests for Korean titles:

> Selling world English rights helps Korean authors sell in other places because a complete English translation can be commissioned and then shared with others. Many foreign editors do not have Korean readers or translators so they read the English translations and translate from the English rather than directly from the Korean.[16]

EBOOKS

With the arrival of ebooks, English language publishers have already seen an uplift in sales of their books in international markets. There is the possibility of reaching all parts of the world, without the need for intermediaries to facilitate the distribution of physical books. A publisher which holds the global rights to a title can offer it as an ebook right around the world, whilst looking to sell rights in local languages. For publishers such as Michael Bhaskar at Profile Books, 'The markets are much more international than they have ever been in the past, so you have to think about books in a global sense, whereas I think previously most publishers around the world thought in a national sense.'[14]

There are some markets where English language books compete directly with local language editions. The Netherlands is a prime example, where a Dutch publisher will aim to have the translated edition available as close as possible to the publication there of the English edition. But a reader may well be tempted to read the book in English if an ebook is readily available at an attractive price. Rüdiger Wischenbart sees price as being influential in markets such as the Netherlands and Scandinavia, where there is already a high level of reading in English:

> In these markets you have such a significant number of people prepared to read in English, that publishers need to consider whether to translate a book from English because the main group of readers may have read that book already. On the one hand it is timing, but it is also pricing. An English language ebook will be available at a very low cost to the local populations everywhere. The local publisher has much higher costs from the translation but also from producing the book in a small print run.[18]

From the viewpoint of Slovenia, Miha Kovač says that 'English books represent competition to Slovenian publishers, and this means that ebooks in English are a very serious problem.'[19]

It is also possible to imagine the translation being commissioned by the originating publisher as part of the original production, if they are willing to extend their financial risk. Just as a film or app can be distributed with a range of language options, an ebook could be made available with a choice of language or suite of languages. At the press of a button you could display a bilingual edition, with text on facing pages. If a publisher wished to produce an ebook in any language requested, what are the prospects for machine translation? Could it be done automatically on request, according to customer preference? At the present time this looks undesirable for fiction, where ease of reading is sought, even should the reader be willing to lose some of the meaning of the original along the way.

For non-fiction, where you might be simply after the information and not the smoothness of the reading experience, there are machine translators that do a pretty good job and may offer 'good enough' content. Most prominently, Google Translate can offer some very good results, because it has the benefit of scanning the web for previous translations of a phrase – often those might have been carried out by a professional translator. This artificial intelligence is based on the crowd-sourcing efforts of many people, and Jaron Lanier bemoans the impact: 'The act of cloud-based translation shrinks the economy by pretending the translators who provided the examples don't exist. With each so-called automatic translation, the humans who were the sources of the data are inched away from the world of compensation and employment.'[20]

As more machine translations are used, however, the waters are made murkier as Google cannot necessarily discriminate between the sources as to their quality.[21] The Malaysian Ministry of Defence relied on Google Translate to produce English language pages on its website, and the phrase 'pakaian yang menjolok mata', which means 'revealing clothes' in Bahasa Malaysia, was translated as 'clothes that poke eye'.[22]

In his book *The Last Lingua Franca*, Nicholas Ostler describes a study which analysed the outcome of a 12-year project by the European Union to produce a machine translation system amongst the nine languages then used by member states (the report appeared in 1990). It was clear that the project had not produced a functioning system, but even the final report itself had ambiguities. In the French version of the report, the project's work was described as 'insuf-fisant' (insufficient); in the English version the word used was 'inadequate'.[23] Such nuances highlight the difficulties of perfecting an automated system.

In 2012 Google Translate offered translations between 64 languages, including Latin, Tamil, and Welsh. Again it is only able to do this by relying on the primacy of the English language, and using it as a bridge language. As David Bellos comments:

> The service that Google provides appears to flatten and diversify interlanguage relations beyond the wildest dreams of even the EU's most enthusiastic language parity proponents. But it is able to do so only by exploiting, confirming and increasing the central role played by the most widely translated language in the world's electronic databank of translated texts.[24]

Bellos points out that English-language detective novels may well have been translated into both Icelandic and Farsi, offering the opportunity to find a match between sentences in the two languages. He suggests that the real wizardry of Harry Potter is the way the books enable text to be translated from Hebrew into Chinese. Over time the quality of this method is improving, but even in the medium term there has to remain a place for a human translator who can honour the style and approach of the original author.

GO GLOBAL

Digital developments offer a broader reach for the book, and can offer new opportunities for authors and publishers, not just from Western markets. In 2011 the Chinese publisher Jiangsu Science and Technology Publishing House produced a book app on acupuncture, sold through the Apple store. There was a relatively modest sale of 1,000 units but 60 per cent of the market was in Europe and North America. Liu Feng, their Business Development Director, said that 'Digitized books offer an easier way to introduce books overseas compared to the traditional model.'[25] This traditional model would most likely have been selling the print rights in translation to an overseas publisher.

Users can now more directly feed their thoughts into the writing and publication of books, and the same applies in the area of translations. Customer sales and feedback can inform decisions about which titles should be translated, and Amazon has its own imprint, AmazonCrossing, built upon this idea. There are forums to which suggestions can be posted, and the programme's editorial team can spot likely projects through examination of Amazon's own data on sales and customer ratings.

Digital can offer benefits in those countries without a developed infrastructure around the distribution of physical books. A range of content can be accessed directly from domestic publishers, but also from companies operating on a global scale. The tendency towards globalization is a concern for all of those keen to see the preservation of local identities and cultures. The issues are not unique to the book, and many consumers will want to participate in the trends around the latest mobile device, movie, or blockbuster teen fiction. However, the collapse of physical retail for books in some countries, which is being accelerated by the growth of ebooks, and the rise of global bestsellers, are not healthy for the diversity of local book markets. So far the growth of ebooks carries with it benefits for titles in English, which can command a global reach. Whilst it is good for books to be seen as successful, and holding their own against other media, there is the risk of homogenization and little alteration to the imbalance in the flow of translations. The importance remains of interventions to smooth the passage of authors and books between cultures. These include state subsidies for translations and programmes which bring exposure for writers at events or in the media in other countries.

42 The Globalization of Literature

Suman Gupta

The role of publishing in the global spread of English in the late twentieth century can hardly be underestimated. In numerous ways this contributes to the prospects for English studies [...], including the possibility of dispensing with Englishness from English studies and Americanness from American studies. Equally, though, the centring of the global publishing industry in English in the United States and the United Kingdom may well undermine that envisaged possibility, and perpetuate and extend the cultural imperialism of Englishness and Americanness in new guises. Despite Venuti's dark prognosis of the unevenness of and absences within what is translated for Western readers (mentioned in the previous chapter too), the global cultural capital that English is acquiring and the global reach of publishing in English suggests that translations into English from all languages will pick up further. Anxieties may very reasonably attach to the modes of selection and emphasis that will mediate such increased scope of translations into English. Whether the dominance of English will continue to the detriment of various minority languages that are still used for literary production and consumption, and the industries that serve them, remains to be seen – it seems likely that would happen. These are the predictable paths that seem to lie before us. However, it is worth unpicking some of the complexities and contradictions which lie within these very generalized expectations too – for which the specific context of Indian publishing in English at the beginnings of the twenty-first century is worth pausing on.

A traditionally small English-language publishing industry in India, focused primarily on academic books and textbooks and only in a minuscule way on literary works, has expanded in a significant fashion since about 1990. In a visible way this expansion has taken place with regard to both Indian literary writing in English and translations into English from literature in Indian languages. Various explanations are offered for this. The success of some Indian authors writing in English in international Anglophone markets – such as Salman Rushdie, Vikram Seth, Amatav Ghosh, Arundhati Roy – has drawn attention to the possibilities for literary production that exist in India. Publishers had always been aware that the potential market of English-language readers in India, though confined to a relatively small proportion of the population, is still a large number in absolute terms and growing – in the early twenty-first century this number has been ambitiously estimated to be as large as 200 million. However, the relatively low consumer power of Indians had meant that English-language publishing in India was seldom regarded as a profitable business. With economic growth and increasing affluence in the relevant section of the Indian population at the turn of the century this perception has changed. Towards the end of the twentieth century and early in the twenty-first, therefore, the number of publishers within India who were publishing literary books in English for the Indian market (especially original fiction and translations) had increased many times – in terms both of independent firms (such as Ravi Dayal, Zubaan, Rupa, Katha, Roli, IndiaInk, Stree, Srishti) and of international publishing conglomerates and, later, multinational corporations with bases in India (notably Penguin, HarperCollins, Random House, Hachette Livre). This happy coexistence of growing numbers of independents and multinational corporations hasn't yet turned into the spree of takeovers and mergers seen in the United States and the UK in the 1980s and 1990s, but that could be expected to happen in due course. At this nascent stage of the Indian book industry's expansion, at any rate, international business interest has been evidenced by the drawing up of market profiles, such as that by Rob Francis for the UK Publishers' Association (2003, updated 2008) and Khullar Management's for American businesses (1999). Despite the underdevelopment of the retailing and library sectors and poor regulation of piracy and black markets, it is clearly felt now (in the early twenty-first century) that the Indian book publishing market – especially in English, and including the literary – presents extraordinary promise and opportunities (for a gauging of pros and cons, see the 'documents page' of the *Contemporary Indian Literature in English and the Indian Market* project [2007] at www.open.ac.uk/Arts/ferguson-centre/ Indian-lit/documents/).

All this might appear to make the Indian scene in publishing consistent with global developments, but in terms of on-the-ground realities in literary production and consumption this phenomenon presents certain interestingly complex and contradictory characteristics. For one thing, insofar as this trend focuses on the publication of literature in English, this growth has instigated a drive for producing original literary works of a sufficient diversity – from 'serious literature' to all categories of 'mass market literature' – from *within* India and targeting consumers primarily *within* India. Thus, a spate of popular fictional works by Indian writers have appeared – especially Chetan Bhagat's *Five Point Someone* (2004) and *One Night @ the Call Centre* (2005) and Anurag Mathur's *The Inscrutable Americans* (1991) – which are enormously popular bestsellers in India, but unusually without going through the usual circuit of prior testing in Western markets and without even being made available in the latter. Publishers in India focusing on literary production in English seem at present bent on diversifying popular literary production by Indian authors for Indian readers, in keeping with the profit-driven moulding of the book market seen in the UK and the United States. A 2007 report in the national daily the *Hindustan Times* observed:

> Over the last year or so, V. Karthika, editor in chief at HarperCollins India, has actively sought writers to write the kind of books that Indian writers haven't written in English so far – or at least not in volumes.

> She's looked for writers who'll do chick lit, who'll do thrillers, who'll do contemporary urban stories, who'll write for young adults … In short, writers

who write the kind of books that the majority of us like to read. Books that are not highbrow, that tell a good story without necessarily probing the murky depths of human experience, that entertain and are simply a damn good read. She's succeeded at least to the extent that, in the space of one year, HarperCollins India has 50 new books to offer the reading public on a wide variety of subjects. A greater variety than Indian writing in English has ever had at one time before.

(Gulab 2007)

In a curious way, therefore, it appears that the extension of the global book industry into India is functioning now by *containing* the Indian market – by developing book circulation in all its facets (authoring, editing, designing, distributing, marketing, retailing) *within* India. Customizing Indian literary products for Indian readers seems to be the motto underlying these developments. This is noteworthy because it demonstrates the paradoxical fashion in which globalization of the publishing industry can result in the containment of a certain variety of literary production and consumption (a 'certain variety', of course, because international mass-market books such as the Harry Potter series or Dan Brown's *The Da Vinci Code* [2003] were marketed and consumed in India as successfully as anywhere else) or in the indigenization of Indian English writing and Indian literature in translations as a brand. It may be surmised that these developments, especially insofar as Indian English literature is implicated, are likely to initiate reconsideration of postcolonial literary theory and criticism as currently conducted in the academy. That, however, is too complex an exercise to be undertaken here – the point here is to register the possibility.

There are other ways too in which the globalization of the book industry as it embraces India seems to open up unexpected possibilities. One of the consistent fears about globalization processes has been that they lead to a homogenization of culture – evidenced, for instance, in misgivings about the survival of vernaculars and minority indigenous linguistic cultures before the relentless expansion of global languages such as English. This is a particularly sensitive issue in a markedly multilingual context such as India. The gradual incorporation of Indian literature markets within the global publishing industry, however – though instigated by the status of English therein – seems to promise some revitalization of publishing in Indian languages too. Thus Sarah Brouillette, in an article published in 2007, observes:

Transnational firms now commit to publishing the same vernacular languages they were once engaged in marginalising, as they recognise that English is not the only globalisable South Asian language. The structures of production and circulation that exist within the dominant Western publishing market, having so readily incorporated South Asian writing in English, may well treat vernacular works in much the same fashion. Such texts serve a myriad of functions: they can be exported to or locally produced for communities of South Asians living either in the region or abroad, or sold to those who are more competent or comfortable in the vernacular as well as those who want to maintain the alternative cultural cache that comes with continued support for one's 'mother tongue'. A celebrated and romanticised localism is just as marketable as an ostensibly delocalised cosmopolitan English-language writing. This is something that the transnational companies operating in South Asia are now beginning to realise, and there is little doubt that they will quickly absorb and expand the existing markets of vernacular literatures, establishing those new rules for the game, from lower price points to more lavish marketing, that will make it hard for the many existing smaller firms to compete.

(Brouillette 2007: 37)

She notes the intention of several multinational publishing corporations operating in India to start publishing in Indian languages other than English.

Leaving this digression on the Indian publishing industry behind and returning to general observations on the globalization of the publishing industry and its impact on literature: what appears to be called for is an approach to the relationship between globalization and literature not from *within* literature and literary studies but, so to speak, on the surface of both from *outside*. Of course, that is a rhetorical way of stating the matter. Even approaching it thus would effectively mean bringing the surface of literature and literary studies and the agents working upon them inside literature. This may sound like a rhetorical conundrum but is, in the present context, very much worth engaging more energetically than is customary. Literary studies has so far intervened in the mediations between authors/texts/readers and broad historical/ideological/cultural contexts to only a limited extent, and with little attention to the exigencies of markets and circulations. Book and publishing history and studies of reading practices and attention to textual media (e.g. arising from the implications of digitization and hypertext) are areas affiliated to literature and literary studies that come closest at present to apprehending the impetus of markets and circulations. Useful as those are, for what I have in mind these are still rather limited approaches to the matter and are in themselves yet incompletely excavated fields. When Bryant programmatically called for a consistent understanding of 'fluid texts', he listed the agents he saw as contributing to the production of textual fluidity – 'writers, editors, publishers, translators, digesters, and adapters' (Bryant 2002: 4); interestingly, some of these agents still remain invisible in literary studies, even in the field of book history and text editing. But, beyond that, even the processes working on the surface of literature that book historians have registered (if not explored) are limited by a kind of fetishization of texts. The overdetermined attention to the concretizations of texts (in notebooks, typescripts, proofs, codices, specific editions, cassettes, audio CDs, digitized surfaces, etc., of author versions, editor versions, editions, translations, adaptations, screenplays, hypertexts, etc.), and to the industries that are implicated in the literary product as product, effectively downplays the depth and range of the industries surrounding literature and acting upon literary circulation. A fuller apprehension of the latter would involve coming to grips with the fluidity not only of texts but also of authors and readers, and with the notion that it is not only texts that are concretized and produced by industrial processes but also authors and readers. Literary texts, literary authors and literary readers are all industrial products, all commodities in the circulatory matrix of literature and literary studies, and the industrial sectors involved are not one and the same. To a great extent the industrial sectors overlap – the book publishing industry, the media industry and the academic sector (which increasingly works along advanced capitalist industrial lines) have crucial roles in the production of fluid authors, texts and readers – but other sectors which do not overlap are also involved, working with distinct economic rationales and prerogatives.

Stanley Fish's argument, that literary interpretation is conducted not in terms of encounters between critics and texts but in terms of 'interpretive strategies' which exist already in 'interpretive communities' (Fish 1980), had an immediate plausibility – despite objections raised by reader-response theorists (such as Iser 1989; equally Fish [1989] also objected to Iser's formulations). Within that formulation could be recognized something of the practical experience of most academic literary critics, who really do acquire and share and employ in an institutional fashion a critical discourse which instantiates a sense of disciplinary communal belonging. Fish's idea obviously also extends to an apprehension of readerly fluidity: not just literary criticism but all kinds of reading employ 'reading strategies' which are in some sense pre-given and which operate through 'reading communities'. Readers, like academics, really do form communities, and come together with different senses of akinness or communal belonging – in, for instance, virtual or real fan-sites, book clubs, coffee-table discussions, poetry or literature festivals, informal or formal public readings and bookshops, or, more individualistically (and yet with a kind of shared sensibility), by following certain genres. And equally, corporations of various sorts – certainly in the book and media and academic industries, but also in those connected to public relations and advertisement and celebrity, in those for cultural products (films, images, art, music, etc.) connected to literature, and sometimes in those producing consumer products that can be branded through literary association – seep into and begin to produce such reader communities. They operate by shaping reading spaces, by categorizing readers as niche markets, by turning reading into lifestyle indicators. These operations have something to do with the manner in which publishers' catalogues and shelves in bookshops categorize books for the attention of target audiences. They have something to do with the manner in which various coffee-vending chains provide spaces in bookshops or spaces for readers. They have something to do with media celebrities endorsing literary books for their followings (for instance, through the 'book clubs' of UK television breakfast-show hosts Richard and Judy and US chat-show host Oprah Winfrey). The associations unwind in an enormously complex web of readerly fluidity that does not just happen spontaneously but is manufactured by a range of industries.

Similarly, authors are also constantly and explicitly manufactured. This argument has come up already in connection with the depiction above of fictional authors, especially in Rowling's characterization of Gilderoy Lock-hart. The dissociative quality of late twentieth-century literary celebrity that was remarked above is very much part of this authorial fluidity, of authors being manufactured. The degrees to which authors' public images and appearances and statements are now engineered by corporate entities and their agents (literary agents, publishers, media persons, advertisers, product designers and commodity pushers of various sorts working in collaboration) to appeal to certain readers and their expectations is an as yet under-explored area. This process of manufacturing authors according to market contexts is, obviously, coeval with manufacturing readers. The production of one is in some sense the production of the other, and both unravel in ways that are unregistered *within* literature and literary studies and yet surely influence the pursuit of both not just in material ways but at textual and interpretive levels too. An aspect of this process, with obvious effects on literature and literary studies, which has received some critical attention has to do with literary prizes. Literary prizes are sometimes rather obvious brand investments by corporations with little stake in literature or literary studies: the Man Booker, Costa, and Orange literary prizes come immediately to the minds of English-language readers as modes of selling brands through literary association. But, besides that, it has been observed consistently that literary prizes, whether through corporate sponsorship or otherwise, increasingly make literary reputations and market value through means that have less to do with literary content than with surrounding rituals and controversies. In 1986 Adair had observed that, while the Booker Prize increases sales for shortlisted books, its mode of doing so was at the expense of literary evaluation:

> Since it was essential for the success of the Booker Prize that the world of books as a whole be implicated in its prestige, it became necessary, paradoxically, almost to underplay the importance of individual novels and their authors and concentrate instead on the *year*, in other words, to invest books with the concept of *vintage* (an idea cribbed, aptly enough, from the French: the Booker might reasonably be regarded as the British Goncourt). For if a book is the intellect's loaf of bread, why should it not also be its wine, that inevitable 'poetic' complement of bread? The rest is, as they say, history; now, every October, during the run-up to the prizegiving itself, the classic connoisseurial anxieties can be heard expressed: Is it a good year? A disappointing year? A vintage year? (Adair 1986: 146)

In a paper in 2002 on literary (and other culture) prizes, James English observes a kind of spreading of Booker Prize-like tactics, focusing on the effect of controversies or 'scandals' (such as authors refusing to accept prizes):

> While the Booker is possibly the most talked-about of high-cultural prizes, the relationships to criticism, scandal, and the field of journalism are largely unexceptional. [...] Indeed, we find other prizes more and more often being compared to the Booker, usually in order to suggest the 'Bookerization' of the whole cultural-prize phenomenon. So chat when a 'scandal' or 'row' breaks out in connection with some literary or arts prize these days, those who attack and denigrate or ... embarrass the prize arc less likely to be perceived as acting within the long tradition of sincere animosity between artists and bourgeois consecrations – artistic freedom fighters on the old model of art versus money – and

more likely to be seen as players in a newer cultural game whose 'rules' and 'sides' are more obscure and of which the Booker happens to be the best known, and hence the most generic, instance.

(English 2002: 118–19)

In English's account, then, no gesture is possible in the early twenty-first century by an artist or author which isn't incorporated into the market logic of prizes, and that logic operates irrespective of the content of the literature which or stance of the author whom it seems to promote. Both are *produced*, so to speak, by the market logic of literary prizes and their mediations or mediatizations. English extends this argument, with a great deal of useful information and further analysis of the industrial processes underlying and cutting into literary prizes, in his book *The Economy of Prestige* (2005).

Another area which registers the fluidity of authors and texts with global effects on literature and literary studies, and has received a modicum of scholarly attention, is that of international property regulation. It is well known that, from the Berne Convention of 1886, the first multilateral copyright agreement between sovereign nation-states, to the Agreement on Trade-Related Aspects of Intellectual Property Rights (TRIPS) of the World Trade Organization of 1994, the regulation of the rights of authors (among other kinds of 'creators') and publishers (among other kind of cultural industries) at a global level has come to be increasingly uniformly regulated and policed. The manner in which copyright law has attempted variously to 'fix' (reduce) authorship, in a rational and purposive legal discourse which is indifferent to literary analysis or estimation, is redolent with illustrations of the fluidity of both literary texts and literary authors. In fact the attribution of authorial rights could be seen as a mode of producing authors and texts (including literary) – or of stabilizing authors and texts against the grain of their fluidity – through means which have little to do with the prerogatives of literature and literary studies. Along with the purely juridical rationale of this process, under conditions where culture industries (such as literary publishing) are becoming increasingly globalized and consolidated, the international regulation of intellectual property rights coheres with such globalization and consolidation. Indeed, the effects of such intellectual property regulation is often seen as having substantially the same effects on cultural production as those Schiffrin had observed on literature in the context of global market-driven publishing. Ronald Bettig, for instance, in a wide-ranging study of the effect of international property rights regulation on cultural production, *Copyrighting Culture* (1996), foresees:

> new rules governing intellectual property [that] will greatly facilitate the process of global commodification of human intellectual and artistic creativity. Cultural activities, in particular, will continue to be incorporated into the global market system, produced and sold primarily for their exchange value. This commodification will lead to an even greater concentration of copyright ownership in the hands of the global cultural industries. The profit orientation of these

industries leads them to produce and distribute homogeneous cultural products. Their market power, in turn, fosters the erosion of national, regional, ethnic and group autonomy, undermines democratic participation in cultural expression, and increases inequalities between people and nations.

(Bettig 1996: 226–27)

Again, it is mainly in book and publishing history vis-à-vis literature and literary studies where the working of copyright law on conceptualizing texts, authors, readers – on the very constitution of literature – is occasionally discussed at present.

A systematic examination of market processes which work *upon*, as I have put it, literature and literary studies, without being evident *within* these is an enormous project which is just beginning to be undertaken. This project needs to engage with textual, readerly and authorial fluidities, and the points of concretization in these, through a complex network of corporate and market agents and interests. The foothold into this area that has already been enabled in book and publishing history is a fruitful one, but should be expanded to develop a more nuanced and less predeterminedly text-centred sense of the industries and markets that incorporate literature. Though the influence of new digital media on cultural processes has been profound – and has so to speak been manifested *within* literature and literary studies – the area of printed book publishing in the global market still provides, and will continue in the foreseeable future to provide, a broader understanding of the markets and industries underlying literature. The situation may increasingly become otherwise for the academic pursuit of literary studies, but the circulation of literary texts appears to be embedded in the form of the printed book – which devolves into textual and readerly and authorial fluidities – in still dominant ways. Taking stock of the impact of digitization and the development of the internet on publishing, John B. Thompson, in *Books in the Digital Age* (2005), discerns three phases. The first phase was one of the 'inflated expectations of the mid-1990s', when the demise of the printed book was foreseen in favour of cheaper production and circulation of texts through electronic means, and enormous investments were made accordingly. The second phase, around late 2000, was one of disappointed expectations and scepticism, with only limited growth of the electronic book market and the bursting of the dot com bubbles. The third and current phase, according to Thompson, is of cautious experimentation:

The areas where electronic delivery of book content has failed to live up to expectations (such as general trade books) have been sidelined and attention focused increasingly on those areas (reference, professional and scholarly publishing) where the prospects for electronic delivery seem more promising. [...] The phase of cautious experimentation is generally premised on the assumption that printed books will remain the principal source of revenue for most book publishers for the foreseeable future.

(Thompson 2005: 311)

It may therefore be expected that, while the printed book will continue to be the principal mode of concretizing literary texts, the digital form may become the dominant medium of the literary studies text. The globalization of the industries that impinge *upon*, rather than immediately *within*, literature and literary studies needs to be examined accordingly.

But all that remains within the realms of possibility. The note on which I wish to conclude this study is clear already: ultimately the relationship between globalization and literature is arguably most immediately to be discerned not in terms of what is available *inside* literature and *within* literary studies but in terms of the manner in which globalized markets and industries act *upon* and from *outside* literature and literary studies. This requires a great deal more attention than it has yet received *within* literature and literary studies.

43 The Global Literary Field and Market Postcolonialism

Sarah Brouillette

What *kind* of commodity is a book? The average novel is not a commodity in the way that, say, Coke is a commodity, because the word 'book' implies a variety of distinct products – there are currently several million separate titles in print – whereas Coke implies uniformity. With a book, too, there is presumably more room between articulation and reception, more space for the consumer to construct meaning, and each book product contains a distinct symbolic content. 'Books' are not just books; the word stands in for an assemblage of separate entities, and variety in content leads to complexity of ordering and distribution, and in turn to special technologies for stock control and consumer profiling. Moreover, books cannot move easily across borders due to linguistic and cultural differences that impede easy dissemination. Coke is Coke wherever it goes. Barring a few basic changes to its packaging and design, the content is the same, whereas books require translation and what Eva Hemmungs Wirtén has termed 'transediting.'[1] Notwithstanding all this, isn't Coke itself a complex carrier of different symbolic material, and isn't its meaning as a product something that varies with consumption? And can't the ambiguities of a literary work be reduced to insignificance in certain circumstances, its meaning turned into the embodiment of a singular ideology? Moreover, isn't there a global network of readers of English-language literary works that makes transediting largely unnecessary, as communities across the globe access the newest Salman Rushdie title with relative ease?

In 2004, at the time of publication of *The New Media Monopoly*, the seventh update of the most cited study of contemporary media concentration, Ben Bagdikian could declare that five 'global-dimensions firms' controlled all mass media on a global scale. These are 'Time Warner, by 2003 the largest media firm in the world; The Walt Disney Company; Murdoch's News Corporation, based in Australia; Viacom; and Bertelsmann, based in Germany.' Even a number as small as five, though, understates these firms' collective power, since despite some obvious competition each is intertwined with the other. They 'have similar boards of directors, they jointly invest in the same ventures, and they even go through motions that, in effect, lend each other money and swap properties when it is mutually advantageous.'[2] Book publishing, the mass media's key predecessor, arguably the first global information system, and 'a less flamboyant branch of the cultural industries,'[3] is not exempt from this concentration.

Bertelsmann, for example, is the largest book publisher, with 10 per cent of all English language book sales worldwide. It is in general the world's third largest media conglomerate, with major shares in both AOL and barnesandnoble.com. In 1998 it acquired Random House, one of the largest publishers of literary fiction, with upwards of 100 houses in 13 countries under its umbrella, including Alfred A. Knopf, Pantheon, Fawcett, Vintage and Doubleday.[4] Random House is in fact a good indicator of the changing dimensions of the publishing landscape during the twentieth century. Established in 1927 when Horace Liveright sold the Modern Library to Bennett Cerf, and originally thriving due to the booming paperback fiction market, it went on to acquire Knopf, Vintage, and other imprints in 1960–1, before being sold to RCA in 1965. In 1980 RCA sold the company to Newhouse, then Newhouse to Advance Publications, and in 1998 it became a part of Bertelsmann. In 2000 Random House's US$2 billion sales accounted for about 12 per cent of Bertelsmann's total revenues.[5] It remains a German company, but throughout the 1990s a third of its global sales revenue was earned in the US. It owns media companies producing magazines, books, and newspapers, as well as radio stations and television networks, and also printing and paper plants worldwide, including Offset Paperback Mfrs. in Pennsylvania, where one out of every five paperbacks produced in the US is printed.[6]

Corporatization in the publishing industry has occurred in a few key phases, and was in its early stages primarily a British and American phenomenon.[7] In the 1960s book publishing companies were bought by firms that did not specialize in media; they were particularly attractive to the electronics and defense industries (GE, IBM, RCA), which hoped to make inroads in textbook publishing, and wanted access to information for distribution in the new electronic formats. These 'electronic invaders' purchased existing firms, but also caused other anxious publishing houses to merge. Most of these initial acquisitions failed, and major industries divested themselves of publishing houses soon after acquiring them. In the 1980s the same houses were merged frequently with the film and video industries, until they were finally primarily concentrated in communications firms (like Bertelsmann), with a few absorbed within conglomerates (such as Pearson, which continues to do business in oil and banking, for example, while operating newspapers like *The Financial Times* of London and magazines like *The Economist*, as well as Penguin, and therein the New American Library and Viking, to name but two). These communications firms, alternately called TNMCs (Transnational Media Corporations), or 'the media' in popular parlance, commonly see themselves as existing to use all available formats, or all available media vehicles, to disseminate 'information, education, and entertainment.'[8] Getting under way in the European industry later in the 1970s, the concentration process then became significantly international, as the Traditional Market Agreement between the US and the UK collapsed, and European firms made inroads into lucrative markets where 'common ownership of the English language' had long made British and American publishers 'each other's largest customers.'[9]

Accounts of the process of corporatization have for the most part been articulated by people with direct experience in the book industries, who tend to depict a past of idyllic cultural work untainted by the pursuit of wealth. Jason Epstein, an early Doubleday editor and one of the founders of the *New York Review of Books*, is one such industry insider. He depicts recent developments in media concentration as a betrayal of publishing's 'true nature,' as it gradually, and 'under duress from unfavorable market conditions and the misconceptions of remote managers,' assumed the characteristics of a standard business. Epstein maintains the fairly conventional belief that publishing was and should be more like 'a vocation or an amateur sport in which the primary goal is the activity itself rather than its financial outcome.'[10] His condemnation of changes in the industry is characterized most notably by his avowedly urban insistence that the source of the general plight of contemporary culture is the very existence of the suburbs. The urban represents a 'natural diversity' that has been undermined by 'an increasingly homogenous suburban marketplace, demanding ever more uniform products.'[11] Whereas books 'have always needed the complex cultures of great cities in which to reverberate,' in the suburbs culture is not so much defective as overwhelmed by 'morally neutral market conditions.'[12] Ideas like these have much currency within the industry itself, and are best understood as a more recent version of a long-standing generative trope that has for centuries pitted economic considerations against what is 'truly' literary. They are also somewhat misconceived.

Books are a major industry, and concentration has by no means meant that fewer cultural products are finding their way to the market. Instead, as Herb Schiller has argued, if we have witnessed a marked 'acceleration in the decline of nonmarket-controlled creative work and symbolic output,' there has still been major growth in the 'commercial production' of culture.[13] Despite fears about the demise of reading, in the face of pressures from competing media the number of titles published worldwide every year in fact continues to grow. A number of factors have contributed to the continued presence of books as a competitive media. Media synergy has meant that publishing houses, operating within larger corporations, have been guaranteed promotion through tie-ins with television, film, and the internet. Technologies like offset lithography, film-setting, and later computer-setting have replaced metal or rubber plates, making smaller print runs economically viable. Management of distribution systems has vastly improved since International Standard Book Numbers (ISBNs) were introduced globally in 1967–8, allowing for barcoding and making it easier for bookstores to control stock. Efficient stock control has been further encouraged by the narrowing range of available publishers, as well as by the tele- and then electronic ordering taking precedence since the late 1970s.[14] These technological developments have made it possible for publishers and bookstores to cater successfully to smaller and smaller portions of the reading public, and the synergies of corporatization have provided more venues and opportunities for niche marketing. So while some feared that minority readers, for example, would be abandoned or ignored as media concentration became more prevalent, in fact, as Randall Stevenson argues, publishers recognized that they could not afford to ignore any segment of the reading public, and in response they have continually sought ways to access readers as members of specific and identifiable reading communities.[15]

In short, in recent years corporatization has often gone hand in hand with a trend toward greater diversity, as concentration has been significantly offset by a parallel formation of new companies. In turn, as Elizabeth Long points out, growing levels of affluence and education for the generations coming of age since World War II have guaranteed a 'much more diverse and sophisticated set of reading publics' than a 'massification model' might allow.[16] Critiques of the concentration or commercialization process often overlook this fact, in favour of expressing what Long describes as an anxiety that 'cultural diversity and innovation, serious literature and critical ideas, may be suppressed just as effectively by the mechanisms of mass marketing as by more visible forms of censorship.' Critics may agree that conglomerates demand rationalization and 'editorial accountability to the corporate hierarchy,' but publishing has always been a blend of or balance between commercial and other interests, and there is no sense in which the commercialization process can be considered strictly a phenomenon of the postWorld War II era.[17]

Moreover, if 'multinational' simply defines any company with partner divisions in two or more countries, then the British and American publishing industries have long operated multinationally, whether through mutual trade with one another or through the establishment of branch offices in diverse areas of the world. In addition, it is wise to distinguish between globalization and internationalization in publishing. In a globalization model, markets for 'already produced media products' are 'extended from certain centres in developed countries to other developed and developing countries.'[18] Global operations are facilitated by acceptance of the doctrine that information should flow freely across borders, by laws that allow for foreign ownership and control of media systems, by non-restrictive banking laws 'facilitating currency conversion and capital movement,' as well as by aspects of copyright law.[19] In contrast, internationalization involves significantly more reciprocal trade in products, and for real success requires the existence of a stable domestic industry which includes numerous indigenous producers. This often entails an agency system through which major publishing companies deal with offices on a local level. The parent company may retain control but profits circulate within the local market. A major firm that deals with a variety of local agents may see the feasibility of setting up, alternatively, their own local branch, thus rerouting profits to the parent company, a procedure which leads to true globalization. Scrutiny of the globalization process requires understanding the various ways companies deal with international partners, if they do at all; it should also entail analysis of how what counts as local content relies on and is marketed through the global cultural industries, and vice versa.

Granted, corporatization has changed the way publishers think about the task they perform, by changing the way manuscripts are acquired, turned into books, and marketed and sold. Though there may continue to be a growing number of publishing houses in general – *Books in Print* lists over 73,000 in 2003[20] – if more than 50 per cent of the publishing industry is run by between five and seven encompassing firms that on average make US$500 million each year, that leaves almost no income for those thousands remaining.[21] The consequence of this concentration is not so much that there are no alternative or smaller successful companies, but that the conglomerates control the rules of the game, having access to those aspects of publishing and marketing that require significant capital. As Bagdikian points out, it is the big conglomerates that have the power to acquire 'credit from big banks for expansion and acquisitions, bidding for manuscripts, negotiating and paying for shelf space and window displays in book shops which increasingly are owned by national chains, mounting national sales staffs, buying advertising, and arranging for author interviews in the broadcast media.'[22] Publishing firms that traditionally aimed for a profit margin between 1 and 4 per cent are now forced to achieve 12 to 15 per cent to keep pace with the other media companies belonging to the larger conglomerates in which they are situated. The major conglomerates, moreover, have distribution firms under their umbrellas. These firms often negotiate directly with the monster bookstore chains, selling print runs of a size inconceivable to smaller publishing houses and independent bookstores alike, and negotiating 'co-op' deals to advertise potential bestselling titles in specific key merchandising areas.[23]

This parallel process of concentration and diversification within the publishing industry, a characteristic tension within most forms of media conglomeration, has a number of possible implications. First, in ways I return to at length below, Jason Epstein is not alone in imagining that he is a part of a process that has fundamentally changed the status of books as cultural products. Despite the specific nuances of emerging corporate structures, the dominant narrative within the industry itself is one in which corporatization has significantly changed the way literature is marketed, and has contributed to the 'blockbuster' phenomenon through which particular authors become central to the imaginations of readers. Regardless of its purchase on reality, authors have imbibed this narrative as well, in part because they are now thoroughly organized as a self-conscious class of quasiprofessionals. Those whose works are published in the Anglo-American marketplace have little choice but to belong to major organizations that advocate for authors' rights and express their concerns in publications like *The Author*. These organizations, such as the Society of Authors and its sister groups outside the UK, work to keep authors abreast of developments in the industry, and in recent years they have raised significant political questions about industry corporatization.

Second, if the dissemination of a specifically literary tradition remains a goal for the dominant firms, it is largely because a niche audience exists to make that tradition financially viable. Its characteristics are easily gleaned through rationalized sales systems, and then appealed to through strategic target marketing. Long speculates that 'high culture [...] is now being dealt with in publishing as one specialized aspect of a less hierarchical and more fragmentary cultural totality.'[24] That is, what Robert Escarpit called the 'cultured circuit,' made up of 'persons having received an intellectual training and an esthetic education [...], having sufficient time to read, and having enough money to buy books with regularity,'[25] has clearly become a niche within the larger publishing industry. That niche is one that can be reached through specifically global corporate operations. Indeed one way to combat fears about corporatization in the publishing industry is to point to the market triumph of 'serious' literary fiction as a distinct publishing category. Since the 1970s increasing amounts of such fiction have managed to reach bestseller or even 'fastseller' status, and by the middle of the 1990s more than 100 literary titles per year were selling at least 100,000 copies in the UK. Commercial viability has been encouraged and accompanied by a number of phenomena, including the spread of major chain bookstores and the emergence of the trade paperback format that 'contrived to enhance the consumer profile' of 'serious' work.[26] Publishers often divide their lists into lead and non-lead titles, promoting only the former with any seriousness, circulating bound proofs to reviewers up to six months in advance of a new publication, and developing promotional portfolios that include biographical information about their respective authors and sales figures for their other works. It is now quite common to treat literary works as blockbuster lead titles in just this way. In Britain there are abundant media available for promotion or review, including the *Times Literary Supplement*, the *London Review of Books*, W.H. Smith's *Bookcase*, and the *Bookseller*, as well as a variety of literary weeklies and book review pages in various daily and Sunday papers, not to mention book-related programming on the BBC and Radio 4. Equivalents in the US include the *New York Review of Books*, the *New York Times Book Review*, and pages in papers like the *Boston Globe* and the *Village Voice*. Online, both the *Guardian Unlimited* (www.guardian.co.uk) and *Salon* (www.salon.com) are extremely popular with market readers of literary fiction and with industry professionals.

Within this niche of literary fiction for a cultured audience, further divisions exist. With methods previously exclusive to specialist publishing, trade fiction houses have registered the value of perceiving readers as belonging to particular communities of interest which can be segmented and targeted with specific marketing. Gardiner notes that publishers' catalogues and display spaces in bookstores are now more likely to feature generic subdivisions categorizing literary titles ('chick lit' is a commonly cited example). She also notes that these genres are established across publishing houses through bibliographic codes that unite disparate titles with, for example, similar features of format and cover design.[27]

It is with this in mind that the proliferation of postcolonial literatures within the Anglo-American market can be explained in part as an aspect of the twinned processes of niche fragmentation and market expansion in the global publishing industry. There remains some truth in a claim made by executives at Bertelsmann that their German communications megalith is less a global company than an international 'network' of national firms, in the sense that a truly global commodity 'must be able to travel easily around the world with only the most modest cosmetic retouching to appeal to local customers.'[28] However in recent years it has become possible to speak of the cosmopolitan, elite readers of English-language literary fiction as consumers of a truly global commodity in need of little alteration for local consumption. Postcolonial literatures have had something to do with this. They facilitate the sort of incorporation of niche audiences that allows for global market expansion within transnational publishing, much though that extension keeps the locus of production in a few key cities in the developed world.

This works in a number of ways. In 2004 'In Full Colour' appeared as a supplement in *The Bookseller*, the journal of the UK book trades, and presented the results of a survey of minority representation in the English publishing industry. Though its first lines state that the subject is a 'moral issue' as well, the emphasis of the remaining pages is undoubtedly the commercial implications of neglecting diversity. Researched and produced in association with *decibel*, an Arts Council of England initiative to promote cultural diversity, the report makes a few major claims based on a survey distributed to publishing industry employees. One is that the industry's workforce and manuscript acquisition trends remain 'unrepresentative' of ethnic communities in England, and especially of metropolitan London's 29 per cent minority population. In turn, those minority writers whose works have made up a growing percentage of the lists of the major publishers are said to feel the effects of a certain ghettoization, as a largely white industry forces them 'to write about multicultural issues.'[29] The other is that the industry has a commercial responsibility to correct these imbalances. In fact the publishing professionals who make up *The Bookseller*'s major readership are appealed to through continual reference to the market implications of any neglect of the necessity of significant improvements in representing diversity. It is said that there are minority markets for literature that publishers will certainly fail to reach if they continue to lack the staff 'who have an inside knowledge of those markets.'[30] In fact ethnic groups are taken to be more appealing potential markets for publishers than the white majority. Arts Council of England surveying has shown that minorities do more than average amounts of creative writing and visit libraries at rates higher than the overall national average. It is noted in particular that the South Asian population exceeds all norms in mobile phone and personal computer ownership and in internet access, modes of consumption considered indicative of a generally elevated level of investment in 'lifestyle commodities' like books and films.

The report promotes Race for Opportunity as a potential corrective. A network of 'over 180 UK organizations working on race and diversity as a business agenda,' to which W.H. Smith, the BBC, the Guardian Media Group, and 'education' conglomerate Pearson PLC all belong, Race for Opportunity encourages the business community to recognize the commercial value of managing diversity. In chairman Allan Leighton's words, 'communities equal customers and potential employees.'[31] It is the larger publishers that are meant to form the vanguard of this activity, since they have the resources to engage in the kind of market research and employee diversification that will ensure their success within a changing market. The report cites Random House and Penguin Books as two publishers making notable efforts to access minority markets, at least in part through actively recruiting employees from minority populations. For example, Penguin's 'diversity project' actively seeks participants for its work experience program at schools with a high percentage of minority ethnic students. Penguin director Helen Fraser explains, 'A workforce that mirrors the population, especially urban populations where the majority of books are sold, will be able to tap into the whole market.'[32]

As *The Bookseller*'s report suggests, publishers now recognize the commercial necessity of attracting minority ethnic writers within metropolitan locations. Companies solidify their dominant positions by incorporating postcolonial writers for global distribution, and also by opening branch offices in the regions from which their authors emerge. These offices attract local authors who would likely seek publication abroad in any case, and they distribute them at the local level while also arranging international publishing contracts for global release. A good example is Penguin Books, which is incorporated within Pearson PLC. Penguin opened branch offices in India in 1985, where it represents Vikram Seth, Arundhati Roy, Vikram Chandra, and Upamanyu Chatterjee, amongst others; in Ireland in 2002, where it aims to take advantage of the popularity of 'local interest' titles in the region, and to 'harness the talent of the authors to a professional organisation which has its sights set on the international stage';[33] and in South Africa in the 1970s. Similarly, the Macmillan group, owned by the German company Holtzbrinck, includes Pan Macmillan South Africa and Australia, and has countless other offices engaged in the worldwide distribution of mainly textbook titles and academic and reference works, and also of literary fiction in a variety of languages.

The more literature associable with specific national or ethnic identities enters the market, the more the market, despite increasing concentration and globalization, can make the claims to inclusivity and universality that justify its particular form of dominance. Expanding markets for literatures in English have depended on the incorporation of a plurality of identities for global export. Paul Jay's statement that 'English literature is increasingly postnational'[34] needs to be tempered by awareness of the market that this postnationality serves. If contemporary writing is produced in a postnational, global flow of deterritorialized cultural products appropriated, translated, and recirculated worldwide,' as Jay states, that 'flow' is not untapped, but is instead checked by observable hierarchies.[35] While it may be true that the organization of the study of literature around national divisions is increasingly outmoded, and that attention to the cross-border traffic in texts and their contents is the better path for future literary scholarship, it remains the case that the expansion of the market for English literatures has been mostly an Anglo-American phenomenon. Products from a plurality of locales are incorporated into the central metropolitan locations of New York and (decreasingly) London. Despite the undoubted prominence of works by writers not simplistically identifiable as Anglo-American, the locus of production and consumption that drives the trade, and hence the economic beneficiaries of its operations, remains centered in the Anglo-American metropolizes. It doesn't help that much critical scholarship originates in those same metropolitan locations; this is the new 'international division of labour' that Biodun Jeyifo identifies.[36] It is for all of these reasons that one might be forgiven for thinking that the distinction between 'World' literature and 'Western' literature has never been more tenuous.[37]

The kind of postcolonial writing most often picked up for global distribution has certain characteristics. It is typically novels, currently the best selling literary genre. Writing in European languages, and especially in English, is privileged. As Gordon Graham argues, 'the unacknowledged tide that has carried the corporations into many lands is the speed with which the English language has increased its dominance as the world's main commercial language.' Successful firms 'are either based in countries where English is the native language, or have taken deliberate decisions to move out of their own language cultures.'[38] In 2003 Graham noted that five times more books are translated from English into other languages than vice versa. He claims that in order for 'foreigners' to be read within the Anglo-American market they either have to write in English, or win the Nobel Prize, which is seemingly the only evaluative guarantee that one's work will be translated.[39] UNESCO states that 50 per cent of all translation is from English into other languages, and that only 6 per cent of translation is into English,[40] though these figures mean less when one considers that there are simply more books published in English to begin with, and that the more books published in English the lower the rate of translation into English will seem.[41]

A more salient statistic may be, in this case, the amount of English literary fiction that is read *in English* across the globe. Indeed some of my own rationale for referring to an Anglo-American marketplace rather than a Euro-American one stems from the general dominance of English. This is in line with Pascale Casanova's recent concession that in moving from literary internationalism to commercial globalization, major European publishing centres like Paris are losing ground to a more 'polycentric,' pluralistic literary field which is nonetheless increasingly organized around London and New York, in part due to the commercial triumph of the English language.[42] Though major transnational media firms like Bertelsmann may be headquartered in Europe, their publishing companies release a great deal of material in English, which is more and more the global vernacular of literary fiction despite the fact that it is not the world's dominant first language. Eva Hemmungs Wirtén's explanation is convincing: 'English is the vernacular of the world because power is assigned in the interstices between linguistic supremacy *and* control of the industries that capitalize on content, information, knowledge, or other assets of intellectual property *in that language*.'[43]

In addition, a growing consensus holds that celebrated postcolonial writers are most often those who are *literary* in a way recognizable to cosmopolitan audiences accustomed to what Timothy Brennan identifies as the 'complexities and subtleties' of a very specific kind of 'great art.'[44] In Casanova's terms, the pole that dominates 'world literary space,' which has to be reached to achieve literary consecration, defines itself in opposition to those underdeveloped literary worlds still 'dependent on political – typically national – authorities.' Various kinds of formalism, for example, seem to be privileged over realism 'in all its forms and denominations – neonaturalist, picturesque, proletarian, socialist.'[45] Moreover, if literary writing that addresses the politics of specifically Third World nations has become its own niche in the Anglo-American market, in part because readers want to be educated to a certain degree about 'other' realities – so that political material becomes eminently marketable – the texts that fulfil that interest most often accord with a broadly anti-imperialist political liberalism. This is, as Brennan writes, a liberalism 'that openly and consciously seeks to throw off what it considers to be the clichés of the postwar rhetoric of third-world embattlement.'[46] It often entails 'a harsh questioning of radical decolonization theory; a dismissive or parodic attitude towards the project of national culture; a manipulation of imperial imagery and local legend as a means of politicising "current events"; and a declaration of cultural "hybridity".'[47]

Brennan's characterization of cosmopolitanism as '*local* while denying its local character' is similar to Masao Miyoshi's discussion of what he calls the 'TNC class,' made up of the employees of transnational corporations in their guise as efficient managers of 'global production and consumption, hence of world culture itself.' Miyoshi describes that class as presumably 'clear of national and ethnic blinders,' but 'not free of a new version of "ideologyless" ideology,' the ideology of cultural management.[48] Much of Miyoshi's argument about the role that academics should play in articulating an opposition to the 'TNC class' relies on analogies he makes between it and academic professionals themselves, who are also 'frequent fliers and globe-trotters,' addicted to a sanitizing discourse of pluralism and an identity politics which is, in his view, a form of collaboration with the processes of transnational capitalism.[49] This increasingly common reading of the general parameters of cosmopolitanism – its liberalism, pluralism, and seeming congruity with multinational capitalism – is echoed in Arif Dirlik's picture of postcolonial literature as a feature of capitalist accumulation in the culture industries, and as part of the way the metropolitan university asserts control of its many peripheries. As I discussed previously, Dirlik and others tend to claim that the distinguishing features of celebrated postcolonial writing coincide with the concerns of metropolitan critics in general, concerns which encourage an adherence to a largely inadequate or utopian politics of hybridity and postnationality. In turn it is no great surprise that metropolitan critics and postcolonial authors alike have tended to negotiate positions that recognize, deflect, or interrogate their own complicity in this general situation.

To review, several things characterize the postcolonial literature that achieves the greatest success in the current market: it is English-language fiction; it is relatively 'sophisticated' or 'complex' and often anti-realist; it is politically liberal and suspicious of nationalism; it uses a language of exile, hybridity, and 'mongrel' subjectivity. What is the function of writers' biographies in additionally ensuring their success within the market? Celebrated postcolonial writers are typically situated in relation to a number of underdeveloped locales, such that what Brennan calls the 'banners' of geographical affiliation are always in sight: 'Being from "there" in this sense is primarily a kind of literary passport that identifies the artist as being from a region of underdevelopment and pain.'[50] Writers like Rushdie are made to 'present their own "Third World" identities as a mark of distinction in a world supposedly exempt from national belonging.'[51] In fact these writers in part succeed because of their ostensible attachment to specific locations. In effect the trumpeted 'complexity' of successful postcolonial literary production is a sign of a '[l]iterary sophistication [...] doubly authoritative because it is proof of overcoming *that* to join *this*.'[52]

Works Cited

Achebe, C., 1996 [1958]. *Things Fall Apart*. Oxford: Heinemann (African Writers Series: Classics in Context).

Adair, G., 1986. 'Le Booker nouveau est arrivé', in, *Myths and Memories*. London: Fontana, pp. 144–47.

Adversis Major, Short History of Educational Books Scheme; Staples Press, 1949.

Alberge, Dalya. (1995) 'Heavyweight Publishers Vie for Virago'. *The Times* [UK] 25 Oct.: 3.

Allen Lane, King Penguin, J.E. Morpurgo; Hutchinson, 1979.

Anderson, C. and M. Wolf., 2010. 'The Web is dead. Long live the Internet'. *Wired*, 17 August. Online: www.wired.com/magazine/2010/08/ff_webrip/all/1 (accessed 21 February 2012).

Appiah, K.A., 1991. 'Is the post – in postmodernism the post – in postcolonial?'. *Critical Inquiry*, 17, 336–57.

Asad, T. (ed.), 1972. *Anthropology and the Colonial Encounter*. Atlantic Highlands, NJ: Humanities Press.

Ballou, R.O., 1946. *A History of the Council on Books in Wartime, 1942–1946*. New York: Privately printed.

Barthes, R., 1974. *S/Z*. Paris: Éditions du Seuil, 1970. *S/Z*, Trans R. Miller. New York: Hill and Wang.

Baxter, Sarah. (1995) 'Why Did the Apple Crumble?' *Observer* [UK] 29–Oct.: Review, 9.

Ben-David, J. and R. Collins, 1966. 'Social factors in the origins of a new science: The case of psychology'. *American Sociological Review*, 31 (4), 451–465.

Benkler, Y., 2006. *The Wealth of Networks: How Social Production Transforms Markets and Freedom*. New Haven, CT: Yale University Press.

Bettig, R.V., 1996. *Copyrighting Culture: The Political Economy of Intellectual Property*. Boulder, CO: Westview Press.

Bhagat, C., 2004. *Five Point Someone*. New Delhi: Rupa.

Bhagat, C., 2005. *One Night @ the Call Centre*. New Delhi: Rupa.

Bhagwati, J., 2004. *In Defense of Globalization*. New York: Oxford University Press.

Bhaskar, M., 2011. 'Digital publishing start-ups'. *Google Docs*, 28 November. Online: https://docs.google.com/document/d/lvcPBUincOjwgIQBjq_qhMPb9QYitgeyl6gOU MlhWQUw/edit (accessed 29 December 2012).

Bhaskar, M., 2011. 'Towards paracontent: Marketing, publishing and cultural form in a digital environment'. *Logos: Journal of the World Publishing Community*, 22 (1).

Bolter, J.D., 2001. *Writing Space: Computers, Hypertext, and the Remediation of Print*. Mahwah, NJ: Lawrence Erlbaum Associates.

Bookseller. (1985c) 'Virago Bookshop: "Stylish and Fun"'. 5 Jan.: 15.

Bookseller. (1995b) 'Little, Brown Pips Bloomsbury in Battle for Virago'. 10 Nov.: 8.

Bookseller. (1995d) 'Virago Loses Another Virago'. 13 Oct.: 6.

Bourdieu, P. and A. Darbel, 1969. *L'amour de l'art. Les musées d'art européens et leur public*. Paris: Minuit.

Bourdieu, P., 1971. 'Le marché des biens symboliques'. *L'Année Sociologique*, 22, 49–126.

Bourdieu, P., 1985. 'The market of symbolic goods'. *Poetics*, 14, 17–22 and 33–43.

Bourdieu, P., 1993. *The Field of Cultural Production: Essays on Art and Literature*, ed. R. Johnson. New York: Columbia University Press.

Bourdieu, P., 1996. *The Rules of Art*. Cambridge: Polity Press, pp. 141–173.

Brouillette, S., 2007. 'South Asian literature and global publishing'. *Wasafiri*, 22 (3), 34–38.

Buckingham, Lisa. (1995) 'Women's Imprint Virago Sold'. *Guardian* [UK] 3 Nov.: 4.

Callil, Carmen. (1986) 'The Future of Feminist Publishing'. *Bookseller* 1 Mar.: 850-2.

Caro Baroja, J., 1964. 'El ritual de la danza en el Pais Vasco. Revista de Dialectologia y Tradiciones Populares', Tomo XX, Cuadernos 1° y 2°.

Castells, M., 2010. 'The rise of the network society'. 2nd edn. Chichester: Wiley-Blackwell.

Cloyd, J.S. and A.P. Bates., 1964. 'George Homans in footnotes: The fate of ideas in scholarly communication'. *Sociological Inquiry*, 34 (2), 115–128.

Cole, J.Y. (ed.), 1984. *Books in Action: The Armed Services Editions*. Washington, DC: Library of Congress.

Collectors' Society, 1974–1996.

Coser, L. A., C. Kadushin and W. W. Powell, 1982. *Books: The Culture and Commerce of Publishing*. New York: Basic Books.

Council on Books in Wartime Records, Public Policy Papers, Department of Rare Books and Special Collections, Princeton University Library, Princeton, NJ.

Cravan, A., 1966. Quoted by A. Breton. In: *Anthologie de l'humour noir*. Paris: J.J. Pauvert.

Dalley, Jan. (1995) 'Was Virago Too Successful?' *Independent on Sunday* [UK] 29 Oct.: 21.

Darnton, R., 1982. 'What is the history of books?'. *Daedalus*, 111 (3), 65–83.

Davies, Margaret Llewelyn, ed. (1977) *Life as We Have Known it*. [1931] Virago Reprint Library. London: Virago Press.

Davis, K.C., 1984. *Two-Bit Culture: The Paperbacking of America*. Boston: Houghton Mifflin.

Delacroix, E., 1923. *Oeuvres littéraires*, Vol. 1. Paris: Crès.

Doctorow, C., 2011. 'Publishers and the Internet: A changing role?'. *Guardian*, 30 June. Online: www.guardian.co.uk/technology/2011/jun/30/publishers-internet-changing-role/print (accessed 30 June 2011).

Durrant, Sabine. (1993) 'How We Met: Carmen Callil and Harriet Spicer'. *Independent* [UK] 23 May: Review, 93.

Education in the Forces 1939–1946, N. Scarlyn Wilson; University of London, 1948.

Eisenstein, E., 1979. *The Printing Press as an Agent of Change: Communications and Cultural Transformations in Early Modern Europe*. 2 volumes. Cambridge: Cambridge University Press.

English, J.F., 2002. 'Winning the culture game: Prizes, awards, and the rules of art'. *New Literary History*, 33 (1), 109–35.

English, J.F., 2005. *The Economy of Prestige: Prizes, Awards, and the Circulation of Cultural Value*. Cambridge, MA: Harvard University Press.

Evening Standard. [UK] (1995) 'Official: The Feminist Dream is Dead'. 13 Sep.: 8.

Everywoman. (1987) 'Upheavals in Women's Publishing'. Sep.: 11.

Ezard, John. (1995) 'Virago Facing Sale after Rows and Recession'. Guardian [UK] 25 Oct.: 3.

Febvre, L. and H.-J. Martin, 1958. *'L'Apparition du Livre'*. Paris: A. Michel.

Febvre, L. and H.-J. Martin, 1976. *The Coming of the Book: The Impact of Printing 1450–1800*. London: Verso.

Fifty Penguin Years, Linda Lloyd Jones, Jeremy Aynsley, Penguin, 1985.

Finkelstein, D. and A. McCleery (eds), 2006a. *The Book History Reader*. London: Routledge.

Firth, R., 1963. *Elements of Social Organization*. Boston, MA: Beacon Press.

Fish, S., 1989. 'Why no one's afraid of Wolfgang Iser', in *Doing What Comes Naturally: Change, Rhetoric and the Practice of Theory in Literary and Legal Studies*. Oxford: Clarendon Press.

Foucault, M., 1977. 'What is an author?' in *Language, Counter-Memory, Practice: Selected Essays and Interviews*, Trans D.F. Bouchard and S. Simon. Ithaca, NY: Cornell University Press, 113–38.

Francis, R., [2003] 2008. *Publishing Market Profile: India*. Rev. ed. London: UK Publishers Association.

Gannett, L., 1946. Books, in J. Goodman (ed.) *While You Were Gone: A Report on Wartime Life in the United States*. New York: Simon and Schuster, pp. 447–463.

Garner, Helen. (1995) The First Stone, Some Questions About Sex and Power. Sydney: Picador.

Gerrard, Nicci. (1993) 'Sisters on the Shelves': *Observer* [UK] 13 Jun.: 61.

Goodings, Lennie. (1993) 'Cleaning the Office, Changing the World'. *Bookseller* 4 Jun.: 26–7.

Greenway, J., 1964. *Literature among the Primitives*. Hatboro: Folkore Associates.

Guardian. [UK] (1997) 'Wayward Girls & Wicked Women'. Virago advertising insert. 7 Jun. 1–16.

Gulab, K., 2007. 'Desperately Seeking Authors', *Hindustan Times*, 23 September; also at: www.open.ac.uk/Arts/ferguson-centre/indian-lit/documents/pub-doc-kushal-gulab-sept07.htm.

Hauser, A., 1951. *The Social History of Art*, Vol. II. New York: Vintage Books. Translated from the German by S. Godman.

Heim, M., 1993. *The Metaphysics of Virtual Reality*. New York: Oxford University Press.

———., 1987. *Electric Language: A Philosophical Study of Word Processing*. New Haven, CT: Yale University Press.

Hench, J.B., 2009. A D-Day for American books in Europe: Overseas Editions, Inc., 1944–1945, in D.P. Nord, J.S. Rubin and M. Schudson (eds), *The Enduring Book: Print Culture in Postwar America, Volume 5 of A History of the Book in America*. Chapel Hill: University of North Carolina Press.

Hench, J.B., 2010. *Books as Weapons: Propaganda, Publishing, and the Battle for Global Markets in the Era of World War II*. Ithaca, NY: Cornell University Press.

Henry, Scott. (1995) 'Taming of the Shrew'. *Australian* 27 Oct.: 13.

Hill, A., 1988. *In Pursuit of Publishing*. London: John Murray in Assoc. with Heinemann Educational Books.

Hope, S., 1997. *Human Nature: Agricultural Biodiversity and Farm-Based Security*. Ottawa: Rural Advancement Foundation International.

Irele, A., 1990. *The African Experience in Literature and Ideology*. Bloomington, IN: Indiana University Press.

Iser, W., 1978. *The Act of Reading: A Theory of Aesthetic Response*. London: Routledge & Kegan Paul.

Iser, W., 1989. 'Interview 42', in *Prospecting: From Reader Response to Literary Anthropology*. Baltimore: Johns Hopkins University Press.

Jamieson, J., 1947. Armed services editions and GI Fan Mail. *Publishers' Weekly*, 12(July), 148–152.

Jones, Nicolette. (1992) 'Harriet Spicer – The Punctilious Professional'. *Bookseller* 3 Jan.: 20–3.

Junod, H., 1927. *The Life of a South African Tribe*. London: Macmillan.

Kelly, K., 1999. *New Rules for the New Economy: 10 Ways the Network Economy Is Changing Everything*. London: Fourth Estate.

Khullar Management and Financial Investment, 1999. *India: Book Publishing*. Washington, DC: US Department of State.

Kotei, S.I.A., 1981. *The Book Today in Africa*. Paris: Unesco.

Lane, M. and J. Booth, 1980. *Books and Publishers: Commerce against Culture in Postwar Britain*. Toronto: Lexington Books.

Lanier, J., 2011. *You Are Not a Gadget: A Manifesto*. London: Penguin.

Lethève, J., 1959. *Impressionistes et symbolistes devant la presse*. Paris: Armand Colin.

Lévi-Strauss, C., 1969. *The Raw and the Cooked: Introduction to a Science of Mythology: I*, Trans John and D. Weightman. New York: Harper & Row.

Lewis, J., 2005. *The Life and Times of Allen Lane*. London: Viking.

Lindfors, B., 1990. 'The teaching of African literatures in anglophone African universities: An instructive canon'. *Matatu*, 7, 41–55.

———., 1993. 'Desert gold: Irrigation schemes for ending the book drought', in D. Riemenschneider and F. Schulze-Engler (eds), *African Literature in the Eighties*. Amsterdam: Rodopi, 27–38.

Lizarríbar, C.B., 1998. *Something Else Will Stand Beside It: The African Writers Series and the Development of African Literature*. Ann Arbor, MI: UMI.

Lowry, Suzanne. (1977) 'Three's Company'. *Guardian* [UK] 19 Aug.: 9.

Lyotard, J.F., 1984. *The Postmodern Condition: A Report on Knowledge*, Trans G. Bennington and B. Massumi. Minneapolis: University of Minnesota Press.

Macaskill, H. (1990) 'Virago Press: From Nowhere to Everywhere'. *British Book News* Jul.: 432–5.

Maja-Pearce, A., 1992. 'In pursuit of excellence: Thirty years of the Heinemann African Writers Series', *Research in African Literatures*, 23 (4), 125–132.

Malinowski, B., 1926. *Myth in Primitive Psychology*. New York: W.W. Norton and Co.

Mathur, A., 1991. *The Inscrutable Americans*. New Delhi: Rupa.

Mazrui, A.A., 1996. Perspective: The muse of modernity and the quest for development, in P.G. Altbach and S. Hassan (eds.), *The Muse of Modernity: Essays on Culture as Development in Africa*. Tenton: Africa World Press.

McGuire, H. and B. O'Leary (eds), 2012. *Book: A Futurist's Manifesto: A Collection of Essays from the Bleeding Edge of Publishing*. Boston: O'Reilly Media.

McKnight, C., Richardson, J., and Dillon, A. 1988. *The Authoring of Hypertext Documents*. Loughborough: Loughborough University of Technology/HUSAT Research Center.

McPhee, Hilary. (2001) *Other People's Words*. Sydney: Picador.

Miller, C.T., 1990. *Theories of Africans: Francophone Literature and Anthropology in Africa*. Chicago, IL: University of Chicago Press.

Miller, D.J., 1996. *Books Go to War: An Exhibition at the University of Virginia.* Charlottesville, VA: Book Arts Press.

Miller, M., 2012. 'Android tablet marketshare up 10%'. Zdnet. 27 January. Online: www.zdnet.com/blog/mobile-gadgeteer/android-tablet-market-share-up-10-ipad-down-10-through-2011/5430 (accessed 3 February 2012).

Morrison, E., 2012. 'The self-epublishing bubble'. *Guardian*, 30 January, Online: www.guardian.co.uk/books/2012/jan/30/self-e-publishing-bubble-ewan-morrison (accessed 30 January 2012).

Murray, S., 2007. 'Publishing studies: Critically mapping research in search of a discipline'. *Publishing Research Quarterly*, 22 (4), 3–25.

Nettelbeck, C.W., 1991. *Forever French: Exile in the United States, 1939–1945.* New York and Oxford: Berg.

Norden, Barbara. (1993) 'Coat of Many Colours'. *Everywoman* Jun.: 15–16.

Owen, Ursula. (1988) 'Feminist Publishing'. *Publishing – The Future.* Ed. Peter Owen. London: Peter Owen. 86–100.

Owen, Ursula. (1998b) Interview Simone Murray. London. 21 Dec.

Pagels, H.R., 1989. *The Dreams of Reason: The Computer and the Rise of the Sciences of Complexity.* New York: Bantam.

Paulson, W.R., 1988. *The Noise of Culture: Literary Texts in a World of Information.* Ithaca, NY: Cornell University Press.

PCS Newsletters, The Penguin Collector, Miscellanies; The Penguin Collectors Society.

Penguin Portrait: Allen Lane & the Penguin Editors 1935–1970, Steve Hare; Penguin Books, 1995.

Piaget, J., 1950. *Introduction à l'épistémologie génétique*, Vol. III. Paris: P.U.F.

Pilger, J., 1998. *Hidden Agendas.* London: Vintage.

Pitman, Joanna. (1995) 'Mother of All Rows'. *The Times* 18 Nov.: Magazine, 27–8, 30, 32.

Porter, Henry. (1995) 'The Feminist Fallout that Split Virago'. *Daily Telegraph* [UK] 3 Nov.: 1, 25.

Pringle, Alexandra. (1996) Interview with Simone Murray. London. 8 Aug.

Proudhon, P.J., 1939. 'Contradictions économiques'. Paris: Rivière. 1846.

Rawsthorn, Alice. (1995) 'Virago Sold to Time Warner'. *Financial Times* [UK] 3 Nov.: 7.

Reeves, Maud Pember. (1979) *Round About a Pound a Week.* [1913] Virago Reprint Library. London: Virago Press.

Robin, R., 1995. *The Barbed-Wire College: Reeducating German POWs in the United States during World War II.* Princeton, NJ: Princeton University Press.

Said, E.W., 1985. *Beginnings: Intention and Method.* New York: Columbia University Press.

Sainte-Beuve, 1867. 'L'Académie Francaise'. In: *Paris-Guide, par les principaux écrivains et artistes de la France*, Paris: A. Lacroix, Verboeckhoven et Cie. T.I. pp. 96–97.

Sartre, J.P., 1948. *Qu'est-ce que la littérature?* Paris: Gallimard.

Satterfield, J., 2002. *The World's Best Books: Taste, Culture, and the Modern Library.* Amherst: University of Massachusetts Press.

Scanlon, Joan and Julia Swindells. (1994) 'Bad Apple'. Trouble & Strife 28: 41–6.

Schücking, L.L., 1966. *The Sociology of Literary Taste.* London: Routledge and Kegan Paul. Translated from German by E. W. Dickes.

Shakespeare, Sebastian. (1995) 'When Viragos Fall Out'. *Evening Standard* [UK]14 Sep.: 12.

Shirky, C., 2002. 'Weblogs and the mass amateurisation of publishing'. *Shirky.com*, 3 October. Online: www.shirky.com/writings/weblogs_publishing.html (accessed 5 January 2012).

Showalter, Elaine, (1978) A Literature of Their Own: British Women Novelists from Brontë to Lessing. [1977] London: Virago Press.

South African National Bibliography 1994 and 1995, State Library, Pretoria, South Africa.

Spicer, Harriet. (1996) Interview with Simone Murray. London. 16 Jul.

Spiers, J., 2007. *Serious about Series: American Cheap 'Libraries', British 'Railway' Libraries, and Some Literary Series of the 1890's.* London: Institute of English Studies.

Spivak, G.C., 1987. *In Other Worlds: Essays in Cultural Politics.* New York: Methuen.

Squires, C., 2007. *Marketing Literature: The Making of Contemporary Writing in Britain.* Basingstoke: Palgrave Macmillan.

Sutherland, J., 1998. 'Publishing history: A hole at the centre of literary sociology'. *Critical Inquiry,* 14 (3), 574–589.

The Bantam Story, Clarence Petersen; Bantam Books, 1975.

The Book of Paperbacks, Piet Schreuders; Virgin, 1981.

The History of Army Education 1939–45, W.E. Williams; unpublished monograph, P.R.O. WO 277.

The Prisoner of War magazine, published by The Red Cross.

The Red Cross and the White, H. St John Saunders; Hollis & Carter, 1949.

The Road to 1945; British Politics and the Second World War, Paul Addison; Pimlico, 1994.

The Scottish Red Cross, George Pratt Insh; Jackson & Co, 1952.

The Services Central Book Depot, October 1939 – June 1943, Report by Lt.-Col. R.D. Jackson; Imperial War Museum archives.

Thibault., 2010. 'Search engine share by country'. *Them.pro*, 27 July. Online: www.them.pro/Search-engine-market-share-country (accessed 21 February 2012).

Thompson, J. B., 2005. *Books in the Digital Age: The Transformation of Academic and Higher Education Publishing in Britain and the United States.* Cambridge: Polity.

Thompson, J. B., 2010. *Merchants of Culture: The Publishing Business in the Twenty-First Century.* Cambridge: Polity, 2010.

Travis, T., 1999. Books as weapons and "The Smart Man's Peace": The work of the council on books in wartime. *Princeton University Library Chronicle*, 60, 353–399.

Traynor, Ian and Giles Foden. (1998) 'German Giant Buys Random House'. *Guardian* [UK] 24 Mar.: 1.

Twenty-Five Years; Penguins Progress 1935–1960; Penguin, 1960.

Unwin, V. and Currey, J., 1993. 'The African writers' series celebrates thirty years'. *Southern African Review of Books*, March/April 1993, 3–5.

Virago publicity pamphlet. (1996) 'A Short History of Virago, 1973–1995'. London: Virago Press.

Vitet, L., 1861. *L'académie royal de peinture et de sculpture, étude historique.* Paris: Michel Lévy.

Watt, I., 1957. 'The rise of the novel'. *Studies in Defoe, Richardson and Fielding.* Harmondsworth: Penguin Books.

Williams, Raymond. (1983) *Keywords: A Vocabulary of Culture and Society.* 2nd edn. London: Flamingo.

Wu, T., 2011. *The Master Switch: The Rise and Fall of Information Empires.* London: Atlantic.

Zittrain, J., 2008. *The Future of the Internet: And How to Stop It.* London: Allen Lane.

Notes

2 THE TRIALS OF A PUBLISHER

1 *Best-Sellers: Are They Born or Made?* (London: George Allen & Unwin Ltd., 1939).

3 THE MARKET OF SYMBOLIC GOODS

1 Here, as elsewhere, the laws objectively governing social relations tend to constitute themselves as norms that are explicitly professed and assumed. In this way, as the field's autonomy grows, or as one moves towards the most autonomous sectors of the field, the direct introduction of external powers increasingly attracts disapproval; as the members of autonomous sectors consider such an introduction as a dereliction, they tend to sanction it by the symbolic exclusion of the guilty. This is shown, for instance, by the discredit attaching to any mode of thought which is suspected of reintroducing the total, brutal classificatory principles of a political order into intellectual life; and it is as if the field exercised its autonomy to the maximum, in order to render unknowable the external principles of opposition (especially the political ones) or, at least intellectually to 'overdetermine' them by subordinating them to specifically intellectual principles.

2 'As for criticism, it hides under big words the explanations it no longer knows how to furnish. Remembering Albert Wolff, Bourde, Brunetière or France, the critic, for fear of failing, like his predecessors, to recognize artists of genius, no longer judges at all' (Lethève 1959: 276).

3 In this sense, the intellectual field represents the almost complete model of a social universe knowing no principles of differentiation or hierarchization other than specifically symbolic distinctions.

4 It is the same, at least objectively (in the sense that no one is supposed to be ignorant of the cultural law), with any act of consumption which finds itself objectively within the field of application of the rules governing cultural practices with claims to legitimacy.

5 Thus Proudhon, all of whose aesthetic writings clearly express the petit-bourgeois representation of art and the artist, imputes the process of dissimilation generated from the intellectual field's internal logic to a cynical choice on the part of artists: 'On the one hand, artists will do anything, because everything is indifferent to them; on the other, they become infinitely specialized. Delivered up to themselves, without a guiding light, without compass, obedient to an inappropriately applied industrial law, they class themselves into genera and species, firstly according to the nature of commissions, and subsequently according to the method distinguishing them. Thus, there are church painters, historical painters, painters of battles, genre painters – that is, of anecdotes and comedy, portrait painters, landscape painters, animal painters, marine artists, painters of Venus, fantasy painters. This one cultivates the nude, another cloth. Then, each of them labours to distinguish himself by one of the competing methods of execution. One of them applies himself to drawing, the other to colour; this one cares for composition, that one for perspective, yet another for

costume or local colour; this one shines through sentiment, another through the idealism or the realism of his figures; still another makes up for the nullity of his subjects by the finesse of his details. Each one labours to develop his trick, his style, his manner and, with the help of fashion, reputations are made and unmade' (Proudhon 1939: 271).

6 The emergence of the theory of art which, rejecting the classical conception of artistic production as the simple execution of a pre-existent internal model, turns artistic 'creation' into a sort of apparition that was unforeseeable for the artist himself – inspiration, genius, etc. – undoubtedly assumed the completion of the transformation of the social relations of production which, liberating artistic production from the directly and explicitly formulated order, permitted the conception of artistic labour as autonomous 'creation', and no longer as mere execution.

7 It can be seen that the history leading up to what has been called a 'denovellisation' of the novel obeys the same type of logic.

8 'As long as the opportunities on the art market remain favourable for the artist, the cultivation of individuality does not develop into a mania for originality – this does not happen until the age of mannerism, when new conditions on the art market create painful economic disturbances for the artist' (Hauser 1951: 71).

9 If these analyses can equally obviously be applied to certain categories of avant-garde art critics, this is because the position of the least consecrated agents of a more consecrated field may present certain analogies with the position of the most consecrated agents of a less consecrated field.

10 More generally, if the occupants of a determinate position in the social structure only rarely do what the occupants of a different position think they ought to do ('if I was in his place...'), it is because the latter project the position-takings inscribed into their own position into a position which excludes them. The theory of relations between positions and position-takings reveals the basis of all those errors of perspective, to which all attempts at abolishing the differences associated with differences in position by means of a simple imaginary projection, or by an effort of 'comprehension' (at the back of which always lies the principle of 'putting oneself in someone else's place'), or again, attempts at transforming the objective relations between agents by transforming the representations they have of these relations, are inevitably exposed.

11 *La Quinzaine Littéraire*, September 15, 1966.

12 E. Lalou, *L'Express*, October 26, 1966.

13 It was thus to demonstrate that the development of psychology in Germany, at the end of the 19th century, can be explained by the state of the university market, favouring the movement of physiology students and teachers towards other fields, and by the relatively lowly position occupied by philosophy in the academic field, which made it a dream ground for the innovative enterprises of deserters from the higher disciplines (cf. Ben-David and Collins 1966).

14 Short-term movements in the cultural value stock market ought not to dissimulate the constants, such as the domination of the most theoretical discipline over those more practically orientated.

15 We should pay particular attention to the strategies employed in relation with groups occupying a neighbouring position in the field. The law of the quest for distinction explains the apparent paradox which has it that the fiercest and most fundamental conflicts oppose each group to its immediate neighbours, for it is these who most directly threaten its identity, hence its distinction and even its specifically cultural existence.

4 PARATEXTS: THRESHOLDS OF INTERPRETATION

1 *Palimpsestes* (Seuil, 1981), 9.
2 And undoubtedly in some other languages, if this remark by J. Hillis Miller, which applies to English, is to be believed: '"Para" is a double antithetical prefix signifying at once proximity and distance, similarity and difference, interiority and exteriority, ... something simultaneously this side of a boundary line, threshold, or margin, and also beyond it, equivalent in status and also secondary or subsidiary, submissive, as of guest to host, slave to master. A thing in "para," moreover, is not only simultaneously on both sides of the boundary line between inside and out. It is also the boundary itself, the screen which is a permeable membrane connecting inside and outside. It confuses them with one another, allowing the outside in, making the inside out, dividing them and joining them' ('The Critic as Host,' in *Deconstruction and Criticism*, ed. Harold Bloom et al. [New York: Seabury Press, 1979], 219). This is a rather nice description of the activity of the paratext.
3 [The French title of this book is *Seuils*, which means 'thresholds'.]
4 This image seems inevitable for anyone who deals with the paratext: 'an undefined zone ... where two sets of codes are blended: the social code as it pertains to advertising, and the codes producing or regulating the text' (C. Duchet, 'Pour une socio-critique, ou Variations sur un incipit', *Littérature* 1 [February 1971], 6); 'an intermediary zone between the off-text and the text' (A. Compagnon, *La Seconde Main* [Seuil, 1979], 328).
5 Philippe Lejeune, *Le Pacte autobiographique* (Seuil, 1975), 45. What follows this phrase indicates clearly that the author was partly aiming at what I am calling paratext: '... name of author, title, subtitle, name of series, name of publisher, even the ambiguous game of prefaces.'
6 I now say *texts* and not only *works* in the 'noble' sense of that word (literary or artistic productions, in contrast to nonliterary ones), as the need for a paratext is thrust on every kind of book, with or without aesthetic ambition, even if this study is limited to the paratext of literary works.
7 The notion of 'peritext' overlaps with that of 'périgraphie', proposed by A. Compagnon, *La Seconde Main*, 328–56.
8 Even so, I must add that the peritext of scholarly editions (generally posthumous) sometimes contains elements that do not belong to the paratext in the sense in which I define it. Examples of such elements would be extracts from allographic reviews (see the Pléiade edition of Sartre, the Flammarion edition of Michelet, and so forth). [The word 'allography' in its various forms refers to a text (preface, review, etc.) that one person writes for another person's work.]
9 Here I will disregard the sometimes pronounced technical (bibliographic and bibliophilic) differences among *first trade edition*, *original [limited] edition*, *editio princeps*, and so on, to summarily call the earliest one *original*.
10 [Allais (1854–1905) was a humorist who wrote light verse, tales, and sketches.] *Anthumous* is the term Allais used to designate those of his works that had appeared in a collection during his lifetime. We should also remember that *posthumus*, 'after burial', is a very old (and wonderful) false etymology: *postumus* is merely the superlative of *posterus* ['following' (compar. *posterior*: 'following after'; superl.: 'hindmost, last')].

6 MERCHANTS OF CULTURE

1 The notion of publishers as gatekeepers of ideas is developed by Lewis A. Coser, Charles Kadushin and Walter W. Powell in *Books: The Culture and Commerce of Publishing* (New York: Basic Books, 1982), discussed further below.

2 The practice of allowing booksellers to return stock for full credit has a long history in Europe but was used rarely and half-heartedly by American publishers until the Great Depression of the 1930s, when publishers began experimenting seriously with returns policies as a way of stimulating sales and encouraging booksellers to increase stock-holdings. In spring 1930, Putnam, Norton and Knopf all introduced schemes to allow booksellers to return stock for credit or exchange under certain conditions, and in 1932 Viking Press announced that orders for new books would be returnable for a credit of 90 per cent of the billed cost (see John Tebbel, *A History of Book Publishing in the United States*, vol. 3: *The Golden Age between the Two Wars, 1920–1940* (New York: R. R. Bowker, 1978), pp. 429–30, 441). The practice of returns subsequently became a settled feature of the book trade and marks it out as somewhat unusual among retail sectors.

7   THE DIGITAL CONTEXT AND CHALLENGE

1 See Morrison (2012).
2 In the words of McGuire and O'Leary, 'We are now effectively replicating this ["paper-based"] model for digital: Publishers send files to distributors and retailers, who sell those files to readers, who download them onto various devices and read them when and where they like' (2012: 2).
3 See Thibault (2010).
4 See www.ebizmba.com/articles/social-networwebsites (accessed 1 March 2012).
5 See Miller (2012).
6 Viewed in this light Big Tech's corporate strategy becomes clear – they are all playing for total platform dominance, hence Google in browsers and operating systems (Chrome), Apple in retail (the Appstore), Amazon in tablets and cloud computing and app stores (the Kindle Fire), Microsoft in search engines (Bing). Everyone in a patent war; everyone in market segments outside their original competencies.
7 Another associated network effect is the 'cluster effect' usually associated with geographical business and innovation clusters like Silicon Valley (appropriately) or the City of London. Clusters of products or services, like Google's suite of tools or Amazon's devices and services also create a cluster effect where the value of each is increased by the presence of the others, so encouraging centralisation.
8 Unquestionably worse for Zittrain (2008). Not only is the generativity nullified but perfect legal enforcement, enabled in such systems, could give rise to mass censorship, total surveillance, immediate injunctions and absolute regulability.
9 Ironically, of course, it was 'Ma Bell' that created the framework for the digital revolution that would up-end the entire industry.
10 Wu (2011: 273) is cautiously optimistic; the stakes are so huge, and the players so varied 'this time around, as compared to any other, the sides are far more evenly matched.'
11 Furthermore we might view the centralisation of the Internet as what Deleuze and Guattari (2004) called 'territorialization'. New 'lines of flight' create new 'segments' that are basically occupations. However, they also hold open the possibility of 'territorialization', which chimes with the counter-currents of digital culture.

8   AGENTS AND THE FIELD OF PRINT CULTURE

1 On this point see Bonham-Carter, *Authors by Profession*, 1: 133, 169.
2 Henry Holt, 'The Commercialization of Literature,' 583.

3 Curtis Brown, '"The Commercialisation of Literature" and the Literary Agent,' 357.

4 Curtis Brown, '"The Commercialisation of Literature" and the Literary Agent,' 358.

5 We need to be careful when examining Watt's client lists as presented in his own advertising efforts because they are somewhat misleading. They name clients for whom he did minimal work – Hardy and Oliphant, for example – or who moved on to other agents – Bennett and Wells, for example – alongside those for whom he did a great deal of work – Collins and MacDonald, for example. The lists' obvious purpose was to convince writers and publishers of Watt's importance and prominence, and listing famous individuals, even if he did little work for them, enhanced his credibility. Interestingly, the AP Watt web site continues this practice of listing famous authors as clients, including Arnold Bennett, who moved to the Pinker Agency very early in his career and remained a loyal client of Pinker's well into the 1920s.

6 Harry Ricketts, *The Unforgiving Minute*, 150.

7 Martin Seymour-Smith, *Rudyard Kipling*, 124.

8 Seymour-Smith, *Rudyard Kipling*, 124. Prior to the meeting with Watt, Kipling had already published a substantial number of short stories, many of which appeared in the six volumes of stories that he published for the Indian Railway Library with A.G. Wheeler and Company. The stories that appeared in these volumes, according to Seymour-Smith, put 'Kipling on the international map' (91), thereby contributing to his status as a rising literary star.

9 Quoted in Ricketts, *The Unforgiving Minute*, 157.

10 James Hepburn says that Watt 'served as Besant's own agent from 1884 onwards' (*The Author's Empty Purse*, 43).

11 D.S. Higgins indicates in his biography of Haggard that in January of 1886 Watt's first major task as Haggard's agent was to untangle a contract between Haggard and J. and R. Maxwell that gave 'them the right to bring out cheap editions of all [Haggard's] books written within five years' (*Rider Haggard*, 89).

12 Peter McDonald notes that Doyle began using the Watt agency in late 1890, a fact borne out by the Watt-Doyle correspondence in both the Berg Collection in New York and the Watt Records at Chapel Hill (*Literary Culture and Publishing Practice, 1880–1914*, 138).

13 The Watt Records at Chapel Hill contain contracts and correspondence from the majority of Watt's clients during the period under scrutiny in this book. When one scrolls through the index to materials, Yeats and Strindberg are joined by other experimental writers such as T.S. Eliot, Henry James, and D.H. Lawrence, making it appear as if Watt did take an interest in a larger number of experimental writers than my argument suggests. But the amount of actual work his firm performed for these writers is limited – two contracts related to Eliot's edited volume of Kipling's verses; one contract for a volume of Henry James stories; and two contracts for Lawrence stories. In the cases of James and Lawrence, they were both represented for longer periods of time by Watt's younger rival, James B. Pinker, though Lawrence eventually parted company with Pinker on acrimonious terms.

14 Despite their protestations about the deleterious effects of agents' growing influence, by 1910 most publishers used agents extensively to procure new material, and if the agent had a reputation for supplying material that sold well, his clients were at a distinct advantage when compared to an unknown author making a direct submission.

9   DISEMBODIED IMAGES: AUTHORS, AUTHORSHIP AND CELEBRITY

1 W.K. Wimsatt, Jr and Monroe C. Beardsley, 'The Intentional Fallacy', in W.K. Wimsatt, Jr, *The Verbal Icon: Studies in the Meaning of Poetry* (Lexington, KY: University of Kentucky Press, 1954), p. 5.
2 Malcolm Bradbury, 'The Telling Life: Thoughts on Literary Biography', in idem, *No, Not Bloomsbury* (London, André Deutsch, 1987), p. 311.
3 Peter Washington, *Fraud: Literary Theory and the End of English* (London: Fontana, 1989), p. 50.
4 Roland Barthes, 'The Death of the Author', in idem, *Image/Music/Text*, ed. and tr. Stephen Heath (London: Fontana, 1977), p. 143.
5 Barthes, 'The Writer on Holiday', p. 29.
6 Michel Foucault, 'What is an Author?', in *Language, Counter-Memory, Practice: Selected Essays and Interviews*, ed. Donald F. Bouchard, tr. Donald F. Bouchard and Sherry Simon (Ithaca, NY: Cornell University Press, 1977), pp. 124–6. Raymond Williams also stresses the clear relationship 'between the idea of an author and the idea of "literary property," notably in the organization of authors to protect their work, by copyright and similar means, within a bourgeois market'. See Raymond Williams, *Marxism and Literature* (Oxford: Oxford University Press, 1977), p. 192.
7 Adorno and Horkheimer, 'The Culture Industry', pp. 154, 161.
8 Walter Benjamin, 'The Work of Art in the Age of Mechanical Reproduction', p. 233.
9 Gaines, *Contested Culture*, p. 212.
10 Celia Lury, *Cultural Rights: Technology, Legality and Personality* (London: Routledge, 1993), pp. 62, 51. See also the essays collected in Martha Woodmansee and Peter Jaszi (eds), *The Construction of Authorship: Textual Appropriation in Law and Literature* (Durham, NC: Duke University Press, 1994) for the ways in which copyright law has been affected by the development of new technologies.
11 Braudy, *The Frenzy of Renown*, p. 8.
12 Stuart Ewen, *All-Consuming Images: Style in Contemporary Culture* (New York: Basic Books, 1988), p. 101.

10   'WHAT IS AN AUTHOR?' CONTEMPORARY PUBLISHING DISCOURSE AND THE AUTHOR FIGURE

1 For a recent discussion of 'Lifestyle and personal consumption' see Celia Lury *Consumer Culture* (Cambridge: Polity Press, 1996).
2 Michel Foucault 'What is an Author?' in *Language, Counter-Memory Practice: Selecetd Essays and Interviews* (ed.) Donald Bouchard, trans. Donald Bouchard and Sherry Simon (Ithaca, NY: Cornell University Press, 1977). First published in 1967.
3 Roland Barthes, 'The Death of the Author' in *Image – Music – Text* trans. and ed. Stephen Heath (London: Fontana, 1977).
4 Foucault 'What is an author' ibid.
5 I will give the name *peritext* to … the zone that exists merely by the fact that the book is published and possibly republished and offered to the public in one or several more or less varied presentations … [it] is basically spatial and material Gerard Genette *Paratexts: Thresholds of Interpretation* trans. Jane E. Lewin (Cambridge: CUP, 1997) pp. 16.

6 The Barnes & Noble shop in Union Square, New York, comprises 67,500 square feet of selling space.

7 The new Waterstone's Piccadilly shop which opened on 14 September 1999, has a café, juice bar, licensed bar, restaurant and an events floor, as well as 'numerous sofas, tables and chairs' and Internet stations.

8 *Ominibus* BBC 2 November 1995.

9 *Independent on Sunday* 12 May 1996. Ayrton also draws attention to the phenomena of the small independent publisher who loses an author to a large conglomerate on the promise of a bigger advance and more substantial promotion budget than the independent could entertain as soon as the author has a publishing success. Whilst this is not a new situation, Ayrton, now regretfully regards his independent houses as being *solely* a 'nursery' for fostering talent which is then 'lost' to the major conglomerate publishers as soon as this talent is recognised by critical review and sales by publishers who are not prepared to make this risky first investment (of money *and* time in the case of new writers) but only come into the market once the author's 'value' is clear.

10 Pierre Bourdieu, 'The Market for Symbolic Goods' in *The Field of Cultural Production* (Cambridge: Polity Press, 1993).

11 Andrew Welham. The *Bookseller*. 25 June 1993 pp. 24–5.

12 This view is somewhat discounted by Penguin who claims a 39 percent 'spontaneous recognition' and a further 53 percent 'prompted recognition,' success rate, followed by Mills & Boon at only 9 percent spontaneous and 75 percent 'prompted' recognition: no other publisher achieved any brand recognition worth building an advertising strategy on. Indeed Vintage which has the ambition of being the 'Penguin of the next century' did not score at all (*The Bookseller* 30 April 1999 p. 40).

13 Lucy Ellman, a two-book novelist contributed a weekly opinion column to the *Independent on Sunday* until axed by the incoming editor before the present one, Rosie Boycott, in 1996.

14 Martin Amis covers Wimbledon, snooker and other sporting events for the *Evening Standard*.

15 Academic, educational and SMT book publishing does use a number of response market research strategies available to a product where the market can be defined as 'for use.'

16 *The Information* was published in paperback at £6.99: it was one of the 18 books listed in the 100 paperback best sellers of 1996 at the same price; 7 were £9.99; 1 was £8.99; 2 were £7.99; 61 were £5.99; 4 were £4.99; 3 were £3.99; one was £1.99 and one – *The Highway Code* in at number four – was 99p (*The Bookseller* 10 January 1997 pp. 24–5).

17 See Christine Restall "A breakthrough in the study of women, *Campaign* 22 November 1985 pp. 26–8.

11   WHO ARE YOU CALLING AN AUTHOR? CHANGING DEFINITIONS OF CAREER LEGITIMACY FOR NOVELISTS IN THE DIGITAL ERA

1 Mark O'Connell, 'Why tweet about your novel?' *New Yorker*, 8 August 2014, accessed 8 August 2014, www.newyorker.com/culture/cultural-comment/working-novel-tweeting-writing.

2 Cory Arcangel, 'Elevator Pitch', accessed 7 October 2014, http://novel.coryarcangel.com.

3 Oscar Rickett, 'Working on My Novel – the art of literary procrastination', *Shortcuts Blog*, 3 August 2014, accessed 7 October 2014, www.theguardian.com/books/shortcuts/2014/aug/03/working-on-my-novel-cory-arcangel-literary-procrastination.

4 Dan Piepenbring, 'Working on My Novel', *The Daily* blog, www.theparisreview.org, 28 July 2014, accessed 7 October 2014, www.theparisreview.org/blog/2014/07/28/working-on-my-novel/.

5 John Thompson, *Merchants of Culture: The publishing business in the twenty-first century.* (Cambridge: Polity, 2012, 2nd edn).

6 Jennifer C. Lena and Danielle J. Lindemann, 'Who is an artist? New data for an old question,' *Poetics* 43 (2014), accessed 28 April 2014, doi 10.1016/j.poetic.2014.01.001.

7 Ailsa Craig, quoted in Lena and Lindemann, 'Who is an artist?'

8 Alison Flood, 'Nobel judge fears for the future of western literature,' *The Guardian*, 7 October 2014, accessed 10 October 2014, www.theguardian.com/books/2014/oct/07/creative-writing-killing-western-literature-nobel-judge-horace-engdahl.

9 Maggie Brown, 'The Fifty Shades effect: Women dominate self-publishing,' *The Observer*, 9 November 2014, accessed 18 November 2014, www.theguardian.com/world/2014/nov/09/fifty-shades-of-grey-women-dominate-self-publishing.

10 Susanne Janssen, 'Side-roads to success: The effect of sideline activities on the status of writers,' *Poetics* 25 (1998): 266–7.

11 Allegre Hadida and Thomas Paris, 'Managerial cognition and the value chain in the digital music industry,' *Technological Forecasting & Social Change*, 83 (2014): 84–97.

12 N. Anand and Brittany C. Jones, 'Tournament Rituals, Category Dynamics, and Field Configuration: The Case of the Booker Prize,' *Journal of Management Studies*, 45(6) (2008): 1036–1060.

13 Steve Coll, 'Citizen Bezos', *New York Review of Books*, 10 July 2014, accessed 17 October 2014, www.nybooks.com/articles/archives/2014/jul/10/citizen-bezos-amazon/.

14 Coll, 'Citzen Bezos'.

15 Anand and Jones, 'Tournament Rituals', 76.

16 Michel Foucault, 'What Is an Author?', in *Language, Counter-Memory, Practice,* trans. Donald F. Bouchard and Sherry Simon (Oxford: Basil Blackwell, 1977), 118.

17 Thompson, *Merchants of Culture.*

18 Ann Patchett, *This is the Story of a Happy Marriage* (New York: HarperTorch, 2013), 153.

19 Payments to one's publisher are, of course, not at all unusual for authors working with academic presses; the Hydra uproar underscores how differently trade and academic publishing recognise and reward authorial contributions.

20 Richard Lea, 'Random House accused of '"predatory" contracts for new e-book imprint.' *theguardian.com*, 8 March 2013, accessed 25 October 2013, www.theguardian.com/books/2013/mar/08/random-house-contracts-new-ebook-imprint.

21 The Board of the Science Fiction and Fantasy Writers of America, 'SFWA Response to Hydra Letter,' last modified 8 March 2013, www.sfwa.org/2013/03/sfwa-response-to-hydra-letter/.

22 The Board of the Science Fiction and Fantasy Writers of America, 'SFWA Response to Hydra Letter.'

23 'Frequently Asked Questions', Hydra, Penguin Random House, accessed 17 November 2014, www.readhydra.com/.

24 Laura Dietz, Claire Warwick and Samantha Rayner, 'Auditioning for permanence: Reputation and legitimacy of electronically distributed novels,' *Logos*, 26(4) (2015): 22–36.

25 Thompson, *Merchants of Culture.*

26 Lisa Campbell, 'E-book purchases "up 20% in 2013"', *The Bookseller*, 19 March 2014, accessed 6 May 2014, www.thebookseller.com/news/e-book-purchases-20-2013.html.

27 Digital Book World, 'How Much Money the Biggest Publishers Actually Make,' last modified 16 June 2014, www.digitalbookworld.com/2014/how-much-money-the-biggest-publishers-actually-make/.

28 *From Papyrus to Pixels*, (London: The Economist, 2014), 7.

29 Claire Squires, *Marketing Literature: the Making of Contemporary Writing in Britain*, 2nd ed. (Basingstoke: Palgrave Macmillan, 2009).

30 Thompson, *Merchants of Culture*, 87.

31 Sarah Robbins, 'The Go-To Book Bloggers', *Publisher's Weekly*, May 16, 2014, accessed 11 November 2014, www.publishersweekly.com/pw/print/20140519/62334-the-go-to-book-bloggers.html.

32 Maria Bustillos, 'Jonathan Franzen, come join us!' *Page Turner blog*, 18 September 2013, accessed 25 October 2013, www.newyorker.com/online/blogs/books/2013/09/jonathan-franzen-come-join-us.html.

12　RECONFIGURING THE AUTHOR

1 For a discussion of to what degree hypermedia in both read-only and read-write forms does or does not empower readers, see Landow (2004: 321–376).

2 Marie-Laure Ryan makes some properly forceful observations about extreme claims that hypertext makes readers into writers: 'To the skeptical observer, the accession of the reader to the role of writer ... is a self-serving metaphor that presents hypertext as a magic elixir: "Read me, and you will receive the gift of literary creativity." If taken literally – but who really does so? – the idea would reduce writing to summoning words to the screen though an activity as one, two, three, click ... Call this writing if you wish; but if working one's way through the maze of an interactive text is suddenly called writing, we will need a new word for retrieving words from one's mind to encode meanings' (9). The context of this astute warning makes clear that Ryan mistakenly includes me among critics who believe in the complete merging of reader and writer. As the complete sentence she quotes makes clear, the phrase she emphasizes with italics – '*of ourselves* as authors' – refers to the way linking changes the author's conception of his or her power and authority. In fact, the sentence implies a distinction between readers and authors.

3 See the final sections of chapter 8 for a discussion of the political implications of open hypermedia applications for the Web.

4 Lévi-Strauss's observation in a note on the same page of *The Raw and the Cooked* (12) that 'the Ojibiwa Indians consider myths as "conscious beings, with powers of thought and action"' has some interesting parallels to remarks by Pagels on the subject of quasi-animate portions of neural nets: 'Networks don't quite so much compute a solution as they settle into it, much as we subjectively experience our own problem solving ... There could be subsystems within supersystems – a hierarchy of information and command, resembling nothing so much as human society itself. In this image the neuron in the brain is like an individual in society. What we experience as consciousness is the 'social consciousness' of our neuronal network' (126, 224).

5 Lévi-Strauss also employs this model for societies as a whole: 'Our society, a particular instance in a much vaster family of societies, depends, like all others, for its coherence and its very existence on a network – grown infinitely unstable and complicated among us – of ties between consanguineal families' (*Scope of Anthropology*, 33).

6 Said in fact prefaces this remark by the evasive phrase, 'it is quite possible to argue,' and since he nowhere qualifies the statement that follows, I take it as a claim, no matter how nervous or half-hearted.

7 I originally wrote in 1991 that Heim would be correct only 'in some bizarrely inefficient dystopic future sense – 'future' because today [1991] few people writing with word processors participate very frequently in the lesser versions of such information networks that already exist, and "bizarrely inefficient" because one would have to assume that the billions and billions of words we would write would all have equal ability to clutter the major resource that such networks will be.' The reason for Heim's prescience comes, as we shall observe in chapter 8, from the new technologies of Internet surveillance, web browser cookies, Google-like search tools, and data mining.

8 An example of the way changes in an author's beliefs weaken the value of the author function – the traditional conception of the unitary author – appears in the works of Thomas Carlyle: whereas in *The French Revolution* he clearly accepts the necessity of violence and sympathizes with lower classes, he became increasingly reactionary and racist in his later works. In arguing for the unity of any particular Carlylean text one cannot casually refer to "Carlyle" unless one specifies to which Carlyle one refers.

13   THE BOOK MARKET

1 Whereas a German publisher only spends 3 per cent to 4 per cent of the *cost of production* on advertising, the English publisher spends about 6 per cent of his *turnover* in advertisement, while the American publisher George H. Doran claims to spend 10 per cent of his *gross income* on 'promotion'. This information, obtained from the article 'Publishing' in the *Ency. Brit.* (14th ed.), of course proves nothing, but it does suggest the general proposition that the more cultured a country the less its publishers would have to spend in forcing books on the public attention.

2 A really popular-at-all-levels novel like *The Constant Nymph*, which was the book of the year 1924–5, has only sold a million copies, and those largely in the 6d. Readers' Library edition.

3 These figures are taken from the Report on Public Libraries (1927). It has been suggested to me by an eminent and experienced public librarian that the relative percentages of fiction and non-fiction would be even more disproportionate were it not that librarians, actuated presumably by local patriotism, endeavour to equalize matters by transferring such sections as 'Juvenile Fiction' and 'Classical Novels' over to the non-fiction classifications.

4 The head of a big public library (and in a University town), when asked why there were no novels by D. H. Lawrence on the shelves, replied indignantly: 'I've always tried to keep this library *clean*.'

5 Arthur Waugh, *A Hundred Years of Publishing* (1930), says there are 340 branches of Boots' Library, with a quarter of a million subscribers.

6 When these libraries sell off their out-of-date stock several times a year, the novels are generally worn and shabby, while the other books are 'good as new'.

7 A random instance from *The Times* (24 June 1930): 'In honour of the centenary of the French Romantic movement, the western facade of Notre Dame was brilliantly illuminated by flood-lighting on Sunday evening.' The English general public has never heard of the English Romantic movement, and the governing classes who possibly have would not in any case think of taking up a serious attitude to it. Cf. too the space given in any French newspaper to the death of a man of letters and a purely literary event with the absence of such an interest in England. Also the two main features of English journalism, the Sunday paper and the large-circulation newspaper, are both unknown in France. In contrast to the responsible interest in literature so evident in the French Press, the attention paid by the English journalist to the recent appointment of a Poet

Laureate is significant. The announcement was made on a Saturday, and an inspection of the next day's newspapers showed that not one of the popular Sunday organs thought the news worth mentioning (one published a photograph of the new Laureate without comment), though the appointment was what might be called a popular one. This is what is meant by the assertion on p. 53 that poetry is no longer read.

8 Taken as common to a majority of the following: a flourishing shop in the centre of a market town, a back-street 'paper-shop', the contents of the periodicals rack in a Boots' store, a W. H. Smith shop, a suburban newsagent's.

9 A foreigner's opinion of the English Press is illuminating. The intelligent and open-minded Dibelius (*England*, Cape, 1930) comments on the superior appearance and good workmanship of English newspapers, and concludes: 'In this respect the English standard is very high indeed, certainly higher than the German. But a different picture is given by a comparison of the contents of the newspapers of the two countries. While, in this respect, the better-class English newspaper, like the *Morning Post*, *Manchester Guardian*, or *Daily Chronicle* [now defunct], certainly does not give its readers any more than the *Deutsche Allgemeine*, *Vossische*, the *Frankfurter Zeitung* or *Hamburger Fremdenblatt*, the great mass of English newspapers, even in the metropolis, are incredibly thin and empty. Most of them, in sharp contrast to the half-dozen or so papers with an international reputation, have practically no foreign news, little or no literary or general information, and no magazine page; they are made up of leaders, telegrams, local gossip, and a mass of sporting news. In the provinces, there is the *Scotsman* and *Glasgow Herald* in Scotland, and, in the industrial areas, the *Birmingham Daily Post*, *Liverpool Daily Post*, the *Yorkshire Post*, and the admirable *Manchester Guardian*; but outside this half-dozen there is an almost unbelievable dullness. No one who has not been condemned to read a local sheet of that sort regularly can understand the empty chatter that does duty as the average play or the popular novel ...'

10 In the *Advertiser's ABC* it describes itself in these terms: 'JOHN O' LONDON'S WEEKLY has unique powers of appeal. It is not a paper only for women or only for men; it is a paper for both; for the whole family, and it is calculated to make a direct appeal to clear-thinking people of educated tastes and a discriminating standard of comfort.'

11 The scope of these is best suggested by their own advertisements in the *Advertiser's ABC* (1929): 'It exists to remind its readers that life is not all work and worry; that there is a more leisurely, laughing side which contributes so much to make it worth living. The Editorial policy of the TATLER embraces all the lighter interests of the well-to-do Englishman – Sport, Society, Motoring, Art, the Theatre. It is found in every club and regimental mess, in every private house of substance in every doctor's waiting-room, hotel lounge.' 'The SPHERE is representative of all that is best in English life. The SPHERE is read by the very rich, the moderately rich; and by the ordinary well-to-do folk of intelligence and culture throughout the Empire. It is the Empire's Illustrated Weekly Journal, and is to be found, not only in club-rooms, hotels and libraries, but in the homes of the best people throughout the English-speaking world.' 'The SKETCH was the first expression of an entirely new idea in British Illustrated Journalism. Before its appearance, in 1893, illustrated newspapers devoted themselves almost exclusively to the more serious of current happenings ... It sets itself to provide cheery entertainment for the smoking-room and boudoir, and to illustrate the subjects most commonly discussed when men and women meet after the serious business of the day is done. Its instant and signal success is a matter of history. Inevitably it had many imitators', etc.

12 It may be useful to point out here that there is no reason for supposing that novelettes are bought exclusively by the uneducated and the poor. A list kindly made for me of the private reading-matter in a high-class cramming establishment states that the young

men own all the varieties of film and detective-story magazine mentioned above, 3s. 6d. and 7s. 6d. novels by Rider Haggard, Baroness Orczy, John Buchan, Edgar Wallace, Freeman Wills Crofts, and also, 'There are a great number of 9d. and 1s. paper novels circulating among them, most of them by Edgar Wallace and Oppenheim.'

13 The writer has vainly tried to buy the *Nation and Athenaeum*, *New Statesman*, and *Times Literary Supplement* all over south-western England, and obtained them only (but not invariably) at the bookstalls at big railway junctions. The newsagents in many cases showed no knowledge of the names even. It is worth remembering that in France there are at least three serious literary weekly *newspapers* (i.e. literary journals in newspaper form which review intelligently all the notable poetry and criticism that appears as well as lighter works, and have leading articles on literary movements by distinguished writers), and they can all be bought in the ordinary way in the little provincial towns (and are usually sold out on the day of issue).

14 For illustration see *Is Advertising Today a Burden or a Boon?* (The New Advertiser's Press, 1930).

15 On the contrary, for before the war Messrs Nelson published pocket editions of the classics and good copyright novels (e.g. Jane Austen, George Eliot, Thackeray, the Brontës, in Nelson's Classics, the early Wells, and Henry James and Conrad, in Nelson's Library) at 6d. and 7d. each, that really were well printed and bound.

16 The Manager of the Readers' Library Publishing Co. Ltd, when requested to put the writer into communication with the editor of the series, regretted that he was unable to do so or to furnish any information, so that not only the identity of the distinguished man of letters, but also the principle on which he chooses the volumes for publication, must remain a dark secret.

17 'Edgar Wallace, although so immensely successful in his own line of work, is too modest a man to claim that the mystery story necessarily belongs to the highest form of literature, although some of its examples are assuredly among the best.' – From the introduction to *The Melody of Death*, 'the first book by Edgar Wallace that the READERS' LIBRARY has had the honour to publish.' (1927.)

18 It is interesting to notice that Woolworth fiction has revived 'best sellers' of the last generation with considerable success: Garvice and Hocking appear to sell nearly as well as P. C. Wren and Edgar Wallace.

14   A PUBLISHER LOOKS AT BOOKSELLERS

1 The 'see safe' method – which means that the bookseller buys the books but may return them if he cannot sell them. The 'on sale or return' method – which means that there is no formal sale, until the bookseller returns the unsold copies.

2 The reader should note that the use of terms like 'mob', 'masses', 'herd', is relative. In the book-world the masses consist of a few score of thousands. The proletariat is almost wholly outside it.

15   THE SCANDAL OF THE MIDDLEBROW: THE PROFESSIONAL-MANAGERIAL CLASS AND THE EXERCISE OF AUTHORITY IN THE LITERARY FIELD

1 Strasser, *Satisfaction Guaranteed*, 43.

2 For a discussion of the unevenness of both economic and cultural change, see Raymond Williams's exploration of the operation of dominant, residual, and emergent forms in

Marxism and Literature, 121–27. I prefer Williams's formulation of this set of relationships to the revision of them developed by Terry Eagleton in *Criticism and Ideology*, even though I have appropriated his term 'the literary mode of production' here. Eagleton, it seems to me, posits too mechanical a relationship between economy, cultural production, and ideology despite his explicit desire to avoid a kind of Marxist functionalism. Still, in using Williams's terminology it is important not to give the connotations of progress to emerging modes of production or to think of residual modes as simply retrograde and therefore conservative.

3 I have used the gendered pronoun advisedly here because, like Jane Gaines, Sandra Gilbert, Susan Gubar, Jane Tompkins, Nancy Miller, and many other feminists, I believe the ideology of the writer as literary genius was profoundly gendered. That is to say, writing was analogized as a kind of fathering of the work by means of the phallic pen. This ideology thus excluded the possibility that women might produce as authors. Consequently, writing women were represented as 'lady amateurs,' as 'scribbling women,' and as mere 'local colorists.'

4 In *Marxism and Literature* Williams defines the residual as that which has 'been effectively formed in the past, but is still active in the cultural process, not only and often not at all as an element of the past, but as an effective element of the present.' He notes further that 'thus, certain experiences, meanings and values which cannot be expressed or substantially verified in terms of the dominant culture, are nevertheless lived and practiced on the basis of the residue – cultural as well as social – of some previous social and cultural institution or formation.' See his argument, pp. 121–27.

5 As Bourdieu argues, 'Given that works of art exist as symbolic objects only if they are known and recognized, that is, socially instituted as works of art and received by spectators capable of knowing and recognizing them as such, the sociology of art and literature has to take as its object not only the material production but also the symbolic production of the work, i.e. the production of the value of the work or, which amounts to the same thing, belief in the value of the work' ('The Field of Cultural Production,' in *Field of Cultural Production*, 37).

16 HOW THE BRITISH READ

1 Sutherland, *Fiction and the Fiction Industry*, p. x.
2 Ibid., p. xi.
3 Michael Grant, *Penguin's Progress* (Harmondsworth: Penguin, 1960), p. 20.

17 THE CENSOR'S NEW CLOTHES

1 My definition of censorship is an extension of the *OED* definition. I approach the analysis of censorship from a sociological perspective. Consequently my definition of the term is much broader than definitions which have currency in Liberal free-speech theory. Where free-speech theory is concerned with the formal logic of legal protections of speech rights, I am concerned with analyzing the socio-logics which actually operate in organizing and sustaining real human communities and communications. My definition of the term encompasses all socially structured proscriptions or prescriptions which inhibit or prohibit dissemination of ideas, information, images, and other messages through a society's channels of communication whether these obstructions are secured by political, economic, religious, or other systems of authority. It includes both overt and covert proscriptions and prescriptions.

As a result of this sociological focus, my analyses of censorships in Liberal societies seek to raise consciousness about the form of censorship the Liberal model fails to
address, specifically material or market censorship. Where free-speech theory is concerned about Skokie Nazis, Lyndon La Rouche, and other causes brought to the attention of the American Civil Liberties Union and the courts, I am more interested in the
socially structured silences of political capitalism which almost never receive sustained
public attention but nevertheless render some ideas and their authors un-publishable.
Although the priorities of the ACLU are not my priorities, I do not dispute the legitimacy of Liberal concerns. While I think debates about the kinds of conundrums in
free-speech theory which put Skokie Nazis in the headlines often deflect public attention away from more common and pervasive forms of censorship operating in American
society, I nevertheless believe these debates should continue. I believe that Liberal free-
speech theory has a significant role to play in preserving civil liberties in America. I do
not seek to repeal these liberties but to extend or amend them to include all the people.
To this end, I have cut a far wider theoretical path than do researchers working within
the paradigms of Liberal free-speech theory.

2 Dallas W. Smythe, *Dependency Road: Communications, Capitalism, Consciousness, and
Canada* (Norwood, NJ: Ablex, 1981), 235.

3 There are, of course, the exceptions which Liberals are always eager to celebrate as *proofs*
of press freedom. The hegemonic effect noted by Marxists is not complete. For a perceptive discussion of dialectical counter-currents in capitalist mass media, from a socialist
perspective, see Hans Magnus Enzensberger, *The Consciousness Industry* (New York:
Seabury, 1974).

4 From the perspective of a theory of power-knowledge which recognizes the ubiquity
of constituent censorship in the formation and maintenance of human communities,
repression of Marxist-Leninism (especially Stalinism) within Liberal societies is analo-
gous to suppression of the early Christians by the Romans. Both Marxist-Leninism and
Christianity are monolithic thought systems which are incompatible with the heterodox
assumptions of classic nineteenth-century Liberalism and the polytheistic assumptions
of Roman paganism.

5 Baudelaire quoted by Elemire Zolla in *The Eclipse of the Intellectual* (New York: Funk and
Wagnalls, 1968), 22. For an examination of the politics of the romantic protest, see
Alvin W. Gouldner, 'Romanticism and Classicism: Deep Structures in Social Science,' in
For Sociology (New York: Basic Books, 1973). Nevertheless Baudelaire's protest against
the domination of matter does anticipate to some extent later critiques of the reification
of thought and desire by Lukacs and members of the Frankfurt School.

6 In *Clarel*, Melville laments the plight of humankind in industrial society:

Debased into equality:

In glut of all material arts

A civic barbarism may be:

Man disenobled—brutalized

By popular science—Atheized

Into a smatterer—

For discussion and exemplification of the mass culture/high culture debate, see relevant entries in *Mass Culture: The Popular Arts in America*, edited by Bernard Rosenberg
and David M. White (Glencoe: Free Press, 1957); and *Culture for the Millions*, edited
by Norman Jacobs (Princeton, NJ: Van Nostrand, 1961). See also Herbert Gans's

neo-Liberal defense of pluralism, *Popular Culture and High Culture* (New York: Basic Books, 1974). In contrast to these Liberal critical traditions, 'Critical' theorists have embraced terms like 'the culture industry' (Adorno) and 'the consciousness industry' (Enzensberger) to focus attention on the social contexts of mass production in the cultural area. Although there are also elitist elements in 'Critical' theory, the focus on the social organization of production avoids the blaming-the-victim convention of much corporate-funded communications' 'effects' research.

7 Bakhtin maintains that, 'It can be said, with some restrictions to be sure, that medieval man in a way led *two Lives*: one *official*, monolithically serious and somber; beholden to strict hierarchical order; filled with fear, dogmatism, devotion, and piety; the other, of *carnival* and the *public place*, free; full of ambivalent laughter, sacrileges, profanations of all things sacred, disparagement and unseemly behavior, familiar contact with everybody and everything.' Mikhail Bakhtin, quoted by Tzvetan Todorov in *Mikhail Bakhtin: The Dialogical Principle*. Translated by Wlad Godzich (Minneapolis: University of Minnesota Press, 1984), 78.

Synthetic production of popular culture permits the controllers of culture selectively to mirror and cultivate ideas. It takes some of the ideas and values that circulate among the people, ascribes legitimacy to these ideas and values, then projects them back to the people as their culture. Laughter and cynicism are permitted to go as far as is required to maintain the credibility of the controllers, but they never seriously challenge the system of control. The dog barks but it does not bite.

8 David W. Ewing, *Freedom inside the Organization: Bringing Civil Liberties to the Workplace* (New York: E. P. Dutton, 1977), 3. Presidential directives enacted during the first term of the Reagan Administration subsequently expanded and tightened controls over publications by government employees and former employees. Ewing analyzes formal rights of employees. A large body of sociological research examines both formal and informal constraints on worker autonomy. See, for example, the following standard works in organizational sociology: Alvin Gouldner, *Patterns of industrial Bureaucracy* (New York: Free Press, 1954); C. Wright Mills, *White Collar* (New York: Oxford University Press, 1951); and Charles Perrow, *Organizational Analysis: A Sociological View* (Monterey: Brooks-Cole, 1970). Also see Harry Braverman's *Labor and Monopoly Capital: The Degradation of Work in the Twentieth Century* (New York: Monthly Review Press, 1974) and Michael Burawoy's *Manufacturing Consent: Changes in the Labor Process under Monopoly Capitalism* (Chicago: University of Chicago Press, 1979). These researches indicate that organizational freedom, like income, is distributed hierarchically, with workers in professional and managerial positions generally exercising greater control over the work process than workers who are paid an hourly wage. Marx, of course, presented the classic analysis of the alienation of labor, and members of the nineteenth-century labor movements in Europe and America saw their revolt as a revolt against 'wage slavery.' Contra Marx, Emile Durkheim and his followers saw professionalism as the answer to the alienation of industrial societies. They believed that the autonomy of the professions could serve as anchors for a pluralism which would restrain the excesses of capitalism. See Durkheim's *The Division of Labor in Society* (Glencoe: Free Press, 1947). Recent empirical studies suggest that the 'managerial revolution' is now extending its reach into the professions and reducing or eliminating the autonomy of professionals in such fields as health care and higher education. For an excellent analysis of the corporate restructuring of health care, see Paul Starr, *The Social Transformation of American Medicine* (New York: Basic Books, 1982). For discussion of the managerial revolution in higher education, see Jake Ryan and Charles Sackrey's analytic essays in their jointly authored *Strangers in Paradise: Academics from the Working Class* (Boston: South End Press, 1984).

9 Thorstein Veblen, *The Higher Learning in America* (New York: B. W. Huebsch, 1918).

10 Freud, quoted by Eric Rhode in 'The Outline of a Couch,' *Times Literary Supplement* (London), Nov. 24, 1978, p. 1355.

11 Eli M. Oboler, *The Fear of the Word: Censorship and Sex* (Metuchen, NJ: Scarecrow Press, 1974), 60–62.

12 E. P. Thompson, 'Time, Work-Discipline, and Industrial Capitalism,' *Past and Present* 38 (Dec. 1967), 59–97. Thompson's ideas are provocatively applied to American social history by Stuart Ewen in *Captains of Consciousness* (New York: McGraw-Hill, 1976).

13 Richard Sennett, 'Our Hearts Belong to Daddy,' *New York Review of Books* XXVII (May 1, 1980), 32.

14 See John Cheever, *Falconer* (New York: Knopf, 1977); and Michel Foucault, *Discipline and Punish: The Birth of the Prison* (New York: Pantheon, 1977).

15 George Gerbner, 'Television: The New State Religion?,' *Et Cetera* (June 1977), 147.

16 Herbert I Schiller, *Who Knows: Information in the Age of the Fortune 500* (Norwood, NJ: Ablex, 1981).

17 Georg Lukacs, *History and Class Consciousness* (Cambridge, MA: MIT Press, 1971).

18   PUBLISHERS AS GATEKEEPERS OF IDEAS

1 Kurt Lewin, *Field Theory in the Social Sciences* (New York: Harper and Row, 1951), pp. 186–187.

2 *See*, Lewis Coser, *Men of Ideas* (New York: Free Press, 1965).

3 Even though this article deals with only one of the many institutions that serve gatekeeper functions, it needs to be pointed out in passing that large numbers of lay members of a society also serve to varying degrees as gatekeepers of ideas. When people congregate to exchange ideas, to gossip or to discuss the events of the day, they continually contribute to the molding of public opinion. That opinion is a most potent determinant of receptivity, or lack thereof, for new ideas or new intellectual products. While in modern democratic societies public opinion is shaped, at least in principle, by all citizens (though often guided by a few), in older aristocratic cultures only the educated strata, the first and the second estates, served as molders of opinion, the bulk of the population being relegated to purely consummatory functions in the realm of culture. Cf. Juergen Habermas, *Strukturwandel der Oeffentlichkeit* (Neuwied: Luchterhand, 1962); and Karl Mannheim, *Man and Society in an Age of Reconstruction* (London: Routledge and Kegan Paul, 1940).

4 Victor S. Navasky, 'In Cold Print: Selling Out and Buying In,' *New York Times Book Review*, 20 May 1973, p. 2.

5 Paul M. Hirsch, 'Processing Fads and Fashions: An Organization-Set Analysis of Cultural Industry Systems,' *American Journal of Sociology* 77, no. 4 (1971), p. 652.

6 An anecdote from the movie industry seems pertinent: A movie producer was recently reported as saying that he had five movies in production that year, and one of them would make $10 million. When asked, 'Which one?' he shrugged his shoulders and said, 'That's the only thing I cannot predict.'

7 Arthur L. Stinchcombe, 'Bureaucratic and Craft Administration of Production: A Comparative Study,' *Administrative Science Quarterly* 4 (September 1959), pp. 168–187; and Hirsch, 'Processing Fads,' p. 644.

8 Hirsch, 'Processing Fads,' p. 644. For some recent reverse trends, *see*, Victor S. Navasky, 'In Cold Print: What Is an Editor Worth?' *New York Times Book Review*, 15 April 1973, p. 2.

9 *See*, among others, Robert W. Frase, 'The Economics of Publishing,' in *Trends in American Publishing*, ed. Kathryn Henderson (Urbana, Illinois: Graduate School of Library Science, University of Illinois, 1968); William Miller, *The Book Industry* (New York: Columbia University Press, 1949); Morris Philipson, 'What Is a University Press Worth?' *Encounter* 40 (May 1973), pp. 41–49; Herbert Addison, 'Books and Bucks: The Economics of College Textbook Publishing,' *College Composition* (October 1972), pp. 287–291.

10 *See*, Philipson, 'University Press;' and 'An Interview with Morris Philipson,' *Chicago Literary Review* 2, no. 2 (8 February 1974).

11 *See*, Linda Kuehl, 'Talk with James Laughlin,' *New York Times Book Review*, 25 February 1973; and Linda Kuehl, 'Talk with Mr. Knopf,' *New York Times Book Review*, 24 February 1974.

12 Victor S. Navasky, 'In Cold Print: When Is a Book Dead on Arrival?' *New York Times Book Review*, 21 April 1974.

13 Navasky, 'What Is an Editor Worth?'

14 *See*, Edward Shils, 'Center and Periphery,' in *The Logic of Personal Knowledge: Essays Presented to Michael Polanyi* (London: Routledge and Kegan Paul, 1961), pp. 117–131.

15 *See*, Bruce Bliven, Jr., 'Book Traveller,' *New Yorker* (12 November 1973), pp. 51ff.; and Victor S. Navasky, 'In Cold Print: When Editors and Salesmen Meet,' *New York Times Book Review*, 20 January 1974.

16 Hirsch, 'Processing Fads,' p. 648.

17 Navasky, 'When Is a Book Dead on Arrival?'

18 *See*, Ted Morgan, 'The Making of a Best Seller: Sharks,' *New York Times Magazine*, 21 April 1974, pp. 10–11, 85–96.

19 Philipson, 'University Press.'

20 Hirsch, 'Processing Fads,' p. 652.

21 On authors' discontents, *see*, *New York Times*, 27 November 1972, p. 30.

22 Karl Mannheim, 'The Problem of the Intelligentsia,' in *Essays on the Sociology of Culture*, pt. 2, ed. Ernest Mannheim (London: Routledge and Kegan Paul, 1956).

23 Max Scheler, *Die Wissensformen und die Gesellschaft*, 2nd ed. (Bern and Munich: Francke Verlag, 1960).

24 Florian Znaniecki, *The Social Role of the Man of Knowledge*, with a new introduction by Lewis A. Coser (New York: Harper Torchbooks, 1968).

25 Theodor Geiger, *Aufgaben und Stellung der Intelligenz in der Gesellschaft* (Stuttgart: Ferninand Enke, 1949).

26 Cf. Coser, *Men of Ideas*. For a very fine example of contextual analysis, *see*, Allan Janik and Steven Toulmin, *Wittgenstein's Vienna* (New York: Simon and Schuster, 1973).

27 *See*, however, Robert Escarpit, *The Book Revolution* (London: George Harrap, 1966).

28 For example, David T. Pottinger, *The French Book Trade in the Ancient Regime* (Cambridge, MA: Harvard University Press, 1958).

20 COMBATING CENSORSHIP AND MAKING SPACE FOR BOOKS

1 For a list of political prisoners and activists mentioned in this chapter, see the appendix.

2 Ronnie Kasrils, *Armed and Dangerous: From Undercover Struggle to Freedom* (Johannesburg: Jonathan Ball, 1998), 57–8.

3 Ronnie Kasrils, *The Unlikely Secret Agent* (Auckland Park: Jacana, 2010), 64.

4 Personal interview with Denis Goldberg, 5 March 2003.

5 'Human Rights Commission, Violence in Detention,' in B. McKendrick and W. Hoffmann, eds., *People and Violence in South Africa* (Cape Town: Oxford University

Press, 1990), 410–13; M. Coleman, ed., *A Crime against Humanity: Analyzing the Repression of the Apartheid State* (Cape Town: David Philip, 1998), 43–67.

6 J. Schadeberg, *Voices from Robben Island* (Randburg: Ravan Press, 1994), 48.

7 '18 000 Pages of Documents in Treason Trial,' in *Treason Trial, 1957–1961: Newspaper Clippings; Scrapbook ex libris the Presiding Judge, F.L.H. Rumpf* (Body and Mind Foundation, 1997), unnumbered.

8 Records relating to the 'Treason Trial,' File AD1812, Historical Papers, University of the Witwatersrand. For a detailed record, see Thomas Karis, *The Treason Trial in South Africa: A Guide to the Microfilm Record of the Trial* (Stanford: Hoover Institute, Stanford University, 1965).

9 Lionel Forman, 'You Can Hang for Treason,' in Sadie Forman and André Odendaal, eds., *A Trumpet from the Housetops: The Selected Writings of Lionel Forman* (London: Zed Books, 1992), 100–1.

10 A.M. du Preez Bezdrop, *Winnie Mandela: A Life* (Cape Town: Zebra; London: New Holland, 2003), 138.

11 J. Slovo, *Slovo: The Unfinished Autobiography*, with an introduction by H. Dolny (London: Hodder and Stoughton, 1996), 120.

12 Freda Matthews, *Remembrances* (Bellville: Mayibuye Books, 1995), 57.

13 Albie Sachs, *The Jail Diary of Albie Sachs* (Cape Town: David Philip, 1990), 175.

14 Quentin Jacobsen, *Solitary in Johannesburg* (London: Michael Joseph, 1973), 8–13.

15 Jean Middleton, *Convictions: A Woman Political Prisoner Remembers* (Randburg: Ravan Press, 1998), 68.

16 Zubeida Jaffer, *Our Generation* (Cape Town: Kwela Books, 2003), 131.

17 Carl Niehaus (re: possession of banned publications, 1982), File AK2532, Historical Papers, University of the Witwatersrand Library, Johannesburg, 1.

18 The Congress of the People was organized by the Congress Alliance, led by the African National Congress, and adopted the *Freedom Charter* at Kliptown on 26 and 27 June 1955. Jacob Brits, ed., *The Penguin Concise Dictionary of Historical and Political Terms* (London: Penguin Books, 1995), 55.

19 Helen Joseph, *If This Be Treason: Helen Joseph's Dramatic Account of the Treason Trial, 1956–1961* (Johannesburg: Contra, 1998), 47.

20 Forman and Odendaal, *A Trumpet from the Housetops*, 108.

21 Lionel Forman, *The South African Treason Trial* (London: Calder, 1957); Joseph, *If This Be Treason*, 17.

22 M. Resha, *Mangoana Tsoara Thipa Ka Bohaleng–My Life in the Struggle* (Johannesburg: COSAW, 1991), 187.

23 Jacobsen, *Solitary in Johannesburg*, 244.

24 Tom Lodge and Bill Nasson, *All Here, and Now: Black Politics in South Africa in the 1980s* (Cape Town: Ford Foundation; David Philip, 1991), 307.

25 Interview with Omar Badsha, 11 October 2008.

26 Jacobsen, *Solitary in Johannesburg*, 164.

27 R.D. Vassen, *Letters from Robben Island: A Selection of Ahmed Kathrada's Prison Correspondence, 1964–1989* (East Lansing: Michigan State University Press, 1999), 14.

28 This did not change in Section 6 of the Terrorism Act, which was in effect from June 1967 to July 1982. The Internal Security Act's Section 29, which replaced it, differed very little and detainees remained incommunicado.

29 Ben Turok, *Nothing but the Truth: Behind the ANC's Struggle Politics* (Johannesburg and Cape Town: Jonathan Ball, 2003), 150; P.A. Kgosana, *Lest We Forget: An Autobiography by Philip Ata Kgosana* (Johannesburg: Skotaville, 1988), 38.

30 F. Desai and C. Marney, *The Killing of the Imam* (London: Quartet Books, 1978), 125.

31 F. Meer, *Prison Diary: One Hundred and Thirteen Days, 1976* (Cape Town: Kwela Books, 2001), 33.

32 Vassen, *Letters from Robben Island*, 182.

33 Jaffer, *Our Generation*, 133–5.

34 F. Bookholane, 'Six Years Inside,' in D.E.H. Russell, ed., *Lives of Courage: Women for a New South Africa* (London: Basic Books, 1989), 61–2.

35 M.S. Mogoba, *Stone, Steel, Sjambok: Faith on Robben Island*, ed. T. Coggin (Johannesburg: Ziningweni Communications, 2003), 48.

36 Frank Chikane, *No Life of My Own: An Autobiography* (London: Catholic Institute for International Relations, 1988), 56.

37 T.S. Farisani, *Diary from a South African Prison*, ed. J.A. Evenson (Philadelphia: Fortress Press, 1987), 22, 49, 60.

38 M. Dingake, *My Fight against Apartheid* (London: Kliptown Books, 1987), 114.

39 E. Mashinini, *Strikes Have Followed Me All My Life: A South African Autobiography* (London: Women's Press, 1989), 54, 82, 84.

40 Raymond Suttner, *Inside Apartheid's Prison: Notes and Letters of Struggle* (Pietermaritzburg: University of Natal Press, 2001), 26.

41 Sachs, *The Jail Diary*, 64. This applied also to other books read in detention. When Ruth First was allowed a book of crossword puzzles she restricted herself to one puzzle per day. Ruth First, *117 Days: An Account of Confinement and Interrogation under the South African Ninety-Day Detention Law* (London: Bloomsbury, 1988), 129. Ellen Kuzwayo and her fellow inmates limited their time spent on a book in order to give 'each other the opportunity to read it too.' Ellen Kuzwayo, *Call Me Woman* (Johannesburg: Ravan Press, 1985), 211.

42 James Kantor, *A Healthy Grave* (London: Hamish Hamilton, 1967), 46.

43 Farisani, *Diary from a South African Prison*, 22; S. Jobson, 'Diary of Recent Events,' in B. Schreiner, *A Snake with Ice Water: Prison Writings by South African Women* (Johannesburg: COSAW, 1992), 174; G. ffrench-Beytagh, *Encountering Darkness* (London: Collins, 1973), 269.

44 Neville Alexander, in B. Hutton, ed., *Robben Island: Symbol of Resistance* (Johannesburg: Sached and Mayibuye Books, 1994), 69; Rusty Bernstein, *Memory against Forgetting: Memoirs from a Life in South African Politics, 1938–1964* (London: Viking, 1999), 267, footnote 2.

45 *Raymond Mhlaba's Personal Memoirs: Reminiscing from Rwanda and Uganda*, narrated to T. Mufamadi (Pretoria: Human Sciences Research Council and Robben Island: Robben Island Museum, 2001), 132; du Preez Bezdrop, *Winnie Mandela: A Life*, 150.

46 J. Matakata, *Hills of Hope: The Autobiography of Jama Matakata* (Pietermaritzburgh: Nutrend, 2004), 59.

47 H. Strachan, *Make a Skyf Man!* (Johannesburg: Jacana, 2004), 105. Some male political prisoners did order magazines like *Vogue* and *Women's Own* to deal with the sex drive and relations with women. T. Jenkin, *Inside Out: Escape from Pretoria Prison* (Bellevue: Jacana, 2003), 239.

48 *Island in Chains–Prisoner 885/63: Ten Years on Robben Island As Told by Indres Naidoo to Albie Sachs* (London: Penguin Books, 1982), 53. A *zoll* is South African slang for a hand-rolled cigarette.

49 Government Gazette Extraordinary No. 1326, 31 December 1965. Library facilities and reading privileges at South African prisons preceded the period examined here. Herman Charles Bosman, who was in Pretoria Central Prison in the 1920s, worked in the prison library and had books by Dostoyevsky supplied to him by the Orange Free State library service. H.C. Bosman, *Cold Stone Jug* (Cape Town: Human and Rousseau, 1981), 66;

S. Gray, *Life Sentence: A Biography of Herman Charles Bosman* (Cape Town: Human and Rousseau, 2005), 128. While he was held as a political prisoner at the Fort Prison in Johannesburg in June 1900, James Thompson Bain was reading Thomas Carlyle. See J. Hyslop, 'A Scottish Socialist Reads Carlyle in Johannesburg Prison, June 1900: Reflections on the Literary Culture of the Imperial Working Class,' *Journal of Southern African Studies*, 29 (2003): 639–55.

50 Suid-Afrika, Departement van Gevangenisse, Hoofstuk 26, Wysigingstrokie no. 4/76, Biblioteekdienste en Leesstof, 28 junie 1976 (Ongepubliseerd), Staande Gevangenis diensorder no. B.22.8 (b) (ii).

51 J. Gregory, with Bob Graham, *Goodbye Bafana: Nelson Mandela, My Prisoner, My Friend* (London: Headline, 1995), 105. For an account of how political prisoners undermined censorship, see Archie L. Dick, '"Blood from Stones": Censorship and the Reading Practices of South African Political Prisoners, 1960–1990,' *Library History*, 24 (2008): 1–22.

52 Mogoba, *Stone, Steel, Sjambok*, 45.

53 J.K. Coetzee, *Plain Tales from Robben Island* (Pretoria: Van Schaik, 2000), 86.

54 *South African Prisons and the Red Cross Investigation: An Examination by International Defence and Aid Fund, with Prisoners' Testimony* (London: Christian Action Publications, 1967), 27.

55 Ahmed Kathrada, *Memoirs* (Cape Town: Zebra Press, 2004), 218.

56 Vassen, *Letters from Robben Island*, 95.

57 P.A.G. Reitz, 'Die Plek wat die Openbare Biblioteek Inneem in die: Behandelingsprogram van Gevangenes,' *South African Libraries*, 38 (1970): 176.

58 Hugh Lewin, *Bandiet: Seven Years in a South African Prison* (London: Heinemann, 1974), 81.

59 Lewin, *Bandiet*, 108, 170.

60 Baruch Hirson, *Revolutions in My Life* (Johannesburg: Witwatersrand University Press, 1995), 207; Suttner, *Inside Apartheid's Prison*, 70.

61 Sedick Isaacs Collection (MA/Robben Island Collection/Boxfile 48); Ahmed Kathrada Collection (MA/Ahmed Kathrada Collection/Boxfile 13), Robben Island Archives, Mayibuye Centre, University of the Western Cape, Bellville. Denis Goldberg also obtained a Unisa degree in librarianship. Many political prisoners included courses in librarianship as part of their university studies.

62 Personal interview with Sedick Isaacs, 9 April 2008.

63 Isaacs Collection, Boxfile 48.

64 Kathrada Collection, MA/File 13.3 (non-fiction books) and File 13.4 (fiction books).

65 Kathrada Collection, MA/File 13.1 (list of films).

66 Fatima Meer, *Prison Diary: Hundred and Thirteen Days, 1976* (Cape Town: Kwela Books, 2001), painting no. 3 between pages 64 and 65.

67 Meer, *Prison Diary*, 47–8, 55, 73, 86, 113.

68 'Nelson Mandela's Cell,' *South African Panorama*, 22 (1977): 2.

69 Nelson Mandela, *Long Walk to Freedom: The Autobiography of Nelson Mandela* (London: Abacus, 1994), 491.

70 Mandela, *Long Walk to Freedom*, 595.

71 Personal interview with Denis Goldberg, 5 March 2003.

72 Sachs, *The Jail Diary*, 184.

73 Sachs, *The Jail Diary*, 165, 250.

74 Sachs, *The Jail Diary*, 162.

75 Sachs, *The Jail Diary*, 251.

76 Sachs, *The Jail Diary*, 165.

21 SETTING UP THE PROPAGANDA MACHINE

1 Ironically, Lord Haldane was later forced to resign from the Cabinet for his alleged German sympathies.
2 Lucy Masterman, *C. F. G. Masterman* (London: Cassells, 1939), p. 272.
3 In *British Propaganda during the First World War, 1914–1918* (London: Macmillan, 1982), Chapter 1, M. L. Sanders and Philip M. Taylor speculate that Wellington House was chosen because it had organized a successful publicity campaign to explain the benefits of the National Insurance Act.
4 The list appears in Lucy Masterman's biography of her husband, p. 272.
5 Charles Mallett, *Anthony Hope and His Books* (London: Hutchinson, 1930), p. 243.
6 *The Journals of Arnold Bennett*, ed. Frank Swinnerton (Harmondsworth: Penguin, 1971), p. 379.
7 Hardy did write a few patriotic poems, including 'A Call to National Service,' but his only really abusive remarks about the Germans are the last lines of 'The Pity of It':

> Sinister, ugly, lurid be their fame;
> May their familiars grow to shun
> their name
> And their breed perish everlastingly.
> (*Moments of Vision* [London: Macmillan, 1917], p. 230).

8 Ivor Nicholson, 'An Aspect of British Official Wartime Propaganda,' *Cornhill Magazine* (May 1931): 593–606.
9 The most complete record of the organization, methods, content of British propaganda in the Great War is Sanders and Taylor's *British Propaganda during the First World War, 1914–18*.
10 Public Record Office, London (PRO), Ministry of Information, Files 4/4a.
11 PRO, Inf, 4/11.
12 Cate Haste, *Keep the Home Fires Burning* (London: Lane, 1977), p. 94.
13 Parker's activities in this period are documented in J. C. Adams's *Seated with the Mighty: A Biography of Sir Gilbert Parker* (Ottawa: Borealis, 1979), Chapter 14.
14 PRO, Inf., 4/5.
15 PRO, Inf., 4/11.
16 PRO, Inf., 4/5.
17 PRO, Inf., 4/5.

23 PUBLISHING AND THE STATE: 'BOOKS OF PROPAGANDA VALUE'

1 The National Archives Ministry of Information (hereafter TNA INF) 1/238 E. Bamford to F. Cooper, Ministry of Supply, 30 May 1940. This was written at the time of the campaign against imposing purchase tax on books, and just three weeks before Faber's unproductive meeting with the Chancellor of the Exchequer.
2 TNA INF 1/238 Part C.
3 TNA INF 1/238. Annex to draft letter from Mr Wiltshire to Sir William Palmer, Ministry of Supply, 16 January 1942.
4 TNA INF 1/238 Part C. R.H. Parker to Mr Gates, 1 April 1942.
5 A.S.G. Butler, *Recording Ruin* (London: Constable/Toronto: The Macmillan Company of Canada, 1942), p. 12.

6 OUP Archives PB/ED/009576 Box 1299, file 6900. H. Milford to E. Barker, 23 December 1941.

7 OUP Archives. Nicolas Barker's comment on 1974 correspondence about the book's publishing history.

8 TNA INF 1/247. OPD Books and Booklets in French: quantities adjusted at review meeting 25 May 1945. Revised again on 15 June 1945. It is not absolutely clear from the lists whether or not some of the quantities given are included in earlier figures, or are additional.

9 See Michael Carney, *Britain in Pictures: A History and Bibliography* (London: Werner Shaw, 1955), and Michael Carney, *Stoker, the Life of Hilda Matheson OBE, 1888–1940* (Pencaedu, Llanglynog, Wales: the Author, 1991). Hilda Matheson had been Political Secretary to Lady Astor, Britain's first woman MP, and when Lord Hailey became ill had arranged for completion of his massive *African Survey*, for which she was awarded the OBE. (See Chapter 3, the section 'From Empire to Independence: Africa'.) She was recruited to M16 in 1938.

10 The four members of the advisory committee were Frederick Whyte, Head of MOI's American Division; Lord David Cecil; Sir Ronald Storrs; and Hugh Walpole.

11 During the War, Adprint's sole backer was Lord Glenconner, who also financed Max Parrish when he took over the firm in 1948 after working as an editor for Foges. Eventually, 'Lord Glenconner of the Tennant Group sold his interest in Adprint to Wilfred Harvey of Purnell' (C. Foyle, obituary of his mother, Alice Harrap, in *The Bookseller*, October 1998). I am extremely grateful to Christopher Foyle for notes on Adprint written by his mother (formerly Alice Foyle) who had worked as Secretarial Assistant to Wolfgang Foges. See also Brian Mills, 'Some Notes on the Story of Adprint, *Antiquarian Book Monthly Review*, vol. XIII, no. 10, issue 150, October 1986, pp. 368–73.

12 W.J. Turner in *The Bookseller*, 13 March 1941, p. 2.41.

13 The quotation is from Sir John Squire, *The Bookseller*, 1 October 1942.

14 For example, the monthly lists of 'Books Across the Sea' – what were known as 'Ambassador Books' – show that for the period April–September 1942, Americans living in Britain chose to send their compatriots in the USA copies of Elizabeth Bowen's *English Novelists*, Edith Sitwell's *English Women*, Graham Greene's *British Dramatists* and David Low's *British Cartoonists*, as well as the volumes *British Trades Unions* and *English Social Services*.

15 Society of Authors, minutes of Management Committee meeting, 4 June 1943.

16 Society of Authors, minutes of 15 September 1943.

17 In the minority were Osbert Sitwell, Charles Morgan and Ernest Raymond, who resisted any form of compromise.

18 Society of Authors, minutes for 16 November 1943. Day-Lewis cited a further example: Pilot Press, whose *Target for Tomorrow* series, with some covers designed by Abram Games, was particularly striking visually.

19 Society of Authors, minutes for 15 February 1944.

25   THE AMERICAN PUBLISHER'S SERIES GOES TO WAR, 1942–1946

1 John B. Hench (2009).

2 On Armed Services Editions, see Robert O. Ballou (1946: 64–83), John Y. Cole (Cole, 1984) and Daniel J. Miller (1996).

3 Trysh Travis (1999: 393–5).

4 Gretta Palmer to Council on Books in Wartime, 30 November 1944, Council on Books in Wartime Records, box 26, folder 2, Public Policy Papers, Department of Rare Books and Special Collections, Princeton University Library (hereinafter cited as CBW Records).

5 Lewis Gannett (1946: 460).

6 Kenneth C. Davis (1984: 60–4).

7 Jeremy Lewis (2005: 76–77, 140–2).

8 Davis (1984: 99, 102).

9 ibid.: 65–6.

10 Hench (2009) and Ballou (1946: 83–94).

11 Ron Robin (1995: 91–106).

12 Colin W. Nettelbeck (1991: 58–61) and interview with Emanuel Molho, New York City, 17 May 2007. The firm's website is Frenchbookstore@aol.com.

13 Nettelbeck (1991: 61–4).

14 See John Spiers (2007: 20).

15 Jay Satterfield (2002: 27) and Spiers (2007: 4).

16 Robin (1995: 98).

17 Various documents in CBW Records, boxes 33–40.

18 Davis (1984: 77–9) and Cole (1984: 3–11).

19 Most of the letters are in CBW Records, boxes 31–2. See also Ballou (1946: 80–3), John Jamieson (1947: 148–52), Davis (1984: 75–8) and Cole (1984: 18–20).

20 Ballou (1946: 81), Travis (1999: 393–4) and 'Col. Trautman's Speech, 1 Feb. 1945´, CBW Records, box 38, folder 3.

21 Ballou (1946: 93–4).

22 Spiers (2007: 19).

23 Among scholars currently researching book publishing in the Cold War are Gregory Barnhisel, Amanda Laugesen and Trysh Travis.

24 Spiers (2007: 17).

26 WORLD LITERARY SPACE

1 See Taha Hussein, *Le livre des jours*, with a preface by André Gide (Paris: Gallimard, 1947); Rabindranath Tagore, *L'offrande lyrique*, trans. André Gide (Paris: Gallimard, 1914); and Marguerite Yourcenar, *Mishima, ou la vision du vide* (Paris: Gallimard, 1981).

2 See especially Florence Harlow, *Resistance Literature* (New York: Methuen, 1987).

3 Salman Rushdie, 'The New Empire within Britain,' in *Imaginary Homelands: Essays and Criticism, 1981–1991* (London: Granta, 1991), 130.

4 Édouard Glissant, *Poetics of Relation*, trans. Betsy Wing (Ann Arbor: University of Michigan Press, 1997), 23, 19.

5 Salman Rushdie, *The Satanic Verses* (New York: Viking Penguin, 1989), 398–399.

6 See Valérie Gannes and Marc Minon, 'Géographie de la traduction,' in *Traduire l'Europe*, ed. Françoise Barret-Ducrocq (Paris: Payot, 1992).

27 SCHOOL READERS IN THE EMPIRE AND THE CREATION OF POSTCOLONIAL TASTE

1 J. O. Cutteridge, ed. *Nelson's West Indian Readers*, Vol. 5 (Edinburgh: Nelson, 1928), p. 200.

2 V. S. Naipaul, *The Enigma of Arrival: A Novel in Five Sections* (London: Penguin, 1987), p. 12.

3 Ernst H. Gombrich, *The Story of Art* (London: Phaidon, 1961), p. 374.

4 *The Royal Readers* Special Canadian Series. Third Book of Reading Lessons. With illustrations from Giacomelli and Other Eminent Artists (Edinburgh and Toronto: Thomas Nelson and Sons and James Campbell, 1883), iii–iv. A copy is held in Edinburgh University, Thomas Nelson and Sons Archive at Gen 1728 52.616.

5 Nelson Archive B/2/178 (Buchan Files) to 'H–L of 1917' (G. M. Brown files). Owing to technical problems with the crusher, though, the plant proved a liability, and finally something of an embarrassment. In 1942 it was disposed of to a South American consortium after lengthy and difficult negotiations. Nelson Archive Gen 1728.68.76D.

6 S. B. Watson to G. C. Graham, 31 July 1923. Nelson Archive. Gen 1728.37.471 (Toronto House Letters).

7 J. O. Cutteridge, ed. *Nelson's Geography of the West Indies and Adjacent Lands* (Edinburgh: Nelson, 1931).

8 For Cutteridge's contributions to the Trinidadian educational system, and the reactions to it of the local bourgeoisie, see Carl C. Campbell's *Colony and Nation: A Short History of Education in Trinidad, 1834–1986* (Kingston: Ian Randle, 1992) and also his *Endless Education: Main Currents in the Educational System of Modem Trinidad and Tobago 1939–1986* (Barbados: University Press of the West Indies, 2000).

9 Interview with Keith Sambrook, recorded in Senate House, London, 14 October 2005.

10 Nelsons archive 1/W/MB.

11 Heather Holmes and David Finkelstein, eds, *Thomas Nelson and Sons: Memories of an Edinburgh Publishing House* (East Lothian: Tuckwell Press in association with the Scottish Archive of Print and Publishing History Records and the European Ethnological Research Centre, 2001), p. 93.

12 Ibid., p. 69.

13 Ibid., p. 4.

14 The evidence for this complex imbroglio is contained in file 1728.65.738 of the Nelson archive, soberly entitled 'Celanese'. Much of the correspondence is missing, but from the fragmentary record the following details can be inferred. The Indian enterprise was called the India Paper Pulp Company Limited, and based at Naihati in Bengal, adjacent to an estate managed by a concern known locally as the Bengal Coal Company of 8, Clive Row Calcutta, and in London as Andrew Yule and Co. Limited of 9, Basinghall Street, EC2 (Telegraphic Address: 'Unicorn' or 'Yuletide'). Capital was provided by loans from Nelsons channelled through the so-called Bamboo Company Limited, whose directors were Ian Nelson, J. L. Jardine and Sir Hardman Lever. Lever was also the director of Nelson's auditors, Lever, Honeyman and Company, whose London address was the very same as the Coal Company's: 9, Basinghall Street. Several of the same names turn up as directors of a seemingly unrelated concern known as Yule, Catto and Company, who were accountants to the firm in India. In Trinidad the capital for the paper mill was provided jointly by Nelsons and Morgan Grenfell to Trinidad Paper-Mills Ltd, which of course the former owned. Like the abortive negotiations with British Celanese, the deal was arranged by Abbott, Hoppin and Company of 120, Broadway, New York, whose agent George Whigham just happened to be a director of Morgan Grenfell, as indeed did Thomas Catto who sat with Andrew Yule on the board of Yule, Catto and Company, not entirely unrelated to the Andrew Yule and Company who shared office space with Nelson's auditors. The necessity for the rushed tax return was caused by Nelsons' insistence that their paper mill in India was a rupee company from which they derived no sterling benefit. Throughout all of these dealings Nelsons kept on the right side of the law by ensuring that, though associates of theirs sat on the boards of each of these incestuous concerns, no one enterprise shared precisely the same board of directors or list of shareholders as any other. One common factor is that several of the principals

were ennobled: Thomas Catto as Baron Catto of Cairncatto in the County Aberdeen, Charles Grenfell as Lord St Just in Cornwall. For latter-day John Buchans, a rich plot awaits.

15 Holmes and Finkelstein, *Thomas Nelson*, p. 99.
16 Interview with Sambrook, 14 October 2005.
17 Interview with Sambrook, 2005. Alistair McCleery's Preface to Holmes and Finkelstein, xxi–xxii.

29 AFRICAN LITERATURE/ANTHROPOLOGICAL EXOTIC

1 For different, but equally impassioned, diagnoses of this dilemma, see the essays by Soyinka (1991) and Omotoso (1975); in the wider context of literary publishing in the Third World, see also Altbach (1975).
2 A more detailed treatment is urgently needed of the ideological function of 'the paratextual apparatuses' (Genette 1987) surrounding postcolonial literary works. Introductory studies like Ashcroft et al.'s make occasional mention of paratextual devices like glossaries, arguing that these may serve both to inform the reader and, by drawing attention to what s/he otherwise would not understand, to install cultural difference into the text (Ashcroft et al. 1989: 56–57, 61–64). Equally, however, glossaries and other translational mechanisms might be seen as ways of *domesticating* the text, making it available for what might be euphemistically called 'general consumption'. To date, the only essay that I have come across that deals in any detail with the ideological effects of the paratextual is Wendy Waring's (1995); for a discussion of this essay in the context of the metropolitan packaging of contemporary Aboriginal writing, see Chapter 6 of this book.
3 See, for example, Adewale Maja-Pearce's unabashedly celebratory overview of the first three decades of the AWS: 'In Pursuit of Excellence: Thirty Years of the Heinemann African Writers' Series' (RAL 1992), in which he lauds 'the increasing diversity of voices that have emerged from the continent in recent years' (Maja-Pearce 1992: 130). As Maja-Pearce – who has himself played an important editorial role within the Series – suggests, 'The genesis of the African Writers' Series has become part of the mythology of modern African literature itself' (1992: 125). While this is true, it may also be – as Lizarríbar suggests – part of the problem. The constitutive role played by the AWS in the creation of 'the mythology of modern African literature' is itself in need of critical analysis, precisely the kind of analysis Lizarríbar – however provocatively – presents.
4 See Achebe's eponymous essay in the collection *Hopes and Impediments* (1989a). The question of colonialist biases in Western criticism of African literature is far from resolved, even though the angriest exchanges – often *ad hominem* – probably belong to the period from the late 1960s to the early 1980s.

30 AFRICA WRITES BACK: HEINEMANN AFRICAN WRITERS SERIES – A PUBLISHER'S MEMOIR

1 John St John, *William Heinemann: Century of Publishing 1890–1990* (London: William Heinemann, 1990), p. 519.
2 Ngugi wa Thiong'o, *Homecoming* (London: Heinemann Educational Books, 1975), p. 81.

31   A ROOM OF ONE'S OWN

1 'It remains a strange and almost inexplicable fact that in Athena's city, where women were kept in almost Oriental suppression as odalisques or drudges, the stage should yet have produced figures like Clytemnestra and Cassandra Atossa and Antigone, Phèdre and Medea, and all the other heroines who dominate play after play of the "misogynist" Euripides. But the paradox of this world where in real life a respectable woman could hardly show her face alone in the street, and yet on the stage woman equals or surpasses man, has never been satisfactorily explained. In modern tragedy the same predominance exists. At all events, a very cursory survey of Shakespeare's work (similarly with Webster, though not with Marlowe or Jonson) suffices to reveal how this dominance, this initiative of women, persists from Rosalind to Lady Macbeth. So too in Racine; six of his tragedies bear their heroines' names; and what male characters of his shall we set against Hermione and Andromaque, Bérénice and Roxane, Phèdre and Athalie? So again with Ibsen; what men shall we match with Solveig and Nora, Heda and Hilda Wangel and Rebecca West?' – F. L. Lucas, *Tragedy*, pp. 114–15.

33   'BOOKS WITH BITE': VIRAGO PRESS AND THE POLITICS OF FEMINIST CONVERSION

1 Time Warner became AOL Time Warner after its merger with Internet service provider America Online in January 2000. Little, Brown & Co. UK changed its name to Time Warner Books UK from 1 January 2002, and is a part of the AOL Time Warner Book Group. See www.time-warnerbooks.co.uk/company/company.htm.
2 An equally textbook example of how to reduce complex political and commercial differences to female catfights in order to dismiss feminism appeared in London's *Evening Standard,* complete with pat political homily: 'What happened to Virago is a cautionary tale. It shows that the sisterhood is too fragile for strong individuals. Feminism is fine in principle, but women can still fall out ... Virago is dead. Long live the Viragos' (Shakespeare, 1995: 12).
3 The exact meaning of the term 'radical' within feminist political discourse is a troubled one, as the word has altered in meaning and has, in addition, frequently sustained multiple meanings simultaneously (see Chapter 4 for an extended discussion of this issue). In the twentieth century, the term has contained three distinct meanings: firstly, it describes a non-conformist position to the left of progressive politics; secondly, it has been used to denote the separatist wing of the women's liberation movement, which prioritorised gender over other social categories; thirdly, and simultaneous with these other meanings, the term has continued to be used to denote the subversively non-conformist in a general sense (see Williams, 1983: 251–2). Clearly, when using the term in relation to the capitalist ethos of Virago Press, I intend this third sense of the term, as Virago was never an adherent of collectivist or avowedly separatist politics. In most cases, this terminological distinction will be apparent from the context in which the term is used. Though a slight potential for confusion exists, it seems essential to destabilise the word's received meaning in terms of the standard tripartite classification of feminism into liberal, socialist/Marxist and radical wings. For radicalism in the general sense is by no means confined to self-proclaimedly 'radical' feminist enterprises.

4 The 'Virago's History' page of the imprint's current website gives the date of the press's establishment as 1973, making 2003 the press's thirtieth anniversary. See www.virago.co.uk/virago/virago/history.asp.

5 The conflict in 1991 between The Women's Press's then managing director, Ros de Lanerolle, and the owner of Quartet Books, Naim Attallah, is explored in detail in Chapter 2. At the time of Virago's departure from the Quartet fold in 1976, however, John Booth and William Miller were in charge of the firm; Attallah did not become owner of Quartet until the following year. Yet speaking of Virago's time under Quartet's previous ownership, Ursula Owen recalls that 'a year of that was enough and we realised we had to go off and do our own thing' (1998b).

6 In March 1998 Random House was itself bought by German media conglomerate Bertelsmann for an undisclosed sum. It has since been merged with Bantam Doubleday Dell (also a Bertelsmann subsidiary) and restructured as Random House Inc. (Traynor and Foden, 1998). Virago's architecturally designed signature bookshop had generated positive industry attention upon its opening in January 1985 (*Bookseller*, 1985c: 15).

34 SHE NEEDS A WEBSITE OF HER OWN: THE 'INDIE' WOMAN WRITER AND CONTEMPORARY PUBLISHING

1 Stefanie Cohen, 'Why women writers still take men's names', *The Wall Street Journal*, 6 December 2012, www.wsj.com/articles/SB10001424127887324355904578159453918443978.

2 Amy Fallon, 'VS Naipaul finds no woman writer his literary match – not even Jane Austen', *The Guardian*, 1 June 2011, www.guardian.co.uk/books/2011/jun/02/vs-naipaul-jane-austen-women-writers.

3 Katha Pollit, 'A touch of Franzenfreude', *The Guardian*, 19 September 2010, www.theguardian.com/commentisfree/2010/sep/19/books-franzen- gender-wars-reviews.

4 Ruth Franklin, 'A literary glass ceiling?', *New Republic*, February 7, 2011, www.newrepublic.com/article/books-and-arts/82930/VIDA-women-writen-magazines-book-reviews.

5 Robin Romm, 'Why it matters that fewer women are published in literary magazines', *Slate*, 2 February 2011, www.slate.com/blogs/xx_factor/201l/02/02/vida_study_fewer_female_authors_published_in_literary_magazines.html.

6 Richard Mocarski and Sim W. Butler, 'Where are the women authors? Exploring gender roles' influence on submitting work for publication', *Women and Language*, 37.2 (Fall 2014): 75–81, 7p.

7 Rosemary Marangoly George and Helen Scot, 'A new tail to an old tale: An interview with Ama Ata Aidoo', *Novel*, 26.3(Spring 1993): 297–308. Cited in Barbara Fisher, *Third World Women's Literature: A Dictionary and Guide to Materials in English* (Westport, CT: Greenwood Press, 1995), 249.

8 Leila Aboulela, Interview with the Author, December 11, 2014.

9 Jana Bradley, Bruce Fulton, Marlene Helm, and Katherine A. Pittner, 'Non-traditional book publishing', *First Monday*, 16.8 (2011), http://firstmonday.org/ojs/index.php/fm/article/view/3353/3030.

10 Bradley et al., 'Non-traditional book publishing'.

11 Bradley et al., 'Non-traditional book publishing'.

12 Lynn Neary, 'Self-publishing: No longer just a vanity project', NPR Books, December 19, 2012, www.npr.org/2012/12/19/167448748/self-publishing-no-longer-just-a-vanity-project.

13 Simon Carolan and Christine Evain, 'Self-publishing: Opportunities and threats in a new age of mass culture', *Publishing Research Quarterly*, 29.4 (2013): 281, http://link.springer.com/article/10.1007%2Fs12109-013-9326-3.

14 Carolan and Evain, 'Self-publishing'.

15 Carolan and Evain, 'Self-publishing'.

16 Alison Baverstock and Jackie Steintiz, 'Who are the self-publishers?' *Learned Publishing*, 26.3 (2013): 213. http://dx.doi.org/10.1087/20130310.

17 Susan S. Williams, *Reclaiming Authorship: Literary Women in America, 1850–1900* (Philadelphia: University of Pennsylvania Press, 2006), 1.

18 Mohanalakshmi Rajakumar, 'Women and Writing', Survey, SurveyMonkey.com, 23 November 2013. Accessed online 11 January 2014.

19 Nadia Lee, 'Why Simon and Schuster's Archway Publishing is bad for authors', *NadiaLee*(blog), November 28, 2012, www.nadialee.net/blog/2012/11/28/why-simon-schusters-archway-publishing-is-bad-for-authors/.

20 Lee, 'Why Simon and Schuster's Archway Publishing is bad for authors'.

21 Rajakumar, 'Women and writing'.

22 Rajakumar, 'Women and writing'.

23 'About She Writes Press', *She Writes Press*, accessed 13 December 2014, http://shewritespress.com/about-swp/.

24 Emlyn Chand, Interview with the Author, 15 December 2014.

35   LITERARY PRIZES AND THE MEDIA

1 Frank Kermode, *The Art of Telling: Essays on Fiction* (Cambridge, MA: Harvard University Press, 1983), p. 10. This figure, if accepted, would have to be revised upwards to something in the region of £1.5m by 1996.

2 John Sutherland, *Fiction and the Fiction Industry* (London: Athlone Press, 1978), cites Leonard Woolf on his wife's income from fiction between 1920 and 1924: £106/5/10, £10/10/8, £33/13/–, £40/0/5, £70 exactly (Sutherland, p. 110). The pound of this period had the purchasing power of between £30 and £50 today; thus in the best of these years Woolf's income from fiction was equivalent to a few thousand pounds in today's terms, the leanest equivalent to a few hundred. Woolf was fortunate to have private means, unlike many of her 1990s sisters.

3 These figures were kindly supplied by Lennie Goodings and Sarah White of Virago.

4 Virginia Woolf, *Orlando* (London: Vintage, 1992), p. xv. The figures are quoted as 14,950. The case of Woolf is particularly piquant because from 1 January 1996 a pan-European copyright period of seventy years *post mortem* replaced the half-century that had been mandatory in Britain since 1911. Woolf is among a number of writers who have gone back into copyright until the early twenty-first century as British titles, while copyright in the UK, come or remain out of copyright in the US, where the fifty-year rule will still apply. See Hugh Jones, 'Life Plus Seventy', *Bookseller* (1 April 1994), pp. 20–21. The seventy-year rule will be grist to the mill of the James Joyce Estate, which has been fighting the consequences of the fifty-year copyright rule in a variety of ingenious ways since the early 1990s. Britain's Department of Trade and Industry (DTI) accepted the EU ruling as a *fait accompli* after a minimum of consultation.

5 Dorothy L. Sayers, *Have His Carcase* (1932; rpt. London: Coronet, 1989), p. 9.

37 GENRE IN THE MARKETPLACE

1 My article 'A common ground? Book prize culture in Europe' considers the varying role of literary prizes, and the ways in which research into them can be conducted. In *Javnost The Public* 11:4 (2004), 37–47.
2 Jonathan Taylor, Chairman of Booker plc and The Booker Prize Management Committee, Introduction to *Booker 30: A Celebration of 30 Years of The Booker Prize for Fiction 1969–1998* (Great Britain: Booker plc, 1998), 5.
3 Pico Iyer, in 'The empire writes back', *Time* (8 February 1993), 54–9 sees the Booker Prize at the forefront of the promotion of a new set of post-colonial or 'World fiction' writers (54). Graham Huggan, in *The Post-Colonial Exotic*, particularly in chapter 4, 'Prizing otherness: A short history of the Booker', 105–23, analyses the ironies of the Booker Prize's relation to the colonial past (including Booker's history as a distribution company in Guyana) and post-colonial present.
4 'Prizes and awards', in *Writers' & Artists' Yearbook 1998* (London: A&C Black, 1998), 488–515.
5 Richard Todd, *Consuming Fictions: The Booker Prize and Fiction in Britain Today* (London: Bloomsbury, 1996)
6 Todd, *Consuming Fictions*, 128.
7 Rose Tremain, *Music and Silence* (London: Chatto & Windus, 1999); David Cairns, *Berlioz Volume Two: Servitude and Greatness 1832–1869* (London: Allen Lane, 1999); Seamus Heaney, *Beowulf* (London: Faber and Faber, 1999).
8 Kate Atkinson, *Behind the Scenes at the Museum* (London: Doubleday, 1995).
9 Ted Hughes, *Birthday Letters* (London: Faber and Faber, 1998).
10 Interview with Bud McLintock of Karen Earl Ltd., Director of the Whitbread Book Awards, 30 June 2000.
11 Connor, *The English Novel in History*, 22–23. Michael Hayes makes the same argument in his chapter on 'Popular fiction', in Clive Bloom and Gary Day, eds., *Literature and Culture in Modern Britain. Volume Three: 1956–1999* (Harlow: Longman, 2000), 76–93, 77.

38 SCANDALOUS CURRENCY

1 The three epigraphs are taken from: Philip Howard, 'Curling up with all the Bookers,' *The Times* (London), 19 October 1982, 12; David Lehman, 'May the best author win: Fat chance – A flap over book prizes,' *Newsweek*, 107 (21 April 1986): 86; and Anonymous, 'A Turner for the worse,' *Daily Telegraph*, 29 November 1995, 20.
2 Dustin Hoffman, OBIE Awards, 27 May 1985, New York; Bill Murray, New York Film Critics Circle Awards, 10 January 1999, Windows on the World, New York; Sally Field, Academy Awards, 14 April 1980, Dorothy Chandler Pavilion, Los Angeles.
3 Mick Lasalle, 'MTV Movie Awards goof-off,' *San Francisco Chronicle*, 12 June 1992, D1.
4 Pierre Bourdieu, *Photography: A Middle-Brow Art*, trans. Shaun Whiteside (Stanford: Stanford University Press, 1990), 96.
5 Pierre Bourdieu and Hans Haacke, *Free Exchange* (Stanford: Stanford University Press, 1994), 84.
6 It might seem scandalous, as well, that the other towering figure of European letters, Emile Zola, was passed over. But here the academy was given some latitude owing to the fact that Alfred Nobel was known to have loathed Zola's work.
7 It is likely, as well, that Tolstoy would have declined the prize had they offered it to him in a subsequent year. Not only might he have felt some bitterness toward the

academicians after they gave their inaugural prize to Prudhomme, but, as Carl David af Wirsén noted in his 1902 committee report on Tolstoy, the Russian had recently spoken out more generally about 'the lack of worth, nay, the harm in money prizes.' Anders Österling, 'The literary prize,' in Henrik Schück et al., *Nobel: The Man and His Prizes*, 2nd revised and enlarged edition (Amsterdam: Elsevier, 1962; orig. pub. 1950), 92.

8 In accordance with the logic that we will examine in the next section, however, the Bollingen soon began to reap a symbolic profit from its scandalous visibility, eclipsing the Pulitzer as (to quote the *New York Times*) 'America's most prestigious poetry award.' See James F. English, 'Prizes,' in Eric Haralson, ed., *Encyclopedia of American Poetry: The Twentieth Century* (Chicago: Fitzroy Dearborn, 2001), 580.

9 Anonymous, 'Never mind the plot, enjoy the argument,' *Independent*, 6 September 1994, 12.

10 Richard Brooks, 'Judges trade insults as book award turns into prizefight,' *Observer*, 7 May 1995, 3.

11 Anonymous, 'The Booker Prize,' *Economist*, 15 October 1994, 118; Annalena McAfee, 'Judges split as Kelman wins Booker,' *Financial Times*, 12 October 1994, 12. The tally of 'fucks' is reported in Robert Winder, 'Highly literary and deeply Vulgar,' *Independent*, 13 October 1994, 18.

39   THE FUTURE OF PUBLISHING

1 Martine Prosper, *Édition, l'envers du décor* (Paris: Éditions Lignes, 2009).
2 Paris: Stock, 2009.
3 Prosper, *Édition, l'envers du décor*.

41   THE GLOBAL BOOK

1 Miha Kovač and Rüdiger Wischenbart, 'A myth busted: Bestselling fiction in Europe and Slovenia', *Primerjalna književnost*, Ljubljana, 33(2) (2010).
2 Unpublished study by Sasa Drakulic, cited in Rüdiger Wischenbart, 'Knowledge and its price', *Publishing Research Quarterly*, 22(4) (2007), Winter.
3 Johan Heilbron, 'Structure and dynamics of the world system of translation', paper at the International Symposium on Translation and Cultural Mediation, UNESCO, 22–23 February 2010. Available at www.unesco.org/fileadmin/MULTIMEDIA/HQ/CLT/languages/pdf/Heilbron.pdf, accessed 26 February 2012.
4 ibid.
5 Gisèle Sapiro, 'Globalization and Cultural Diversity in the Book Market: The case of literary translations in the US and in France', *Poetics* 38 (2010), 430.
6 Ibid., 433.
7 Data on bestsellers was supplied to the author by Carlo Carrenho of PublishNews, which compiles regular charts available at www.publishnews.com.br/
8 Heilbron, op. cit.
9 See www.rochester.edu/College/translation/threepercent/
10 See www.rochester.edu/College/translation/threepercent/index.php?id=4712, accessed 28 September 2012.
11 Lawrence Venuti, *The Translator's Invisibility: A history of translation*, 2nd edn, (Abingdon: Routledge, 2008), 5.

12 Interviewed by Nicholas Wroe, *Guardian*, 29 December 2012.

13 Interviewed by the author, 14 January 2013.

14 Dalkey Archive Press, *Research into Barriers to Translation and Best Practices: A study for the Global Translation Initiative*, March 2011. Available at www.dalkeyarchive.com/html/WYSIWYGfiles/file/Global%20Translation%20Initiative%20Study.pdf, accessed 20 December 2012.

15 Interviewed by the author, 23 January 2013.

16 Interviewed by the author, 5 March 2013.

17 Interviewed by the author, 20 December 2012.

18 Interviewed by the author, 20 December 2012.

19 Interviewed by the author, 23 January 2013.

20 Jaron Lanier. *Who Owns the Future?*, Penguin, 2013, loc 316 of 5429.

21 Francesco Pugliano, 'Microsoft, Google, and the future of Machine Translation', from blog *Localization in Silicon Valley*, 28 October 2011. http://rosecourt.wordpress.com/2011/10/28/microsoft-google-and-the-future-of-machine-translation/, accessed 5 October 2012.

22 The *AMO Times*, 28 January 2012. Available at www.theamotimes.com/2012/01/28/malaysian-eye-poked-over-google-translate-fail/, accessed 5 October 2012.

23 Nicholas Ostler. *The Last Lingua Franca: English until the return of Babel* (London: Penguin, 2010), 257–58.

24 David Bellos, *Is That a Fish in Your Ear? Translation and the meaning of everything*, London: Penguin, 2011, 264 of 377 in ebook.

25 Huo Lee, in China Publishers Magazine, *Special Report for the London Book Fair 2012*, page 23. Available at http://publishingperspectives.com/2012/04/sponsored-post-report-from-china-publishers-magazine/?utm_source=feedburner&utm_medium=feed&utm_campaign=Feed%3A+PublishingPerspectives+%28Publishing+Perspectives%29, accessed 20 December 2012.

43 THE GLOBAL LITERARY FIELD AND MARKET POSTCOLONIALISM

1 Eva Hemmungs Wirtén, *Global Infatuation: Explorations in Transnational Publishing and Texts: the Case of Harlequin Enterprises and Sweden* (Uppsala: Section for Sociology of Literature at the Department of Literature, Uppsala University, 1998). Transediting can be thought of as the way glocalization works in the publishing world, as an original text is edited and altered to appeal to a variety of localities that would be less receptive to it otherwise.

2 Ben Bagdikian, *The New Media Monopoly* (Boston: Beacon Press, 2004), 3–4.

3 Herbert I. Schiller, *Culture, Inc.: The Corporate Takeover of Public Expression* (Oxford: Oxford University Press, 1989), 36–7.

4 Ben Bagdikian, *The Media Monopoly*, 6th edn. (Boston: Beacon Press, 2000), 126; Eva Hemmungs Wirtén, *No Trespassing: Authorship, Intellectual Property Rights, and the Boundaries of Globalization* (Toronto: University of Toronto Press, 2004), 85.

5 Ibid., 87.

6 Richard J. Barnet and John Cavanagh, *Global Dreams: Imperial Corporations and the New World Order* (New York: Simon & Schuster, 1994), 69.

7 For recent general accounts of the process of media concentration in the publishing industry, not cited in the body of this chapter, see Beth Luey, 'The impact of consolidation and internationalization,' in *The Structure of International Publishing in*

the 1990s, eds. Beth Luey and Fred Kobrak (New Brunswick, NJ: Transaction Publishers, 1992), 1–22; Douglas Gomery, 'The Book Publishing Industry,' in *Who Owns the Media? Competition and Concentration in the Mass Media Industry*, 3rd edn., eds. Douglas Gomery and Benjamin M. Compaine (Mahwah, NJ: Lawrence Erlbaum Associates, 2000), 61–145. For stringent commentary on the same, in addition to Bagdikian, see, for example, Mark Crispin Miller, 'The publishing industry,' in *Conglomerates and the Media*, eds. Patricia Aufderheide et al. (New York: New Press, 1997), 107–33; Ted Solotaroff, 'The literary-industrial complex,' *New Republic* (8 June 1987), 28–45; Leo Bogart, *Commercial Culture: The Media System and the Public Interest* (New York: Oxford University Press, 1995). Laura J. Miller attempts to keep up with the breathless pace of changes in ownership patterns ('Major Publishers with North American Holdings,' 1 August 2006 http://people.brandeis.edu/~lamiller/publishers.html).

 8 Gordon Graham, 'Multinational publishing,' in *International Book Publishing: An Encyclopedia*, eds. Philip G. Altbach and Edith S. Hushino (New York: Garland, 1995), 243–6.

 9 Ibid., 244.

10 Jason Epstein, *Book Business: Publishing Past, Present, and Future* (New York: W.W. Norton, 2001), 4.

11 Ibid., 12–13.

12 Ibid., 13, 26.

13 Schiller, *Culture, Inc.*, 32.

14 Randall Stevenson, 'A golden age? Readers, authors, and the book trade,' in *Oxford English Literary History*, Vol. 12, *1960–2000: The Last of England?* (Oxford: Oxford University Press, 2004), 129–30.

15 Ibid., 149.

16 Elizabeth Long, 'The cultural meaning of concentration in publishing,' in *The Structure of International Publishing in the 1990s*, eds. Beth Luey and Fred Kobrak (New Brunswick, NJ: Transaction Publishers, 1992), 99.

17 Ibid., 94.

18 Rowland Lorimer and Eleanor O'Donnell, 'Globalization and internationalization in publishing,' *Canadian Journal of Communications* 17 (1992), 494.

19 Ibid., 500.

20 *Books in Print 2003–2004*, Vol. 8, *Authors S–Z/Publishers & Indexes* (New Providence, NJ: Bowker, 2003), vii.

21 Bagdikian, *Media Monopoly*, 19.

22 Ibid.

23 André Schiffrin, 'The corporatization of publishing,' *The Nation* (3 June 1996), 32.

24 Long, 'Cultural meaning,' 98.

25 Robert, Escarpit, *Sociology of Literature*, 2nd edn., trans. Ernest Pick (London: Frank Cass, 1971), 59.

26 Richard Todd, *Consuming Fictions: The Booker Prize and Fiction in Britain Today* (London: Bloomsbury, 1996), 13–14. In the UK, Terry Maher had much to do with these developments. Todd (123–4) notes that Maher's Pentos company acquired Dillon's in 1977 and turned it from a university bookshop into a major retailer of a wide variety of books. Rival chain Waterstone & Co. Ltd., later Waterstone's, founded in 1982 and run by W.H. Smith from 1989, eventually took over Dillon's. When Pentos collapsed in 1995 there were approximately 150 Dillon's branches in the UK; and in 1996 there were 103 branches of Waterstone's in the UK and Ireland. cf. Maher's *Against My Better Judgment: Adventures in the City and in the Book Trade* (London: Sinclair-Stevenson, 1994), his own account of the role of Dillon's in changing English publishing and in destabilizing the

Net Book Agreement, an industry standard that regulated cover prices in the English book trade until 1995, forbidding price reductions by retailers.

27 Juliet Gardiner, 'Reformulating the reader: Internet bookselling and its impact on the construction of reading practices,' *Changing English* 9 (2002), 162–3.

28 Barnet and Cavanagh, *Global Dreams*, 79.

29 'In full colour: Cultural diversity in book publishing today,' ed. Danuta Kean, supplement, *The Bookseller* (12 March 2004), 3.

30 Ibid., 5.

31 Ibid., 7.

32 Ibid., 10.

33 'Penguin to set up new publishing venture in Ireland,' 1 August 2006 www.penguin.ie/static/cs/uk/503/pressrelease/penguin_ireland.pdf.

34 Paul Jay, 'Beyond discipline? Globalization and the future of English,' in *Globalizing Literary Studies*, ed. Giles Gunn, spec, issue of *PMLA* 116 (2001), 33.

35 Ibid., 41.

36 Biodun Jeyifo, 'On Eurocentric critical theory: Some paradigms from the texts and subtexts of post-colonial writing,' in *After Europe: Critical Theory and Post-Colonial Writing*, eds. Stephen Slemon and Helen Tiffin (Sydney: Dangaroo Press, 1992), 107. It is worth noting that scholarship on the history of the book has largely reflected this division. Having paid ample attention to North American and Western European histories, it is only beginning to turn to colonial and postcolonial topics (Mary Hammond and Robert Fraser, 'Conference Report I: The colonial and postcolonial history of the book,' *SHARP News* 13.2 [2004], 1–2).

37 Harald Weinrich, 'Chamisso, Chamisso authors, and globalization,' *PMLA* 119 (2004), 1344.

38 Graham, 'Multinational publishing,' 247.

39 Gordon Graham, 'Press file,' *LOGOS* 14 (2003), 166.

40 *Index Translationum*, UNESCO, 1 August 2006 www.unesco.org/culture/xtrans/html_eng/index6.shtml, and cited in Anthony Pym, 'Two principles, one probable paradox and a humble suggestion, all concerning percentages of translation and non-translation into various languages, particularly English,' 1 August 2006 www.fut.es/~apym/on-line/rates/rates.html, par. 1.

41 Ibid., par. 10.

42 Pascale Casanova, *The World Republic of Letters* (Cambridge, MA: Harvard University Press, 2004), 164.

43 Wirtén, *No Trespassing*, 54.

44 Timothy Brennan, *Salman Rushdie and the Third World: Myths of the Nation* (Basingstoke: Palgrave Macmillan, 1989), 36–7.

45 Casanova, *World Republic of Letters*, 108, 197.

46 Timothy Brennan, *At Home in the World: Cosmopolitanism Now* (Cambridge, MA: Harvard University Press, 1997), 39–40.

47 Timothy Brennan, 'Cosmopolitans and Celebrities', *Race and Class,* 31 (1), July 1989, 7.

48 Masao Miyoshi, 'A Borderless World? From Colonialism to Transnationalism and the Decline of the Nation State', *Critical Enquiry*, 19 (4) Summer 1993, 742.

49 Ibid., 750. Slavoj Žižek similarly states: 'the privileged *empty point of universality* from which one is able to appreciate (and depreciate) properly other particular cultures [...] is the very form of asserting one's own superiority,' since what appears to be 'the hybrid coexistence of diverse cultural life-worlds' is in fact 'the form of appearance of its opposite, of the massive presence of capitalism as *universal* world system' ('Multiculturalism, Or, the cultural logic of multinational capitalism,' *New Left Review* os 225 [1997], 46). It

is worth noting that each of these positions is significantly predicted by *The Communist Manifesto's* claim that 'The bourgeoisie has through its exploitation of the world market given a cosmopolitan character to production and consumption in every country. [...] From the numerous national and local literatures, there arises a world literature' (Karl Marx and Friedrich Engels, *The Communist Manifesto*, trans. Samuel Moore [London: Penguin Classics, 1985], 83–4). cf. Erich Auerbach's lament that 'man will have to accustom himself to existence in a standardized world, to a single literary culture, only a few literary languages, and perhaps even a single literary language' ('Philology and *Weltliteratur*,' *Centennial Review* 13 [1969], 3).

50 Brennan, *At Home in the World*, 38.
51 Brennan, 'Cosmopolitans and celebrities,' 2.
52 Brennan, *At Home in the World*, 38.

Index

Page numbers in italics and bold typeface refer to information in figures and tables respectively.
Names spelt 'Mc' are filed as if 'Mac'.

market impact, 53, 81, 245, 299
resale of, 81
editors, 2
author relationship, 15, 74–75, 129, 130
career mobility, 130
decision-making, 115, 118–119, 128, 129, 272, 274
gatekeeping, 79
review copies of books, 15
targets and profit, 272
Edward Arnold Publishers Ltd., 162–163
Eliot, T. S., 252, 262
Ellison, Ralph, 119
Enoch, Kurt, 179
epitext, 9, 32
Epstein, Jason, 302–303, 305
Equatorial Publishers, 206, 207
Escarpit, Robert, 305
ethnicity, 119, 244, 245, 268–269, 306–309
Evans, 206, 209, 219
Ewen, Stuart, 70
Ewing, David W., 121
experimental art, 20–21, 25, 65, 66, 238, 321

F
Faber, Geoffrey, 2, 89–90, 102–105, 113
Facebook, 53, 54, 55, 56, 78, 245, 246
feminism, 3, 223–224
A Room of One's Own (Woolf), 223, 225–229
publishers in the global south, 3, 223, 230–234
self publishing, 224, 243–247
theory of gatekeeping, 9, 36–44
Virago Press, 224, 235–242, 253
'Fiction' (Arcangel), 78
field of cultural production, 17
see also field of restricted production
field of large-scale cultural production, 8, 17, 21–22, 75
field of restricted production, 8
in modern literary marketplace, 75–76
positions and position-taking, 22–30
structure and functioning, 8, 17–22
Fighting Forces Series, 152, 179
films
awards, 261
book tie-ins, 59, 99–100, 251, 253, 274, 303

celebrity culture, 68–69
corporatisation, 55, 301
cultural value, 22, 107, 112
industry centralisation, 55
magazines, 97
prison library (apartheid South Africa), 148
Fish, Stanley, 258, 296
Fleming, Ian, 254
Foges, Wolfgang, 169, 171
Ford, Ford Madox (Ford Madox Hueffer), 151, 155, 165
Foucault, Michel, 60, 68, 72, 84, 85, 87, 115, 123
Foundation Books, 207, 209
Fowles, John, 251
Fox, John, 11
Frankfurt School, 68, 69
Frank, Waldo, 108
Franzen, Jonathan, 82
freelancers, 47, 48, 49
The French Lieutenant's Woman (Fowles), 251
Freud, Sigmund, 121

G
Gaines, Jane, 69
Galsworthy, John, 147, 156, 252
gatekeeping
book reviews, 109
by publishers, 2, 9, 10, 43–44, 46–47, 79, 115–116, 118–119, 126–132, 274
critics of Book-of-the-Month Club, 109, 110, 111
digital disruption of, 9, 56, 79–80
feminist theory of, 9, 10, 36–44
marketing and promotion, 95–96, 115–116, 131–132
postcolonial context, 3–4
Genderpress, 232
genre, 35, 249, 250, 256–259, 260, 296
gentleman publishers, 2, 3, 8, 10, 102, 113, 127, 271
George Allen and Unwin, 8, 14, 163–164, 165
George, Lloyd, 155, 163
globalisation
Africa, effects in, 214, 267–268, 276–283, 308
authors, readers and texts as industrial products, 295–298, 299

Kermode, Frank, 252
Kipling, Rudyard, 65, 156, 252
Knopf, Alfred A., 128
Knopf Group, 274, 302
Korean authors, 289
Kovač, Miha, 284, 288, 289

L
Lady Chatterley's Lover (Lawrence), 3, 116,
　133–141
Lane, Allen, 90, 113–114, 137
Lanier, J., 53, 54, 290
large-scale cultural production *see* field of
　large-scale cultural production
Larsson, Steig, 284, 288
Lawrence, D. H., 94, 137, 138
　Lady Chatterley's Lover, 3, 116, 133–141
Lawson, Mark, 263
Leavis, Q. D., 2, 89, 90, 93–100, 113, 114
Lee, H. O., 157
Lee, Nadia, 246
Leon, Ruth, 263
Lévi-Strauss, Claude, 86
literary agents, 1, 2
　author image, 296
　Britain in Pictures series, 171
　marketplace transformation, 59, 61,
　　63–66
　in the publishing value chain, 45,
　　46, 47
　and the trials of a publisher, 12–13
literary prizes, 3, 249–250
　Booker Prize *see* Booker Prize
　corporate brand investment, 297
　disdain for, 260
　game rules, 260–261, 264–265
　and genre, 249, 250, 256–259, 260
　Nobel Prize in Literature, 65, 193, 219,
　　221, 249, 252, 260, 262, 308
　paratext, 35
　postcolonial authors, 219, 256
　scandals, 250, 261–265, 297–298
　transformative power of, 249,
　　251–253, 308
literary quality
　booksellers as the 'midwife of literature',
　　89–90, 102–105
　levelling, concern about, 79–80
　in Liberal Critical Tradition, 120–121
　literary agents, 63, 64–65

and market expansion, 63, 90,
　106–114, 120
public reading habits (England, 1932), 89,
　93–101
see also cultural capital
literary theory, 59, 60, 67–68, 72,
　83–88, 294
Lizarríbar, Camille, 210–212, 214
Locke, W. J., 156
Lolita (Nabokov), 136
Long, Elizabeth, 303–304, 305
Longman
　in Africa, 188, 203–204, 205, 206, 207,
　　208–209, 219
　in India, 211
　war pamphlets, 167
Lord of the Flies (Golding), 251
Lotte in Weimar (Mann), 184
Lucas, E. V., 156
Lü Jiamin *see* Rong, Jiang
Lury, Celia, 69
Lyotard, Jean-François, 84

M
Macaulay, Rose, 170
McBain, Alexander, 138
machine translation, 268, 289–290
Mackail, J. W., 156
MacLehose, Christopher, 288
Macmillan
　in Africa, 188, 205, 206, 219, 308
　antitrust cases, 79
　author remuneration, 80–81
　paperback revolution, 114
　wartime publishing, 151, 157, 161, 167
　worldwide distribution, 308
Mahfouz, Naguib, 221
Maillu, David, 207
Mair, G. H., 157
Maison Française, 180–181
Man Booker Prize, 249, 297
Mandela, Nelson, 144, 149, 218
market censorship, 3, 115
　commercial editorial decisions, 115,
　　118–119, 128, 274
　electronic panoptics, 123–124
　employees, 121, 122
　marketing and promotion as, 115–116,
　　131–132, 304
　political exiles, 119–120